HUMAN GEOGRAPHY
behavioural approaches

D. J. WALMSLEY and G. J. LEWIS

HUMAN GEOGRAPHY

behavioural approaches

Longman
London and New York

Longman Group Limited
Longman House, Burnt Mill, Harlow
Essex CM 20 2JE, England
Associated companies throughout the world

Published in the United States of America
by Longman Inc., New York

First published 1984

British Library Cataloguing in Publication Data
Walmsley, D. J.
Human geography.
1. Anthropo-geography
I. Title II. Lewis, G. J.
304.2 GF41

ISBN 0-582-30091-6

Library of Congress Cataloging in Publication Data
Walmsley, D. J.
Human geography.

Bibliography: p.
Includes index.
1. Anthropo-geography — Philosophy. 2. Anthropo-geography — Methodology. 3. Environmental psychology.
I. Lewis, G. J. II. Title.
GF21.W34 1984 304.2 83-13590
ISBN 0-582-30091-6

Set in 9/11 pt Linotron 202 Plantin
Printed in Singapore by
Selector Printing Co (Pte) Ltd

For
Jennifer, Adam and Rachel
Vivien, James and Natasha

CONTENTS

List of figures		**viii**
List of tables		**ix**
Preface		**x**
Acknowledgements		**xii**
Part One: Introduction		**1**
1	Geography and behaviour	3
Part Two: Macro-scale approaches		**17**
2	Modelling economic behaviour	19
3	People and space	25
4	Models of man	37
Part Three: Micro-scale approaches		**41**
5	Environmental information	43
6	Decision-making	54
7	Image and behaviour	63
Part Four: Case studies of Micro-scale behavioural approaches		**79**
8	Consumer behaviour	81
9	Urban living	89
10	Industrial location	100
11	Adaptation to hazards	109
12	Leisure and recreation	118
13	Stress and pathology	127
14	Migration and residential mobility	135
15	Voting behaviour	145
Part Five: Humanistic Approaches		**153**
16	Experiential environments	155
Bibliography		**164**
Index		**190**

LIST OF FIGURES

1.1 The primitive view of environmental perception 5
1.2 Environmental perception and behaviour 6
1.3 The process of environmental cognition 8
1.4 Constraints on behaviour 13
3.1 The Burgess model of city structure 26
3.2 Social space in four British towns, 1971 29
3.3 The stages of factor analysis 30
3.4 Factorial ecology of Leicester, 1966 31
3.5 Cluster analysis for Leicester, 1971 33
3.6 A typology of neighbourhoods 34
3.7 Insanity rates in Chicago, 1930–31 35
3.8 Schizophrenia in Nottingham, 1963–69 35
5.1 Ontogenetic development of spatial awareness 47
5.2 The learned environment 50
5.3 The diffusion of innovations 52
6.1 The filtering of environmental information 55
6.2 The mind as a 'black box' 56
6.3 A communication model of the mind 56
6.4 The behavioural matrix 58
6.5 A model of consumer decision-making 60
6.6 Single and multiple choice decision-making 61
6.7 The managerial matrix 62
7.1 A conceptual model of man–environment interaction 63
7.2 The image of Armidale, New South Wales 66
7.3 The regression lines between subjective and objective distance for a random sample of ten students 69
7.4 Styles of cognitive mapping 71
7.5 The preference surface of Inverness school leavers 74
7.6 Influences on action space 75
7.7 A typology of time 76
7.8 A one day life-path in time-space 77
8.1 Revealed space preference 82
8.2 Influences on consumer behaviour 83
8.3 Consumer information and usage fields 84
9.1 A hierarchy of social spaces 90
9.2 Activity patterns for the purchase of groceries in Belfast 92
9.3 Local intimacy scores in Leicester 95
9.4 Perceived neighbourhoods in Adamsdown, Cardiff 96
9.5 The neighbourhood quotient 97
10.1 A model of industrial location decision-making 102
10.2 External contacts of central London offices 105
10.3 Spatial learning and organizational growth 106
10.4 The Swedish contact surface in 1970 107
10.5 The multiplier effect of specialized information 108
11.1 Human adjustment to natural hazards 110
11.2 Natural and humanly induced hazards 112
11.3 The processing of information about hazards 114
11.4 A typology of groups in post-hazard situations 116
12.1 Leisure-time activities 119
12.2 Hypothetical changes in activity preferences with age and education 121
12.3 A conceptual model of recreational behaviour 122
12.4 The linkage between location and awareness 123
12.5 Life cycle influences on recreational behaviour 124
13.1 The optimal level of stimulation 128
13.2 Physical pathology in Chicago 130
13.3 The diffusion of measles in Akron 131
13.4 The cycle of disadvantage 134
14.1 Determinants of migration 137
14.2 Life cycle changes and likely residential mobility within a city 138
14.3 A model of relocation decision-making 140
14.4 Inspected residential vacancies in Leicester 143
14.5 A general model of migration 143
15.1 The amplification of majority voting through contagion 149

LIST OF TABLES

1.1 A typology of man–environment interaction 11
3.1 Constructs in social area analysis 28
3.2 Factor loadings in Leicester, 1966 30
5.1 The formal content of personal construct theory 51
5.2 Types of spatial information 53
6.1 Types of decisions 57
6.2 Business decisions and motivations 62
10.1 Location principles 103
11.1 Types of adjustment to natural hazards 111
12.1 The emergence of a society of leisure 118
12.2 The use of time 119
14.1 Causes of residential mobility 137
14.2 The life cycle and residential mobility 138
16.1 Gurvitch's levels of social reality 162

PREFACE

In the last twenty years there has appeared a massive volume of geographical literature concerned with how man comes to know the environment in which he lives and with the way in which such knowledge influences subsequent spatial behaviour. For the most part, however, attempts to review this research have been overly concerned with cognition and with images. They have therefore told us a great deal about how man builds up cognitive maps but have at the same time overlooked a number of important issues such as how man derives information from his environment, how he uses public and private information channels, how he evaluates environmental information in making decisions, and how preferred behaviour may be suppressed as a result of environmental and temporal constraints. The present book seeks to rectify this situation by addressing these issues and by taking a broad perspective that emphasizes the variety and range of the behavioural approaches adopted in the study of man–environment interaction. Particular attention is paid to the philosophical basis for behavioural research in human geography. This is because we believe that human geography in the last couple of decades has tended to be preoccupied with the methodological 'How?' at the expense of the philosophical 'Why?'. Insufficient attention, in other words, has been given to the philosophical foundations of behavioural research. This is not to say that the book propounds a single philosophical orientation or advocates a particular research paradigm. Rather an attempt is made throughout to illustrate the variety of approaches that have been adopted. Thus although we have a leaning towards the transactional–constructivist position that highlights the way in which spatial behaviour is mediated by environmental knowledge, attention is also paid to other philosophical approaches, notably the recent spate of humanistic perspectives. Likewise the book stresses that behavioural research should be seen as complementing rather than supplanting other approaches in geography: for example, the study of everyday spatial behaviour within cities cannot ignore the findings of so-called 'structural' approaches such as social area analysis, just as studies of travel behaviour can never overlook aggregate level spatial interaction models. The micro-scale study of individual decision-making units does nevertheless have advantages, in our opinion, over both structural approaches and the aggregate level pursuit of 'statistically average man'. Principal among these advantages is the fact that micro-scale study affords the opportunity for an authentic model of man that highlights distinctly human characteristics and activities thereby dispensing with the notion of the mind as a 'black box' (implicit in many analyses of behaviour in the aggregate) and with the idea that individuals are powerless in the face of reified concepts like class and culture. The rationale for, and advantages of, micro-scale behavioural approaches are in fact explored at length in both substantive chapters on human information processing and in a number of case studies. Inevitably the choice of case studies had to be selective, and several themes, such as agriculture, welfare, and planning, were considered, but given the limits of time and space, they had to be omitted. As for readership, it is hoped that the book will be useful to all students of geography, particularly those doing undergraduate courses with a behavioural emphasis, as well as to other social scientists, planners, and designers with an interest in environment and behaviour.

The book has had a somewhat protracted development, as befits a joint effort of authors separated by 12,000 miles. The idea for the book arose when the two of us were together at the University of New England in 1979. Refinement of the idea took a considerable time and it was not until late 1981 that work on the project began. Fortunately, study leave arrangements in 1982 allowed the friction of distance to be overcome, first when Gareth Lewis visited Flinders University and then when Jim Walmsley visited the University of Leicester. We are grateful for the support of all three universities and for the constructive comments that many of our colleagues made during the writing of the book. In particular we would like to thank David Lea, Murray McCaskill, Cliff Ollier, and John Paterson for their support and encouragement. Typing of the manuscript made heavy demands on the patience and time of Denise Cumming, Karoly Lockwood, and, above all, Bev Waters and to all three of them we are extremely grateful. Likewise we are equally grateful to Kate Moore and Ruth Rowell, for preparing the figures so expertly, and to Terry Garfield for supervising the cartographic and reprographic procedures. Above all, though, we would like to thank our families for their unending love and support.

D.J.W.
G.J.L.
Leicester, Christmas 1982.

ACKNOWLEDGEMENTS

We are grateful to the following for permission to reproduce copyright material:

Addison Wesley Publishing Company for figs 9.1, 13.1 from figs 5.1, 7.1 (J. D. Porteous, 1977); editor, Geografiska Annaler for fig 8.3 from fig 2 (R. B. Potter, 1979); Annual Reviews Inc for Table 1.1 adapted from Table 1 (D. Stokols, 1978); Edward Arnold Ltd for fig 1.2 from fig 8 (R. M. Downs, 1970a), fig 5.2 from fig 3 (R. G. Golledge 1978); fig 13.4 from fig p 227 (D. T. Herbert, 1977) & Table 10.1 from Table p 212 (Stafford 1972); Australian Academy of Science for fig 11.2 from fig 19.1 (M. Williams, 1979); editor, Australian Geographical Studies for fig 7.7 from Table 1 p 224 (D. J. Walmsley, 1979); Cambridge University Press for fig 7.5 from fig 9 (P. Gould & R. White, 1968); editor, Economic Geography, Clark University for fig 7.6 from fig 1 (F. Horton & D. R. Reynolds, 1971), figs 11.1, 11.3 from figs 3, 4 (R. W. Kates, 1971), fig 12.3 from fig 1 (H. Aldskogious, 1977), fig 13.2 from fig 2 (G. F. Pyle & P. H. Rees, 1971) & fig 13.3 from figs 6, 10 (G. F. Pyle, 1973); editor, Irish Geography & the author for fig 9.2 from figs 10.6, 10.7 (F. W. Boal, 1969); Helen Dwight Reid Educational Foundation for fig 12.2 from fig 2, p 32 (Hendee et al, 1971); the author, Robert E. L. Faris for fig 3.7 from map II p 24 (R. E. L. Faris & H. W. Dunham 1939); The Geographical Association for figs 6.1 a/b from figs 5, 6 (W. Kirk, 1963); Hutchinson Publishing Group Ltd for fig 10.5 from fig 3.1 (A. Pred, 1977a) & Table 12.2 from Table, p 14 (I. Cosgrove & R. Jackson, 1972); Hutchinson Ross Publishing Co for fig 5.1 from fig 3, P 149 (G. T. Moore & R. Golledge, 1976); Institute of British Geographers for fig 1.4 from fig 4 (J. A. Giggs, 1973), fig 3.8 from fig 1 (J. Eyles, 1971) & Table 14.1 from Table V (J. R. Short, 1978a); Longman Group Ltd for fig 9.4 from fig 23.5 (D. T. Herbert, 1975) & fig 10.2 from fig 8.7, p 79 (J. B. Goddard, 1978); the author, R. Maw for fig 12.4 from diagram 19 (R. Maw & D. Cosgrove, 1972); The MIT Press for fig 7.4 from fig 23.2, p 437 *Planning Urban Growth & Regional Development*, Rodwin 1967, & Table 11.1 from Table 3.1 (G. F. White & J. E. Haas, 1975); Ohio State University Press for fig 14.5 from fig 1, p 31 (A. L. Mabogunje, 1970); Oxford University Press for fig 1.3 from fig 3.4, p 42 (J. R. Gold, 1980); Penguin Books Ltd for fig 15.1 from fig 5.3, p 260 (P. J. Taylor & R. J. Johnston, 1979) & Table 5.1 summarised from pp 202–3 (D. Bannister & F. Fransella, 1971); Plenum Publishing Corporation for fig 9.5 from fig 4 (T. Lee, 1968); Population Association of America for fig 14.1 from fig 2 (A. Speare jr, 1974); Prentice-Hall Inc for Table 12.1 based on material from p 181 (J. F. Murphy, 1974); Routledge & Kegan Paul Ltd for fig 12.5 from diagram p 22 (R & R Rapoport, 1975); Royal Dutch Geographical Society for fig 3.4 adapted from figs 3,4 (G. J. Lewis & W. K. Davies, 1974) & fig 7.1 from fig 1, p 252 (D. Pocock, 1973); Sage Publications Inc & the authors for fig 1.1 from fig 1 (D. Stea & M. Downs, 1970); the editor, Environment and Planning and the author, M. J. Taylor for fig 10.3 adapted from fig 1 (M. J. Taylor, 1977); the editor, Lund Studies in Geography for fig 6.4 adapted from fig p 25 (A. Pred, 1967) & fig 10.4 adapted from fig p 97 (A. Pred & G. E. Törnqvist, 1973); University of Chicago Press for fig 3.1 from chart II p 55 (R. E. Park, E. W. Burgess & R. D. McKenzie, 1925); University of Durham for fig 6.5 adapted from fig p 3 (R. Hudson, 1976a); editor, Papers and Proceedings of Regional Science Association for Fig 8.2 from fig 6 (D. L. Huff, 1960); John Wiley & Sons Ltd for fig 3.3 adapted from fig 6.3 (R. J. Johnston, 1976) & fig 10.1 from fig 7.1 (J. Rees, 1974).

Part One

INTRODUCTION

Behavioural research in human geography began in the 1960s. Its origins can be found in the dissatisfaction that was widely felt with normative and mechanistic models of man–environment interaction based on such unreal behavioural postulates as rational economic man.

Basically behavioural approaches are non-normative and focus on the information-processing and acted-out behaviour of individual decision-making units. The scale and nature of such studies varies enormously. Early work tended to concentrate on either overt behaviour (e.g. travel patterns) or on environmental perception (e.g. mental maps) but in recent years the scope of research in behavioural geography has widened considerably to take in the scientific analysis of attitudes, decision-making, learning, and personality as well as humanistic examinations of the meaning that attaches to place and to landscape. Not surprisingly, there are parallels to be seen between what is happening in human geography and what is happening in other disciplines. Psychology, for example, has an increasing number of practitioners who argue that the discipline should break away from its preoccupation with the behaviourist tradition and with artificial laboratory experiments and look instead at behaviour as it occurs in natural situations. This viewpoint is clearly seen in ecological psychology and, particularly, in environmental psychology and the links between these branches of the discipline and behavioural research in human geography are quite close.

One of the consequences of close links with psychology has been the adoption by geographers of psychological terminology. Very often this borrowing process has proceeded in a cavalier fashion. The term 'perception', for instance, is widely used and abused in the geographical literature. In many cases it describes a process that would be better labelled 'cognition'. Loose terminology, and a fascination for what goes on in the mind at the expense of acted-out or observable behaviour, has brought behavioural researchers in human geography a great deal of criticism. It has been pointed out for example that the links between attitudes and perceptions on the one hand and spatial behaviour on the other are neither clear nor direct. More fundamentally, behavioural geography has been charged with viewing the environment as given, and hence with overlooking man's capacity to change the world in favour of a value system that supports the *status quo*. Despite these criticisms behavioural geography has many practitioners. The distinction between objective and behavioural environments, that was postulated by early researchers, is a persistent and helpful one, as is the distinction between images and schemata. What seems to be needed in behavioural geography therefore is a greater attention to the philosophical and epistemological foundations of behavioural research so that a framework or paradigm can be devised that will bring together its varied research efforts.

Part One looks at the origins, growth, and present state of development of behavioural geography, particularly in relation to trends in other disciplines. It also outlines some of the objections that have been raised to behavioural research, the reply that has been made to those objections, and the current problems faced by behavioural researchers.

Chapter 1

GEOGRAPHY AND BEHAVIOUR

Human geography has changed markedly since 1945 (Johnston 1979). The areal differentiation school of thought, which emphasized the delimitation of regions and the study of the characteristics that made them distinct, waned in popularity after having been the dominant geographical paradigm for much of this century. In its place came the quantitative revolution and the search for laws and theories. The application to geography of principles from both scientific method and the philosophy of science appeared to promise much (Harvey 1969a). A focus on the inter-relationship between form and process, and in particular on the way in which behavioural processes brought about spatial patterns, encouraged geographers to turn their attention to model building. In human geography such models were probably best developed in what has become recognized as the locational or spatial analysis school of thought which sought to examine phenomena such as settlement patterns and the location of economic activity in terms of geometry and mathematics (Haggett 1965). In many cases such model building derived its inspiration from micro-economics and was normative in approach in that it stipulated the spatial patterns that should obtain given a number of assumptions about the processes that were supposesdly operating. Commonly, the centre of attention was a set of omniscient, fully rational actors operating in a freely competitive manner on an isotropic plane.

There have always been critics of normative model building in human geography and of attempts to develop the discipline along the lines followed by the natural sciences. Initially such criticisms came from an old guard who defended areal differentiation as the core geographical method and from those who believed that the goal of value-free, 'scientific' human geography was both undesirable and unrealistic (N Smith 1979). Increasingly, however, criticism emerged from within the ranks of the practitioners of modern quantitative human geography. Disquiet focused on the fact that many normative models are grossly unrealistic in that they ignore the complexity of real world situations and instead concentrate on idealized behavioural postulates such as rational economic man. At the same time many models are overly deterministic in so far as they rely on simple mechanistic processes and thereby overlook the fact that individuals have different attributes and motivations and respond in varying ways to different environmental characteristics (Porteous 1977: 138). Above all, the development of sometimes elegant models of spatial form and process has had little relevance for human geographers increasingly committed to using their skills in the solution of pressing societal problems. It is not surprising, therefore, that dissatisfaction with the progress of the quantitative revolution in human geography, and qualms about the acceptablity of normative models, have led to a number of developments within the discipline. For example, some researchers have turned away from the philosophy of science and sought guidance in moral philosophy. As a result, they have addressed themselves to questions of justice and equity (Harvey 1973). Others have abandoned the search for postulates of individual behaviour as a basis for understanding spatial form and have preferred to develop non-normative aggregate level approaches that are exemplified by spatial interaction models which conceptualize individual choice as a random process subject to certain overall constraints (Wilson 1971). Yet another approach – and the one that is the principal focus of attention in this book – has taken the view that a deeper understanding of man–environment interaction can be achieved by looking at the various psychological processes through which man comes to know the environment in which he lives, and by examining the way in which these processes influence the nature of resultant behaviour.

A behavioural emphasis in human geography is not of course entirely new: after all, the landscape school in North American geography focused on man as a morphological agent and, similarly, advocates of human geography as a type of human ecology owed much to the possibilist philosophical position that stressed the significance of choice in human behaviour (Haggett 1965: 11–12). What distinguishes modern behavioural research in human geography from earlier work is the primacy afforded to individual decision-making units, the importance given to both acted-out (or overt) behaviour and to the activities that go on within the mind (covert behaviour), and a non-normative stance that emphasizes the world as it is rather than as it should be under certain theoretical constraints. This new orientation has posed philosophical and methodological questions that have never before been tackled seriously by geographers. Yet it would be wrong to view behavioural geography, as it has come to be known, as a completely distinct branch of the discipline because it has tended to complement rather than supplant existing approaches. The subjects on which behavioural research has focused are often the same as those studied by both location theorists and relevance-orientated social geographers (e.g the provision of urban services, travel patterns, migration). Even model building remains an important research strategy, albeit with a positive rather than a normative goal. In order to appreciate how this situation has come about, and why a behavioural emphasis is thought necessary by many researchers, it is important to review the development of behavioural approaches in geography.

The development of behavioural approaches in human geography

To Gold (1980: 3) behavioural geography is the geographical expression of *behaviouralism*, which is itself a movement within social science that aims to replace the simple, mechanistic conceptions that previously characterized man–environment theory with new versions that explicitly recognize the enormous complexity of behaviour. In a very fundamental sense, then, the behavioural approach in human geography is a point of view rather than a rigorous paradigm: its underlying rationale lies in the argument that an understanding of the spatial distribution and pattern of man-made phenomena on the earth's surface rests upon knowledge of the decisions and behaviours which influence the arrangement of the phenomena rather than on knowledge just of the positional relations of the phenomena themselves (Golledge *et al.* 1972: 59). In other words, morphological laws that describe geometrical patterns are insufficient for understanding how those patterns came into being. Process can only be uncovered if attention is directed to the decision-making activities of the actors involved in creating a given pattern (Johnston 1979: 117).

Early reviews of the behavioural approach in human geography pointed out that two types of study were dominant: analysis of overt behaviour patterns (often travel patterns) and investigations of perception of the environment (Gould 1969). The former tended to be based on an inductive approach that sought to observe reality as a prelude to arriving at generalizations which described the behaviour under study and so the emphasis was on discovering the general in the particular. This approach therefore differed from normative model building which usually began from the opposite perspective with simplified assumptions that were then used as axioms from which deductions could be made (as, for instance, when the practice of distance minimization is deduced from the postulate of rational economic man). The same inductive element was evident in perception studies, the assumption being that comprehension of the way in which an individual perceives his environment would help in understanding that individual's behaviour (Brookfield 1964). No *a priori* assumptions were made about the perception process; rather details of the perceived environments were carefully elicited through a variety of techniques. The mind was thought of very much as a black box and researchers had only the most primitive notions as to how the perception process worked (Fig. 1.1).

As the rationale for a behavioural approach became more acceptable, the range of issues that were studied grew broader. By 1972 Golledge, Brown, and Williamson were able to identify five dominant areas of behavioural research in human geography: studies of decision-making and choice behaviour (especially locational choice, route selection, and patronage patterns); analyses of information flows (particularly in relation to innovation and diffusion); models of search and learning (often derived from theories in psychology); examinations of voting behaviour; and perception research (focusing on hazard perception, image formation, and mental maps). By this time too it was becoming evident that the behavioural approach was developing a number of salient characteristics: it was multidisciplinary in outlook; it focused upon individuals rather than groups or organisations; it emphasized the difference that invariably existed between the cognitive image of an environment and the so-called 'objective' environment; and it postulated a mutually interacting relationship between man and his environment whereby man shaped the environment and was subsequently shaped by it (Gold 1980: 4).

By the 1970s the range of behavioural studies of

Fig. 1.1 The primitive view of environmental perception. *Source*: Stea and Downs (1970, 5).

man–environment interaction was so large and varied as to present problems of classification (see Wood 1970). One popular approach was to categorize studies according to the geographical scale with which they were concerned (Saarinen 1976). A more fundamental and more important distinction can, however, be made according to whether studies are *empirical* or *humanistic* in orientation: the former strive for objectively verifiable measurement and for intersubjective consensus whereas the latter rely on description and literal reconstruction to reveal the self-evident meanings of different environments (Downs and Meyer 1978). These approaches represent, in other words, two very different paths to a behavioural emphasis in human geography. Their existence illustrates very clearly that there is no one behavioural approach to the study of man and his environment.

Empirical research

One of the first topics to be studied by geographers from a behavioural perspective that emphasized the decision-making process was human adjustment to natural hazards. Researchers at the University of Chicago, motivated by a desire to improve flood-plain planning and management, conducted a number of studies into how flood-plain dwellers evaluated the risks in the environment (see White 1945; 1964). What emerged from these studies was a picture of man as a boundedly rational animal: there were few signs of individuals consciously maximizing economic considerations but ample evidence of occasions when limited experience led to less than optimal behaviour (Kates 1962). In short, it became obvious from these studies that, in relation to hazard adjustment, men make choices between what they believe to be alternative courses of action but that the choice process is only boundedly rational in intent and is, in any event, based on limited and perhaps inaccurate information which is evaluated according to predetermined criteria that reflect both the experience and the whims of the individual concerned (Johnston 1979: 113–14).

The idea of bounded rationality has its origins in economics (Simon 1957). It refers to the tendency for man to simplify highly complex problems which he cannot fully comprehend and then to attempt to act rationally within this simplified model of reality. The idea was taken up by Wolpert (1964) who showed that, as a result of imperfect knowledge and a degree of aversion to uncertainty, farmers in central Sweden generally achieved only two-thirds of their potential output. To Wolpert, this suggested that the farmers were *satisficers* who, confronted with a problem, sought to find a satisfactory rather than an optimal course of action. No doubt encouraged by this result, Wolpert (1965) turned his attention to behavioural aspects of the decision to migrate and suggested that a full understanding of migration flows would demand consideration of the set of places of which an individual is aware (action space), the desirability and usefulness of each place to the individual (place utility), the motivation and the goals of the decision-maker, and the stage the decision-maker had reached in his life cycle. This need to consider behavioural variables in migration had been noted earlier by Hägerstrand (1957) and was taken up again when that author made a plea for regional scientists to consider people and not just locations (Hägerstrand 1970). However, on this occasion, Hägerstrand argued that behavioural studies should consider time as well as space and should pay particular attention to the way in which movement is inhibited by transport constraints and other commitments that vary temporally (Pred 1977b). Hägerstrand, in other words, demonstrated a difference that has emerged between North American and Scandinavian behavioural geography: the former tends to focus on sovereign decision-makers actively choosing from among environmental opportunities while the latter highlights the way in which individuals react to constraints (see Thrift 1981).

Work on bounded rationality and satisficing is typical of much behavioural research in human geography in that it tends to work 'backwards' from observable behaviour to make inferences about the mental processes that operate in the mind. Thus geographers have frequently used terms like 'attitude' and it has often been naïvely assumed that knowledge of attitudes will facilitate prediction of behaviour. There has, in other words, been a tendency for geographers to adopt psychological terms without reflecting fully on what they involve: for example, it is risky to talk of attitudes without recognizing that an attitude comprises a cognitive component (knowledge), an affective component (feeling), and a behavioural component (outcome or action) (O'Riordan 1973; Svart 1974). Perhaps the most commonly adopted psychological terms in geography have been 'perception', 'cognition', and 'learning'. Indeed, a great deal of the early work in behavioural geography assumed that individuals derived information about the environment through perception and evaluated this information in terms of a value system to arrive at a cognitive image in respect of which decisions were made, much in the manner described in Fig. 1.2. Attempts to measure, in a verifiable way, the image that people hold in their minds generated a vast literature (Downs and Stea 1977). The idea of environmental cognition is in fact so central to behavioural research in geography that it is dealt with at length later (see Part Three).

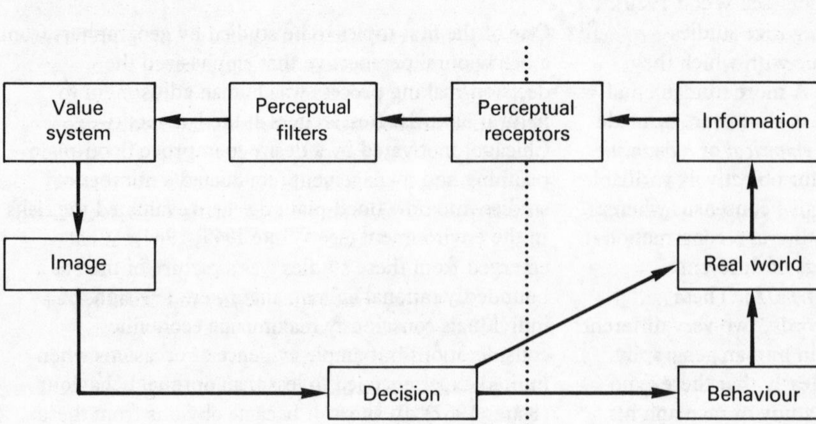

Fig. 1.2 Environmental perception and behaviour. *Source:* Downs (1970a, 85).

Humanistic research

The concern for interpreting observable behaviour in terms of what goes on in the mind, that is evident among empirical researchers in the scientific tradition, is also apparent in those branches of geography which adopt a humanistic approach. However, with this type of inquiry, the scientific goals of replicable and verifiable measurement are generally discarded in favour of an emphasis on understanding the world as seen through the eyes of the individuals whose behaviour is to be understood. Prominent among such work have been studies of landscapes (e.g. Lowenthal and Prince 1964; 1965). In this sense a landscape is something that is all around, something that is being continuously created and altered (often unconsciously as much as through conscious design), and something that is imbued with symbolic and cultural meaning (Meinig 1979a). The study of how landscape is interpreted is therefore integral to an understanding of man's relationship to his environment because changes in the landscape give clues to changing evaluations of the environment (Prince 1971; Lowenthal 1975). This fact has of course been recognized by historical geographers for a long time and a good deal of effort has gone into contrasting myth and reality in the views of landscape held by early settlers in new lands (see Watson and O'Riordan 1976). To a significant degree this sort of historical reconstruction draws on Boulding's (1956) concept of an image as a simplified and distorted representation of reality.

Images of landscape and of the environment obviously change over time. In fact so important are these changed conceptions of environment held by common people that Wright proposed a new field of study – *geosophy* – to take account of them. His proposal rested on the contention that 'geographical knowledge of one kind or another is universal among men, and is in no sense a monopoly of geographers' (Wright 1947: 13). He also pointed out that there are no totally unexplored lands left on earth and suggested that the coming geographical frontiers are to be found instead in the *terrae incognitae* in the minds of men. The idea of subjective worlds, partly private and partly shared, emerged again in the work of Kirk (1952; 1963) who distinguished between phenomenal and behavioural environments: the former refers to 'real' situations and the latter to the 'psycho-physical field' in which facts are arranged into patterns or structures and evaluated in line with cultural influences. To Kirk (1963: 365), the environment has 'shape, cohesiveness and meaning added to it by the act of human perception'. What Kirk proposed, therefore, was that all men have personal worlds but that there also exist consensus views (Lowenthal 1961). By adopting this position Kirk brought Gestalt theory from psychology into geography and did much to bring into focus questions about the nature of explanation in behavioural research.

Acceptance of the fact that individuals have personal worlds encouraged geographers to look at the environment from an experiential perspective. For example, Tuan (1974a) introduced the term *topophilia* to describe the affective bond that develops between people and place. Place in this sense is a centre of meaning that varies in scale from a piece of furniture to a nation state (Tuan 1975a). Exactly how the meaning that a place holds for an individual is to be uncovered is of course a difficult problem. In one sense it demands a humanistic perspective that focuses on the earth as the home of man and geography as the mirror of man (in that knowledge of human nature may be deepened by studying man's relations with his environment) (Tuan 1971). In another sense it implies that geographers may have to turn to philosophical approaches to explanation that they have so far ignored. Tuan (1972) has suggested, for instance, that structuralism and existentialism may be studied with benefit by geographers: the former seeks to identify human thought patterns that transcend cultural differences while the latter sees man as striving to define a self that is given neither by nature nor by culture. Other writers have argued for an apparently less rigorous, idealist position, derived from history (Collingwood 1956), that involves rethinking the thoughts of the people whose behaviour is under study in order that the researcher can explain human actions in a critical and analytical way (Guelke 1974).

A framework for research

The sort of approach advocated by the humanists has not attracted large numbers of devotees. Instead most behavioural researchers in geography have preferred to stay within the methodology and framework in which they themselves were schooled. Empiricism and scientific method have therefore remained strong. Indeed, even within the 'scientific school' researchers have shown a predilection for generalization rather than description. For example a distinction has been drawn between the examination of *behaviour in space* (where actions are largely a function of the particular environment in which they occur) and the study of *spatial behaviour* (which seeks to identify general principles that apply independently of context), and research has concentrated overwhelmingly on the latter (Rushton 1969a).

The search for general principles and laws has led investigators in many directions. As a result there has been a plethora of specific studies but very little progress towards the formulation of an overall framework that ties together individual research efforts. Yet such a framework is essential if research is to be other than piecemeal and if knowledge about man–environment interaction is to be cumulative. An early attempt at a framework, specifically for locational decision-making, was Pred's (1967) development of the behavioural matrix, the axes of which represented the quantity and quality of information available to a decision-maker and the decision-maker's ability to handle that information. Individuals could be schematically assigned to this matrix in any position from rational economic man to rank incompetent. Unfortunately, however, the axes proved difficult to define in operational terms and the matrix is probably best remembered for the stimulus that it gave to the search for other frameworks.

After Pred, the main framework for research in behavioural geography focused on environmental cognition. The rationale for looking at cognition is a simple one: 'if we can understand *how* human minds process information from external environments and if we can determine *what* they process and use, then we can investigate how and why choices concerning those environments are made' (Golledge and Rushton 1976: viii). To unravel the process of cognition is not, however, an easy task, partly because of an ever-present feeling that how we interpret the environment and how we behave is obvious (Downs and Stea 1977: xiii). As a result it is a major achievement to analyse what is often taken for granted and to come up with answers to questions such as how we know the world about us, how we learn about the environment, and how this learning influences our everyday lives.

One conceptual framework that describes the 'how' and the 'what' of environmental cognition has been provided by Gold (1980) (Fig. 1.3). This framework proposes that information from the environment is filtered as a result of personality, cultural, and cognitive variables to form two sorts of cognitive representation: *images* (which are pictures of an object that can be called to mind through the imagination) and *schemata* (which are the frameworks within which environmental information derived from experience is organized). Although important and useful, the distinction between images and schemata is one that has often been overlooked and many writers have preferred to talk about the general activity of *cognitive mapping* which is generally taken to encompass those 'processes which enable people to acquire, code, store, recall, and manipulate information about the nature of their spatial environment' (Downs and Stea 1973c: xiv). Despite sounding specific, the actual process of cognitive mapping is very much an unknown quantity. Little is known, for example, of the neurophysiological processes involved and, as a result, the mind is widely regarded as a 'black box' (Stea and Downs 1970). Psychological

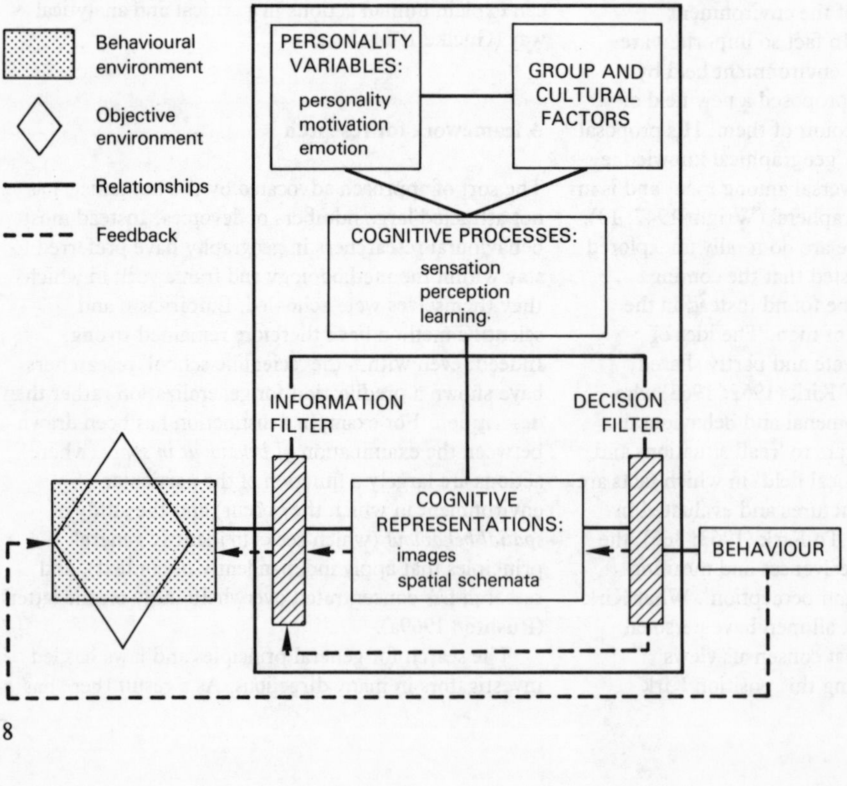

Fig. 1.3 The process of environmental cognition. *Source*: Gold (1980, 42).

make-up, physiological make-up, culture, and the state of arousal of a person are thought to be important in influencing that person's cognitive maps but to date there is little or no empirical proof of this (Pocock 1973).

A major problem inhibiting studies of images and schemata is that of conceptualizing the environment under study, that is, the problem of deciding just which elements within the environment elicit a response from individuals and hence are worthy of study. Gold's (1980) framework suggests that there exists an 'objective' and a 'behavioural' environment. A similar but slightly more complex classification came from Porteous (1977) who recognized phenomenal environments (physical objects), personal environments (perceived images of the phenomenal environment), and contextual environments (cultural beliefs and expectations that influence behaviour). Sonnenfeld (1972) went even further and proposed four levels at which the environment should be studied: the geographical (the world); the operational (those parts of the world that impinge upon a man, whether or not he is aware of them); the perceptual (the parts of the world that man is aware of as a result of direct and indirect experience); and the behavioural (that part of the perceptual environment that elicits a behavioural response). Perception is obviously a critical determinant of the nature of some of these environments. In fact it can be thought of as 'an all-pervasive and supremely important intervening variable in any analysis of the spatial expression of human activities' (Golledge *et al.* 1972: 73). It is a term used by geographers to refer to the product of the sensory encoding of information that usually leads to learned and relatively stable conceptions of the environment (Pocock and Hudson 1978: 1). In this sense, a perceived environment can be thought of as a monistic surface on which decisions are based (Brookfield 1969). Conceptually, this is fine. It is, however, extremely difficult to prove or disprove. In fact one of the problems with the behavioural approach in geography is that conceptual thinking has gone ahead faster than the testing of such thinking. This accounts in part for why the behavioural approach has not attained the prominence that many predicted (Burton 1963). However, before looking at criticisms of the behavioural approach it is important to note that developments in geography have not occurred in isolation but rather have parallels in other disciplines.

Behavioural approaches in other disciplines

The field of man–environment interaction is a burgeoning multidisciplinary one that has attracted a wide variety of researchers. For example, sociologists have examined images of cities (Strauss 1961) and urban behavioural environments (Orleans 1973), and anthropologists have looked at physical settings in order to understand more fully the sociocultural characteristics of the people living within those settings (Hall 1966; Murton 1972). Above all, psychologists have become interested in the field. For the most part, however, this is a recent development and for the greater part of this century psychologists made little contribution to furthering understanding of man–environment relations. There are a number of reasons for this. First, psychologists have tended to be interested in processes in general rather than in relation to specific objects. Thus they have looked at cognition as a mental process rather than at environmental cognition (although some of the general principles can obviously be applied in the environmental context) (Moore and Golledge 1976b: 20). Secondly, psychologists have tended to be committed to a laboratory-based experimental tradition that has limited their attention to small-scale and often artificial environments (Pocock and Hudson 1978: 20). Finally, and most important, a great many psychologists have worked within the *behaviourist* school of thought which has therefore circumscribed the sorts of problems to which they have addressed themselves. Although there is no one behaviourist approach (Watson 1924; Skinner 1974), the position does have two basic tenets: it seeks to be objective and it argues that only those events that can be observed and empirically specified have any legitimacy in a science of human behaviour (Ittleson *et al.* 1974: 65). No place is allowed for concepts like 'need' or 'feeling'. As a result, the approach tends to be reductionist in that complex situations are reduced to simple bonds between stimuli and responses (S–R bonds). The environment, in other words, is specified only as a set of stimuli to which individuals respond in a more or less deterministic manner. Not surprisingly, much of the experimentation on which S–R theory in particular, and behaviourist research generally, is based has been conducted with animals. As a result, its extrapolation into the realm of human behaviour necessitates what Koestler (1967: 30) has trenchantly described as a 'ratomorphic' view of man. In short, behaviourist theories are elegant but unhelpful when it comes to understanding real world man–environment interaction (Getis and Boots 1971). The same can be said for many of the attempts to explain human behaviour in terms of its biological bases (Nelson 1974), despite the apparent resurgence of such a view in the guise of sociobiology (Wilson 1978).

It would be wrong, of course, to characterize all psychology as having been conducted within the behaviourist tradition. Indeed, it is to work outside mainstream psychology that many behavioural geographers have turned for inspiration. For example, Kelly's (1955) conception of man as a protoscientist, who comes to terms with his world by devising *constructs* to help him understand it, has proved tremendously stimulating and has resulted in a number of applications of personal construct theory that are examined later (see Ch. 5). An even more fruitful source of inspiration has been Gestalt psychology (see Koroscil 1971). Part of the appeal to geographers of the Gestalt approach lies in the importance it attaches to perception. Gestaltists argue that perception proceeds according to innate abilities which organize environmental stimuli into coherently structured forms or patterns (Gold 1980: 11). Thus each person has a behavioural environment which is the environment as perceived. Although each individual perceives uniquely, the resultant behavioural environments have much in common because they are derived from both common neurological mechanisms that are innate in people and from common superimposed socializing experiences (Ittelson *et al.* 1974: 68). One of the most prominent Gestalt psychologists was Lewin (1936; 1951) and his work is frequently cited by geographers because he was acutely aware of the significance of the environment and of the way in which the nature of the behavioural environment influenced man's action. Lewin in fact thought of human behaviour as a stream of activity that resulted from the interaction of factors within the person (needs, values, feelings, predispositions) with external factors as perceived in a given behavioural setting (Ittelson *et al.* 1974: 69). The unit of study was therefore man together with his environment and Lewin devised the notation $B = f(P,E)$ to demonstrate the way in which behaviour is a function of the person and the environment. This interaction of the individual with his behaviour setting is sometimes known as the *life space*: it is a cognitively structured psychological field that extends from the past, through the present, and into the future (Pocock and Hudson 1978: 5).

Gestaltists are not the only psychologists to focus on man and his behavioural setting, and life space is not the only concept that has been used to describe that focus. For example, Sprout and Sprout (1957) introduced the term *milieu* to encompass the human and nonhuman tangible objects, the social and cultural phenomena, and the images that impinge on behaviour. Likewise, a number of researchers have argued for a 'psychology of situations' that pays explicit attention to the physical–geographical, biological, and socio–cultural environments that mediate actual behaviour (Magnusson 1981). More significantly, Lee (1968; 1976) borrowed the notion of *schema* from neurology and used it to characterize the inner representations that individuals have of external environments. Lee's (1976: 36) argument was that 'just as every thing must be some*thing*, so it must also be some*where*'. Thus individuals build up *socio-spatial schemata*, which they can add to or modify, for coming to terms with their everyday environment. Precisely how people do this is of course a critical consideration in the design professions and architects in particular have put a great deal of effort into studying this problem (Altman 1975). Generally speaking, such work has concentrated on small-scale structures and therefore on *place* rather than space (Canter 1977). As a result it has been prone to emphasize the idea of *images*. As introduced by Boulding (1956: 17), an image is built up by an individual from information derived from the enveloping social and physical milieu of the individual over his or her entire life history. The problem for architects has been to find what makes a structure or area imageable. In this they have been helped by the work of Lynch (1960) who showed, in a study of North American cities that has subsequently been replicated in several countries, that the image of a city can be resolved into nodes (meeting places), paths, landmarks, edges or barriers, and areas. In this sense an image of a city fulfils several functions: it plays a social role in that it provides the emotional security that goes with a sense of belonging; it offers a means of organizing knowledge; and it presents a ready reference for quick and easy movement.

Another approach that emphasizes the influence of environment on behaviour is to be found in *ecological psychology*. This branch of psychology asserts that real world conditions cannot be simulated in contrived situations and that psychologists must therefore break away from their traditional role as 'operators' (who create situations to which subjects have to react) and take on the role of 'transducers' or, in other words, interpreters of behaviour as it occurs (Barker 1965). The focus of attention in ecological psychology is the *behaviour setting*. This setting is bounded in space and time and has a structure that relates physical, social and cultural phenomena in such a way as to elicit common or regularized forms of behaviour (Ittelson *et al.* 1974: 70). Examples of ecological psychology are to be seen in Barker's (1968) attempts to relate the structural properties of classrooms to the behaviour *en masse* of schoolchildren in that setting. Of particular interest is the fact that some settings seem to be *undermanned* (in that there are too few participants to maintain behaviour at an optimal level) whereas other settings appear to be *overmanned* (with a result that some participants can feel redundant and unimportant).

Table 1.1 A typology of man – environment interaction *Source*: Adapted from Stokols (1978, 264)

		Form of transaction	
		Cognitive	Behavioural
Phase of transaction	Active	*Interpretive* Cognitive representation of the spatial environment Personality and the environment	*Operative* Behaviour modification to adapt to the environment Human spatial behaviour (personal space, territoriality, crowding)
	Reactive	*Evaluative* Environmental attitudes Environmental assessment	*Responsive* Human responses to the physical environment Ecological psychology

Of greater interest to the geographer than ecological psychology has been *environmental psychology*. This is a relatively new branch of psychology that shares with the ecological perspective the view that the object of study should be real world rather than laboratory behaviour (Craik 1968; 1970). Environmental psychology has in fact a dual origin: it began partly as a result of a realization that psychology generally had had little to say, in the face of increasing environmental problems, about man's impact, through design and planning, on his environment (Proshansky *et al*. 1970b; Wohlwill 1970), and partly as a result of the discovery of engaging scientific puzzles in the fields of environmental perception, cognition, and assessment, environmental personality, and environmental adaptation (Craik 1977). According to Ittelson *et al*. (1974: 12 – 14), the discipline is now at the stage where it can be characterized by eight assumptions in respect of the environment:

1. The environment is experienced as a unitary field.
2. Man is an integral part of the environment rather than an object in it.
3. All physical environments are inescapably linked to social systems.
4. The influence of the environment on individuals varies with the behaviour in question.
5. The environment often operates below the level of awareness.
6. There may be significant differences between the 'observed' and 'real' environments.
7. Environments can be cognized as a set of mental images.
8. Environments have symbolic value.

In simple terms, environmental psychology seeks to be of applied value by aiming to tell designers something of how man experiences the environment (Craik 1973). It is however far from deterministic in its approach in that it explicitly recognizes that man is a goal-directed animal who influences the environment and is influenced by it.

As with behavioural research in human geography, the range of issues with which environmental psychologists have been concerned is very broad and a variety of behaviours has been examined at a number of scales and with a fair degree of methodological eclecticism. One means of describing this work has been provided by Stokols (1978) who argued that man – environment relations can be differentiated in terms of whether they involve a cognitive or a behavioural transaction and whether the focus is on man actively interpreting the environment or on man reacting to environmental attributes. In this way it is possible to develop a fourfold typology of interpretive, evaluative, operative, and responsive studies (Table 1.1). Clearly, on this basis a great deal of behavioural research in human geography can be designated as interpretive or evaluative in emphasis, as is shown by attempts to describe images, schemata, mental maps and preference surfaces. In view of this similarity between the disciplines it is worthwhile noting the claim that environmental psychology has a chance of both promoting the welfare of man and of jerking establishment research out of its ever deepening rut of statistical trivialization (Mercer 1975: 52). Whether the same can be said of behavioural geography is uncertain and its impact on geography in general can only really be assessed by examining commentaries on the current state of research.

Environment, cognition, behaviour

In the 1960s the development of a behavioural approach in geography appeared to offer much. Both Burton

(1963: 157) and Brookfield (1969: 51) spoke of studies of perception as a rival to the quantitative revolution in terms of the significance of the viewpoint that they provided. Such enthusiasm has not however been universal. From early times Harvey (1969b) expressed doubts as to whether the unravelling of choice behaviour would be any more rewarding than the conceptualizing of human actions as the result of a stochastic decision process. In his view such statistical generalizations might be quite adequate for the purpose at hand in most geographical research. More recently, Cullen (1978) has criticized geographers for ignoring time as a behavioural dimension and for approaching most studies from the point of view of comparative statics. Even harsher criticism has come from those who believe that most behavioural research belies a commitment to the *status quo* (Massey 1975b). This radical perspective argues that the behaviour and the environment under study in geographical research is usually taken as a 'given', rather than as something 'produced' by an existing social structure, and hence little or no attention is paid to possible alternative behaviours under different circumstances. In the view of Jensen-Butler (1981), this weakness will be inevitable so long as behavioural geography is ontologically grounded in idealism rather than materialism. Others have argued that the failings in behavioural geography lie in methodology rather than ontology.

According to Cullen (1976), behavioural geography should be absolutely fundamental to studies in location theory, regional science, and planning but is instead something of an intellectual backwater. He attributes this situation to the fact that behavioural researchers have rather blindly borrowed the scientific paradigm that was popular in human geography generally and then let that paradigm determine the nature of the problems that were to be investigated. Thus the independent – dependent variable format of much scientific endeavour is reflected in the way in which behavioural geography focuses on an object and then invokes a cognitive image through which people make sense of the object. In Cullen's view, the ubiquity of this framework is also its principal failing: it can be applied in a wide variety of cases because it is almost wholly lacking in content, explains nothing, and generates no testable hypotheses. His solution is to focus on the individual *qua* individual and to try to understand mental processes at that level.

A similar argument for breaking away from the mechanistic perspective of the quantitative revolution has been advanced by Bunting and Guelke (1979). In their view, too great an emphasis on images rather than behaviour has meant that behavioural geography has not produced the results that were expected of it. They lay the blame for this on weaknesses in the theoretical framework which has been adopted in most studies and they argue that, by assuming that man reacts to his environment as he perceives and interprets it through previous experience and knowledge, behavioural geography has all too often put too much emphasis on ego-centred interpretations of the environment. Specifically, they are critical of two assumptions on which a great deal of behavioural research in geography is based. The first assumption is that there exist identifiable environmental images that can be accurately measured. Bunting and Guelke object to this on a number of grounds: it is not clear what terms should be used for describing an image; it is not clear whether an environmental image can be extracted without distortion from the totality of mental imagery; not enough effort has gone into checking and validating the methods by which images are elicited; and too much emphasis has been placed on 'a quest for numerical precision where such precision is unrelated and unrelatable to any real situations' (Bunting and Guelke 1979: 455). The second critical assumption is that there exist strong relationships between revealed images or preferences and actual, real-world behaviour. Bunting and Guelke's objection to this is that it is an unfounded assumption because extremely little research has looked at the congruence between image and behaviour.

Bunting and Guelke's comments provoked a counter-attack by several very prominent researchers who had used the behavioural approach. For example, Rushton (1979) accused Bunting and Guelke of drawing a caricature of behavioural geography, while Saarinen (1979) responded by pointing out that the problems of measuring images were overdrawn and by suggesting that the subject matter with which Bunting and Guelke were concerned was but only one small part of a newly developing interdisciplinary field which transcends geography. In a similar vein, Downs (1979) made the point that behavioural geography has come a long way in a short time. Of course it would be wrong to see Bunting and Guelke's argument as a rejection of all that behavioural geography stands for since their main concern was to assert the primacy of overt behaviour over mental imagery as a focus of geographical attention. Briefly, they argued that geographers should begin with what is known, with what one can measure with confidence, and with what can be directly sensed and then move on to a consideration of vague and difficult to measure images and thoughts which may provide the keys to understanding overt behaviour (Bunting and Guelke 1979: 458).

Where Bunting and Guelke differ from mainstream

behavioural geography is in their assertion that it is better to observe behaviour and then infer what goes on in the mind than to postulate mental processes and phenomena and then look for manifestations of those processes and phenomena. This difference of opinion harks back to one of the most basic problems in modern geography, that is, how to relate form and process. Olsson (1969) introduced the term 'geographic inference problem' to refer to the problem of relating form (which is usually a macro-scale phenomenon) to process (which is usually specified at the micro-scale) at a satisfactory level of aggregation. His suggested solution of using many-valued logics has found few adherents (Olsson 1970). More prosaic attempts to use mental models derived at the individual scale as in input for models of aggregate behaviour patterns at the macro-scale have met with a similar lack of success (Hudson 1976b). This failure to find a satisfactory way of relating form and process means that behavioural researchers in geography must be on their guard against the dangers of *psychologism* (Mills 1970), that is, the fallacy whereby social phenomena are explained purely in terms of the mental characteristics of individuals. This is particularly important because one of the most telling criticisms yet made of behavioural geography is that it frequently views man as *homo psychologicus* and tends to treat environmental behaviour as a one-dimensional phenomenon to the extent that the economic, social and political considerations that act concomitantly with environmental influences are frequently overlooked (Thrift 1981). Only when the whole range of influences is assessed and analysed will a full understanding of real world behaviour be possible (Bunting and Guelke 1979: 461). In this context Mercer (1972) has suggested that the focus of attention for behavioural geographers should be the multi-faceted *situation* in which behaviour occurs and the way in which meaning is ascribed to both the situation and the resultant behaviour. The *taken-for-granted world* might be particularly important in this context but it is invariably overlooked (Ley 1977). What geographers need is perhaps a geographical imagination, parallelling sociological imagination (Mills 1970), to enable them to take account of the individual's recognition of the role of space and place in his own biography, and of the way in which transactions between individuals and between organizations are affected by the space that separates them (Eyles 1971: 243). In this way it might be possible to appreciate how social and spatial institutions attract meanings which serve to constrain behaviour. A simple characterization of how this can happen is presented in Fig. 1.4. Clearly, position in the social structure (class) influences access to society's resources. This is reflected in position in the spatial structure (suburb or residence), which in turn affects both the image that is held of the environment and access to spatial resources. Individuals undoubtedly have preferences for different behaviour patterns but whether these preferences are revealed in behaviour, or simply repressed, depends on the range of spatial opportunities that are available, given the constraints that are operating. The dichotomy between revealed and repressed preferences is of course only schematic and in reality it is much more likely that constraints will restrict the level of activity (rather than repress it) or will lead to compensatory behaviour whereby individuals do something other than their most preferred activity (Klingbeil 1980).

It is important for behavioural researchers in

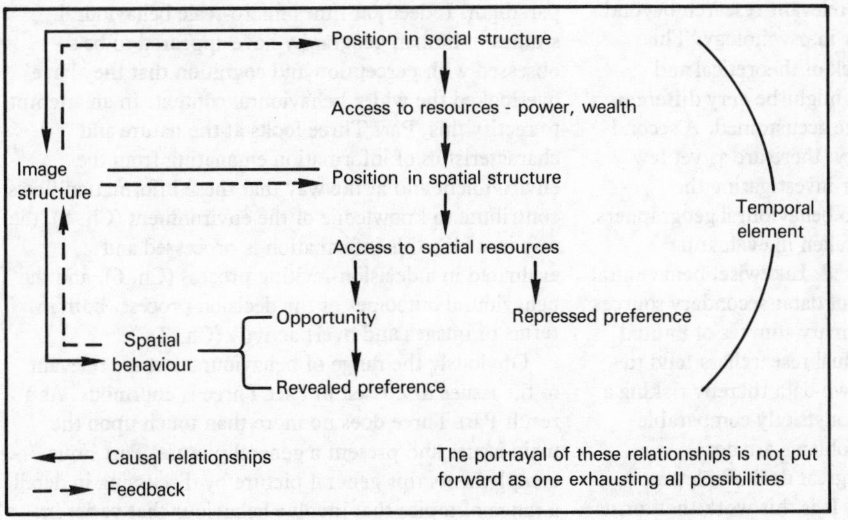

Fig. 1.4 Constraints on behaviour. *Source*: Eyles (1971, 246).

geography to appreciate that their focus of study is man interacting with a complex, multidimensional environment, because this perspective will prevent them from concentrating on the spatial factor alone and will hence stop them adopting a form of *spatialism* that is not dissimilar in some respects from the deterministic doctrine of environmentalism (Guelke 1977). In order to take up this wider perspective, behavioural geographers must be prepared to disregard some of the research done over the last two decades and to temper their enthusiasm for generating yet more data on mental maps and cognitive images. Instead they need to reflect on the basic questions that have stimulated researchers across a number of disciplines: How does man come to know the environment in which he lives? How does that knowledge change over time? How does knowledge of the environment influence behaviour? In pondering these questions behavioural geographers must recognize that the question of how people come to know an environment is part of the more general epistemological question of how a subject comes to know an object (Moore and Golledge 1976b). They must therefore address themselves to the philosophical question as to whether knowledge comes from the environment through the senses, whether knowledge is innate and therefore precedes experience, or whether it comes from the interaction of the individual with his environment. The last of these sounds the most plausible. If it is adopted, the behavioural geographer needs to look at how individuals derive information from the environment, what information is derived, how information is used in the mind, and how the processing of information influences overt behaviour in constrained circumstances. A great many problems must be faced in this sort of approach. To begin with, geographers must be aware of relevant research beyond their own discipline, especially in psychology. This means that they must take stock of theoretical and philosophical frameworks that might be very different from the ones to which they are accustomed. A second problem relates to methodology: there are as yet few generally accepted methods for investigating the questions that are of interest to behavioural geographers and hence great care must be taken in evaluating whatever methodologies are used. Likewise, behavioural geography suffers from a lack of data: secondary sources are usually of no value and primary sources of limited availability. As a result individual researchers tend to fall back on generating their own data thereby risking a situation where data sets are not strictly comparable from study to study. These problems are not insurmountable and already a great deal of relevant research has been undertaken. It is this work that forms the source material for much of this book.

The scope of the book

The book has a simple structure. It is divided into five parts. Part One has described the origins of behavioural research in human geography and its parallels in other disciplines. It has shown that, in large measure, behavioural research has focused on individuals and on the way individuals interact with their surroundings. In order to appreciate why these micro-scale process-orientated behavioural studies are important it is necessary to compare them with macro-scale approaches. This is the scope of Part Two. Essentially human geographers have adopted one of two sorts of macro-scale approach. The first are studies of behaviour in the aggregate, exemplified by spatial interaction models (Ch. 2). The second are structural approaches that posit autonomous macro-structures as causal agents in determining individual human behaviour. These structures can be differentiated into two kinds: politico-economic structures and socio-spatial structures. The former, like spatial interaction models, have a largely economic frame of reference and so are examined in Chapter 2. The latter are discussed in Chapter 3, largely in relation to urban social space. Both approaches have a number of weaknesses that relate, in the main, to the neglect of individual behaviour. Chapter 4 reviews these weaknesses and considers the criteria by which models of man should be evaluated.

It is an awareness of the weaknesses of the macro-scale approach that has encouraged many human geographers to turn to micro-scale behavioural approaches. Because work in this field is still in its infancy, and because it ranges over an enormous subject matter, there has not yet emerged one overriding paradigm. Indeed, at times micro-scale behavioural studies in human geography have appeared to be so obsessed with perception and cognition that they have overlooked the wider behavioural context. In an attempt to rectify this, Part Three looks at the nature and characteristics of information emanating from the environment and at the way that these information flows contribute to knowledge of the environment (Ch. 5), the way in which this information is processed and evaluated in a decision-making process (Ch. 6), and the behavioural outcomes of the decision process, both in terms of images and overt activity (Ch. 7).

Obviously the range of behaviours that are relevant to the issues discussed in Part Three is enormous. As a result Part Three does no more than touch upon the main issues and present a general picture. Part Four complements this general picture by discussing in detail a range of topics that involve behaviour that varies in periodicity, in terms of whether it is obligatory or discretionary, and in the terms of the type of environment involved. The topics covered are consumer behaviour (Ch. 8), urban living (Ch. 9), industrial location (Ch. 10), adaptation to hazards (Ch. 11), leisure and recreation (Ch. 12), stress and social pathology (Ch. 13), migration and residential mobility (Ch. 14), and voting behaviour (Ch. 15).

The problems that are inherent in micro-scale, process-orientated behavioural research are discussed as and when appropriate during Part Four. For the most part these problems have been overcome within a positivistic framework that highlights the importance of 'scientific method'. Increasingly, however, behavioural researchers have come to appreciate that there are non-positivist approaches that can contribute to an understanding of man's relationship to his environment through emphasizing subjectivity. Part Five explores just what these alternative approaches have to offer.

Part Two

MACRO-SCALE APPROACHES

Until recently geographical interest in man–environment interaction focused on aggregate patterns of behaviour rather than on man as an individual animal. At the centre of attention were the general features that could be observed when a group of individuals interacted with their surroundings. The study of individual action was, in other words, subordinated to the study of overall group patterns from which could be derived the behavioural characteristics of 'statistically average man'. This approach is clearly seen in the development of a variety of spatial interaction models that investigate how the flow of humans and human artefacts (e.g. phone calls) between places diminishes as the distance between places increases. Although traditionally based on an analogy with Newtonian physics, these models have now been shown to have a common foundation in information theory and statistical mechanics. The development of such models rests on the rationale that there are characteristics of aggregate spatial behaviour that are observable irrespective of the particular identity of the individuals under study. This is possible in so far as individuals are assumed to adopt a common, largely economic frame of reference in deciding where to go and what to do. In short, spatial interaction models postulate that there are macro-scale features of human spatial behaviour that can be identified by studying man in the aggregate.

Some geographers have gone beyond this view and have argued that there exist macro-scale phenomena which influence human behaviour but which do not result from the mere aggregation of individual actions. This view is best seen in political economy in general and structural marxism in particular. The latter argues that social phenomena (which include much of the behaviour studied by geographers) can only really be understood if they are seen as part of a superstructure that is related to the material needs or mode of production on which society is based. This, then, is a structural approach: it ignores individual values, ideas, and action in favour of autonomous macro-structures (e.g. class, culture) which are seen as major determinants of human behaviour. Another macro-scale structural approach to have had a major impact on human geography is that which emphasizes the effect of social space and neighbourhood structure on individual behaviour. With its origins in the Chicago School of human ecology, and manifestations in social area and factorial ecologies of city structure, this approach highlights the relationship between social milieux and social pathologies (e.g. crime), especially in inner city areas. It suffers, however, from the fact that the causal links between neighbourhood structure and individual pathological behaviour are unclear. In fact, the failure of structural approaches generally to relate the macro-scale and the micro-scale in any truly meaningful way has stimulated a good deal of debate about the appropriateness of various models of man in geographical research. In particular attention has focused on holism, individualism, structuralism, and determinism.

Part Two examines the strengths and weaknesses of macro-scale approaches. Chapter 2 looks primarily at economic behaviour and therefore evaluates both spatial interaction models and structural marxism. Socio-spatial structures are the subject of attention in Chapter 3. The weaknesses of both sorts of macro-scale, structural approaches, and the need for an authentic model of individual behaviour, are examined in Chapter 4.

Chapter 2

MODELLING ECONOMIC BEHAVIOUR

Human geography is concerned with the way in which man interacts with his environment. The idiographic approach, which focused on an individual place and the human activities associated with that place, has nowadays given way to a nomothetic approach that attempts to find the general in the particular in order that statements can be made about man–environment interaction such that these statements will obtain over a wide variety of specific cases. This search for generality has invariably involved model building and two approaches have been prominent. These may be termed the aggregate–behavioural and the structural. The former involves studies of interaction over distance that are popular in economic geography, are linked to location theory, and are frequently derived from deterministic gravity models. In simple terms such studies seek a functional or statistical relationship between external stimulus variables (e.g. city size) and responses (e.g. migration) in a repertoire of human spatial behaviour (Pipkin 1981a). The goal in such studies is not, however, to understand the behaviour of any given individual so much as to understand the behaviour of 'statistically average man', that is to say, the overall features that emerge in an aggregate pattern of behaviour (Hudson 1976b). Spatial interaction models are, then, macro-scale models in the sense that they attempt to identify order in the spatial behaviour of collections of individuals. They are not explicitly concerned with what motivates each individual to behave in a certain way. The same can be said of structural models. These models strive to understand the way in which a society organizes itself without necessarily concerning themselves with the individuals that make up society. Two general sorts of structural models have been popular among geographers: those deriving from structural marxism and those focusing on the organization of social space. The former are very much concerned with economic behaviour and are examined in the later part of the present chapter. The latter, with their emphasis on social areas and social milieux, are the subject of attention in Chapter 3.

Models of spatial interaction

Over a century ago Carey (1858) suggested that the laws of physics could be applied to the study of human behaviour since the flow of people or of human artefacts (e.g. trade, telephone calls) between locations can be explained by the laws of gravitation. The application of the *gravity model* was fundamental to early studies of spatial interaction and more recently in an approach that has become known as 'social physics' (Ajo 1953). Although most social scientists would now frown on the idea that the complexities and subtleties of human behaviour can be reduced to simple physical laws, the gravity model has continued to attract interest. In its simplest form the model can be expressed as follows:

$$I_{ij} = \frac{k\,(P_i\,P_j)}{D_{ij}{}^{b}}$$

where I_{ij} = the interaction between town i and town j
P_i and P_j = the population of towns i and j respectively
D_{ij} = the distance between town i and town j
k = a constant
b = an exponent.

In short, according to the gravity model the interaction between two places is determined by the population of those places (a surrogate measure for mass) and the distance between the places raised to a power (most commonly squared). The enumerator in the equation measures the potential for interaction and the denominator the impedance function. For example, if town i had a population of 7 and town j a population of 8, then there would be 56 potential interactions. The extent to which these potentials are realized is determined by the impedance function. The model can be varied to fit different circumstances by defining distance in terms of geography, time, or money. In this way the model has been applied with success to predict such interactions as inter-city migration, traffic flows, telephone calls, and trade (Olsson 1965). It has even been reformulated in probabilistic rather than deterministic terms (Huff 1963).

Closely related to the gravity model proper are *potential models*. If the gravity model is applied in relation to an individual person rather than a town then one of the two population figures in the enumerator of the gravity model can be set at unity. Moreover, if the impedance function is set at the square of the distance (as is common in many gravity models) then the potential interaction of an individual with a place can be calculated from

$$I = \frac{P}{D^2}$$

where I = interaction
P = the population of the place in question
D = the distance of the individual from the place in question.

This means that, if two places are equidistant, an individual will have more potential interaction with the bigger place. Perhaps a more significant use for this potential model is in describing the total potential interaction of an individual in a given place with a broad area of his surrounding environment. This can be done by calculating the total potential interaction of an individual at a given place with all surrounding places. When this information is displayed cartographically for a number of places a *population potential surface* results (Jakle *et al.* 1976: 115).

Many variations on the gravity model have been suggested in the study of spatial interaction (Batty 1976a). For example, in the field of consumer behaviour Cadwallader (1981) has suggested a 'cognitive gravity model' whereby interaction is directly proportional to subjective evaluations of the attributes of a shopping centre and inversely proportional to cognitive distance. The idea that individuals evaluate what is important, and the notion that such evaluation is reflected in aggregate spatial behaviour, have antecedents in Stouffer's (1940; 1960) *intervening opportunities model*. According to this model, the number of people going a given distance is directly proportional to the number of opportunities at that distance and inversely proportional to the number of intervening opportunities. In other words, the number of people travelling a given distance is directly proportional to the percentage increase in opportunities at that distance. Stouffer successfully tested his model in relation to residential mobility in Cleveland, Ohio. He also suggested that the model was useful in predicting the selection of colleges by undergraduates, the selection of marriage mates, and vacation travel (Stouffer 1960).

One of the main problems with Stouffer's model is that of measuring 'opportunities'. Adequate data are seldom available. As a result, the intervening opportunities model has not attracted the attention that has focused on the gravity model with its more easily measured elements of distance and population. The gravity model is not however without its problems. Although it is lawlike (in that it is based on an invariable and general relationship between the concepts of mass and distance), the gravity model is not embedded in any wider scientific theory (Amedeo and Golledge 1975: 29). It does not, for instance, allow for the application in social science of any general *theory* from physics. It remains simply an empirical regularity that satisfactorily describes human spatial behaviour in a number of contexts. The appellation 'gravity model' is therefore a misnomer because there is no way in which energy force fields can be invoked to explain why the observed pattern came about (Schneider 1959). Moreover, because the model is calibrated to fit different circumstances, both the constant and the exponent in the equation have been found to vary considerably. As a result, like all models that are derived from observations in a given study area, the gravity model provides mere quantitative description of the history of the recent past for that study area and reveals little of a generalizable nature (Louviere 1981). It is therefore dangerous to use the gravity model as a basis for planning since, in a very fundamental sense, it describes only the *status quo*; changes in behaviour are assumed to reflect what people want to do and the environment is assumed to be arranged or planned to accommodate desired behaviour (Burnett 1981). Moreover, description is only in aggregate terms. There is no behavioural base to the gravity model. In fact what the model says about behaviour is essentially a circular argument: if many people go to a place, it must be attractive; and because it is attractive, many people go there (see King and Golledge 1978: 290).

Statistical mechanics

In overall terms, the sort of spatial interaction model characterized by the gravity model and the intervening opportunities model asserts that interaction (I_{ij}) between an origin zone *i* and a destination zone *j* for a particular flow is directly proportional to the demand requirements generated in origin zone *i* (D_i), directly proportional to the number or size of the opportunities in zone *j* (O_j), and proportional to some function of the distance or cost involved in travelling from *i* to *j* (Cordey Hayes and Wilson 1970). In formal terms this can be expressed as follows:

$$I_{ij} = k\ D_i\ O_j f(C_{ij})$$

It should be noted however that traditional gravity models are only one part of a family of spatial interaction models (Wilson 1971). Classical Newtonian physics, on which the traditional gravity model is based, works well where the basic parameters of the system can be specified, as in the prediction of flows between two distinct and discrete towns. It is less than satisfactory, however, when it comes to predicting interaction between a large number of elements (as, for example, with interaction within a system of cities). In such cases, the branch of physics known as *statistical mechanics* may provide a better basis for spatial interaction models than that afforded by Newtonian mechanics.

The field of statistical mechanics has been explored by Wilson (1970a) who has shown that many spatial interaction models have a common foundation in information theory and can be constructed by an *entropy maximization procedure*. In other words, in Wilson's view there is a common theoretical base to all models of spatial interaction and the difference between models appears to be essentially one of emphasis and approach (Cordey Hayes and Wilson 1970: 37). The central notion of entropy maximization is one that is quite difficult to come to terms with. What it involves is a method for making the best estimate of a probability distribution from the limited information that is available, given a situation where everything that is known about a system can be expressed as a series of constraints. Entropy maximization therefore provides a way of saying something about the overall state of a system while not overlooking the fact that uncertainty surrounds the individual elements within the system (Wilson 1970a). In other words, it is the macro-properties of the system that are the focus of attention in statistical mechanics and a state of maximum entropy can be thought of as the most probable state within a system.

Although the notion of entropy maximization sounds simple, the mathematics on which it is based is extremely difficult. Gould (1972), for example, described Wilson's (1970a) book as the most difficult geography book he had ever read. The key to Wilson's approach is the idea of *the most likely state*, which is best understood by considering a matrix denoting individuals travelling between origins and destinations. Such a matrix can be examined at three scales: the micro-scale where a record is made with individual names within each cell of the matrix; the meso-scale where a total is entered in each cell of the matrix; and the macro-scale where only the column and row totals of the matrix are known (Wilson and Kirkby 1975). Clearly, there are many possible micro-states associated with each meso-state, and likewise many possible meso-states for each macro-state. In principle it would be interesting to investigate micro-scale behaviour. In Wilson's view such an approach is however impractical because a matrix of ten individuals and four destinations can generate one trillion configurations (Gould 1972). The only reasonable way to work, it is argued, is to focus on the macro-scale and to try to identify the most probable macro-state. The most likely macro-state is of course that which accommodates the greatest number of meso-states (just as the most probable meso-state is that with the greatest number of micro-states associated with it). Entropy maximization provides a method of calculating which states are most probable. For example, for any distribution, the number of possible configurations is given by

$$W(T_{ij}) = \frac{T!}{\underset{i,j}{\pi}\ T_{ij}!}$$

where $W(T_{ij})$ = the number of configurations that trips can take
T = the total number of trips
T_{ij} = the trips in the cells of the matrix.

This equation is usually subjected to constraints, notably in terms of the fact that the number of trips emanating from each origin zone is known as is the number of trips terminating in each destination zone.

The entropy maximization model of spatial interaction has been applied with success by Batty (1970a; 1970b) in a study of both the English midlands and north-west England. It has also been suggested that the model could be used as a basis for a reformulation of Reilly's law of retail gravitation so as to take account of simultaneous competition between a multiplicity of shopping centres (Batty 1976b). In Wilson's (1970b) opinion, the entropy maximizing methodology holds a number of advantages over the traditional gravity model: in the first place it breaks away from the deterministic analogy with gravity and therefore provides a broader statistical foundation for model building; secondly, it provides a means of both improving spatial interaction models in particular situations and extending the realm of such models to include complex situations that have been beyond the realm of traditional gravity formulations; and finally it provides a stimulus which will lead to the development of more dynamic models to replace the essentially static equilibrium models available at present. Of course not all commentators share Wilson's enthusiasm. Van Lierop and Nijkamp (1980), for instance, evaluated gravity models and entropy models on methodological, theoretical, logical, and practical criteria and compared them with logit models (where the chance of a certain alternative being chosen by a certain trip-maker is determined by the utility of that alternative compared to the utility of all other alternatives) and probit models (where the probability of a trip being made is related to the attitude of the trip-maker which is in turn related to a series of variables that measure personal characteristics). Their conclusion was that there was little to choose between gravity and entropy models and that both were inferior to logit models. This suggests that an approach that pays some attention to individual evaluation is to be preferred to the approach of statistical mechanics. A similar point of view has been expressed by Hudson (1976b) who has drawn attention to the fact that, in entropy maximization, individual decisions are treated as random phenomena. Macro-scale description, in other words, fails to provide any understanding of why individuals behave in the way that they do. Wilson (1970a) has anticipated this criticism by suggesting that disaggregation of entropy models will improve their level of 'explanation' but the fact remains that, with the approach of statistical mechanics, individual decisions are interpreted as random events that are not deserving of attention in their own right.

Structural perspectives

A general criticism that can be levelled at most models of spatial interaction is that they focus on behaviour in its own right and therefore overlook the extent to which behaviour might be constrained by the wider social, economic, and political context in which it occurs. That is to say, what individuals may be observed as doing in a given area may simply be what they are permitted to do by the overall circumstances in which they find themselves operating. As a result, in the eyes of many researchers, a true understanding of human behaviour can only be achieved if attention is paid to the nature of the *structures* within which individuals operate (Cox 1981). There is however no one structural perspective. Some authorities have suggested that there are innate structuring capacities in the human mind through which the individual comes to terms with the surrounding social and physical environment (Piaget 1970; Levi-Strauss 1966). Others, particularly in geography, have argued that spatial structural effects (such as group or neighbourhood affiliation) can be viewed as independent variables in the explanation of such phenomena as voting patterns (Rumley 1979). Another view, which has become more popular in recent years, is that individual behaviour is constrained by the political economy or social formation in which it occurs. Each of these views is deserving of attention. For example, spatial structural effects are examined in Chapter 3 and the structuring capacity of the mind is touched upon in Chapter 5. Discussion of the political economy perspective is appropriate to the present chapter because, in a fundamental sense, it is yet another macro-scale model of economic behaviour.

Structural marxism

A complex and confusing terminology has developed among political economists as different writers have either displayed a fair degree of eclecticism in their choice of source material or have highlighted subtle nuances in interpretation. In simple terms, the political economy perspective adopts a holistic approach to the study of society and argues that the institutions and ideas that are characteristic of society cannot be understood as separate from the underlying material needs of society. Within this perspective, political economy can be viewed at a variety of scales: the world economy can be seen as the scale of reality, the state and the nation as the scale of ideology, and the city as the scale of experience (Taylor 1982). In all cases, however, the superstructure of society is seen as founded on, and intricately related to, material needs. It is therefore reasonably legitimate to label the political economy perspective as one that advocates structural marxism, although there are obviously some individuals who would describe themselves as political economists but not marxists.

The term 'marxist' is of course a vague one. Thompson (1978), for example, has noted no fewer than four usages for the term: as a set of doctrinal beliefs applicable to any and all situations; as a method of analysis, based on Marx's dialectical notion of thesis – antithesis – synthesis, that provides insights into the functioning of society; as one of the 'great ideas' developed in the course of human history; and as an on-going and evolving intellectual tradition. Perhaps a more telling distinction is Gouldner's (1980) differentiation of *scientific* and *critical marxism*. The former involves attempts to develop a general body of theory that can be applied universally while the latter uses historiographic study to gain understanding of specific events. It is the former – scientific marxism – that has been adopted by geographers in the study of political economy. Although interpretations vary, this form of structural marxism can be summarized in simple terms. All social phenomena (e.g. institutions, ideology, government) are part of a 'social formation' that is a superstructure founded on the prevailing 'mode of production' which is the term given to the material economic base for life. Everything in the superstructure derives from the mode of production. Moreover, each mode of production builds up internal contradictions and dialectical accommodation of these contradictions leads to the replacement of one mode of production by another. Thus, according to Marx, there exists an historical sequence that proceeds from tribalism to feudalism, to capitalism, and ultimately to socialism. This is of course a very crude summary of a very complex theory (Harvey 1973; Peet and Lyons 1981). Part of the appeal of structural marxism in geography seems to lie in its usefulness in making sense of many of the ills that currently bedevil advanced, industrial economies (Peet 1977). Certainly the approach has provided useful insights into the structuring of the housing market (Harvey and Chatterjee 1974) and into the role of capital (Harvey 1978). The approach has, however, come in for stern criticism. Ley (1978: 46) has pointed out, for example, that structural marxism depends on a materialist epistemology that emphasizes functional economic relations, and it therefore reduces the position of values, ideas, and individual human action to the status of epiphenomena that are merely derivative of the mode of production and its consequent power relations. As a result of this 'inauthentic model of man', marxism deals in categories that are only imperfect reflections of the world of everyday life and consequently there is often a low degree of correspondence between the world of the marxist commentator and the world of everyday experience (Ley 1978: 50). Many structural marxists in geography have in fact chosen to work at developing the general theory of political economy rather than at examining real events in specific places and at specific times (Johnston 1980).

The most thorough and telling criticism of structural marxism in geography has come from Duncan and Ley (1982). They begin by drawing a distinction in social science research between individualists and holists. The former argue that large-scale social phenomena (e.g. culture, capitalism) are the products of the actions of the individuals who participate in these phenomena and hence explanation of these phenomena can theoretically be reduced to statements about individual behaviour. Holists, in contrast, believe that such reduction is theoretically impossible and that large-scale social phenomena have an existence in their own right that is unrelated to the conscious actions of the participating individuals. In terms of this dichotomy, structural marxism, particularly the work of Althusser (1969) and Castells (1977; 1978) that has been so popular among geographers, is firmly in the holist school of thought. Duncan and Ley challenge the autonomy of macrostructures that is inherent in the holist view. They argue that such macrostructures are ultimately reducible to cumulative human actions: 'though individuals may not be free to transcend their social context, neither are they passive agents of a larger force such as "culture", the "logic of capitalism", or the "mode of production"' (Duncan and Ley 1982: 32). This is not to say that macrostructures can be ignored. Rather the message is that these structures form the context not the cause of behaviour and are, in any case, ultimately traceable to individual actions.

Duncan and Ley identify a number of specific weaknesses in the marxist position. To begin with, structural marxism is overly influenced by an organicist mode of thinking. For example, marxists hold that the analytical approach is inadequate, that the whole determines the nature of the parts, and that the parts of a political economic system cannot be understood in isolation from the whole because the parts are dynamically interrelated and interdependent. This holistic view usually involves *reification*, whereby the whole and the parts (e.g. mode of production, class, capitalism) are seen, not as mental concepts or abstractions, but rather as things that have substance and causal efficiency. In other words, power, activity and sometimes intentionality are ascribed to mental constructs. Moreover, 'the reified categories of the marxists are not only granted a life of their own, but they also have a purpose, or a telos: they move toward some historically determined end' (Duncan and Ley 1982: 37). As a result an element of teleological or functional reasoning enters marxist writings, largely through the use of evolutionary terminology. Phenomena such as the mode of productions are seen to evolve in certain ways because these ways are deemed essential to their survival. The tautology implicit in such a view makes it empirically untestable.

As a result of their holistic perspective, structural marxists are opposed to the idea of sovereign decision-makers. However, in attempting to illustrate how structures influence behaviour, they have rendered man as a non-decision-maker. Consequently there is a deterministic flavour in much marxist literature to the extent that social structures are seen to instill in individuals a habitual way of thinking in order that they might carry out the will of the structure. 'Each class is given a type of consciousness or ideology which individuals appear to internalize *en masse*' (Duncan and Ley 1982: 40). In other words, individuals are viewed as varying only according to their placement in a given social class within which thinking and behaviour are standardized. This sort of conceptualization of individuals emphasizes economic rationality and therefore has closer parallels with neoclassical economics than most marxists care to acknowledge. In view of this it is hardly surprising that those researchers in the vanguard of marxism in geography were often the same ones that had been in the vanguard of the movement towards positivism and quantification. A preoccupation with economic matters also results in structural marxists taking a rather distorted perspective on reality. In the words of Duncan and Ley (1982: 45), 'to collapse the range of social experience to the outworking of deep economic structures is to present an impoverished view of the social, cultural, and political realms of life'. Given this blinkered view it is not surprising to find that much of the marxist literature in geography uses fragments of reality to illustrate theory rather than using theory to provide insights into the real world.

In short, marxist work in geography 'has maintained a model of mechanism in which the actors themselves have no say: they become puppets who dutifully act out the roles prepared for them by the theorist' (Ley 1980: 11). Hidden, transcendental structures are seen as directing the course of history. According to Ley (1980), there are a number of errors inherent in such a view. To begin with the structuralist approach commits an epistemological error to the extent that it denies the importance of the subjective. Associated with this is a theoretical error whereby the power of human consciousness and human action to redirect the course of events is devalued. Thirdly, there is an existential error encountered whenever questions of meaning are presented as questions of theory and technique. Finally, structural marxism is guilty of a moral error in viewing individual humans as passive units in an overall plan.

In summary, it is clear that the very same errors and shortcomings inherent in spatial interaction models are also evident in structural marxism. As a result, neither statistically average man nor marxist man provides a very satisfactory basis for the study of human spatial behaviour.

Chapter 3

PEOPLE AND SPACE

A traditional concern of human geographers has been the way in which the interrelationship between people and their physical and social environments manifests itself in spatial terms (Haggett 1965; Johnston 1979). In large measure this interrelationship has been studied as a macro-scale phenomenon and attention has focused on the patterns that can be observed in aggregate behaviour. Thus there have developed the sort of models of spatial interaction describing how man overcomes the friction of distance that were outlined in Chapter 2. Distance has, in other words, been interpreted as having a major influence on human behaviour. Space, in the form of area or territory, is similarly significant in that it can lead to the development of distinctive social milieux which, as well as being of interest in themselves, are important in that they mould the attitudes and shape the behaviour of residents (Pocock and Hudson 1978).

Most geographical analysis of space has been inductive, whether it be by simple map distribution comparisons or by more sophisticated multivariate techniques. Essentially, areal patterns are explained by means of a coincidence or correlation with a number of 'independent' factors and, invariably, the generalizations to emerge from such studies are to the effect that '*x* is a result of *a*, *b*, *c* . . .'. In view of the diversity of human activities analysed in this fashion, and the variety of geographical scales employed, it is impossible within the confines of this chapter to illustrate all the work that has been done. Instead, attention will be limited to a few selected examples of investigations of the nature and significance of social space, mainly in western cities. This exercise, together with the work reviewed in Chapter 2, will lay the foundation for an assessment of the strengths and weaknesses of macro-scale structural approaches to the study of human behaviour (Ch. 4). A number of more extensive reviews of urban social space are readily available elsewhere (Herbert 1972; Herbert and Johnston 1976a; 1976b; Berry and Kasarda 1977; Knox, 1982).

Space and the urban environment

Traditionally, social scientists have viewed the artificiality, strangeness, and diversity of the urban environment as fundamental conditioners of individual behaviour and social organization within the city (Lewis 1981a). Much of this tradition stems from the attempts by philosophers such as Tönnies, Simmel, Weber, and Durkheim to interpret the effect the Industrial Revolution had on urban living (Michelson 1970). In simple terms, these writers argued that pre-industrial society was characterized by small homogeneous groups of people who performed similar tasks and had similar interests that led them to think and behave alike, thereby giving rise to a uniform way of life (Lewis 1979). The coming of the Industrial Revolution resulted in new forms of production and ways of living centred around economic specialization and advancements in modes of communication and transportation. It therefore involved the agglomeration of large numbers of people from diverse backgrounds, a concomitant increase in the number of people and variety of situations with which individuals were in contact, and the emergence of a greater division of labour. In such a situation the sustaining of close primary relationships with friends and relatives became more difficult and, at the same time, social differentiation resulted in a divergence of life styles which weakened group consensus and cohesion and threatened to disrupt the existing social order. Formal controls commonly emerged to counter these disruptive trends. Often these controls worked but where they failed there was, according to theorists, an increase in what has become known as social disorganization and deviant behaviour.

In the inter-war period these ideas were modified and developed in two schools of thought that had a significant impact on human geography. The first comprised the researchers of the Chicago School of human ecology under the leadership of Park (1936). Like the earlier theorists, these sociologists believed that urbanization created new societies, new ways of living, and different types of people in 'a mosaic of little worlds which touch but do not interpenetrate' (Park 1936: 608). The distinctiveness of the contribution of the Chicago School lies in its conception of the urban environment as a form of social organism in which individuals struggle for survival in a way similar to the struggles that go on in the plant and animal kingdoms. The basic concept of this biological analogy is that of *impersonal competition* between individuals and groups for desired locations within the city. This competition operates through the market mechanism and results in variations in land rents and leads to a *segregation* of different groups according to their ability to pay the rents of different sites. Therefore, the predominance of a particular group within a particular part of the city results from its relative ability to compete for space. The human ecologists also saw functional relationships between individuals as being *symbiotic* and, where these relationships were localized, there emerged 'territorial units whose distinctive characteristics – physical, economic and cultural – are the result of the unplanned operation of ecological and social processes' (Burgess 1920: 458). Such territorial units were termed *natural areas*, or *communities*. With the passage of time the relative attractiveness of location changes, as does the competitive power of different groups. As a result natural areas and communities disappear in some parts of the city only to reappear in other parts. Again biological concepts such as *invasion* and *succession* were employed to describe the manner in which these changes took place. These concepts were summarized by Burgess (1920) in his model of residential differentiation and neighbourhood change (Fig. 3.1). The resultant zonation of the city was viewed by Burgess as arising from the differential economic competitiveness of different functions and different social groups, whilst the segregation of small groups within each zone (e.g. the ghetto, Chinatown) arose as a result of a symbiotic relationship based on language, culture, or race. In short, this model described both the dynamic process whereby cities grew and changed, and the spatial arrangement of land uses and social groups.

The second school of thought to look at the impact of urbanization on society was that associated with Wirth, and particularly with his influential paper on urbanism as a way of life (Wirth 1938). According to Wirth the social and psychological consequences of increasing

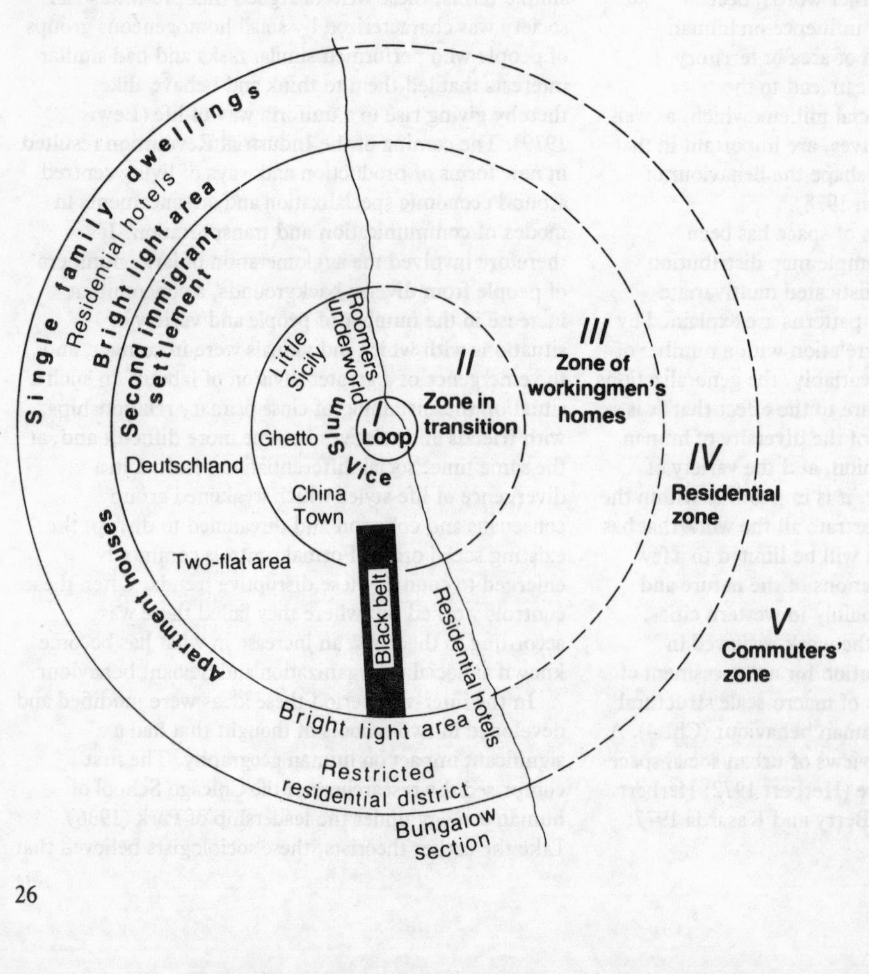

Fig. 3.1 The Burgess model of city structure. *Source*: Park, Burgess and McKenzie (1925, 55).

urbanization stem from three factors: increased population size; increased population density; and increased heterogeneity (or differentiation) of populations. Put simply, this means that, at the personal level, the individual has to face – and cope with – the abundant and varied physical and social stimuli that derive from a large, dense, and highly diverse environment. Although coping strategies can take many forms, certain types of behaviour become 'normal'. For example, many urban residents tend to become aloof, impersonal, and indifferent in their relationships with others. Likewise, many suffer from anxiety and nervous strain that is attributable to stimuli in the urban environment. Furthermore, the resultant loosening of personal bonds often leaves individuals lacking support in times of difficulty and free to pursue ego-centred behaviour. The effect, on the one hand, is an increase in the incidence of loneliness and mental illness and, on the other hand, an increase in the level and diversity of what might be called deviant behaviour.

In addition, Wirth (1938) suggested that the city's size, density, and heterogeneity provide the basis of social change. A division of labour and the residential differentiation of the urban population leads to a separation of activities between home, school, workplace, friends, and relatives, thus weakening the support and control of the family, friends, and neighbours, leading to an absence of social control and an increase in social disorganization. As a result of this weakening of social norms society has developed 'rational' procedures such as criminal codes and institutions like welfare agencies to provide the necessary support and control. Yet, according to Wirth, this new order cannot replace a communal order entirely and, as a result, a condition known as *anomie* develops: some people are unclear about what the new order involves.whilst others disregard it entirely, thereby creating another basis for deviant behaviour.

Despite the obvious relevance of the human ecology school of thought to the study of social space, and its significance in the development of human geography, it was heavily criticized during the 1940s and 1950s and, as a result, almost slipped into oblivion. Much of the criticism focused on the biological analogy of the ecologists, with many arguing that it involved an excessive reliance on competition as a basis of social organization. In these terms the failure of studies to identify the concentric zones and natural areas predicted by the theorists was attributed to the unreality of the underlying propositions (Timms 1971). A further serious weakness of the ecological approach has been its failure to consider cultural and motivational factors, as was illustrated by Firey (1945) in his classic study of 'sentiment and symbolism' in Boston. What Firey argued was that the status and social structure of Beacon Hill, The Common, and the Italian North End could be attributed in large measure to symbolic and sentimental factors. In other words, Firey emphasized that social values often overshadow economic competition as the basis of socio-spatial differentiation. This view was not of course entirely original because Park and his followers certainly recognized social forces when they distinguished two levels of social organization: the biotic, which was controlled by impersonal competition; and the cultural, which was based on a consensus of social values. The latter was conceived as a superstructure over the former (Robson 1969). Both were seen as entities that could be treated separately. However, in their own studies the early ecologists tended to emphasize the biotic at the expense of the cultural, which understandably contributed to the decline of the traditional ecological approach to urban analysis.

During the 1960s geographers once again became interested in the social environment of the city. In part this was due to changes within human geography itself and to the prominence of urban issues (congestion, renewal, ghettos) in the world of politics. In part also it arose from reformulations of the original concepts of the urban ecologists (Timms 1971). For example, Hawley (1950) revised the ecological perspective by conceiving of it as the study of the development and structure of communities, thereby 'emphasizing the functional interdependence within communities that results from collective adaptation to competition'. (Knox 1982: 39). In a somewhat different vein Schnore (1965) elaborated upon the underlying basis of the work of the urban ecologists, and suggested, like others, that the ecological approach should be conceived as a framework for analysing the spatial organization of urban residents. Within human geography these ideas have been developed along three particular lines of enquiry:

1. Studies of the spatial distribution of population that highlight social, economic, and demographic characteristics.
2. Studies of the so-called 'natural areas', or communities, involving both 'objective' surveys as well as more 'subjective' participatory investigations.
3. Studies which focus on social problems (e.g. mental health, crime, and delinquency) within certain parts of the city.

Urban social areas

Over the last twenty years attempts to identify the nature of social areas within cities have involved increasing levels of statistical sophistication, often based on multivariate techniques (Knox 1982). In turn, the distribution of the social areas has been interpreted largely in terms of Burgess's zonal hypothesis and its later derivatives (Herbert 1972). However, of crucial significance in the study of urban social areas was the development by Shevky, Bell, and Williams, in their attempt to determine 'community areas' in Los Angeles and San Francisco, of what has become known as *social area analysis* (Shevky and Williams 1949; Shevky and Bell 1955). Shevky and his followers realized that a single variable such as occupation or education was not truly diagnostic and so they developed a classificatory criterion based on a series of postulates about social differences in post-war United States. Using many of Wirth's ideas it was argued that urban social differentiation was the product of an increasing scale of society which involved three major trends: (1) changes in the range and intensity of relations; (2) increasing differentiation of functions; and (3) increasing complexity of social organization. These trends, according to Shevky *et al.*, resulted, respectively, in changes in the division of labour with a growth in clerical, and managerial employment, changes in family life style with an increase of female employment, and changes in the composition of local populations as a result of greater mobility and, consequently, greater spatial segregation. Evidence of these trends was sought by translating each into a construct – Social Rank, Urbanization, and Segregation – which was then measured by a series of census-derived variables (Table 3.1). For each construct an index was derived based on an unweighted average of standardized scores for each variable. The classification of each census tract was derived by the plotting orthogonally of the social rank and urbanization indices, divided into four equal parts so as to provide sixteen different types. A further division was provided by above and below average scores on the segregation index. Figure 3.2 illustrates such social space diagrams for four towns in Britain and provides a comparative summary of their social composition. By mapping these results it is possible to identify social areas that 'generally contain persons having the same level of living, the same way of life, and the same ethnic background', which, in turn, leads to the conclusion that 'persons living in a particular type of

Table 3.1 Constructs in social area analysis

Statements relating to the character of industrial society (aspects of increasing scale)	*Concomitant trends*	*Changes in the structure of the social system*	*Constructs*	*Census measures designed to reflect constructs in previous column*	
Change in the range and intensity of relations	Changing distribution of skills (lessening importance of manual productive employment, growing importance of clerical, supervisory, managerial employment)	Change in the arrangement of occupation based on function	Social rank (economic status)	Occupation Education Rent	Index 1
Differentiation of function	Changing structure of productive activity (decline of primary production, growing importance of city-central relations, declining importance of household as an economic unit)	Changes in life style – movement of women into urban employment – development of alternative family patterns	Urbanization (family status)	Fertility Women in the labour force Single-family dwelling units	Index 2
Complexity of organization	Changing composition (increased spatial mobility, changes in age and sex structure, increasing heterogeneity of population)	Redistribution in space – changes in dependent population ratio- isolation and segregation of groups in the population	Segregation (ethnic status)	Racial and national groups in relative isolation	Index 3

Source: Adapted from Shevky and Bell (1955)

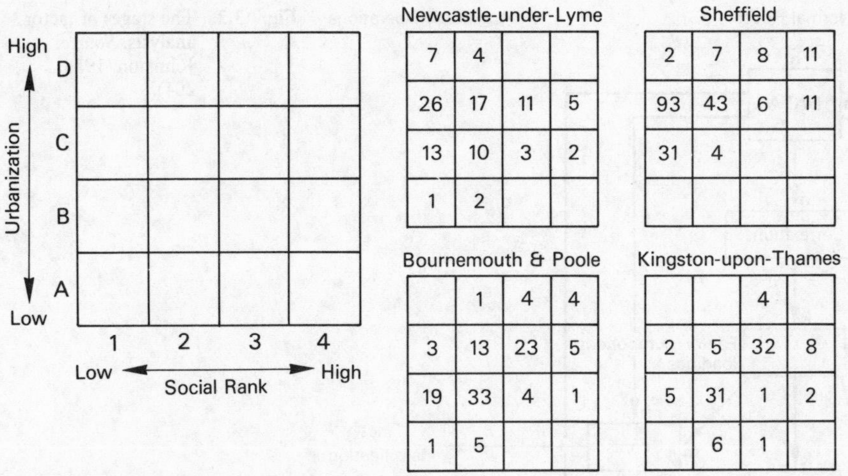

Fig. 3.2 Social space in four British towns, 1971. The numerals refer to the distribution of enumeration districts classified according to the constructs of social rank and urbanization.

social area systematically differ with respect to characteristic attitudes and behaviours from persons living in another type of social area' (Shevky and Bell 1955: 20).

In a detailed review of the social space schema Timms (1971) outlined many of its shortcomings, particularly emphasizing its tendency to conceive of social change largely in economic terms and to ignore differences in people's social values and in access to power. Moreover, according to Udry (1964) there is little evidence to suggest that a theory of societal change can be translated into a typology of social areas and hence attempts to reveal how homogeneous social groups located in different parts of a city are doomed to failure. Empirical testing has however revealed that the social area methodology stands up rather well to the extent that the indices measuring each construct appear statistically independent whilst the variables representing each construct are often closely related (Bell 1958a; Van Arsdol *et al.*, 1958). The only substantive doubt has been over the unspecified correlation between occupation and fertility, which has led Anderson and Egeland (1961) to question the nature of the urbanization construct. It should be noted, however, that much of the support for social area analysis has come from North American cities and beyond these there remains considerable disquiet over the schema's validity; for example, in Western Europe the whole issue of ethnic segregation is a matter of debate (Timms 1971). Partly as a response to these difficulties and the rapid growth in computer technology during the late 1960s, social area analysis was superseded by *factor analysis* as a means of identifying the major dimensions of social differentiation in cities. In contrast to the essentially deductive theory of the social area schema, factor analysis is an inductive device with which to analyse the relationships between a wide range of social, economic, demographic, and housing characteristics, with the object of establishing what common patterns, if any, exist in the data. The procedures involved are summarized in Figure 3.3. Within human geography the technique first came to prominence in attempts to validate the hypotheses implicit in social area analysis. For example, Anderson and Bean (1961) investigated whether the inclusion of additional variables altered the three basic constructs, and found, in Toledo, Ohio, that additional data led to the division of the urbanization construct into two parts. This was followed by several other early studies, notably Gittus (1964), Sweetser (1965a; 1965b) and Schmid and Tagishira (1965), and a proliferation of subsequent work (see Knox, 1982).

The nature of factor analysis can best be illustrated with reference to one example, the case of Leicester in 1966 (Lewis and Davies 1974). The study employed fifty three census-derived variables, on an enumeration district basis, to represent the broad spectrum of the city's demographic, social, economic, and housing structure. Using a varimax rotation of a principal axes solution, the input variables collapsed into eight major dimensions, which together accounted for 72 per cent of the variance in the initial data set (Table 3.2). Of these components the first three were particularly interesting. Component I revealed high loadings on variables reflecting socio-economic status such as income, education, occupation, and material possession. In contrast, Component II represented a life-cycle dimension, contrasting the distribution of older persons with those of large households, young children and economically active males, and Component III suggested an association of variables measuring levels of mobility, including migration and journey-to-work.

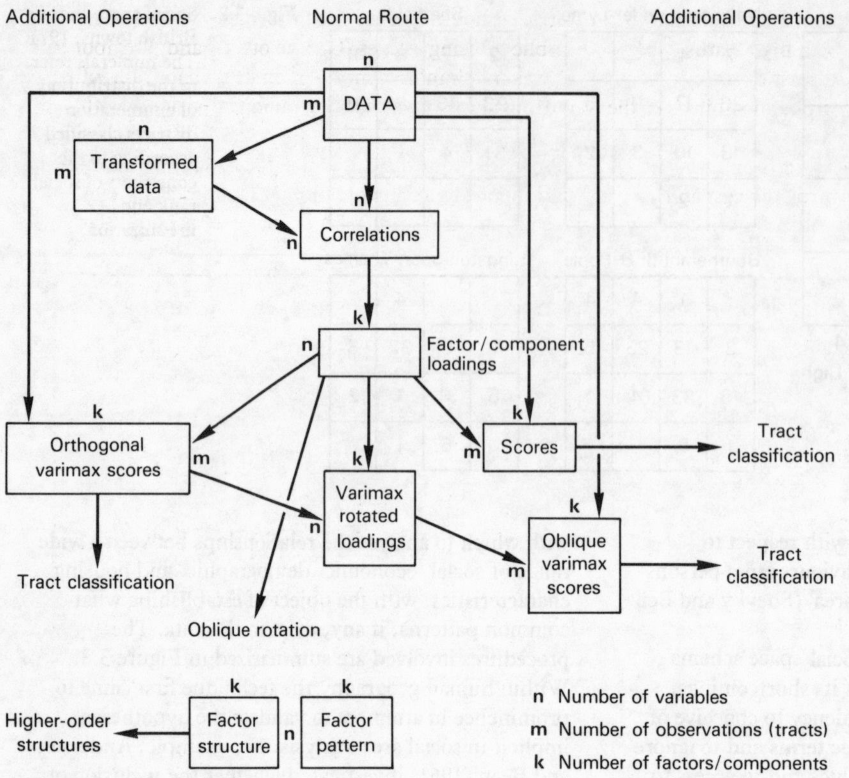

Fig. 3.3 The stages of factor analysis. *Source*: Johnston (1976, 204).

Table 3.2 Factor loadings in Leicester, 1966

Component I. Socio–economic status
+0.85 Two-car households
+0.85 High social class
+0.84 Employers-managers
+0.78 High car ratio
+0.75 Professional workers
+0.71 Intermediate nonmanual workers
+0.65 Distribution-service workers
+0.63 Car commuters
+0.61 Owner occupiers
+0.32 Government workers

–0.40 Irish
–0.56 Foremen-skilled workers
–0.58 Pedestrian commuters
–0.59 Tenants unfurnished property
–0.66 Non-car households
–0.69 Industrial workers
–0.69 Unskilled manual workers
–0.83 Low social class
–0.82 Personal service-agricultural workers
Per cent variance explanation = 17.6%

Component II. Stage in life cycle
+0.77 Old aged
+0.71 Middle aged
+0.59 Rooms per person
+0.48 Households with pensioners
+0.42 Tenants unfurnished property
+0.37 Sparse occupancy households
+0.35 Owner occupiers
+0.33 Pedestrian commuters

–0.55 Mature adults
–0.58 Council tenants
–0.81 Large households
–0.85 Children
–0.93 Single ratio
Per cent variance explanation = 9.9%

Component III. Mobility
Positive – None

–0.31 One-person households
–0.41 Mature adults
–0.53 New residents
–0.41 Households sharing dwellings
–0.65 Recent movers
–0.65 Local movers
–0.82 Single person movers
–0.93 Movers within five years
–0.96 Female movers
Per cent variance explanation = 8.2%

Source: Adapted from Lewis and Davies (1974, 198)

Figure 3.4(a) reveals that Component I had an identifiable sectoral distribution with high status residents concentrated to the south-east of the city centre and in a number of new peripheral suburbs to the north and west, whilst low status areas were concentrated in a zone stretching from the south-west and west across the inner city towards the east and north-east, thereby linking the late-nineteenth century terraced housing areas with the inter-war and post-war public housing estates. On the other hand, Component II was much more concentric in its distribution, often cutting across these socio-economic divisions, with young families predominating on the city's periphery, giving way towards the centre to an older population, and thence to a zone of younger families again close to the city centre (Fig. 3.4b)). The latter is particularly

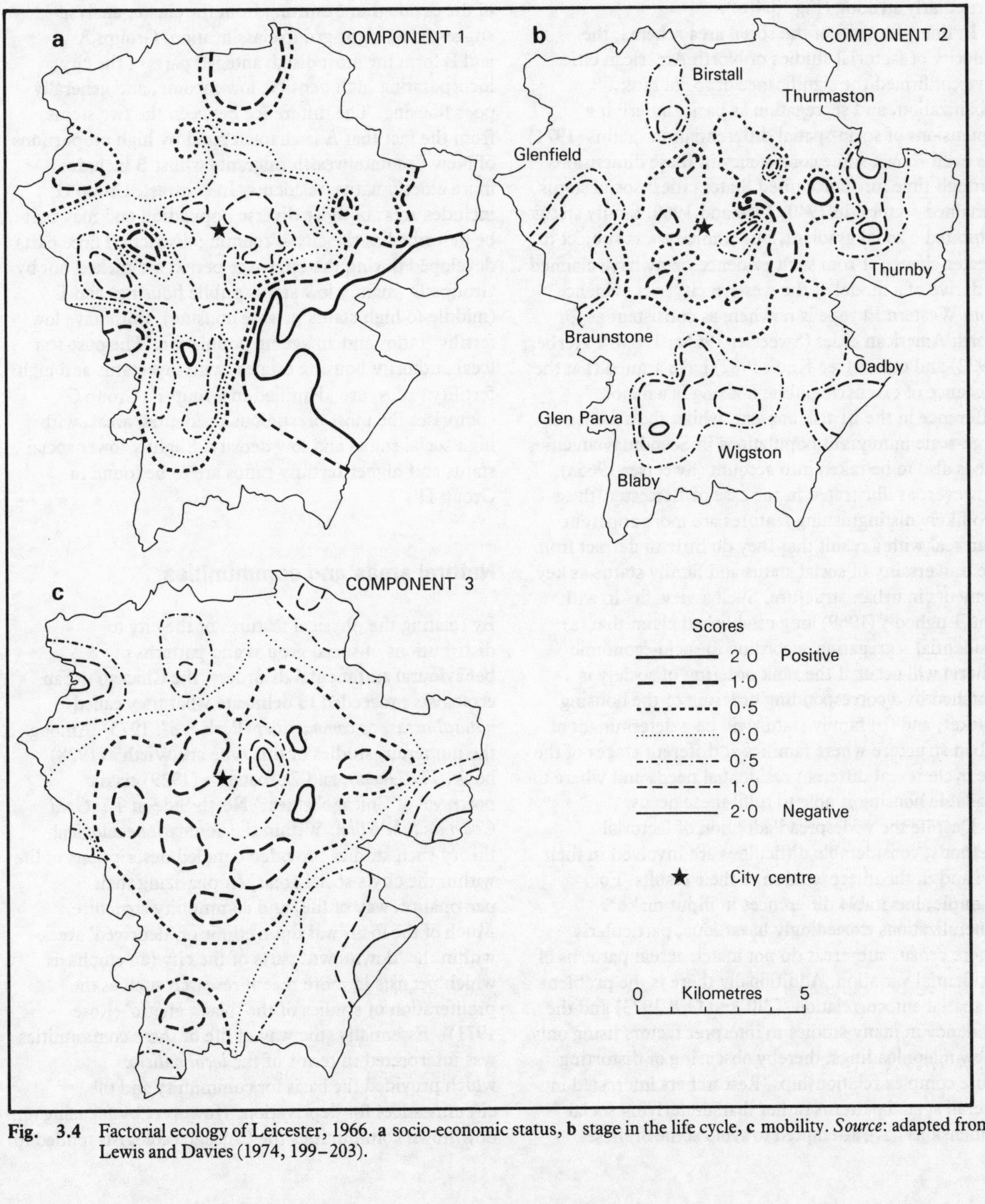

Fig. 3.4 Factorial ecology of Leicester, 1966. **a** socio-economic status, **b** stage in the life cycle, **c** mobility. *Source*: adapted from Lewis and Davies (1974, 199–203).

interesting since it reflects the recent influx of immigrants, particularly from the Indian sub-continent. The mobility dimension (Component III) reveals a much more complex pattern: it identifies not only the recency of the immigrant settlement and the development of new suburban private and public estates but also the high turnover in many middle-class neighbourhoods. The immobility of the older population of the intermediate concentric zone is particularly striking (Fig. 3.4(c)).

In line with tests of the social area schema, the majority of factorial studies of North American cities have confirmed the significance of social rank, urbanization, and segregation as basic underlying dimensions of socio-spatial differentiation. Salins (1971) has even shown some consistency in these dimensions through time for four United States cities: social status remained sectoral in 1940, 1950 and 1960, family status exhibited a zonal gradient, but ethnicity was subject to greater change. From such evidence many have claimed to derive of a model of the western city, yet evidence from Western Europe is nowhere as consistent as for North American cities (Sweetser 1965a; 1965b). Herbert (1972) and others (see Knox 1982) have argued that the existence of extensive public housing is a major difference in the British context, whilst the absence of large-scale immigrant populations in Scandinavian cities needs also to be taken into account (Sweetser 1965a). However, as illustrated in the case of Leicester, these two likely distinguishing features are more apparent than real with a result that they do little to detract from the universality of social status and family status as key elements in urban structure. Such a view fits in with Abu Lughod's (1969) long established claim that (a) residential segregation according to socio-economic criteria will occur if the rank ordering of society is matched by a corresponding ordering of the housing market; and (b) family status will be a determinant of urban structure where families at different stages of the life cycle reveal different residential needs and where the available housing is able to fulfil these needs.

Despite the widespread adoption of factorial methods, considerable difficulties are involved in their use and in the interpretation of their results. For example, inevitable differences in input make generalizations exceedingly hazardous, particularly where census sub-areas do not match actual patterns of residential variation. Additionally there is the problem of spatial autocorrelation (Cliff and Ord 1973) and the tendency in many studies to interpret factors using only a few major loadings, thereby obscuring or distorting more complex relationships. Researchers interested in overall spatial patterns rather than underlying social dimensions have attempted to avoid some of these difficulties by adopting grouping procedures, such as cluster analysis and multiple discriminant analysis, which provide a classification of census sub-areas (Johnston 1978b). Figure 3.5 shows the result, again for Leicester, for a cluster analysis of factor scores for each area on the leading components (socio-economic status, mobility, life cycle, ethnicity, and housing quality) of an analysis, similar to that in Fig. 3.4, but this time based on 1971 data. Visual inspection of the dendogram resulting from the cluster analysis suggested an eight-group classification. Groups A and B form the most disadvantaged parts of the city incorporating high density, low income, and generally poor housing. The difference between the two stems from the fact that A is characterized by high proportions of New Commonwealth migrants whilst B includes more elderly native residents. In contrast, Group C includes areas of more diverse population and may best be described as the city's 'rooming district'. Those parts developed during the inter-war period are picked out by Groups D (mainly low status public housing) and E (middle to high status private housing). Both have low fertility ratios and an ageing population. The post-war local authority housing estates, with low status and high fertility ratios, are identified in Group F. Group G comprises the most prestigious residential areas, with high social status and low density. Slightly lower social status and higher fertility ratios are to be found in Group H.

Natural areas and communities

By relating the physical features of the city to distributions of social groups and patterns of behavioural and mental disorders, the Chicago urban ecologists proceeded to delineate what they called *natural areas*, or *communities* (Park *et al.* 1925). Among the numerous studies of this type are Wirth's (1928) book, *The Ghetto*, and Zorbaugh's (1929) classic portrayal of Chicago's 'near' North Side in *The Gold Coast and the Slum*. Within the context of ecological theory such studies provided detailed descriptions of life within the city's social areas, emphasizing their personality, way of life, and community structure. Much of the focus was upon ethnic or 'deprived' areas within the 'downtown' parts of the city (an emphasis which persists in more recent research such as the proliferation of studies of the 'black ghetto' (Rose 1971)). Essentially, the way of life of these communities was interpreted in terms of the *local milieux* which provided the basis for community and the circumstances for deprivation. However, by focusing on downtown communities the Chicago ecologists tended to

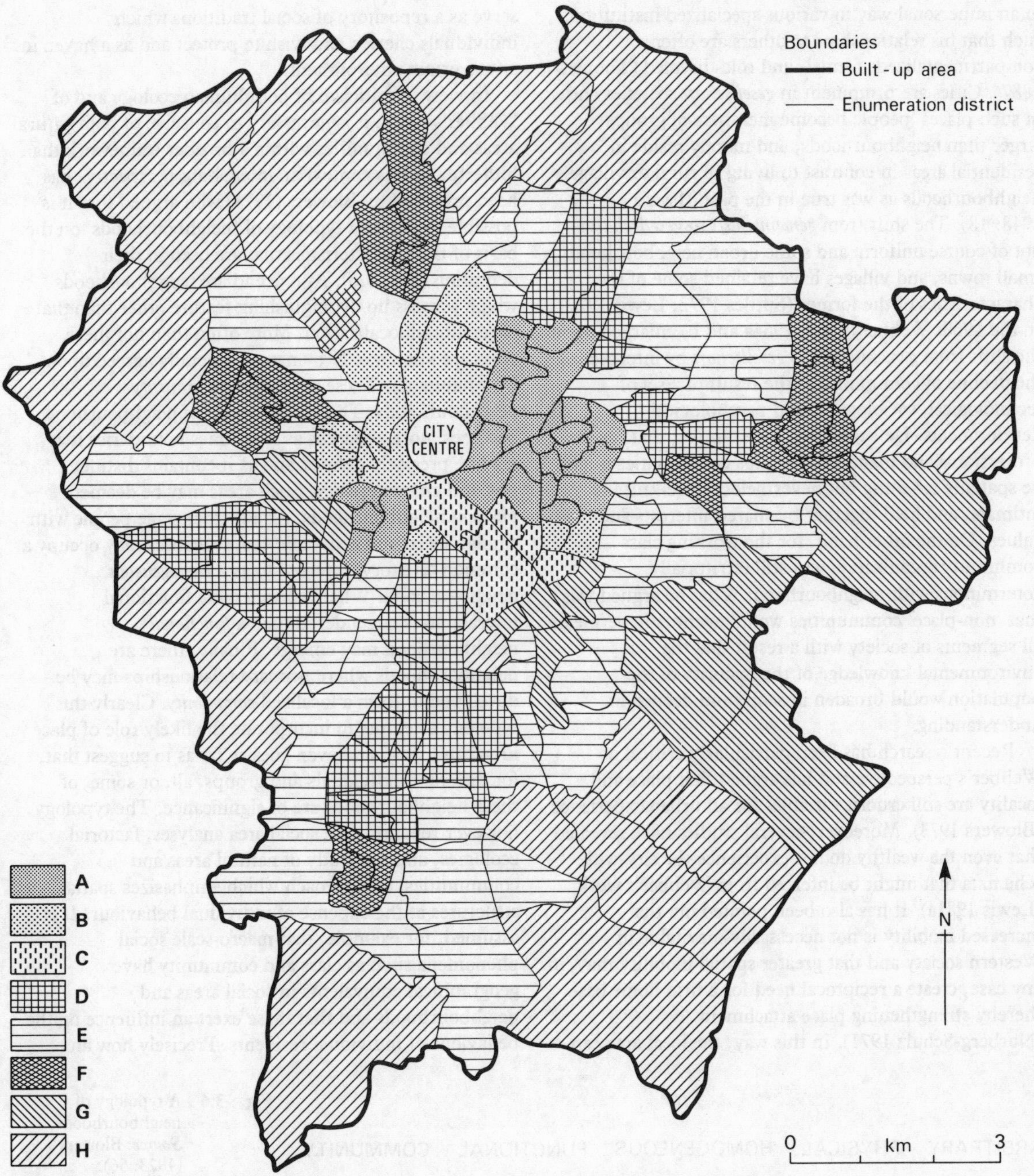

Fig. 3.5 Cluster analysis for Leicester, 1971. *Source*: Lewis (1981a, 42).

ignore other urban communities which differed in social structure, way of life, and territoriality (Theodorson 1961). As a result when later researchers considered these communities the ecological approach was found wanting and the concept of a natural area became less tenable (Kilmartin and Thorns 1978). In its place, attention switched to the impact of urbanization and industrialization in altering community organization. This impact is best appreciated in the context of a continuum model with, at one end, a *gemeinschaft* society, that is a territorially-related community that is socially homogeneous and bound together by a tightly knit pattern of primary relationships, and, at the other end, a *gesellschaft* society where an individual participates in an impersonal way in various specialized institutions such that his relationships to others are often compartmentalized, formal, and role-directed (Tönnies 1887). Cities are prominent in *gesellschaft* societies and in such places 'people become members of groups larger than neighbourhoods, and merely reside in residential areas in contrast to living in rural or village neighbourhoods as was true in the past' (Isaacs 1948: 18). The shift from *gemeinschaft* to *gesellschaft* is not of course uniform and some urban neighbourhoods, small towns, and villages have retained some of the characteristics of the former (Suttles 1972; Lewis 1979). In the 1960s Webber (1963; 1964a and b) enlarged upon the shift from *gemeinschaft* to *gesellschaft* by interpreting the decline of community as the result of a set of technological, sociological, and psychological developments. He suggested, for example, that for the professional and managerial groups communities might be spatially far-flung but nevertheless close-knit, intimate, and held together by shared interests and values. On the other hand, for the working class community organization was still territorially coterminous with neighbourhood. What he argued was that 'non-place' communities would eventually permeate all segments of society with a result that the environmental knowledge of the majority of the population would broaden in scope and deepen in understanding.

Recent research has been particularly critical of Webber's perspective and has argued that place and locality are still crucial variables for all urban experience (Blowers 1973). Moreover, several studies have revealed that even the wealthy do not experience the city-wide schemata that might be inferred from Webber's work (Lewis 1981a). It has also been pointed out that increased mobility is not necessarily inevitable in Western society and that greater spatial mobility may, in any case, create a reciprocal need for a firm home base, thereby strengthening place attachment (Norberg-Schulz 1971). In this way, the local area can serve as a repository of social traditions which individuals cherish and wish to protect and as a haven in an uncertain environment.

In view of criticism of both human ecology and of Webber's work, it is necessary to conceive of both natural areas and communities within a broader framework than hitherto. In this context an interesting perspective has been provided by Blowers (1973) who argued that it is possible to devise a typology of 'neighbourhoods' on the basis of the characteristics that are used in their definition (Fig. 3.6). At one end are neighbourhoods which possess no distinguishing feature other than that of territorial localization. More often than not these areas are known only by names generally agreed upon by inhabitants. These are therefore *arbitrary* neighbourhoods. The spatial aspect of neighbourhood becomes more apparent as it assumes boundaries that may be precisely defined and as it contains distinct physical characteristics. Such areas may be deemed *physical* neighbourhoods. At a further stage people with similar social and economic characteristics may occupy a common territory, referred to as a *homogeneous* neighbourhood. Where considerable functional interaction is engendered then a *functional* neighbourhood may emerge. Finally, there are neighbourhoods where primary relationships may be developed to form a localized *community*. Clearly this typology attempts to incorporate the likely role of place in urban living, and even goes as far as to suggest that, for different individuals and groups, all, or some, of these neighbourhoods are of significance. The typology however remains, like social area analyses, factorial ecologies, and the study of natural areas and communities, an approach which emphasizes spatial structures at the expense of individual behaviour. It is assumed, for example, that macro-scale social phenomena such as class and community have geographical equivalents in social areas and neighbourhoods and that these exert an influence on the behaviour of individual residents. Precisely how an

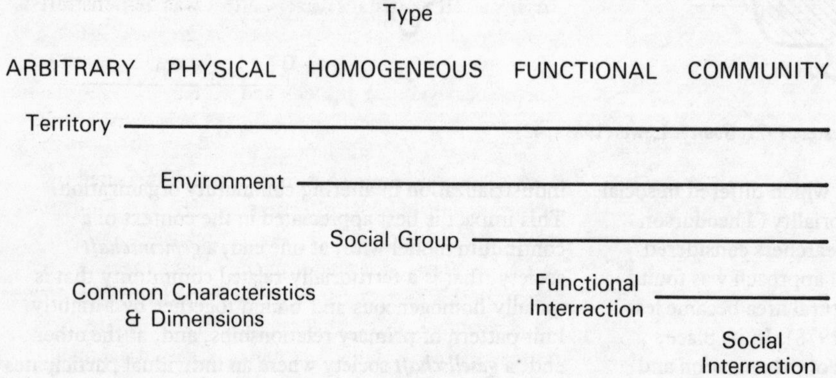

Fig. 3.6 A typology of neighbourhoods. *Source*: Blowers (1973, 56).

intellectually abstract construct like class (that describes aggregate features but involves more than mere aggregation) can influence the behaviour and actions of the individuals that make up society is seldom explored. Only in the 1970s, with the advent of 'socially relevant geography', did researchers address themselves to the problem of how individuals in socially deprived milieux overcome their disadvantage. Until that time research in social geography was overwhelmingly concerned with the description of aggregate features of city structure.

Social issues and social milieux

The current concern among geographers with urban deprivation has its intellectual antecedents in studies by urban ecologists of issues such as mental disorders, delinquency, and prostitution. The prime concern in such work was the identification of the incidence of social issues and the description of the physical and social environment which generated their occurrence.

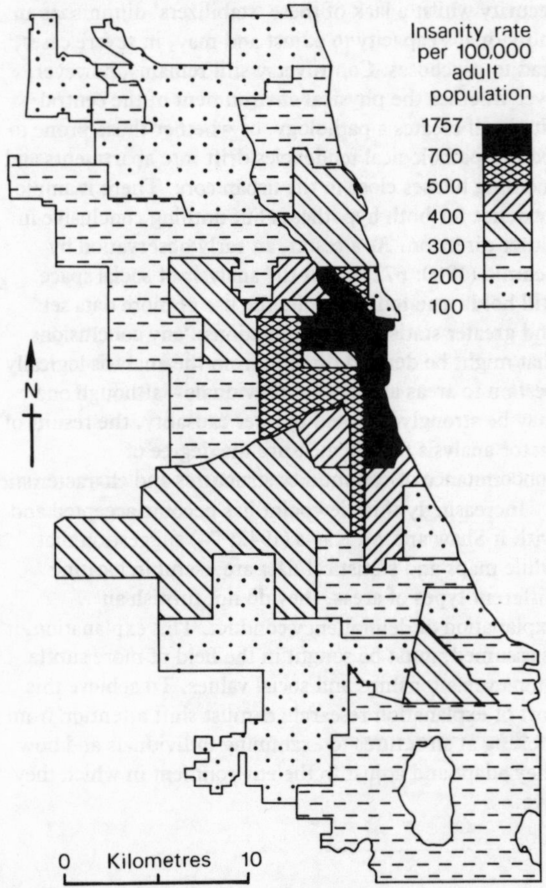

Fig. 3.7 Insanity rates in Chicago, 1930–31.
Source: Faris and Dunham (1939, 24).

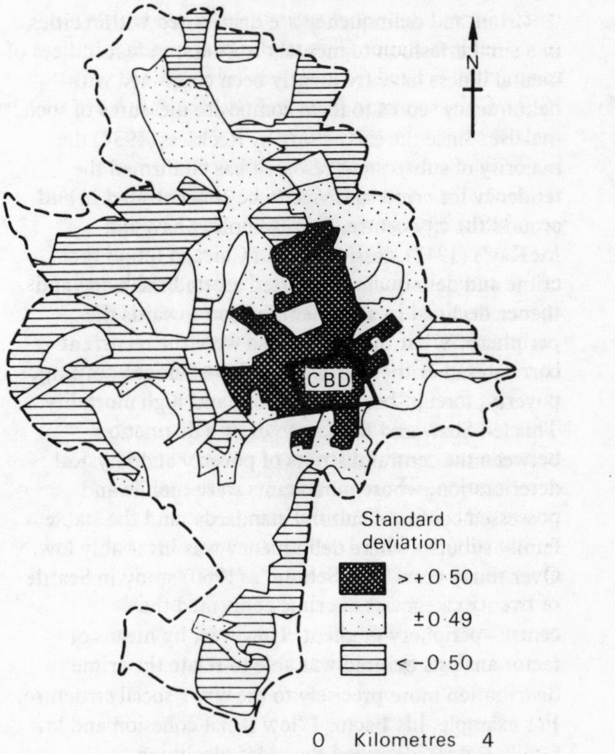

Fig. 3.8 Schizophrenia in Nottingham, 1963–69.
Source: Giggs (1973, 62).

The implication was that an understanding of social milieux would lead to an understanding of social problems.

An example of this type of research was Faris and Dunham's (1939) study of several types of mental disease and associated pathologies including schizophrenia, manic depression, alcoholism, drug addiction, senility, and psychoses in Chicago and Providence, Rhode Island. Apart from the case of manic depression, the highest incidence of mental disorder was found in the heart of the city, and, by combining the rates for specific disease categories into a general insanity rate, a distance decay effect was demonstrated whereby the lowest rates were at the greatest distance from the city centre (Fig. 3.7). These results confirm the earlier evidence of Shaw and McKay's (1929) classic study of delinquency areas and have been supported by a large number of subsequent studies (Dunham 1937). Central city dominance is most vividly illustrated by schizophrenia which, according to Faris and Dunham (1939), was found in high rental apartment districts, skid row areas, and predominantly black areas. More recently this pattern has been confirmed by Giggs (1973) in Nottingham, where 68 per cent of schizophrenia patients lived within 4 kilometres of the city centre (Fig. 3.8).

Crime and delinquency are distributed within cities in a similar fashion to mental disorders; in fact indices of mental illness have frequently been combined with delinquency scores to form composite measures of social malaise. Since the early study by Reckless (1934) the majority of subsequent research has confirmed the tendency for crime and vice to be concentrated in and around the city centre. For example, Shaw and McKay's (1942) classic study in Chicago found that crime and delinquency occurred around the Loop and thence declined in a gradient fashion towards the periphery. What they noted also were the recurrent correlates of crime, particularly sub-standard housing, poverty, foreign-born population, and high mortality. This led Shaw and McKay to draw a distinction between the central districts of poverty and physical deterioration, whose inhabitants were mobile and possessed confused cultural standards, and the stable family suburbs where delinquency was invariably low. Over thirty years later Schmid's (1960) study in Seattle of twenty categories of crime confirmed the centre–periphery gradient. However, by means of factor analysis Schmid was able to relate the crime distribution more precisely to the city's social structure. For example, his Factor I (low social cohesion and low family status) identified the older, declining neighbourhoods of low status that were characterized by weak family structure and crimes such as car theft and shoplifting. Factor II (low social cohesion and low occupational status) picked out population groups with relatively high proportions of unskilled labourers, unemployed, and Negroes and associated these with fighting, robbery, non-residential burglary and disorderly conduct. Factor III (low family status and low economic status) had high scores in census tracts containing large numbers of unmarried and unemployed men and was regarded by Schmid as the crime dimension *par excellence* because it was associated with a wide range of crime indices.

The centre-periphery dichotomy in the incidence of several urban pathologies has traditionally been explained in terms of the physical and human milieux of the city. Initially much emphasis was placed on a physical environmental explanation generally involving noise, pollution, and inadequate housing conditions. Admittedly noise is particularly high in and around the city centre but as yet its relationship with various forms of pathology has not been clearly demonstrated. On the other hand, McHarg (1969) and Esser (1971) have revealed links between levels of physical and chemical pollutants, which are highest over city centres, and both physical and mental abnormalities. However, with greater pollution control this causal link may be of declining significance. The question of housing has been reviewed by Schorr (1963) who concluded that housing conditions clearly influenced physical and mental health, especially where the housing quality is extremely inadequate. Wilner and Walkley (1963) confirmed this view when they found that, of forty studies, twenty six showed positive associations between housing conditions and health. Of course, an obvious explanation of the high incidence of pathology relates deviant behaviour to poverty and overcrowding. It is little wonder, therefore, that Martin (1967) concluded that if overcrowding, air pollution, and poor socio-economic conditions were eliminated, other factors were of little influence in determining the incidence of ill-health. The vicious circle of poverty, physical blight, and deprivation is often encompassed by the term 'social disorganization' and seen, in that context, as a cause of mental illness. For example, McNeil (1970) has suggested that having employment, education, and a stable marriage promotes security whilst a lack of these 'stabilizers' diminishes an individual's capacity to adjust and may, in severe cases, lead to psychoses. Controversy still remains, however, over whether the physical environment of the central city itself creates a pathology, or whether those prone to exhibit pathological tendencies drift into apartments and rooming houses close to the urban core. There is ample evidence for both hypotheses but nothing conclusive in either direction. As a result, an early observation by Schmid (1960: 672) about the analysis of social space still holds true today despite the use of more data sets and greater statistical manipulations: 'any conclusions that might be derived directly from the analysis logically pertain to areas and not to individuals – although one may be strongly tempted to infer causality, the results of factor analysis merely measure the degree of concomitance of community structures and characteristics'.

Increasingly this viewpoint has become accepted and with it Shaw and McKay's (1942: 74) suggestion that while maps and statistical data are useful in locating different types of areas, they do not furnish an explanation of delinquency conduct. This explanation, it is assumed, must be sought in the field of more subtle human relationships and social values. To achieve this sort of explanation researchers must shift attention from looking at structures to examining individuals and how they adapt and adjust to the environment in which they live.

Chapter 4

Models of man

Macro-scale models of human spatial behaviour have a number of shortcomings. Spatial interaction models, such as the gravity model and similar formulations, in some circumstances provide a reasonable description of the empirical regularity that is to be seen in the movement patterns of aggregates of individuals but they offer little by way of explanation. They therefore give little insight into why individuals come to act in a certain way. Likewise structural marxist approaches adopt a holistic rather than an individualistic stance. They place great faith in transcendental structures as the motivating force in the functioning of society and they subjugate individuals to a passive role in a system dominated by the relationship between the mode of production and the associated superstructure. Spatial structural models fare little better. An emphasis on social space as a macro-scale phenomenon, and on the identification of social areas, runs the risk of committing the ecological fallacy, that is, attributing macro-scale characteristics of an area to all individuals living within that area when there is often ample evidence to show that area characteristics are carried by only a minority of residents (Hamnett 1979). It is not surprising therefore that many geographers have argued that the discipline should break away from a preoccupation with the macro-scale and pay at least some attention to the micro-scale of the individual.

Hägerstrand (1970) has pointed out that geography and regional science have tended to look upon a population as made up of 'dividuals' rather than 'individuals'. There has, in other words, been a tendency to compartmentalize people into aggregate categories and to lose track of their existence as individual human beings. Hägerstrand suggests that this situation can be corrected by focusing on the middle ground between biography and aggregate statistics, namely the individual's 'path' through time and space (see Ch. 7). In this way the needs and wants inherent in individual life paths can be related to space-oriented constraints in the provision and accessibility of opportunities for need fulfilment. Micro-scale study can therefore be seen as complementing macro-scale study.

The problem of relating the macro-scale (e.g. urban structure) to the micro-scale (e.g. the behaviour of individuals) has of course preoccupied geographers for some time. Olsson (1969), for instance, coined the expression 'geographical inference problem' to refer to the difficulties involved in trying to relate macro-scale form to micro-scale process at a satisfactory level of aggregation (see Ch. 1). Several methodologies have been put forward for tackling this problem. Gould (1963) has advocated a game theoretic approach for investigating how individuals develop strategies for combating environmental uncertainty and how such strategies manifest themselves in macro-scale features such as land use patterns. More recently Burnett (1978b) has investigated Markov models of how individuals adapt to environmental change with a view to describing aggregate travel within urban spatial structures. None of these approaches has been particularly successful. Watson (1978) has attributed this failure of macro- and micro-scale studies to complement each other to the fact that they are based on different methodological and philosophical positions. Researchers in the spatial analysis tradition, who work at the macro-scale of spatial structures, see individual spatial behaviour as so complex as to be indeterminate and therefore impossible to study. In the view of these researchers, it is more efficient to study the generalized patterns that emerge in aggregate behaviour than it is to look at individual processes. Studies of individual behaviour, in other words, are deemed to be impossible, unnecessary, misleading, and ultimately unsuccessful since what is important to society can be seen in aggregate patterns (Watson 1978). The opposite view is of course that macro-scale studies are unsuccessful. The fact that such studies ignore individual behaviour means that they cannot hope to establish causal relationships between the environment and human actions. They are therefore of limited explanatory and predictive power.

Moreover they tend to ignore phenomena such as cognition which cannot be measured at the macro-scale but which are nevertheless important.

The choice which researchers make between micro- and macro-scale inquiry is characteristically very much a private act of faith. 'Aggregate analyses are economical when human behaviour is indeterminate, or highly repetitious, or highly constrained by space, time and the environment' (Watson 1978: 44). Moreover, they provide a necessary first step in the study of any form of man–environment interaction. However, they are insufficient in themselves because aggregate patterns are only truly meaningful if their interpretation is soundly based on knowledge of individual behaviour. Yet herein lies a problem: most studies of individual behaviour have borrowed the research methodology of macro-scale spatial analysis and have therefore placed undue reliance on the approach to problem formulation and hypothesis testing that is handed down indirectly from the natural sciences. This emphasis has precluded consideration of a number of alternative approaches to the study of human spatial behaviour and has led to a situation where behavioural geography, instead of being an integral and fundamental part of studies of location theory and urban planning, is something of an intellectual backwater (Cullen 1976). Far too much attention has been paid to generalization through aggregation. For example, it has been standard practice to take an element in the environment (e.g. a shopping centre) and to try to measure people's image of that element. This presupposes that images can be committed to paper in experimental situations and that individual images can be aggregated to a meaningful group view. The generality of this approach is one of its strengths. It is also its main failing: 'it can be applied, as indeed it has been applied, to a whole variety of different situations because it is almost wholly lacking in content' (Cullen 1976: 399).

Despite the fact that micro-scale studies of individual behaviour deal with a subject matter that is very different from the holistic perspective of the structuralists, they have generally adhered to the deterministic approach that is characteristic of much macro-scale research. For example, individuals are popularly viewed as organisms whose behaviour can be fully explained by reference to the combined effects of a set of environmental stimuli to which the individual passively and predictably responds in a manner similar to the way in which a Newtonian mass responds to the gravitational forces exerted upon it (Cullen 1976: 401). As a result, little early work in behavioural geography paid much attention to the *meaning* that an environment has for an individual and to the way in which meaning can influence the use to which an environment is put. Subjective meanings simply did not lend themselves to the research methodology that was borrowed from the spatial analysis school of thought. As a result, despite pleas such as Hägerstrand's (1970), human geography remained preoccupied, until relatively recently, with macro-phenomena such as cities, shopping centres, and land use generally.

One of the factors inhibiting the consideration by human geographers of the individual *qua* individual has been a reluctance to think about the question of what models of man should be incorporated into geographic research. To a certain extent this situation is now changing. Agnew and Duncan (1981: 45) have pointed out that all social scientists, whether they engage in the explanation of human activity *per se* or the results of human activity, necessarily adopt – albeit sometimes only implicitly – one of several models of man. These models can be differentiated from each other by reference to the three dimensions of *holism* versus *individualism*, *structure* versus *action*, and *determinism* versus *freewill*. The distinctions between the polar ends of these continua are interesting and worthy of note.

The individualistic viewpoint holds that large-scale social phenomena are simply the sum of the behaviours of the many individuals that participate in these phenomena. In contrast, holists argue that such phenomena are to be explained in terms of their own autonomous, macroscopic level of analysis. Put simply, the distinction is one between looking at individuals and looking at concepts such as 'culture' or 'mode of production'. Likewise the distinction between a structure-orientated approach and an action-orientated approach amounts to a choice between explanation based on autonomous and reified concepts and explanation based on the action of individuals. In support of their view, structuralists point to those regularities occurring in social group behaviour which can be observed even with changes in group membership. The persistence of such regularities precludes, it is argued, explanation in terms of the attitudes and intentional actions of particular individuals. The structures which are thought to be important are, in other words, outside the individual. There are therefore *transcendental structures* and they are manifest in social science in at least three examples: the structural–functional view that there are self-regulating social structures (such as organizations) that seek an equilibrium that is entirely separate from the wishes of the people comprising the structure; the anthropological notion that cultures continually evolve towards a state of greater complexity; and the structural marxist idea that the social structure of advanced capitalism is inexorably driven along a preordained path (Agnew and Duncan 1981: 47). Each of these examples involves an element of teleological argument and in each case human action is subordinate to transcendent societal structures. In short, the action of individuals is seen as the *product* of transcendental structures. Opponents of this view argue that structures should not be reified and treated as subjects; rather regularities in social life are ultimately caused by individual and collective action. People are seen as the active forces behind structures which, therefore, have no power other than that created and endowed by people (Agnew and Duncan 1981: 48). Taken to its extreme, such an argument focuses only on the attitudes, ideas, and behaviour of individuals and therefore overlooks the social origin of intentions and desires. Fortunately such an extreme view is rare except perhaps in those branches of economic geography that have fêted to concept of rational economic man. Similarly, the extreme positions of determinism and freewill are now rare and social science can generally be characterized either by the view of man as an active creator and sustainer of the social order or by the view of man imprisoned by norms, values, and roles determined by the social and cultural system (Agnew and Duncan 1981: 48).

Human geography has, at various times, taken different positions along these three dimensions. For instance, much of North American cultural geography can be thought of as holistic, structural and deterministic to the extent that, in the eyes of many researchers, it was a culture, viewed as being something greater than the sum of its component parts, that was the focus of attention and not the individual actions of the persons carrying that culture. Similarly, structural marxism, as was shown in Chapter 2, can be characterized as holistic, structural, and deterministic: the structure determines the places and functions occupied and adopted by the agents of production who themselves are never anything more than the occupants of those places and functions. In short, both cultural geography and marxist geography reify structures that put the human world outside the power of human agency (Agnew and Duncan 1981: 51). In contrast, early behavioural initiatives involving the postulate of rational economic man (Pred 1967: 5–10) can be thought of as individualistic, action-orientated, and deterministic. The focus of attention was on the overt behaviour of individual actors. Unfortunately, however, the omniscience implied in economic rationality meant that individuals could only act in one way (the most rational way) in any given situation. A similar deterministic flavour marred the stimulus-response learning theories in which geographers were interested for a time (Golledge 1969): human cognition was regarded as a 'black box' and man was viewed as an animal unable to transcend his reflexes and therefore at the mercy of environmental stimuli (Agnew and Duncan 1981: 51).

What seems to be needed is an approach that is individualistic, action-orientated, and which allows man a modicum of free will and a degree of latitude in interpreting, and ascribing meaning to, the environment. Unfortunately the development of such models of man has not been an easy task because a number of weaknesses have been common in much of the research that has been undertaken: for example, many model builders have been unclear as to which aspects of behaviour should be measured, many have failed to consider a full range of explanatory variables, many have used vague operational definitions or surrogate variables for rather vague mental concepts, and many have overlooked the extent to which behaviour is constrained by the environment in which it occurs (Burnett 1981). In fact it was not until relatively recently that behavioural geographers began to make an explicit distinction between the *sensate behaviour* that results from individual, conscious decisions and the *non-sensate behaviour* that is to be observed in the type of macro-scale population flow studied in gravity models (Amedeo and Golledge 1975: 348).

In the eyes of many researchers the foundations for individualistic, action-orientated models that allow man to come to terms with his environment in a non-deterministic way are to be seen in behavioural studies based on transactional–constructivist philosophy. Before such a view can be advanced, however, it is necessary to dispense with some of the misconceptions, misinterpretations, and misrepresentations that have surrounded behavioural approaches in human geography. Golledge (1981) has dealt with these misconceptions at some length. He observed that behavioural studies in geography began in the 1960s when researchers realized that, in order to exist in and to comprehend an environment, people learn to select and organize critical subsets of information from the mass of experiences open to them. It is this information processing that is of interest in behavioural research. The goal of behavioural studies is not therefore to define a new sub-discipline but rather to provide a new perspective on much of the existing geographical domain. Moreover, the scientific goal of behavioural studies in geography has been to find the general in the particular. This is very different from calculating average characteristics for non-sensate aggregate behaviour. Therefore to confuse the behavioural approach with macro-scale model building is to misrepresent the approach. Likewise to argue, as some have done, that behavioural studies in geography are 'behaviouristic' (in the Watsonian sense of reducing everything to stimuli and responses) is to grossly misrepresent reality because the fact is that the rationale for the behavioural approach expressly seeks to avoid deterministic interpretations of man–environment interaction. Similarly, it is wrong to suggest that geographers are only concerned with overt behaviour because a great deal of effort has gone into studying the decision processes from which overt behaviour results. Of course, this is not to say that behavioural studies in geography are free from weaknesses. This is far from the case: there is still too facile an equation drawn between 'behavioural geography' and 'environmental perception'; there is still insufficient attention paid to epistemology; there are still problems in the interdisciplinary transfer of concepts and methods; and there is still little attention given to examining the degree of congruence between image and behaviour. However, to misrepresent behavioural research in geography as deterministic or macroscopic is to do a great injustice to a considerable volume of research. Part Three introduces the main features of this research.

Part Three

MICRO-SCALE APPROACHES

Any micro-scale behavioural interpretation of how man interacts with his environment must pay attention to the manner in which information is derived from the environment. In particular research needs to focus on the environment as a source of information, the psychological processes involved in handling information in the mind of man, and the overt behaviour that results from these psychological processes. Several problems are encountered in this field of study: the environment that is crucial to behaviour varies from individual to individual; little is known about how environmental information is stored in the brain; and the link between information and behaviour is often difficult to pin down. In part these problems arise because geographers have spent a considerable amount of time talking about what goes on in the mind but have given very little consideration to what is meant by 'mind'. Part Three attempts to rectify this and addresses the concept of mind directly. The notion that information flows from the environment through the senses is rejected, as is the idea that knowledge is innate and precedes experience. Instead 'reality' is seen as something constructed in the mind of man while man is engaged in an indivisible relationship with his environment. From this transactional–constructivist point of view, man's relations with his environment can be studied in three time frames: the phylogenetic (concerned with the development of man as an animal); the ontogenetic (concerned with the development, especially intellectual development, of human beings); and the microgenetic (concerned with human adaptation to environmental change). This developmental perspective on man–environment interaction generally holds sway nowadays in behavioural approaches in human geography. Even territoriality, which in the animal world is largely innate, has been shown in the human world to be a learned response to small-scale environments that satisfies basic human needs for security and identity. Knowledge of larger areas also involves a learning process as man comes to terms with his situation by imposing a structure on an otherwise chaotic reality. Not surprisingly, therefore, great attention has been paid by behavioural researchers in human geography to environmental cognition.

One of the principal uses of environmental information is in arriving at decisions relating to spatial behaviour. Decision-making, in other words, involves the translation of motives into overt action within the context of available information. Of course such decision-making involves a whole range of activities from problem solving to habitual behaviour and in trying to understand these activities geographers looked first at stimulus-response learning and Gestalt psychology. Neither of these approaches pays much attention to what actually goes on in the mind which, instead, is viewed very much as a 'black box'. As a result geographers have tended to turn away from psychology and to look at work done by other social scientists on satisficing and boundedly rational behaviour. One of the principal reasons why many decision-makers satisfice rather than optimize is that they operate under a number of constraints. Individuals are not sovereign decision-makers: many have personalities and attitudes that impose severe restrictions on the amount of information that they are capable of handling, and many find that the information available to them is severely constrained by social class, technology, culture, and the political system. In short, individuals operate in an uncertain environment. As a result many human geographers have advocated that behaviour be viewed in probabilistic terms. Such an approach suffers, however, the same weakness as the 'black box' view of man–environment interaction: it reveals little about the actual bases for decisions. One way of rectifying this is to look at utility, and especially place utility. Variants of utility have in fact been used in a number of models of decision-making. The generality of such models tends to be limited however because of the tendency for the behaviour of individuals to be different in both degree and kind from the behaviour of institutions and organizations.

The assumption behind models of decision-making is that the processing of information serves as a basis for overt behaviour. In many cases this information processing does not influence behaviour directly but rather affects how the mind construes the environment. It influences, in other words, the image that is held of an environment. The concept of an image is not of course unique to geography because the suggestion has been made elsewhere in social science that all behaviour is dependent on an image. In geography, it is the imageability of the environment, particularly at the city scale, that has attracted a good deal of attention. For example, researchers have been enthusiastic in the study of cognitive distance, designative images of what is where, and appraisive images (the meanings evoked by the physical environment). Despite enthusiasm, confusion about the main elements in environmental images, uncertainty about how images change over time, and methodological difficulties have led to a situation where it is perhaps better to think in terms of spatial schemata than in terms of images.

Chapter 5 looks at the general nature of micro-scale behavioural research into man–environment interaction. Particular attention is paid to the philosophical underpinnings of this work and to advocacy of a transactional–constructivist approach to the study of spatial awareness at both small and large scales. The way in which information derived from man's transactions with his environment is used in reaching decisions in relation to spatial behaviour is described in Chapter 6. There are two outcomes from decision processes that are of special interest to human geographers: environmental images and overt behaviour, particularly in relation to life paths through time space. These are explored in Chapter 7.

Chapter 5

ENVIRONMENTAL INFORMATION

It is a fundamental proposition of behavioural approaches in human geography that man derives information from his environment and processes that information in such a way as to provide a basis for overt behaviour. Environmental information is, in other words, fundamental to survival, to everyday living, and to the maintenance of a sense of well-being. In short, it is central to most basic human needs (Maslow 1954).

The study of how humans use information about their environment has generated an enormous volume of literature (Moore 1979). Much of the early work spoke in terms of 'perception' and focused overwhelmingly on the notions of 'perceived environment' and 'mental map'. This use of the term 'perception' created confusion in that it differed markedly from the usage that had evolved in experimental psychology where perception was usually taken to mean the impinging of environmental stimuli on the human sense organs. Geographical use of the term 'perception' covered both this sort of immediate response to a stimulus and the more general awareness that is not contingent upon an immediate stimulus and to which the term 'cognition' is more appropriately applied. It may in fact be best to think of both perception and cognition as contributing to knowledge of the environment, the former providing *figurative knowledge* (images resulting from direct contact) and the latter *operative knowledge* (information that has been structured through a variety of mental operations) (Moore and Golledge 1976b). Certainly environmental information is gained through all the senses (Stea and Blaut 1973) and is stored in some way in the memory, as is demonstrated by man's ability to recall knowledge of environments that are not immediately present (Gould and White 1974).

The question of how man comes to know the environment is a fundamental epistemological problem. At issue are not only man's awareness and information but also the impressions, images, and beliefs that people have about environment (Moore and Golledge 1976a). In terms of environmental knowing, there are few objective facts. Rather information about the environment is sought and collected in a subjective and purposeful way that reflects the needs and values of the individual concerned. In other words, how an individual approaches the environment determines what he finds. Thus, in recent years environmental psychology has shifted its emphasis from the dictum that 'seeing is believing' to the point of view that 'believing is seeing' (Proshansky *et al.* 1970a: 101–2). As a result of that shift the environment is not seen just as another variable to be thrown into a multiple regression model but rather as the *raison d'être* of a whole class of behaviour (Downs 1976: 74). In this connection Ittelson (1978) has suggested three foci for the study of the urban environment: the city as a source of information; the psychological processes involved in the use of this information; and the resulting varieties of urban experience. This threefold classification can be extended, through inclusion of the environment itself, into a fourfold listing of the interrelated elements that need to be considered in any examination of how man uses environmental information:

1. The nature of the individual, and in particular the psychological processes that are used to cope with information.
2. The nature of the environment from which information is drawn.
3. The manner in which the individual seeks out information in the environment.
4. The way in which the environment provides an arena within which overt behaviour is acted out (Walmsley 1972a: 43–9).

Each of these is worth examining in detail.

Very little is known about how individuals cope with environmental information. In many studies the mind has been looked upon as a sort of 'black box': the environment has been manipulated, resultant behaviour observed, and imputations made as to how the mind works (Burnett 1976). More commonly in geographical studies it has been assumed that individuals are rational economic men who seek to optimize their overt behaviour. Clearly such a proposition is unreal in that it ignores unpredictable change in the environment and makes wholly unacceptable claims about man's ability to handle information (Wolpert 1964). Unfortunately, the substitution of 'bounded rationality' for omniscient rationality does little to improve the situation in that it leaves unspecified the information-processing capacity of the individual human (see Ch. 6). In this connection Sagan (1977) has argued that the human brain is characterized by 10^{13} synapses capable of carrying 'yes/no' information and that the brain is quite able to process 100 such bits of information per second. Conversely, Miller (1956) has suggested that the channel capabilities of the brain restrict individuals to about seven alternatives when discriminating between absolute judgements along a single dimension. What both these sources seem to imply is a link between the functioning of the brain and mathematical information theory (see Shannon and Weaver 1949). Although frequently cited, such theory has no relevance to the development of environmental knowledge because it is concerned with how much information a *message* has, not with how much information an *individual* has (Ackoff and Emery 1972: 145). In short, little is known about how environmental information is stored in the brain. Milgram (1973) has put forward the idea that size distortions in mental representations of the environment may in some way be proportional to the molecular storage units used for different realms of the environment, but this remains no more than a suggestion despite some support from Sadalla and Staplin (1980b) to the effect that the length of routes with more remembered attributes (and hence more stored information) were consistently overestimated relative to simpler routes. Of course such neurophysiological explanations overlook the fact that how individuals handle environmental information is influenced to at least some extent by their needs and the degree of need arousal (Ittelson *et al.* 1974: 84), their 'cognitive set' (the way they think about the environment) (Leff and Gordon 1974), and by the extent to which they are 'space sitters' or 'space searchers' (Gould 1975).

The nature of the environment from which information is drawn has been studied in depth by Ittelson *et al.* (1974: 105–9) and their conclusions can be summarized briefly.

1. Environments have no fixed or given boundaries in space or time, the boundary at any one point in time being a product of the information generated through the interaction of the individual with his surroundings.
2. Environments provide information through all the senses (although sight is probably dominant (see Pocock 1981a)).
3. Environments include peripheral as well as central information.
4. Environments provide much more information than can be handled adequately, largely because much information is either redundant, ambiguous, or contradictory.
5. Environments are defined by, and experienced through, action. That is to say, environmental cognition can never be completely passive because the individual is always part of the situation about which he is gathering information.
6. Environments have symbolic meanings. In particular certain environments are imbued with social meaning and behavioural expectations.
7. Environmental experience always takes on the systematic quality of a coherent and predictable whole.

Although these seven points have a definitive appearance, they should be regarded as no more than generalized assumptions.

No such generalizations have yet been made about the other two elements (information seeking and overt behaviour) that were suggested above as being central to man's use of environmental information although Downs and Stea (1973a) have pointed out that there are three key questions: What do people need to know? What do they know? And how do they get their knowledge? Obviously man needs to know something of absolute and relative location, something of distance and direction, and something of the attributes of the phenomena that exist at different locations. This knowledge tends to be incomplete, distorted, and schematized. Moreover it is based on both direct experience (learning by doing) and vicarious experience (learning through someone else's actions). This much is known. But according to Downs and Stea (1973b: 82) 'we have no idea how spatial information is processed (although we know something about the products of the transformation), how environments are learned (although we know something of the development of spatial cognition), and of inter- and intra-cultural differences in representation'. This is partly because the concept of information is 'one of those intuitively obvious, but extremely slippery, ideas which appear difficult to pin down and measure' (Gould and Lafond 1979: 286). It is also partly because behavioural geographers have frequently conducted their research without any thought being given to the philosophy of mind on which it is based.

Philosophies of mind

Geographers have frequently made inferences about what happens in the mind but very rarely have they stopped to think what is meant by 'mind'. An exception is a review by Burnett (1976: 25–6) which outlined nine beliefs about the mind that are common in the literature on behavioural geography.

1. Minds are valid objects for scientific enquiry.
2. Minds can be described in psychological rather than neurophysiological terms.
3. Stimuli exist outside the mind.
4. Minds observe, select, and structure information about the environment.
5. Minds evaluate environmental information.
6. Minds are the seat of sensations such as stress.
7. Spatial choices are made in the mind according to decision rules.
8. Spatial choice is the cause of overt behaviour.
9. The mental states of different people are comparable.

Burnett considered these beliefs in relation to three philosophies of mind: the *behaviourist* view that mental states can be defined only in terms of overt action, the *materialist* stance that mental states are purely neurophysiological events in the brain, and the *neodualist* position that a description of the mind must take account of both physical and peculiarly mental (and therefore *non*-physical) phenomena. Although some geographical work on cognitive representation has tended towards a materialist standpoint, the vast majority of researchers has emphasized imagery and therefore adopted a neodualist point of view.

How an individual comes to know his environment is of course a special case of the more general epistemological problem of how a subject comes to know an object. In this sense, there are at least three ways of looking at the relationship between behaviour and environment. These have been described in detail by Moore and Golledge (1976b). The first position – *empiricism and environmental determinism* – rests on the assumption that knowledge is built up by encountering the world through the senses. From this point of view the world is seen as acting on people and the environment is viewed as *real* in that it has an objective existence independent of a subject. The second position – *rationalism and nativism* – rests on the contrary assumption that knowledge is innate and that it precedes experience. In other words, this viewpoint holds that the person acts on the world in that the form and meaning of environment are given *a priori*. The environment is thought of as *ideal* in that it exists in the form of innate ideas. The third position – *interactionalism and constructivism* – flows from the work of Kant who distinguished between the *matter* of knowledge (which is acquired through experience) and the *form* or way in which knowledge is organized (which is given *a priori*). To Kant, there are only two ways of knowing: scientific method (with its emphasis on realism, materialism, and the denial of mind) and the exploration of the processes by which reality is formed in the mind (with its emphasis on idealism, phenomenology, and the primacy of mind). However, neo-Kantians accept that reality exists independently of mind but argue that it 'can only be grasped through the effort of particular minds' (Moore and Golledge 1976b: 14). As a result, from this point of view it is only possible to study reality through man and, even then, the study is not of reality *per se* but of reality as a product of the act of knowing. Reality, in other words, is thought of as being *constructed*. Until relatively recently this constructivist position had little impact on geographical studies of environment and behaviour (Livingstone and Harrison 1981).

The transactional–constructivist position

The transactional–constructivist point of view has come to the study of man and environment through the work of environmental psychologists. It differs from a simple interactional perspective in that it refutes any existential and methodological distinction between man and environment and postulates instead that the two are linked in an indivisible relationship (Patricios 1978). Its origins can be traced in Gestalt psychology and in the proposition that the environment is a complex and organized stimulus field that provides the context for human behaviour (Ittelson *et al.* 1974: 81–2). The thrust of the transactional–constructivist position has been summarized by Moore and Golledge 1976b: 14):

> experience and behaviour are assumed to be influenced by intraorganismic and extraorganismic factors operating in the context of ongoing transactions of the organism-in-environment. Transactions between the organism and the environment are viewed as mediated by knowledge or cognitive representations of the environment; but these representations are treated as constructed by an active organism through an interaction between inner organismic factors and external situational factors in the context of particular organism-in-environment transactions.

More generally, man is assumed to be a goal-directed animal whose actions take place in a social and historical context and are based on a construal of past environmental experience (Wapner *et al.* 1973).
Although the transactional–constructivist position has attracted criticism on the grounds that transactions between man and environment are extremely difficult to measure (Pick 1976), it has provided a basis for valuable

insights into both man's evolutionary adaptation to environment and the way in which conceptions of environment change with intellectual development.

Evolutionary adaptation

Kaplan (1973; 1976) has argued that environmental information processing was a necessary skill for the survival of the human species in that it enabled man to adapt to uncertain and dangerous environments. In this sense survival depends on four types of knowledge and four associated responses: where one is (perception and representation); what is likely to happen (prediction); whether it will be good or bad (evaluation); and what to do about it (action) (Stea 1976: 108). The fact that man was able to recognize, anticipate, generalize, and innovate ensured his survival. In particular, an ability to cope with *specific* information (such as that relating to features in the landscape) and to abstract from this in order to get *generic* information (which provides a way of understanding new environments based on experience of reasonably similar situations) gave man an evolutionary advantage. In other words, generic information processing was the key to going from perception to prediction. Kaplan (1976) saw a neurophysiological basis to this process and suggested that the structures in the brain by which information was handled were very similar to the 'neural nets' hypothesized by Hebb (1949; 1966). Briefly, the idea is that there exists a set of elements in the brain that correspond to real world features and that these are linked in such a way that arousal of one element can lead to arousal of a collection of elements. The real world, in other words, becomes a representation in the brain. Although undoubtedly based on man's transaction with his environment and on his construction of that environment in his mind, the neural net hypothesis gives Kaplan's work a materialist flavour that has perhaps inhibited further work in the field, particularly because it is a hypothesis that is very difficult to either prove or disprove. Little is known, for example, about where the concept of space is located in the brain, although the most likely place seems to be the parietal lobe of the right hemisphere (O'Keefe and Nadel 1978). Likewise little is known about whether the ability of males to perform better than female at spatial orientation tasks is linked in any way to brain structure (McGee 1979).

Intellectual development

The argument that environmental information processing plays an important role in evolutionary adaptation (that is, in *phylogenetic* development) has a parallel in the argument that similar processes are important in the development of the individual (that is, in *ontogenetic* development) (Stea 1976: 111). In both cases man is seen as interacting with his environment, in the first place ensuring the survival of the species and in the second place providing for intellectual growth. Intellectual development in this sense implies 'qualitative changes in the organization of behaviour' (Hart and Moore 1973: 250). It has been studied most commonly in relation to child development where there is ample evidence that environmental awareness and understanding improve with age (Siegel *et al.* 1979). At issue are three fundamental problems: how environmental knowledge comes about; whether intelligence is the awakening of *a priori* structures or the gradual accumulation of bits of information; and the nature of the interaction between knowledge and behaviour. In addressing himself to these problems Moore (1976) proposed six postulates to cover the development of environmental knowing.

Moore's first postulate states that environmental knowledge is *constructed* in that individuals invent *structures* in order to enable them to cope with reality. Thus, in the study of environmental knowledge it is impossible to separate the *objects known* from the *process of knowing*, in much the same way that it is impossible to separate a description of the world from the language used in that description (see Whorf 1956). The fact that individuals construct their own realities implies of course an element of subjectivism in the resultant knowledge. In practice, however, it is usually assumed that similar people have similar constructions. The second postulate is that environmental knowledge results from the interaction between factors internal to the individual (e.g. needs, personality) and the demands made on the individual by the situation (e.g. constraints on the appropriate form of behaviour in certain environments). This is closely related to the third postulate which states that individuals adapt to their environment in that they actively seek out and assimilate information. From this perspective the individual and the situation should be viewed as a whole: man imbues the environment with meaning and that meaning then influences his behaviour. Moore's fourth postulate is that transactions with the environment are mediated by previously constructed conceptions. There is, in other words, an element of learning involved in the processing of environmental information to the extent that cognition takes stock of experience. The fifth postulate is that environmental knowledge has different structures at different stages of development. More specifically, the cognitive structure '*precedes*, *selects*, and *orders* the specific parts of environmental experience and behaviour that will be attended to and assimilated' (Moore 1976: 144) with a result that a change of structure will result in a change in the type of knowledge that the individual has. The final postulate argues that the nature of these structures can only be studied by taking account of their genesis and transformation. Such transformation can take several forms, two of the more important of which are *ontogenesis* (developmental changes associated with the life cycle) and *microgenesis* (short-term adaptation to environmental change which can take place over periods as short as a few days) (Pearce 1977).

The idea of developmental changes has been studied mainly in relation to young children. For example, Stea (1976) has suggested that children think of their environment in a Gestalt manner in that they do not memorize routes so much as *understand* the way in which paths are all related. He ties this in with the structure of the brain. The left-hand hemisphere controls language, writing and other linear processes (*propositional functions*) while the right-hand hemisphere controls perception and spatial knowledge (*appositional functions*) and Stea suggests that, as the child develops, there is a shift in dominance from appositional to propositional functions (see Ornstein 1972). As a result Stea believes that an ability to cognize large-scale environments may be developed in children well before they reach school (see Blaut and Stea 1971). Unfortunately the evidence for this is somewhat equivocal (see Fishbein 1976). The idea of hemispheric differences in the brain remains, however, an important one that is potentially capable of accounting for what people find attractive in urban design (P. Smith 1976) and the adoption of either egocentric or domicentric systems of orientation (Sonnenfeld 1982).

From a developmental point of view the study of brain structure has never been as popular as the work of Piaget. In simple terms Piaget argued that there are four general levels of spatial knowing: the *sensorimotor* level based on representation through action (e.g. the manipulation of objects); the *pre-operational* level based on simple mental constructs and intuitive, unco-ordinated images of the world derived from the memory of previously perceived objects; the *concrete operational* level where simple logical thought permits mental representations of the environment that are symbolized and systematic; and the *formal operational* level at which the individual is capable of hypothetico–deductive reasoning and can handle abstract spatial

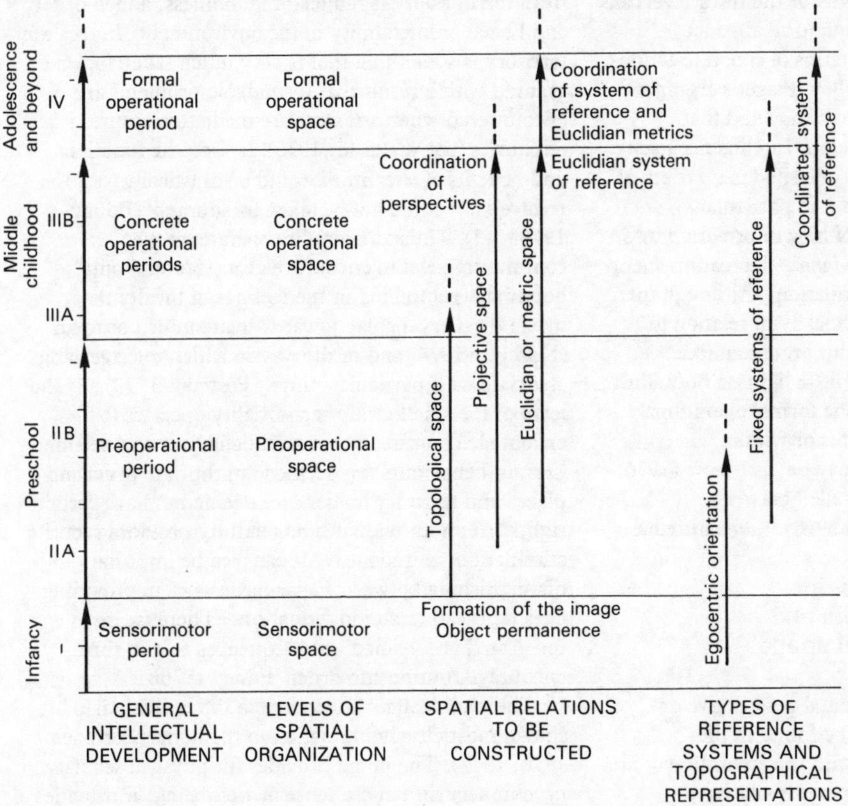

Fig. 5.1 Ontogenetic development of spatial awareness. *Source*: Moore (1976, 149).

notions that are not dependent upon real actions, objects, and spaces (Moore 1976: 148). These levels are sequential in that a child passes through each of them as the child develops (Piaget and Inhelder 1956). Moreover the stages are associated with an ability to handle different sorts of spatial relations; first come *topological* relations (e.g. proximity, separation), then *projective* relations (e.g. objects are thought of in relation to perspectives like straight lines), and finally *Euclidean* or *metric* relations (based on a system of axes and co-ordinates). Figure 5.1 shows that an ability to cope with these sets of spatial relations emerges during the pre-operational period. The figure also illustrates Hart and Moore's (1973) hypothesis that children's understanding of the spatial layout of the environment falls into three stages: an *undifferentiated egocentric reference system* organized about the child's own position and actions; *partially co-ordinated, fixed reference systems* organized around specific places like a home or a town centre; and *operationally co-ordinated and hierarchically integrated reference systems* organized in terms of abstract geometric patterns (Moore 1976: 150). In simple terms, there is a sequence 'from action-in-space to perception-of-space to conceptions-about-space as a function of increasing differentiation, distancing, and reintegration between the organism and its environment' (Hart and Moore 1973: 255). Only at the third level can movement be described in relation to an abstract reference system rather than in terms of concrete actions.

In short, Hart and Moore follow Piaget's argument that adaptation is the key to knowledge and that intelligence is the key to adaptation. Intelligence itself cannot be inherited but what is inherited is a variety of modes of intellectual functioning, in particular *assimilation* (the incorporation of new information into existing schemata) and *accommodation* (the readjustment of schemata in the light of assimilation). Although there is some empirical evidence specifically in relation to spatial information to support this argument (see Acredolo *et al.* 1975), it throws little light on how adult individuals who are already at the formal operational level cope with new environments or with environmental change. There may be, as Moore (1976: 163) suggests, a 'conceptual parallel' between ontogenesis and microgenesis but as yet its nature has not been outlined.

Territoriality and personal space

An alternative to the developmental perspective on environmental knowledge is to be found in the argument that man's relations with the environment are in some way innate. Several popular books have explored the theme of man as a territorial animal (e.g. Ardrey 1967; Morris 1968) and have pointed towards an important question, namely the extent to which ethological studies of the biological bases for behaviour in the natural environment provide clues for the understanding of human behaviour. To ethologists, the concept of territory is linked to the instinct of aggression. A territory is, in other words, a place to be defended on account of its role in providing food and a place for mateship. It is difficult to see simple parallels with this in human behaviour (Malmberg 1980) and the idea has even attracted opposition in biology (see Montague 1968). However, if a territory is thought of as the space around an individual or group which that individual or group thinks of as in some way its own, and which therefore distinguishes it from other individuals or groups, then the concept has at least intuitive appeal in the study of human affairs (Gold 1982).

Edney (1976a) has stressed that human territoriality bears little relationship to aggression but that it is important as a way of organizing behaviour. In this sense territoriality is characterized as the continuous association of a person or persons with a specific place and it operates at three levels: the community; the small group; and the individual. At each level the main benefit from territoriality is reduced randomness, added order, and hence predictability in the environment. In this way territory is something that is very much taken for granted with a result that formidable problems are encountered when attempts are made to measure territories (see Walmsley 1976). In fact 'the functions and benefits of a territory would be drastically reduced if it could not be taken for granted' (Edney 1976a: 43). Thus territoriality operates at the community level to encourage group identity and bonding, exemplified in the feelings of loyalty that urban dwellers display towards their suburb or town (Norcliffe 1974) and in the way in which teenage gangs associate with particular 'turfs' (Porteous 1973). At the level of the small group territoriality operates to encourage congruency between behaviour and setting. Certain behaviours are deemed appropriate to certain places and territory holders are deemed to have certain rights. At an individual level territory provides security, stimulation, and identity. It can also be important in distinguishing between social classes and in providing cues that lead to an individual's behaviour being integrated or 'chained' into sequences that in turn encourage routine and order (Edney 1976b).

The significance of territory to the individual is shown most clearly in relation to the home (Porteous 1976; 1977). The home provides for physical security, psychic security, and a sense of well-being; it provides a threat-free environment in which the territory holder can control and manipulate sensory stimulation; and it provides both an identity and a way of communicating that identity to the outside world. Space, in other words, is assigned meaning and is thereby used as a communication system. Hall (1959; 1966) referred to this non-verbal communication, which differs from culture to culture and of which people are rarely aware, as 'the silent language'. He introduced the term *proxemics* to refer to the human use of space as an elaboration of culture and suggested that research should focus on three things: fixed feature space (the realm of architectural design); semi-fixed features (such as furniture); and informal space (the distances maintained by an individual in encounters with others). Informal space can be resolved into *intimate space* (up to 2 feet); *personal space* (2–5 feet), *social – consultative space* (5–12 feet), and *public space* (beyond 12 feet). Of course these spaces are not spherical about the individual and the distances quoted apply specifically to studies of white, American, middle-class males. There is nonetheless a good deal of support for the existence of these spaces (Sommer 1969). In particular personal space seems to be related to considerations of privacy and freedom (see Westin 1967) with a result that invasion of personal space, either deliberately (e.g. interrogation techniques) or accidentally (e.g. overcrowding), can have discomforting effects.

Knowledge of large areas

Although personal space is undoubtedly important in human behaviour, it operates at such a small scale that it is rarely of direct interest to the geographer, whose concern is more usually with how people come to terms with large-scale environments. Knowledge of large-scale environments has two functions: it facilitates location and movement, and it provides a general frame of reference whereby an individual understands and relates to the environment (Hart and Moore 1973: 274). Such knowledge is generally thought of as being developed over time as the mind imposes structures on the otherwise chaotic reality with which it comes into contact (Golledge 1979). In other words, man structures the present in much the same way as he structures the past (Lowenthal 1975) and in both cases bias results. Bias and subjectivity are inevitable because the percepts (e.g. judgements, interpretations) that result from man's evaluation of his environment are *emergent* in that they express the interaction of the object under consideration (the environment) with the behavioural characteristics (e.g. experience, attitudes) of the subject (Ittelson *et al.* 1974: 86). Interpretation and cognition of the environment are therefore very personal events. They are also very critical events because it is through cognition that man develops an ability to modify his behaviour in relation to a changing environment. In fact Proshansky *et al.* (1970a: 175) have argued that man's cognitive structuring of the environment is organized so as to maximize his freedom of choice in subsequent behaviour. In this sense therefore cognition is probably the single most important psychological process in man–environment interaction (Ittelson *et al.* 1974: 98).

Cognition is based on the extraction of information from the environment. Different people will of course extract different information from the same environment. This does not mean however that it is impossible to generalize about environmental cognition. After all the collection of information about large-scale environments is seriously constrained by distance with a result that people living close together tend to have similar information fields (Hanson 1976; Hudson 1975) and very similar motives for acquiring information (Gold 1980: 48). Thus an understanding of what information the mind processes and uses is central to any investigation of man–environment interaction (Golledge and Rushton 1976: viii). For the most part research in this direction has been theoretical and, despite attempts to look at information overload and urban complexity (Rapoport and Hawkes 1970), most authors have focused on the contribution of learning to cognition.

Environmental learning

There are a great many references in the geographical literature that purport to show how psychological studies of learning can throw light on man–environment interaction. Prominent among these citations have been the *stimulus-response theories* deriving in varying ways from the work of Hull (1952). For example, Stea (1976) has proposed a seven-stage learning model whereby (1) the environment is viewed as a complex of stimuli that (2) act on an organism resulting in (3) a cognitive process within the central nervous system such that (4) a response is learnt and (5) subsequently rewarded or reinforced subject to (6) the organism being disposed in such a way as to make the reward effective with a result that (7) learning can be said to have occurred. There are several problems with this approach: the environment is reduced to the status of a set of stimuli; the central nervous system is regarded as a 'black box' that cannot be investigated directly; and the psychological theory on which the approach is based derives largely from experimentation with animals (see Stea 1973). More important, the approach ignores the transactional–constructivist proposition that man actively creates his reality rather than simply learning an environment (see Golledge 1979).

Dissatisfaction with stimulus-response theories has encouraged geographers to look to the idea of *place learning* and the notion that individuals learn linkages between elements within the environment rather than simple associations between environmental stimuli and resultant behaviour (Tolman 1948). Although this approach is appealing in that it focuses on 'cognitive maps', doubts among psychologists about its logical status tend to have inhibited its adoption (Moore and Golledge 1976b: 9). Instead it is increasingly recognized that the sort of problem that is involved in the learning of large-scale environments is one that has traditionally lain outside the scope of experimental psychology. As a result, researchers interested in large-scale man–environment interaction are likely to have to develop their own models of learning. In this context Appleyard (1973) has suggested that there are three types of knowledge that result from environmental learning:

1. *operational knowledge* concerned with features that are critical to the functioning of the environment (e.g. location of shops, schools);
2. *responsive knowledge* (how people react to features like landmarks);
3. *inferential knowledge*, that is, an ability to generalize and to make inferences that extend beyond what is actually known.

Responsive knowledge is environment-dominant but operational and inferential knowledge are man-dominant and are the product of information derived from personal experience, from contacts, and from the mass media. Of these sources of information, direct experience has been studied most. For example, Golledge (1978) has proposed that learning about an environment takes place primarily as a result of interaction with that environment such that a cognitive representation of the environment is built up over time. First an individual comes to know locations, then links between locations, and then areas around groups of location. The result is the pattern displayed in Fig. 5.2.. Of course interaction does not account for all knowledge; social and historical factors are also important. From this point of view learning about the environment becomes, in essence, the process of compiling information which includes all the spatial relations among environmental elements as well as their socio-economic, cultural or other meanings and significances (Golledge 1978: 81).

The principal danger in viewing environmental learning from this perspective is the temptation to regard the elicitation of the cognitive representation as an end in itself, thereby ignoring the processes that give rise to the representation and the fact that the representation is always in a state of flux. It needs to be remembered therefore that at least five processes are involved in information processing and learning:

1. information filtering (acceptance/rejection of information);
2. shunting (the activation/inhibition of the mental

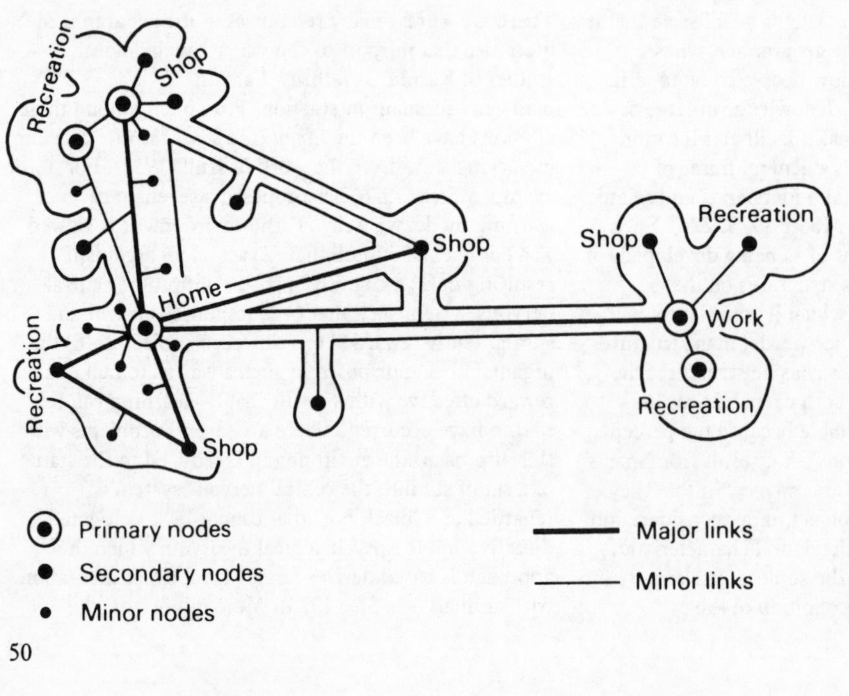

Fig. 5.2 The learned environment. *Source*: Golledge (1978, 80).

processes used to evaluate information);
3. memory (ability to retain information);
4. image building (the development of schemata to handle information);
5. feedback (Bennett and Chorley 1978: 226).

Each of these is important because the environment provides far more information than man can handle. The distinction between information processing in learning and information processing in decision-making is however a fine one and one that tends to mitigate against learning being considered as a process in isolation (see Ch. 6).

Personal construct theory

The way in which places develop meanings for people is a central issue in environmental learning and cognition but one that is not easily accommodated in existing learning theories that are much better equipped to handle the sort of factual information shown in Fig. 5.2. The key problems in coming to terms with 'meaning' involve operational definition of the term, its measurement, and considerations of representivity (Harrison and Sarre 1971). One approach which has appealed to many people as a potentially fruitful way of examining the meaning that the environment has for man is Kelly's (1955) *personal construct theory*. This approach, derived from clinical psychology, assumes that man is a proto-scientist who tries to understand the workings of the world around him (Downs 1976). The theory in fact derives from Brunswik's (1956) suggestion that 'the individual samples his environment perceptually and then tests the accuracy of his perception by trying out the environment through his actions' (Ittelson *et al.* 1974: 110). Because sampling is never perfect, environmental knowledge is never perfect. The fundamental postulate of personal construct theory is that a person's processes are psychologically channelled by the ways in which he anticipates events. From this, eleven corollaries are deduced to show how constructs help in understanding the world (Table 5.1). The difference between personal construct theory and traditional learning theory is perhaps best seen by reflecting on Kelly's distinction between *accumulative fragmentalism* and *constructive alternativism*: under the former perspective, knowledge is obtained by piecing together bits of information whereas under the latter perspective, exemplified by personal construct theory, the world is not seen as fact-filled but rather as a place where man constructs and tests alternative assumptions as to how things work (Downs 1976: 79–80).

Table 5.1 The formal content of personal contact theory

Fundamental postulate A person's processes are psychologically channelled by the ways in which he anticipates events.
Construction corollary A person anticipates events by construing their replications.
Individuality corollary Persons differ from each other in their constructions of events.
Organization corollary Each person characteristically evolves for his convenience in antipating events, a construction system embracing ordinal relationships between constructs.
Dichotomy corollary A person's construction system is composed of a finite number of dichotomous constructs.
Choice corollary A person chooses for himself that alternative in a dichotomized construct through which he anticipates the greatest possibility for the elaboration of his system.
Range corollary A construct is convenient for the anticipation of a finite range of events only.
Experience corollary A person's construction system varies as he successively construes the replications of events.
Modulation corollary The variation in a person's construction system is limited by the permeability of the constructs within whose range of convenience the variants lie.
Fragmentation corollary A person may successively employ a variety of construction systems which are inferentially incompatible with each other.
Commonality corollary To the extent that one person employs a construction of experience which is similar to that employed by another, his processes are psychologically similar to those of the other person.
Sociality corollary To the extent that one person construes the construction process of another he may play a role in a social process involving the other person.

Source: Bannister and Fransella (1971, 202–3)

The constructs that individuals have about the environment can be uncovered in a variety of ways. Perhaps the best known of these is the *minimum context form* whereby phenomena are presented in triads to respondents who are asked to state what differentiates two members of the triad from the third (Fransella and Bannister 1977: 14–19). The resultant constructs are usually expressed as bipolar scales. These constructs can then be listed on one axis of a matrix, the other axis being a listing of the environmental features under study. For example, a group of shopping centres can be evaluated in terms of a number of constructs. Values in the matrix are scores for each element (shopping centre) on each bipolar scale (construct). In other words, the matrix is a grid of the repertoire (rarely more than twenty to thirty) of constructs necessary to describe a given type of environmental feature, hence the term *repertory grid technique*. The technique is not a test because the form and content vary from case to case (Bannister and Fransella, 1971). It is simply a method that puts the least possible number of constraints on an individual as he tries to communicate his understanding of the environment. In fact the flexibility and open-endedness of the technique has led to criticism.

Downs (1976) has pointed out, for instance, that personal construct theory has often been adopted in geography because it affords a ready package rather than because it is deemed theoretically attractive. Moreover, the repertory grid technique only provides for inter-personal comparisons when a common set of constructs and elements is used and yet such a move runs counter to the idiosyncratic focus for which personal construct theory was originally developed. Additionally the theory says little about feedback and its influence on behaviour. Such criticism may however be harsh because the theory has the potential to be developed in the light of application.

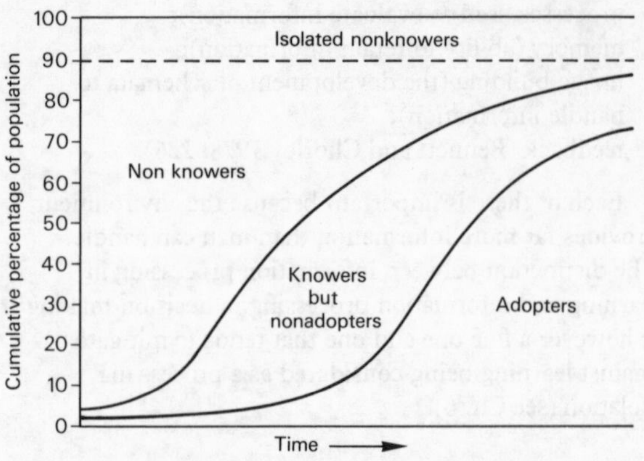

Fig. 5.3 The diffusion of innovations.

Information flows

Personal construct theory has a good deal to say about how individuals use information but it has very little to say about how they acquire information or about how information flows from individual to individual. Yet the subject of information flows has been of interest to geographers ever since Hägerstrand's (1952) seminal work on the propagation of innovation waves. For the most part this information-orientated research has focused on innovation and diffusion. It has usually been assumed, for example, that information about innovations is passed on only through interpersonal communication (the probability of which is influenced by the distance separating individuals), and that different individuals have a differing resistance to innovation. The result of this type of information flow is that diffusion describes an S-curve over time as first early adopters, then late adopters, and finally laggards succumb to the innovation (Brown 1982) (Fig 5.3). In simple terms, diffusion can be likened to a wave that spreads outward from a point of innovation dissipating its energy as it goes (Morrill 1968). Even hierarchic diffusions, where innovations tend to follow the central place hierarchy, can be seen as a special case of the general diffusion process (Brown and Cox 1971; Morrill and Manninen 1975).

This classical view of diffusion has attracted a good deal of criticism in recent years (Brown 1981). Blaut (1977) has stressed that information is not something that lies around in discrete bits but rather something that is part and parcel of the structure of society, with a result that diffusion should be seen as a force for cultural change. A similar theme was taken up by Blaikie (1978) in his argument that information transfer is class-specific and that a focus on regularities in the diffusion process results in a failure to ask vital questions about the ideological, political, and economic origins of innovation. In other words studies of information flow can be criticized from an ideological viewpoint. They can also be criticized in that most of them have concentrated on the macro-scale and only rarely has any attention been paid to the micro-scale and the way individual decision-making units identify and evaluate information sources (see Clark and Smith 1979).

Individuals acquire information from both personal and impersonal sources (Spector *et al.* 1976). Personal sources usually imply a point-to-point information flow and impersonal sources a point-to-area flow (Jakle *et al.* 1976: 121). Personal sources are best illustrated by communication between acquaintances. Despite the emergence in western society of 'community without propinquity' where close ties are maintained with friends who live outside the immediate environment (Webber 1963), most acquaintance-based information flows are heavily constrained to the neighbourhood around the home (Everitt and Cadwallader 1981), the main exceptions being those 'space searchers' (Gould 1975) who travel widely and whose personal experience is thereby broadened. Media-based information flows provide the best example of the use of impersonal sources, although other illustrations are to be found in such things as the advertising of spatial information by estate agents and other organizations concerned with locational decision-making (see Palm 1976a). In all such cases the flow of information is controlled by *gatekeepers* (journalists, editors, agents) who decide what the public should see and hear. Predictably the use to which personal and impersonal sources are put varies from individual to individual according to differences in their needs and cognitive sets (Leff *et al.* 1974). Some generalizations can however be made.

Research into the effects of information on its users has traditionally focused on the question 'who says what, to whom, and how?' and this question can be used to differentiate private information flows from

Table 5.2 Types of spatial information

	Public information	*Private information*
Who?	Skilled professionals (e.g. journalists)	Personal contacts (e.g. friends)
Says what?	Descriptions based on observations	Experiences based on recollections
To whom?	Mass society (e.g. TV viewers)	Primary contact groups (e.g. neighbours)
How?	Broadcasts and publications	Face to face meetings for telephone contact

public information flows (Table 5.2). Private information is exchanged in personal contacts between neighbours on a direct basis usually at a small scale whereas public information involves communication from skilled professionals to a mass society often at a reasonably large scale. This is not to say that public information flows in general, and the media in particular, encourage cultural homogeneity and uniform behaviour. In fact, the impact of public information flows on individuals is not at all clear and a variety of different positions have been adopted (Walmsley 1980). Behaviouralists assume that exposure to things like the media influences both actions and attitudes. That is, the behaviouralist position overlooks the fact that human behaviour is largely goal-directed and assumes that information does something to the people it reaches in an almost deterministic fashion. An opposite position is taken by functionalists who argue that public information fulfils a number of needs (e.g. orientation, reassurance, escape). In other words, public information sources are put to a number of uses from which gratification is derived. Yet a third perspective argues that public information flows have little direct impact on behaviour or attitudes but that they are important in that they tell information users what to think about. In this sense, public information sources set an *agenda* of issues for public consideration (Walmsley 1982b). This is an interesting proposition and it may well be that it has relevance to the distinction that is sometimes made between specific and generic information (Kaplan 1976). Private information flows are ideally suited to the provision of specific knowledge relating to what is where in a reasonably restricted small-scale environment. They are possibly less useful in providing generic knowledge and the ability to extrapolate from a known situation to an unknown situation because many private information flows contain little that is of use in the development of the schemata or mental structures that are necessary for the classification and organization of information. The agenda set by public information flows possibly fulfil this role of providing a schema although the evidence for this is not yet definite (see Walmsley, 1980; 1982b), partly because the nature of public information flows, like private information flows, is changing. Advances in communications technology are continually reducing the friction of distance by making information exchange quicker, cheaper, and more available (Abler and Falk 1981; Falk and Abler 1980). In particular, improvements in telecommunications are likely to have a major impact on private information flows; for example, more telephones are likely to stimulate more social visiting and hence more travel and more private information exchange (Clark and Unwin 1981).

Chapter 6

DECISION-MAKING

In the quest to understand spatial behaviour it is axiomatic that consideration be given to the manner in which decisions are made (Lee 1971). In this sense decision-making can be thought of as the translation of motives into overt action within the context of available information. Without any motivation an individual may be described as inactive, and made up simply of a series of functional characteristics (such as mental and physical abilities and value systems), a series of structural characteristics (such as sex, age, and occupation), and a series of existence variables (such as location and orientation). Decisions arise when an individual is motivated to act by changing needs or changes in the external environment (Huber 1980). With the emergence of a more complex, technologically-based society the nature of decision-making has changed quite markedly. In low-technology societies, both in the past and present, the process of making decisions, the resultant behaviour, and the feedback of information was generally immediate, continuous, and adaptive. In contrast, in modern, high-technology societies individual decision-making often forms part of an intricate network which is difficult to unravel; in many cases it involves not only the individual but also powerful elite groups and institutions, which form a hierarchical nesting of decision authorities, each affecting the other (Hill 1979).

Decision-making can be classified into a number of types, ranging from highly deliberate problem-solving to habitual, subconscious decision behaviour (Moore and Thomas 1976). In general, most decisions tend towards the latter type, largely because of man's inability to process large amounts of information and his predisposition towards minimizing effort (Jarvis and Mann 1977). Simon (1952) has in fact argued that, in order to compensate for these traits, individuals are inclined to simplify the decision process by greatly reducing consideration of alternative courses of action. Certainly this type of decision-making process is commonly used in coping with the trials of everyday living. True problem-solving is however a very different type of decision-making in that it involves confrontation with a problem which requires deliberate thought in a specified direction, whether it be searching or vicarious trial and error, and hence a choice from among a wide range of alternatives. Inevitably such a decision is a highly selective process and the resultant behaviour is often abrupt and substantial. Many problem-solving decisions of this nature represent attempts by man to adapt to changing environmental conditions.

The core of most locational decisions is the notion of choice, which implies a search by individuals among alternatives within the environment (Golledge and Rushton 1976). The criteria for the ultimate choice are invariably relative, rather than absolute, and so the process of spatial choice involves an individual in comparing each alternative with every other one in order to select the one which gives the greatest expected satisfaction. Such choice behaviour is, of course, part and parcel of a continuing learning process that involves both correct and incorrect choices (Golledge 1969). For example, once overt action has taken place individuals tend to restructure their decision processes in the light of the new and additional information so as to confirm and repeat a certain course of action, or lay the foundations for alternative actions. Very often choice behaviour has been conceptualized as involving a ranking procedure whereby all conceivable spatial alternatives are ordered on a scale of preferredness (see Rushton 1969b).

A major consequence of this focus on choice behaviour in human geography has been a plethora of studies of discretionary behaviour, such as shopping and recreational trips, rather than of those activities which are more space and time bound, such as journeys to work and to school (Pipkin 1981b). This suggests that certain forms of behaviour involve much greater choices than others. Also, the range of choices for any one form of behaviour will of course vary for different individuals, with the wealthy having greater choices than the poor, and the young more mobility than the elderly. Inevitably realization of this fact forces attention upon the concept of choice within a wider environment and on the way in which social institutions may constrain individual choices by means of a whole series of 'entry rules' (Moore *et al.* 1976; Pred 1981). First, however, it is essential to appreciate the psychological basis for decision-making.

Stimulus, response, and learning

When attempting to unraval the complexities of decision-making, psychologists generally focus on how input involving information about the environment is transformed into a decision which results in an output in the form of overt behaviour (Carroll and Payne 1976). Of the several approaches to decision-making developed by psychologists two very quickly attracted the attention of geographers: *behaviourism* and *Gestalt theory*.

To a behaviourist, decision-making involves a simple stimulus–response (S–R) relationship, in which a particular response can be attributed to given antecedent conditions. In this perspective the relationship between a stimulus and a response is viewed as arising from a learning process. Thus, by constant repetition a suitable response is reinforced and learnt so that, whenever the particular stimulus is presented, the resultant behaviour is predictable (Wright *et al.* 1970). Although the early behaviourists, such as Watson (1924) and the majority of his followers, did most of their research with animals under laboratory conditions, there has been no lack of individuals inclined to apply S–R theory directly to human behaviour (see Skinner 1971; 1974). This experimental approach has, however, attracted stern criticism, particularly of the way in which behaviourism oversimplifies human behaviour. Koestler (1967) expressed this well when he pointed out that behaviourism was based on a 'ratomorphic' view of man that was no better than the nineteenth century anthropomorphic view of animals. In short, behaviourism overlooks the cultural and socio-economic context of learning (Lee 1976).

Partly as a response to these weaknesses of behaviourism, there emerged Gestalt theory which argued the need to incorporate the individual mind in any consideration of human decision-making. Basically, this theory postulates that perception forms a crucial intervening variable between stimulus and response, and that individuals organize the objects they observe in the environment into patterns, or *gestalten*. Koffka's (1935) claim that behaviour was based on the environment as perceived rather than the environment as it is, was taken by Kirk (1952; 1963) and used as a means of developing a simple geographical decision-making model. In this model Kirk argued that the decision-maker is embedded in a world of physical

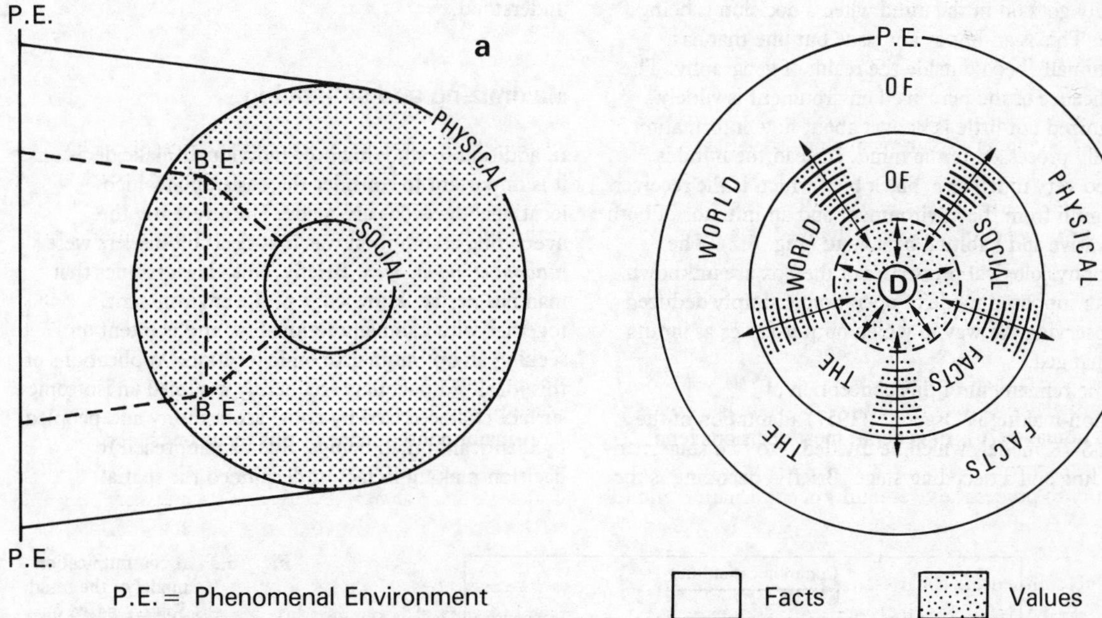

Fig. 6.1 The filtering of environmental information. **a** the behavioural environment **b** the behavioural environment of a decision-taker. *Source*: Kirk (1963, 363 and 367).

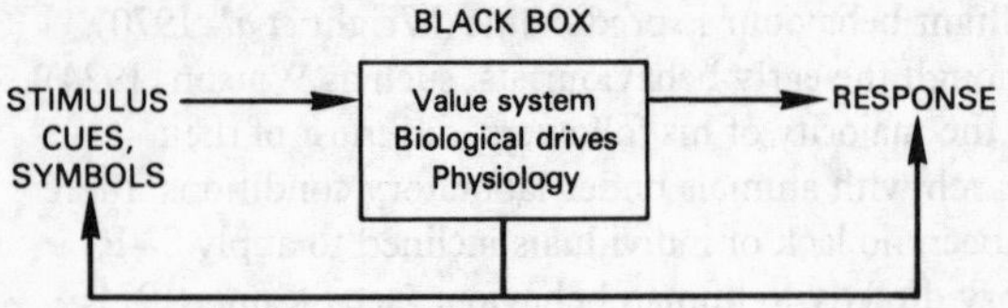

Fig. 6.2 The mind as a 'black box'.

facts and a world of economic and social facts (Fig. 6.1(a)). Both worlds impinge on decision-makers through perception which reflects motives, preferences, and traditions drawn from an individual's social and cultural background. Therefore, the same environment may have quite different meanings to individuals from different cultures, or at different stages in the history of a given culture. These ideas formed the basis of the notion of man as a reasoning and purposive being, who based his decisions on the social and physical facts of the phenomenal environment only after they have penetrated a highly selective filter of values (Fig. 6.1(b)). Such a conception of decision-making emphasizes the point that behaviour is guided, not by the external environment as such, but rather by a distorted psychological representation of it. Despite early suggestions that it was innate, this perceived environment has been shown to be a learned phenomenon (see Lewin 1936).

Both the stimulus-response and Gestalt theories can be regarded as being too limited in their conception of decision-making since they fail to take into account what actually goes on in the mind when a decision is being made. This is an important issue but one that has traditionally been outside the realm of geography. The significance of the perceived environment is widely recognized but little is known about how information is actually processed in the mind. Instead the mind is viewed very much as a 'black box' which is the receiver of stimuli from the environment and an initiator of both innovative and habitual behaviour (Fig. 6.2). The neurophysiological properties of the box are unknown and its supposed mode of operation is simply deduced by observing the way in which output varies as inputs are changed.

One refinement of this conception of decision-making is Osgood's (1957) adaptation of the basic S–R model, which he divided into two stages: an encoding and a decoding stage. Briefly, decoding is the term used to describe the association an individual has with, and his disposition to respond in a certain way to, a particular sign. The eventual response is known as encoding. Such a process involves what have been described as representational mediators. During decoding some physical energy is expended when a stimulus is recoded through nervous impulses before it is interpreted in the 'black box'. On the other hand, in encoding, a motive within the 'black box', after being transmitted to the motor responses, is recoded into physical movements that are the output. Osgood extended this decoding/encoding concept with a communication model (Fig. 6.3). Of course even this model does not make clear exactly what happens in the mind. Indeed, the 'black box' can be characterized as a 'hidden world'. This, of course, is a notion familiar to geographers who have long recognized that the 'terrae incognitae' in the mind may influence behaviour to a much greater extent than actual environmental stimuli (Wright 1974). Essentially what is being argued in this view is that it is not so much what we see, but how we feel about what we see, that is crucial to understanding behaviour (Lowenthal 1961). In other words, 'man has the peculiar aptitude of being able to live by notions of reality which may be more real than reality itself' (Watson 1969: 14). In summary, what the 'black box' concept emphasizes is that spatial behaviour involves not only stimuli and responses but also a complex process of relationship and feedback based on cognitive and physiological processes that are still only vaguely understood.

Maximizing and satisficing

In addition to studying how individuals make decisions, it is important to consider the basis upon which locational decisions are made. Until recently the overriding assumption was that decision-makers were *rational economic men*. Briefly, this view assumes that man has perfect knowledge of the environment, together with complete rationality, and is intent on seeking an optimum economic location. Applications of this idealized postulate frequently assumed an isotropic surface characterized by equal accessibility and peopled by identical human beings. Such an approach to decision-making in fact underpinned the spatial

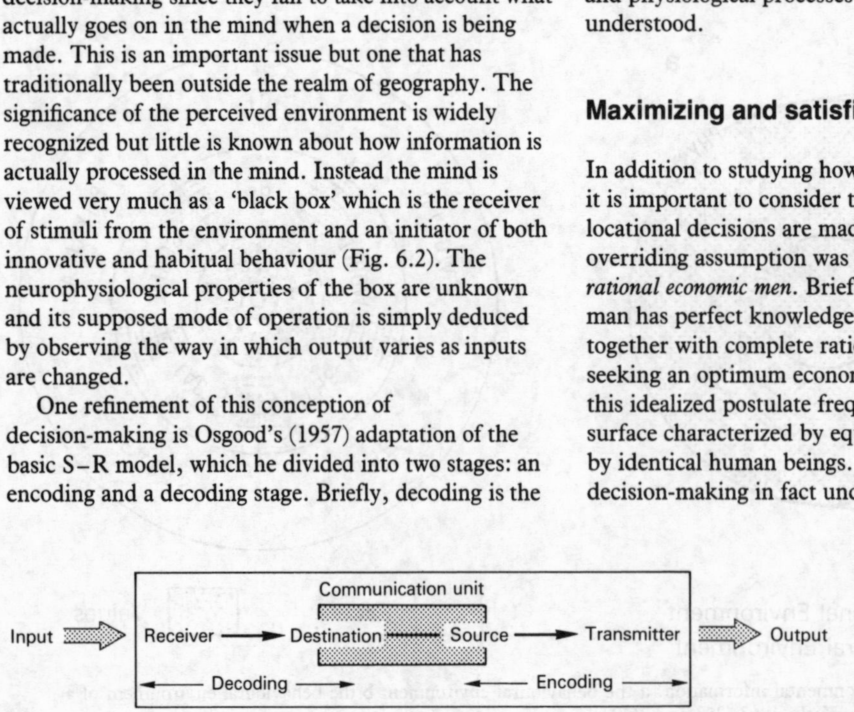

Fig. 6.3 A communication model of the mind. *Source*: based on Osgood (1957, 75–118)

scientific 'revolution' which swept through human geography from the early 1960s onwards. Despite its value in illustrating what should occur under certain conditions, this approach has many shortcomings (see Pred 1967). This has led to questioning of the value of the assumptions upon which the concept of economic man is based (Simon 1959). For example, it has frequently been noted that, in reality, the businessman has only limited information, and is subject to factors that are simply not predictable. In addition, the 'capacity' of the human mind for formulating and solving complex problems is very small compared with the size of the problems whose solution is required (Simon 1957: 198). As a result a certain amount of attention has shifted from the concept of rational economic man to the principle of *bounded rationality*. According to this principle, individuals seek to be rational only after having greatly simplified the choice before them. However, even this view may be unreal in that many individuals may not seek to optimize at all. Rather, given the enormous effort required for searching out and evaluating alternative courses of action, it may be that many decision-makers simply opt for a solution to decision problems that is *satisfactory* in relation to their aspiration levels.

March and Simon (1958: 256) have in fact claimed that most human decision-making, whether individual or organizational, is concerned with the discovery and selection of satisfactory alternatives; only in exceptional cases is it concerned with the discovery and selection of optimal alternatives. According to this view, optimization requires processing several orders of magnitude more complex than those in satisficing. This, then, is the postulate of man as a *satisficer* (Simon 1952; 1957). The conditions for satisfaction are, however, not static, but are adjusted upwards or downwards on the basis of new experience and new aspiration levels. When the outcome of a decision falls short of the decision-maker's level of aspiration, he either searches for new alternatives or adjusts his level of aspiration downwards, or both. The goal is to reach levels that are practically attainable. In other words, the satisficer may evaluate alternatives and assess likely outcomes on a scale that runs from optimistic to pessimistic projections (Table 6.1).

Table 6.1 Types of decisions

Solution	*Characteristics*
Maximum	Optimum; maximum-minimum pay off
Optimistic	Minimum regret at not optimizing
Satisfactory	Good enough within choice range
Pessimistic	Less than satisfactory
Worse-off	Unsatisfactory

An early attempt to verify the satisficing model was Wolpert's (1964) study of actual and potential farm output. This showed that actual labour productivity was substantially less than its theoretical optimum. In fact less than half of the sample farms had labour productivity of more than 70 per cent of the optimal level and, in some areas, productivity fell to 40 per cent of optimum. In other words, the average farmer achieved less than two-thirds of the productivity that his resources would have allowed. On this evidence Wolpert concluded that the concept of satisficing was much more appropriate than that of economic man for explaining the observed behaviour of his sample. Farmers not only lacked knowledge but also, to some extent, were influenced by value systems that emphasized aversion to such uncertainty.

Probability, risk, and uncertainty

With the adoption of the concepts of satisficing and bounded rationality into their analysis of decision-making, geographers began to develop an approach that conceived of spatial behaviour in probabilistic terms. An important contribution to this development was Pred's (1967) *behavioural matrix*. After a detailed critique of the concept of economic man, Pred depicted decision-making outcomes as a function of the quantity and quality of information available in a given situation, and the individual decision-maker's ability to handle this information (Fig. 6.4). In turn each matrix is a function of the environmental system, since this governs both the availability of information and the perception of its usability. The amount of information available can be related to an individual's exposure to the media, an individual's ability to pick out information, and the credibility attached to information sources. Four factors can also be recognized as influencing an individual's ability to use information: the experience of the user; his intelligence; his flexibility and adaptiveness; and his desires, preferences, attitudes and expectations. Generally speaking, placement at the bottom right corner of the matrix results in 'better' locational decisions than placement at the top left-hand corner. However, the matrix does not preclude an individual with little skill and information from making a better locational solution than one who possesses greater ability. Such an eventuality is of course relatively unlikely, hence the emphasis upon probability. In short, although it still incorporates the idea of rational economic behaviour, Pred's matrix affords a permissive framework which allows for the fact that many real world decisions fail to come anywhere near optimality.

Since the impetus given by Pred's model,

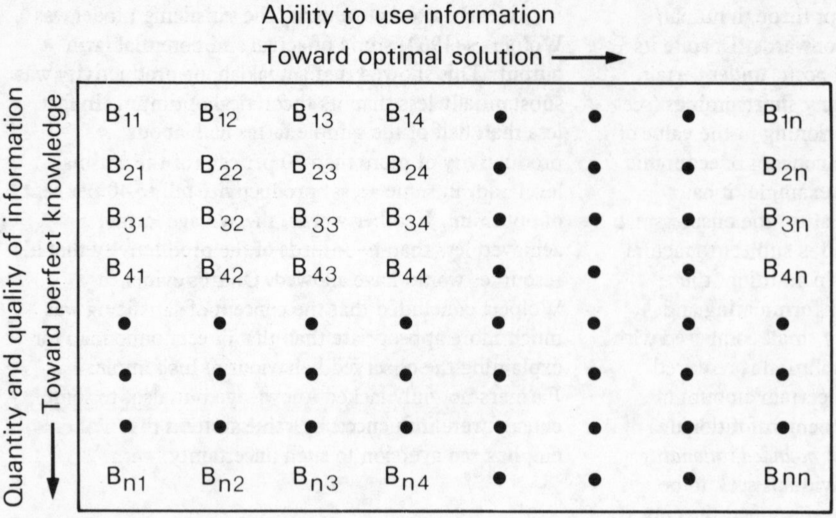

Fig. 6.4 The behavioural matrix. *Source*: Pred (1967, 25).

geographers have attempted to focus more directly on to man's varying ability to predict future events. Inevitably, this involves the incorporation of the concept of *risk*, that is, the notion that all estimates of likely future states are prone to error (Webber 1972). If the probable error is small, then the risk is slight. If the probable error is great, the situation may be described as being 'fairly risky'. Where an individual is unable to make any estimate of future events, that individual can be viewed as operating in conditions of *uncertainty*. Numerous researchers have suggested that, when decision-makers are faced with uncertainty, more often than not they estimate or impute risk in line with their own psychological characteristics (Starr and Whipple 1980). Thus, if an individual is uncertain, the only rational course of action is for him to assign equal probabilities to all 'states of nature'. Alternatively an individual may impute risk by adopting a pessimistic attitude and 'assuming the worst'. In reality, most people are neither optimists nor pessimists, and so Hurwicz (1970) has argued that decision-making probability be studied from the point of view of the 'partial optimist'. In contrast, Savage (1951) has suggested that the object of some individuals is to minimize losses that would be incurred if an unfavourable state of nature occurred. In other words, such people are less concerned about the actual gains than with what they would stand to lose in cases of disaster.

In considering spatial decision-making under conditions of risk and uncertainty, several geographers have adopted formal game theory as a means of simulating the decision process (Alwan and Parisi 1974; Rapoport 1974). Formal game theory should not however be confused with informal gaming, which is a general technique of simulating real-life processes in the form of games with individuals playing the role of real-life participants (Pred and Kibel 1970; Wolpert 1970; Cohen *et al.* 1973). Instead, formal gaming involves the simulation of the probable strategies of various opponents, each trying to obtain certain objectives without any knowledge about the actions of others (Berkman 1965; Gould 1963; Chapman 1974; Amedeo and Golledge 1975). In such games opponents formulate strategies which yield differing pay-offs, depending on the strategies of the others in the game. The strategies and resultant pay-offs are normally indicated in a pay-off matrix. At issue, in other words, are differing chances of success. A similar perspective has been adopted in the use of information theory as a conceptual framework within which to assess the significance of information upon which decisions are based (Marchand 1972; Louviere 1976; Walsh and Webber 1977; Webber 1978).

All of these attempts to incorporate uncertainty into decision-making are essentially probabilistic in their formulation. As an analytic device, probability does increase the predictive powers of the normative perspective. However, as a means of aiding understanding of how decisions are made, it leaves much to be desired. For example, an emphasis on probability fails to unravel the dynamics of spatial decision-making. In particular, it tends to treat the environment as 'given' and tends to ignore the way in which man can modify his environment. Much of the probabilistic strategy relies in fact on what Lipsey (1975) has called the 'law of large numbers'. According to this view, the inconsistencies that are apparent in behaviour at the individual level cancel each other out when behaviour is viewed in the aggregate with a result that uniformity and generality can be observed. Although such a perspective may appear to be reasonable, it has the weakness that it implies that individual decision-makers lack any common or unifying objective. It therefore runs counter to assumption on which much behavioural research in human geography is founded, namely the notion that general principles guide the way in which individuals come to know and interpret their environments.

Utility and preferences

The introduction of the notion of boundedly rational satisficers necessitates the abandonment of the idea of perfect information. It also means a retreat from the position where decision-makers are thought to be profit maximizers. The concept of satisficing remains vague, however, unless some attempt is made to define exactly what is being 'satisfied'. In this regard some guidance may be found in the concept of *utility* that was developed by economists as a common denominator for comparative value. In a series of pioneering papers Wolpert (1964; 1965; 1966) adopted this concept within a geographical context. Specifically he developed the idea of *place utility* which may be defined as the 'net composite of utilities which are derived from the individual's integration at some point in space' (Wolpert 1965: 60). Place utility may be positive or negative, thereby expressing the individual's satisfaction or dissatisfaction with respect to a given place. The operation of place utility in an analysis of spatial behaviour may be illustrated with reference to migration. Where migration is intended and not forced, the argument goes, the migrant will tend to resettle at a destination which offers a relatively higher level of utility than both the place of origin and the alternative places of destination. This higher utility may be expressed in terms of actual characteristics of the place, or it may be the potential of the place as perceived by the migrant. Thus place utility enters the migration decision in two ways: first, in the potential migrant's decision to seek a new residential site arising from dissatisfaction with present utility; and second, as part of the decision as to actually where to search for a new residence. In this sense, then, application of the concept of place utility encompasses the 'subjective expected utility' which individuals ascribe to the different outcomes of decisions (see Graves 1966).

Despite its elegance, the utility concept is extremely difficult to apply. One popular method of attempting to measure utility has been to get individuals to rank order alternative choices in order to arrive at a transitive preference structure (Edwards and Tversky 1967; Lieber 1976). Unfortunately one of the problems with this technique is that it often uncovers intransitive preferences. Such intransitivity may be illustrated by reference to three hypothetical alternatives, A, B, and C: if A is preferred to B, and B to C, and C to A, intransitivity is said to exist. Such intransitivity is particularly common between multi-dimensional alternatives where individual alternatives are often assessed on different dimensions (May 1954). However, the extent of such intransitivity may sometimes be exaggerated because Walmsley (1977) has shown how a majority of Sydney housewives were quite capable of ordering competing shopping centres into a transitive preference ranking. Another problem in applying the concept of utility surrounds the question of whether an individual's preferences are stable through time (Rushton 1976). In particular the concept of utility is difficult to apply when changes occur in the environment or when an individual's knowledge of alternatives changes markedly. In short, changing utility values may be attributable to any one of three factors (changes in the distribution of alternatives, changes in the action space of individuals, and changes in the individual's preference structure) and it is not always clear which combination of these should be the focus of attention.

Models of decision-making

There have been a number of attempts to formulate a general and comprehensive model of decision-making. A significant initial framework was Herbst's (1964) simple behaviour system, which postulated that every decision-making unit has a need set. In geographical terms, this means that individuals located at a given place have needs which are satisfied by that location (e.g. housing needs are satisfied by the dwelling in which the individual resides). If a location fails to fulfil all the needs required of it, stress is generated. Such stress may eventually become transformed into strain, which may be thought of as a force impelling a change in behaviour. According to Herbst, an individual confronted with intolerable levels of strain can adopt one of three courses of action: (1) a change in overt spatial behaviour; (2) an adjustment in the nature of the need set (e.g. reduced aspirations); or (3) an adjustment of the environment (e.g. building extensions to an inadequately small house). Unfortunately Herbst's framework, although attractive through simplicity, does little to suggest how individuals actually learn about the environment in which they live (see Walmsley 1973).

Spatial learning has been the subject of attention in several geographical models (e.g. Horton and Reynolds

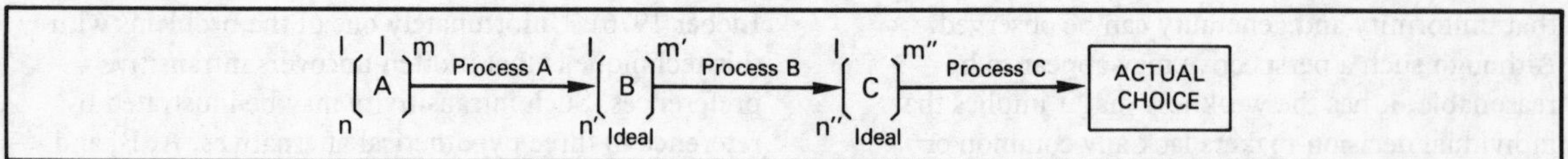

Key:

A	the objective retailing environment.
B	the individual's total knowledge and basic evaluation of the retailing environment and preference (IDEAL) in this respect.
C	the individual's subset of knowledge and evaluation of the environment given certain specific shopping needs as well as preference (IDEAL)
n	total number of shops in the retailing environment
n′	the number of these known to the individual ($n' \leq n$)
n″	the subset of these considered by the individual, given specific shopping needs ($n'' \leq n'$)
m	total number of attributes characterising elements of the retailing environment
m′	the number of personal discriminating constructs developed by the individual ($m' \leq m$)
m″	the subset of these considered by the individual, given specific shopping needs ($m'' \leq m'$)

Process A:
The build-up of knowledge and preferences over time. This implies that both n′ and m′ are a function of time, reaching some asymptotic limit, as is the Ideal shop, aspirations increasing with success, decreasing with failure.

Process B:
The transformation of a subset of this basic environmental knowledge and evaluation, given the existence of certain specific needs. This implies that the elements of n″ and m″ are a function of this motivation.

Process C:
A transformation or mapping function which translates from the location of shops in a person's mental model to an actual choice or choices.

N.B. Feedback loops are omitted from this diagram as the intention is to focus on the determinants of choice at one point in time.

Fig. 6.5 A model of consumer decision-making. *Source*: Hudson (1976, 3).

1971). For the most part, however, no clear link has been specified between learning, cognition, and behaviour. An exception was Hudson's (1976a) model of consumer behaviour which revealed the manner in which individuals learnt about, and chose, opportunities in space. Drawing on Tolman's (1932; 1952) research on cognitive mapping, the field theory of Lewin (1951), and Kelly's (1955) personal construct theory, Hudson's model brought out the relationship between what the individual knows about and the type of shop he or she would ideally like, with the former being evaluated against the latter (Fig. 6.5). The model focused on the objective retail environment, the knowledge and evaluation that an individual has of that environment, and, of course, the actual choice which is finally made. Although this model was initially devised for shopping behaviour, and tested with reference to students, it does have much wider applicability. Unfortunately, however, the model suffers from one important weakness, namely its failure to link choice and satisfaction levels (Jarvis and Mann 1977). A possible solution to this problem is presented in Fig. 6.6, which illustrates decision-making in terms of single and multiple choices, within the context of aspiration levels and satisfactory solutions (Wilson and Alexis 1962). This formulation suggests that when an individual faces only a single choice, three phases are involved in reaching a decision: first, an aspiration level is determined; second, after some searching a limited number of outcomes of alternatives are defined; and third, the alternatives are assessed with a view of finding a solution consistent with the aspiration level. In multiple choice situations the position becomes much more complex as the satisficer attempts to balance aspiration and action. In such cases each new decision is the product of earlier ones. For example, a positive discrepancy between behaviour and aspiration (the case where behaviour is actually better than what was aspired to) (Stage 1 in Fig. 6.6) leads to an upward adjustment of aspirations and a renewal of search produces Stage 2. In contrast, a negative discrepancy (where behaviour falls short of aspirations) leads to a downward adjustment of aspirations and a commitment to search over a wider range of alternatives (Stage 3 of Fig. 6.6). Of course in neither case does the model say anything about the myriad of factors that influence aspirations.

A somewhat different framework for the study of locational decision-making, and one which gives some clues as to what influences aspirations, is Huff's (1960) model of consumer space preference. Although developed to analyse consumer movements, this model has much wider appeal because its holistic perspective highlights major components of the decision process. Briefly, five major components are identified (see also Fig. 8.2):

1. A *desiraderatum*, or a desire for a particular objective, which results from physiological needs and a stimulus drive.
2. A *value system* which determines how an individual's values operate as a filter between his objectives and his eventual decision.
3. *Perception*, or the filtering process through which an

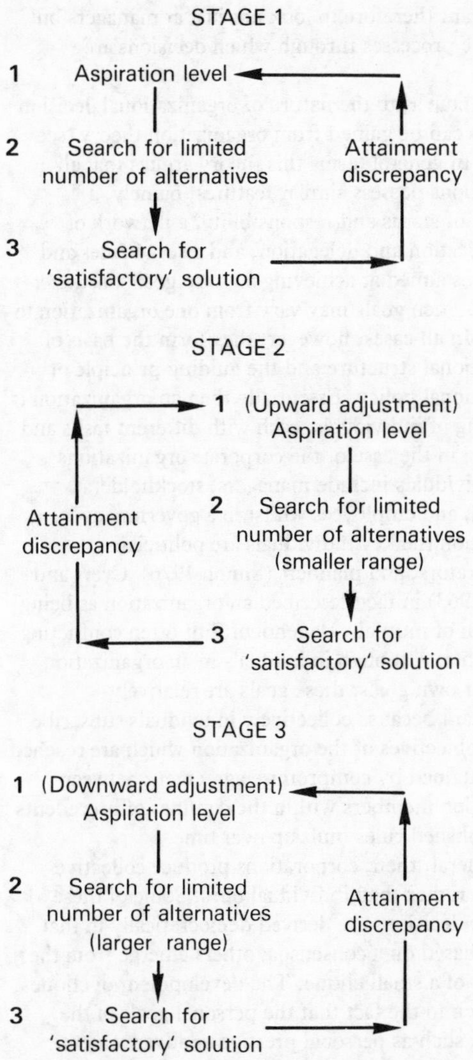

Fig. 6.6 Single and multiple choice decision-making. *Source*: adapted from Wilson and Alexis (1962, 24).

individual selects and distorts information about the location and relative accessibility of different alternative choices.

4. *Movement imagery* which focuses on how an individual perceives his ability to overcome the frictional effect of distance;
5. The *overt behaviour* or movement which results from the evaluation of alternatives.

No matter what behaviour results, there is always a feedback of information which causes a restructuring of perception activities and movement imagery. Huff's model is, in other words, a very broad one. In fact it is probably better thought of as an organizing framework rather than a strict model in that its main function is to highlight the critical elements to be considered in a study of spatial decision-making. Of course the relevance of these elements varies from decision-maker to decision-maker. For example, it would seem reasonable to assume that individuals and small firms are likely to be limited in their ability to acquire and use available information. At this scale, therefore, personality differences might well be a significant factor in accounting for how information is actually used. On the other hand, such factors will be less significant for large organizations since they probably have greater information and, in general, a greater expertise in analysing information. The differences between individual and organizational decision-making are therefore worth examining.

Organisational decision making

Organizational decision-making, like individual decision-making, can be conceptualized in utility terms (Elbing 1978). It warrants separate study however in that organizational decisions are characteristically of a different order of magnitude and a different degree of complexity from individual decisions (Castles *et al.* 1977; Bartlett 1982). As a result the behaviour of business enterprises, large corporations, and government has become of increasing interest to geographers (e.g. Mounfield *et al.* 1982; Hamilton 1974; Hamilton and Linge 1979; Flowerdew 1982).

Within the business world there are at least two groups of important decision-makers: the owner-manager and the manager, both of whom tend to have different motivations and outlook (Harrison 1975). According to Florence (1964) such motivations may be economic, psychological, sociological, or 'alogical' and in each case the entrepreneur differs from the salaried manager (Table 6.2). A similar distinction has been drawn by Blake *et al.* (1962) in terms of a schematic 'managerial matrix' (Fig. 6.7). The axes of this matrix are represented by a concern for profit and a concern for other utilities, and different types of managerial approach can be identified within the matrix. Thus the 'task manager' seeks to maximize profit while the so-called 'country club' management places greater reliance on satisfaction of non-profit orientated concerns. Likewise, 'impoverished management' de-emphasizes profit and other utilities whilst 'team management' attempts to maximize both its own satisfaction and the monetary success of the business. In the middle of the matrix is to be found what is aptly labelled the 'dampened pendulum'; in this area are the managers whose decisions are made partly to achieve personal satisfaction and partly to ensure the business's

Table 6.2 Business decisions and motivations

Motives	*Entrepreneur*	*Salaried manager*
Economic A	Maximum profits	Choice of greater salary
Economic B	Satisfaction – balance of profit and other utilities	Satisfaction – balance of pleasing the shareholder and other utilities
Psychological hobby, boss, and free man	Power seeking, empire building, love of work	Power seeking, fear of others' power
Sociological	Prestige, status-seeking in industry	Identification with firm, prestige from successful firm
Alogical	'His own money to do as he wishes', tradition	No initiative or ideas from outside, tradition

Source: Adapted from Florence (1964)

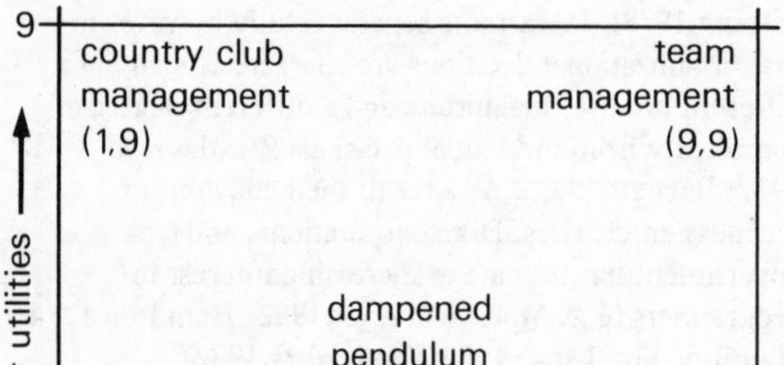

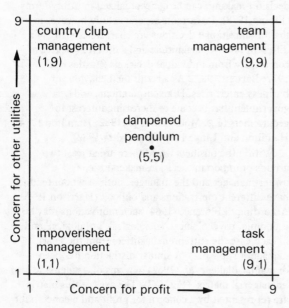

Fig. 6.7 The managerial matrix. *Source*: based on Blake, Mouton and Bidwell (1962, 13).

survival. Of course it would be wrong to place too much emphasis on this type of matrix because, in many respects, the role of the manager is declining in advanced economies as the scale of organizational activity increases and diversifies (Brown *et al.* 1974). It is important therefore to look not just at managers but also at the processes through which decisions are reached.

Some clue as to the nature of organizational decision processes can be gained from organization theory (see Ch. 10). In general terms this theory argues that all organizations possess similar features, namely, a structure of status and responsibility, a network of communication and delegation, and a set of rules and procedures aimed at achieving a group goal (Castles *et al.* 1977). Such goals may vary from one organization to another. In all cases, however, they form the basis of organizational structure and the guiding principle of organizational policy. Essentially then an organization is a grouping of individuals, each with different tasks and authority: in the case of the corporate organizations these individuals include managers, stockholders, suppliers, and employees whilst in a government organization the key individuals are politicians, administrators, and planners (Simon 1976). Cyert and March (1963) in fact described an organization as being a coalition of mutually dependent, but often conflicting, participants. Although individuals in an organization have their own goals, these goals are relatively insignificant because collectively individuals subscribe to those objectives of the organization which are reached and maintained by compromise agreement between organization members within the confines of precedents and established rules built up over time.

In general, then, corporations produce collective decisions rather than individual ones. Some of these collective decisions are derived democratically in that they are based on a consensus; others emerge from the workings of a small clique. The development of cliques owes much to the fact that the personal goals of the manager, such as personal prestige or advancement, often diverge from the general, collective, company goal of profit making (McNee 1960). As a result there often emerges what might be called a 'managerial subculture' which acts as the fulcrum of corporate decision-making. Thus the perceptions and feelings of managerial groups within corporations are frequently accompanied by a degree of corporate autonomy, a particular tradition of planning, and a particular relationship with other corporations and trade unions, as well as with government. The workings of such managerial groups are however extremely complex and individualistic and it is not surprising therefore that there are as yet few general models of organizational decision-making.

Chapter 7

Image and behaviour

It is commonly agreed in behavioural geography that the acquisition of environmental information, and the use of that information in some form of decision-making process, serves as a prelude to overt or 'acted out' behaviour. In many cases, however, the processing and evaluation of environmental information does not influence overt behaviour and human activities directly. Rather these processes operate to change how the mind construes the environment, very much in the way proposed in the transactional–constructivist approach to environmental awareness (see Ch. 5). Thus it is the changed mental construction of the environment that most immediately influences overt behaviour. This point is shown clearly in Pocock's (1973) model of how a perceiver interacts with an environment to create a mental image of that environment: the information status of the environment influences what the individual comes to know about the real world while the individual's psychological, physiological, and cultural make-up determines how that knowledge contributes to the development of an environmental image (Fig. 7.1). Although individual formulations vary from author to author, this model is characteristic of a large volume of research that can be summarized by Gould's (1973a: 183) contention that 'the manner in which men view their spatial matrix impinges upon and affects their judgements to some degree'. This emphasis on man's 'view' of the environment and the resultant mental image encouraged geographers, particularly in the early 1970s, to think in terms of 'environmental perception' and 'mental maps' (see Wood 1970). For example, Downs (1970a) drew attention to 'geographic space perception' as part of the 'behavioural revolution' in the discipline and suggested that research should focus on how man stores spatial information and on the way in which man develops a preference for different activities and locations within the environment.

The idea that behaviour is influenced by man's construal of the environment as some form of perceived mental map is not an entirely new one because in some

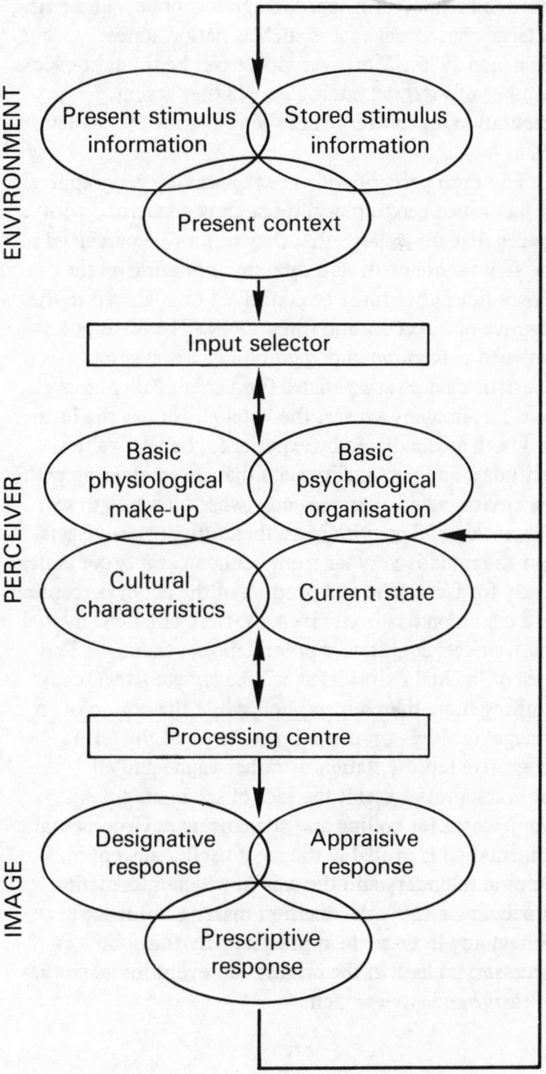

Fig. 17.1 A conceptual model of man – environment interaction. *Source*: Pocock (1973, 252).

ways it has antecedents in Lewin's (1951) proposition that behaviour is a function of a person's 'life-space' (see Ch. 1). Nor is the notion of a mental map an idea that has escaped criticism: Graham (1976) has argued that mental maps have made little contribution to the development of theory in geography because of the incoherence of the central concept, and Lowenthal (1972a) has suggested that work on environmental perception generally is weakened through a lack of commonly accepted definitions, objectives, and mechanisms for applying research results in the realm of environmental design. In part, these problems arise because studies of perception have been conducted at a variety of scales that range from 'room geography', through architectural space, neighbourhoods, and cities, to large conceptual spaces such as nation states (Saarinen 1976). Moreover, space can be thought of in a number of ways depending on whether action, orientation, or imagery is the central issue (Wheatley 1976).

The term perception is used loosely by geographers. In fact much geographical research is concerned with spaces that are so large that they cannot be perceived in the strict sense of stimuli directly impinging on the senses but rather must be conceived or cognized in the absence of direct stimuli (Stea 1969). The distinction between perception and cognition is however an heuristic device rather than a fundamental dichotomy because, in many senses, the latter subsumes the former and both are mediated by experience, beliefs, values, attitudes, and personality such that, in interacting with his environment, man sees only what he wants to see. Perception and cognition are therefore purposive acts and the mind is very far from being an empty container ready for facts. The end product of the act of perception and cognition has been given a variety of labels: mental map; image; cognitive representation; schemata. The idea of 'mental maps' is, as will be shown later, really nothing more than a metaphor, while the notion of an 'image' conjures up mental pictures, and the term 'cognitive representation' is rather vague and all embracing. As a result the idea of schemata as frameworks for coding and structuring environmental information is probably the most useful concept in helping to understand the way in which information processing and spatial decision-making influence overt behaviour. In order to appreciate why this is so it is necessary to look at the origins and evolution of studies of image and environment.

The concept of image

Environmental images can be thought of as learned and stable mental conceptions that summarize an individual's environmental knowledge, evaluations, and preferences (Pocock and Hudson 1978: 3). In this sense an image is a partial, simplified, idiosyncratic and distorted representation that is not necessarily isomorphic to the objective environment (Pocock and Hudson 1978: 33). The study of images is therefore illustrative of a neodualist philosophy of mind (see Ch. 5).

Academic interest in the concept of image first reached prominence with the work of Boulding (1956) who proposed that all behaviour is dependent upon an image built up of information derived from the social and physical milieu (Powell 1978: 17). In this sense an image can be thought of as part of the culture in which it develops. That is to say, an image is both an individual phenomenon and a cultural phenomenon to the extent that similar individuals in similar milieux are likely to have similar images in their minds and hence to exhibit similar forms of behaviour. Boulding's idea of an image was in fact very much in accordance with the spirit of the times. For example, in many ways it complemented Simon's (1957) idea of boundedly rational man arriving at decisions on the basis of simplified models of the real world. As a result, Boulding's work has had a great impact on subsequent research, at least to the extent that his book is cited repeatedly. Powell (1978: 17–8) is however of the view that, despite the citations, Boulding's ideas have not been thoroughly understood. He has therefore drawn attention to the fact that an image is not the simple concept that it is sometimes thought to be but rather is comprised of at least ten main features: a spatial component accounting for an individual's location in the world; a personal component relating the individual to other people and organizations; a temporal component concerned with the flow of time; a relational component concerned with the individual's picture of the universe as a system of regularities; conscious, subconscious, and unconscious elements; a blend of certainty and uncertainty; a mixture of reality and unreality; a public and private component expressing the degree to which an image is shared; a value component that orders parts of the image according to whether they are good or bad; and an affectional component whereby the image is imbued with feeling. Of these features it is the spatial component which has generated most interest from geographers, not only because it is perhaps the most important part of the total structure but also because it appears to be accessible in a way that other parts are not (Boulding 1973: viii).

Geographical studies of spatial and environmental imagery have drawn considerable inspiration from the pioneering work of Lynch (see Appleyard 1978) and in particular from his book on the image of the city (Lynch 1960). In that book Lynch asked respondents in Boston, Jersey City, and Los Angeles to draw a sketch map of their respective cities. The resultant drawings simplified the spatial structure of the environment by omitting numerous minor details and straightening out complex geometrical shapes into more manageable patterns of straight lines and right angles (Day 1976). In fact the simplification process was carried on to such an extent that Lynch was able to argue that the image of the city was organized in terms of five elements: *paths* which are the channels along which individuals move; *edges* which are barriers (e.g. rivers) or lines separating one region from another; *districts* which are medium-to-large sections of the city with an identifiable character; *nodes* which are the strategic points in a city which the individual can enter and which serve as foci for travel; and *landmarks* which are points of reference into which an individual cannot enter (Lynch 1960). According to Lynch, an image of a city based on these elements serves as a basis for interpreting information, as a guide to action, as a frame of reference for organizing activity, as a basis for individual growth, and as a provider of a sense of emotional security (Downs and Stea 1973b: 80). More particularly, Lynch argued that an individual's knowledge of the city is a function of that city's *imageability*, that is, the extent to which it makes a strong impression on the individual concerned. Imageability is, in turn, closely related to *legibility* by which is meant the extent to which parts of the city can be recognized and organized into a coherent pattern. Thus a legible city would be one where the paths, edges, districts, nodes and landmarks are both clearly identifiable and clearly positioned relative to each other. Of course neither prominence nor architectural detail guarantees imageability because places and spaces only become significant when they are given meaning through a combination of usage, emotional attachment, and symbolism (Pocock and Hudson 1978: 31–2). In other words, an image acts back on man by influencing what he sees such that an image can be analysed into at least three components: identity (distinguishing features); structure (pattern); and meaning (evaluation).

The five elements of the Lynchain landscape are by no means as clear-cut as is sometimes implied. For instance, a church may be a node to one person (because it is visited regularly) but a landmark to another person (because it is not visited at all but used for directional wayfinding). Despite this, Lynch's approach has been used with a reasonable degree of success in a wide variety of towns (Fig. 7.2) and only edges have proved to be an elusive characteristic (see Pocock and Hudson 1978: 51). There are nonetheless a number of important criticisms to be made. To begin with, the freehand mapping technique may not be a good method of eliciting the image because it demands a certain level of education, training, and aptitude. Moreover the entire thrust of Lynch's work concentrates overwhelmingly on the visual element of the image at the expense of considerations like sound and smell. This means that not enough attention is given to the functional and symbolic meaning of urban space (Steinitz 1968), largely because Lynch's approach focuses on the passive encountering of the environment rather than on interaction.

A more serious criticism of geographical work on imagery generally is that it has been characterized by 'borrowed methodology, a pot-pourri of concepts, and liberal doses of borrowed theory' (Stea and Downs 1979: 3). As a result there has been little advance in knowledge. In fact Stea and Downs (1970: 6) have highlighted five key issues on which research needs to focus:

1. *Elements of an image*. What are the main elements of an image? How do these interrelate? Is there a common set or do they vary with the particular environment?
2. *Relations between elements*. What are the distance metrics relating elements in cognitive representations? What are the orientation frameworks used to relate elements?
3. *Surfaces*. Do the interrelationships between the elements lead to a surface? Is the surface a continuous or a discontinuous phenomenon?
4. *Temporal nature*. How stable is the image over time? How far backwards or forwards in time do images extend, i.e. what is the temporal rate of information decay? How do images respond to environmental changes? Are there lags in response time?
5. *Covariations with other features*. What is the spatial extent of the image, i.e. what is the spatial rate of information decay? Is there a hierarchy of images according to the particular desired behaviour? How do all these factors vary with cultural, socio-economic, and personality correlates?

Additionally, Canter (1977: 16) has argued that images represent only one type of cognitive experience and that cognition more frequently takes the form of *schemata* that exert an important influence (of which individuals might not be fully aware) on interaction with the environment. The idea of schemata stems initially from Bartlett's (1923) work on memory and has been used by Lee (1968) in his study of how people define and know urban neighbourhoods. This work is however only one illustration of the application of the concept of image in the geographical literature.

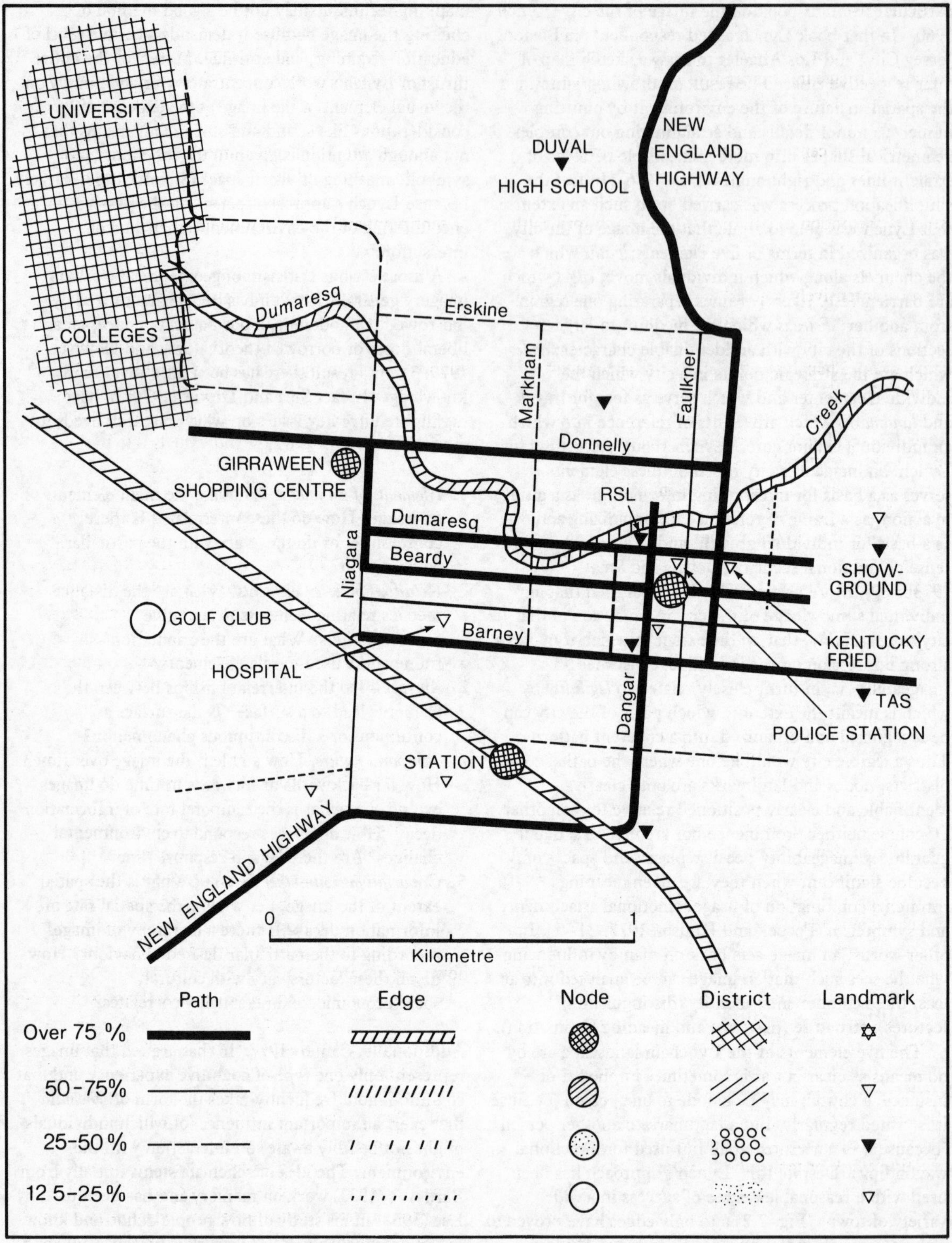

Fig. 7.2 The image of Armidale, New South Wales.

Applications

Possibly the most fruitful area for the application of the concept of image in geographical research is in historical geography and various authors have set about explaining the spread of New World settlement in the eighteenth and nineteenth centuries in terms of the prevailing images of the new lands. For example, Powell (1978) has shown how, at one stage or another, the quest for Arcady, the notion of wilderness, the search for health, and the co-operative ideal influenced the settlement of North America and Australasia. In this context, one of the most intensively studied topics is the image held of the North American Plains (Blouet and Lawson 1975). Bowden (1975), for instance, has illustrated how the image of the Plains varied from that of an agricultural Eden to that of a sandy desert, and how the image held by frontiersmen differed from that held by both newcomers and writers in the eastern states. In a similar vein Jackson (1978) has traced changing Mormon perceptions of Salt Lake Valley from an initially favourable view to one which emphasized the agency of man in overcoming the vagaries of climate. This changing image of nature has also been studied over a much longer time span, and for North America as a whole, by Watson (1976a) in his examination of man's increasing awareness of the fragile nature of wilderness.

Images are particularly important in the development of stereotypes and nowhere is this shown more clearly than in the way in which people develop stereotyped images of regions. Although these images have been analysed at a national level (Boulding 1959), most work has concentrated on a smaller scale. For example, Watson (1976b) has noted that the sectional differences that arose in early colonial America became stronger with time so that New England, the South, and the West all developed a distinctive image. In more contemporary terms, both Jordan (1978) in Texas and Williams (1977) in New Brunswick have shown how perceptual regions are a part of folk culture. Just how these perceptions are created and passed on is not clear. Oral history may be important as may literary sources (Tuan 1976a). Pocock (1979), for instance, demonstrated how the English novel did much to create and perpetuate the image of the north of England as a harsh, polluted and depressed region. Folk culture is also important in determining man's attitudes to landscape (Appleton 1975), not least because of the affective bond, or *topophilia*, that develops between people and places (Tuan 1974a). However, the insular symbology employed in many environmental images makes them hard to understand (Blakemore 1981). Despite these difficulties there have been a number of important studies of the cultural component of environmental images. Perhaps the most notable is Glacken's (1967) examination of how European attitudes to the environment changed from focus on the earth as a purposeful creation to the view that the environment determined human nature, and subsequently to the idea that man has altered the earth.

At a smaller scale, environmental images of cities have attracted a good deal of attention. Although in some senses this work began with Firey's (1945) study of sentiment and symbolism in locational decision-making and planning in Boston, for the most part it has been inspired by Lynch (1960). Buildings, paths, and areas have been the most commonly identified elements of the urban image (Pocock 1975). The topic of paths has attracted particular attention and studies have been made of the way in which the image associated with a path varies with the mode of transport (Pocock 1975). For example, Lowenthal and Riel (1972a) have examined how individuals rate the environment when on a short walk, and Cullen (1961) and Appleyard *et al.* (1964) have looked at the sequential and almost linear image of cities held by car travellers.

To all these studies could be added countless more. Many will in fact be dealt with in Part Four because the concept of image has been one of the most stimulating to enter geography in recent years. For the moment, however, it is important to turn to the methodological problems inherent in the study of environmental imagery.

Methodological difficulties

There are three critical methodological problems in the study of environmental imagery: the question of how to *extract* meaningful information from individuals about large-scale environments; the question of how this information can be *manifest* so as to make obvious the extent of an individual's cognitions; and the question of how to *analyse* this material (Golledge 1976: 300–1). The range of available techniques varies from self report procedures (e.g. sketch maps) to inferences made from indirect judgemental tasks (e.g. the application of repertory grid methodology), and from natural environments to controlled situations (e.g. manipulation of models). However, by far and away the most common approach has been the sketch map of a real world environment. After all this technique is a revealing one because it provides information on the sequence in which elements of the environment were drawn, the connectivities and gaps between these elements, and the style, detail and scale distortions of the image, as well as evidence of emotional attachment or indifference to different parts of the environment (Lynch 1976: vi). There are nevertheless a number of difficulties with the approach. To begin with, it is very time consuming. Moreover it remains unknown to what extent the technique relies on artistic prowess; it may well be that more complete images are drawn by better artists rather than by individuals who are more aware of their environment. This raises the issue of *validity*, that is, whether sketch maps actually provide a true measure of environmental images. In this context the actual instructions given to map drawers may be important in that Lynch (1960) noted a significant difference between sketch maps and maps built up from verbal descriptions. *Reliability*, or the extent to which the results of a sketch mapping exercise are replicable, is another problem. Sketch mapping is a reactive technique in the sense that the drawing of one map of a particular environment will influence the drawing of subsequent maps of the same environment. As a result it is very difficult to replicate a study or, for that matter, to examine the change in an image over time. The best that can be attempted is an inference based on cross-sectional studies and certainly such exercises seem to suggest similarity between images, albeit with some confusion between nodes and landmarks (Norberg-Schultz 1971).

In view of these difficulties, the attitude of geographers to 'the world in the head' has changed somewhat. Many view a mental map not as 'an explanatory construct' but as 'a potentially dangerous nostrum' (Downs 1981). As a result the process of 'mapping' is probably a more important focus of attention than the finished product or map. Given this, it is somewhat surprising that geographers have not paid more attention to *projective techniques* whereby the mapping process can be uncovered. According to Saarinen (1973a) there are five such techniques: association techniques (like word association tests where a response is given to a stimulus); construction techniques (like the Thematic Apperception Test where a subject goes beyond a stimulus and constructs a story); cloze procedures (where individuals fill in the missing parts of a stimulus); choice techniques (such as drawing a neighbourhood on an existing map); and free expression techniques (exemplified by sketch maps). Of these only the free expression techniques have been widely used, possibly because they are well suited to the Lynch-type studies with which many behavioural geographers have been preoccupied. Sketch mapping, in other words, has perhaps been given too much emphasis in geographical methodology because it may well be that it is only appropriate to a small portion of the total number of approaches that geographers have developed in the study of how man comes to know his environment. The full range of these geographical approaches has been classified by Briggs (1973a) into four categories: studies of cognitive distance; examination of designative images of what is known to be where in the environment; analysis of appraisive images that express preference for different parts of the environment; and investigation of activity patterns. Each of these approaches has attracted a good deal of research.

Cognitive distance

Briggs (1973a) has suggested that an image of a city is built up, on the basis of public and private information, from four types of knowledge: knowledge of nodes; knowledge about the closeness of nodes; knowledge of the relative location of nodes; and knowledge of sets of nodes and their interlinking paths. Central to each of these is the concept of distance. One of the first researchers to realize that the notion of distance that people hold in their mind is different from objective distance was Thompson (1963) who discovered that mile and time estimates to shopping centres in San Francisco were overestimated relative to real world distance (see Ch. 8). This finding has since been corroborated in a number of studies thereby leading to the suggestion that cognitive distance is overestimated relative to objective distance irrespective of the mode of transport, city size, or the distance metric (time, road, or straight line distance) used (Pocock and Hudson 1978: 53). The significance of this lies in the fact that cognitive distance is important in influencing three types of trip-making decisions: whether to stay or go; where to go; and what route to take (Cadwallader 1976).

Unfortunately the results of experiments on cognitive distance, although generally pointing to overestimation, are less than clear cut in detail. For example, Pocock and Hudson (1978: 53) have noted that cognitive distance is *underestimated* relative to objective distance beyond a distance of about 7 miles in London and 3½ miles in Dundee. Similarly, Day (1976) has found slight underestimation beyond distances of 1,200 yards in central Sydney, a fact which he attributes to such distances being beyond walking range. Lowrey (1973) has interpreted this sort of marked overestimation of very short distances in terms of the extra effort required to get started on a journey. He has also noted the very considerable range that exists in the regression equations between cognitive and objective distance. These can vary greatly from person to person (Fig. 7.3). A high degree of variance in distance estimates is in fact characteristic of all experiments on cognitive distance. According to Briggs (1976), this idiosyncratic response

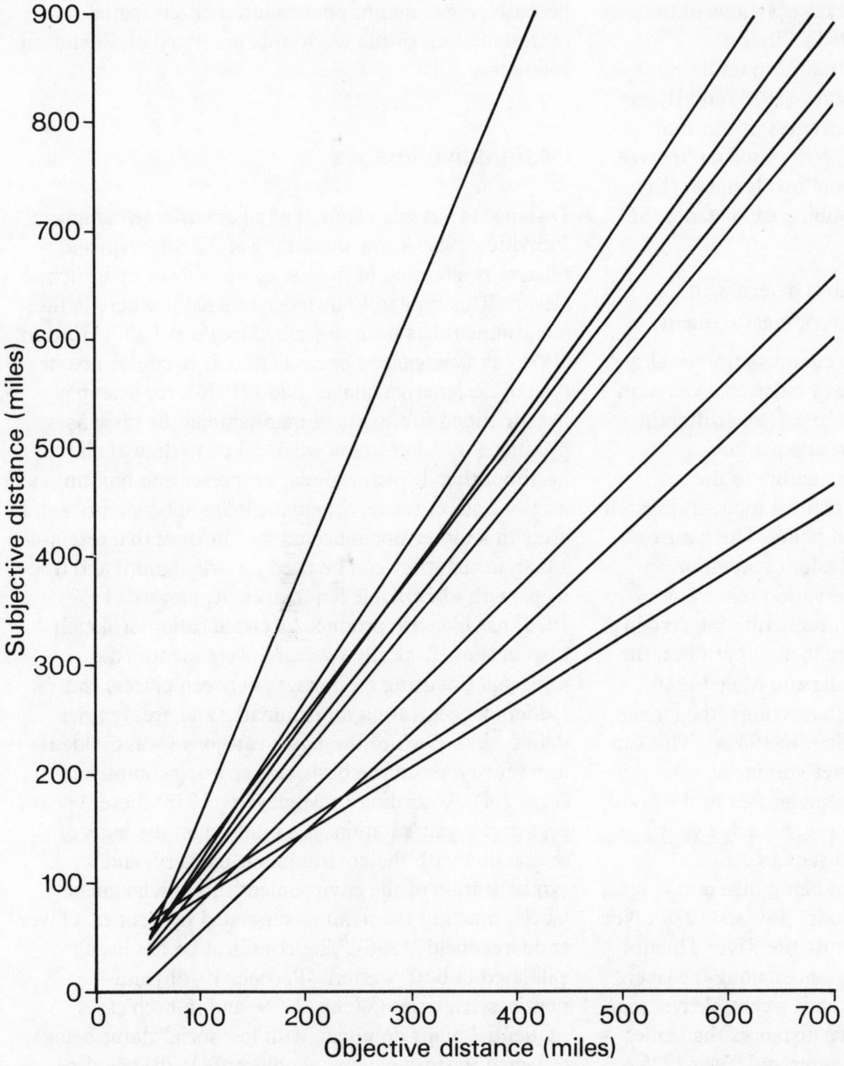

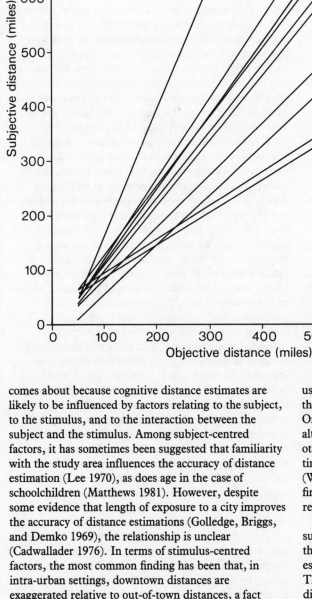

Fig. 7.3 The regression lines between subjective and objective distance for a random sample of ten students.

comes about because cognitive distance estimates are likely to be influenced by factors relating to the subject, to the stimulus, and to the interaction between the subject and the stimulus. Among subject-centred factors, it has sometimes been suggested that familiarity with the study area influences the accuracy of distance estimation (Lee 1970), as does age in the case of schoolchildren (Matthews 1981). However, despite some evidence that length of exposure to a city improves the accuracy of distance estimations (Golledge, Briggs, and Demko 1969), the relationship is unclear (Cadwallader 1976). In terms of stimulus-centred factors, the most common finding has been that, in intra-urban settings, downtown distances are exaggerated relative to out-of-town distances, a fact which may be associated with the denser packing of land uses – and hence the greater number of stimuli – around the central city (Golledge, Briggs, and Demko 1969). Once more, however, the evidence is equivocal because, although the exaggeration has been corroborated in other areas of dense land use (e.g. Ericksen 1975), for time estimates (Burnett 1978a), and in rural areas (Walmsley 1978), Lee (1970) has produced a contrary finding to the effect that out-of-town distances are relatively more exaggerated in Dundee.

In terms of factors relating to the interaction of the subject with the stimulus, two considerations stand out: the attractiveness of the end point of the distance to be estimated; and the nature of the connecting path. Thompson's (1963) pioneering work on cognitive distance established that a positive evaluation of a shop tended to shorten the subjective distance between a consumer and that shop. Similar observations of the way in which the distance to desirable facilities is underestimated relative to the distance to undesirable facilities have been made by Lowrey (1973) and Eyles (1968). In fact such is the pervasiveness of this finding that Ekman and Bratfisch (1965) postulated an 'inverse square root law' to relate emotional involvement (EI) with a place to estimates of the subjective distance (SD) to that place:

$$EI = \frac{b}{\sqrt{SD}}$$ Where the value of b is determined by the arbitrary units of measurement

Unfortunately this 'law', despite claims to universality, is simply an artefact of the range of cities considered in the experiments on which it was based, and different ranges of stimuli give very different equations (Walmsley 1974a). As a result the nature of the connecting path may be a more fruitful topic of research than the attractiveness of the end point. The nature of urban paths has in fact attracted a lot of attention despite Tuan's (1975a: 207) observation that some people can travel a route without remembering certain parts of it. It seems that the more turns a path has, the longer it is estimated to be (Sadalla and Magel 1980), and the greater the number of intersections, the longer it is thought to be (Sadalla and Staplin 1980a). This can be interpreted in terms of a greater volume of information requiring a greater storage area in the brain (Sadalla and Staplin 1980b). However, such a view does not explain why cognitive distances are non-commutative (in the sense of being different lengths when viewed in different directions) (Pocock 1978). Nor does it explain why distances across the River Thames are more over-estimated than distances along the river (Canter 1977: 92), or why cities with a central river tend to have less exaggerated cognitive distances than cities without such central features (Canter and Tagg 1975).

In short, there is no unanimity in the results of experiments on cognitive distance. One possible explanation of this may lie in the methodology employed. Some studies have used straight line distances, others have used road or time distances. Likewise, distance estimates have been elicited in a variety of ways: simple and direct questions; scales graduated in miles; ratio estimates; and inferences from sketch maps. Day (1976) is of the opinion that the nature of the technique makes no significant difference to the results but this finding has been challenged by both Phipps (1979) and Cadwallader (1979). The latter has stressed that the distance estimates provided by a subject are not independent of the way in which these estimates are sought. Moreover, he has suggested that it will be extremely difficult to identify any simple relationship between cognitive and objective distance because people do not possess internalized spatial representations of the world that are based on Euclidean geometry.

Designative images

Distance is but one element of an environmental image. Individuals also know something of the direction and relative positioning of places, as was shown by Lynch (1960). This type of knowledge of what is where in the environment has been described by Pocock and Hudson (1978) as a *designative image*. There is of course no one type of designative image. Ladd (1970), for example, has identified four sorts of maps among the responses produced by adolescents when asked to draw their neighbourhood: pictorial maps representing buildings as part of a street scene; schematic maps showing lines and areas in a rather unconnected way; images that resemble a map in that they can be used for orientation; and true maps with identifiable landmarks. Appleyard (1969; 1970) has likewise produced a classification of sketch map images. Basically two sorts were identified: *sequential* (focusing on linkages between places) and *spatial* (concentrating on landmarks and areas rather than paths). Each of these two categories was divided into four types on the basis of increasing complexity (Fig. 7.4). According to Appleyard (1973) these types of cognitive representations are built up on the basis of interaction with the environment, imagery, and symbolization of the environment through language labels, much in the manner suggested by Bruner, Oliver and Greenfield (1966). The classification has been validated in both western (Pocock, 1976b) and non-western cities (Wong, 1979) and in both cases sequential maps dominate with low social status being reflected in simple maps. Appleyard (1970) has also suggested that over time there occurs a shift from sequential to spatial maps and an associated shift from topology to Euclidean geometry. This point has been corroborated by several authorities (e.g. Moore 1979) but challenged by Spencer and Weetman (1981) who made two contrary findings: first, neighbourhoods tend to be represented in spatial form irrespective of when the maps are drawn; and second, the choice between spatial and sequential maps at the city scale is dictated by respondent preference for mapping style and not by the timing of the map-drawing exercise.

The sort of exercise in which Lynch and Appleyard were engaged is frequently referred to as *cognitive mapping*. The idea of maps in the mind has a long history (see Trowbridge 1913; Tolman 1948). It is however a term with 'tremendous surplus meaning' (Stea 1976: 107). Basically what are referred to as

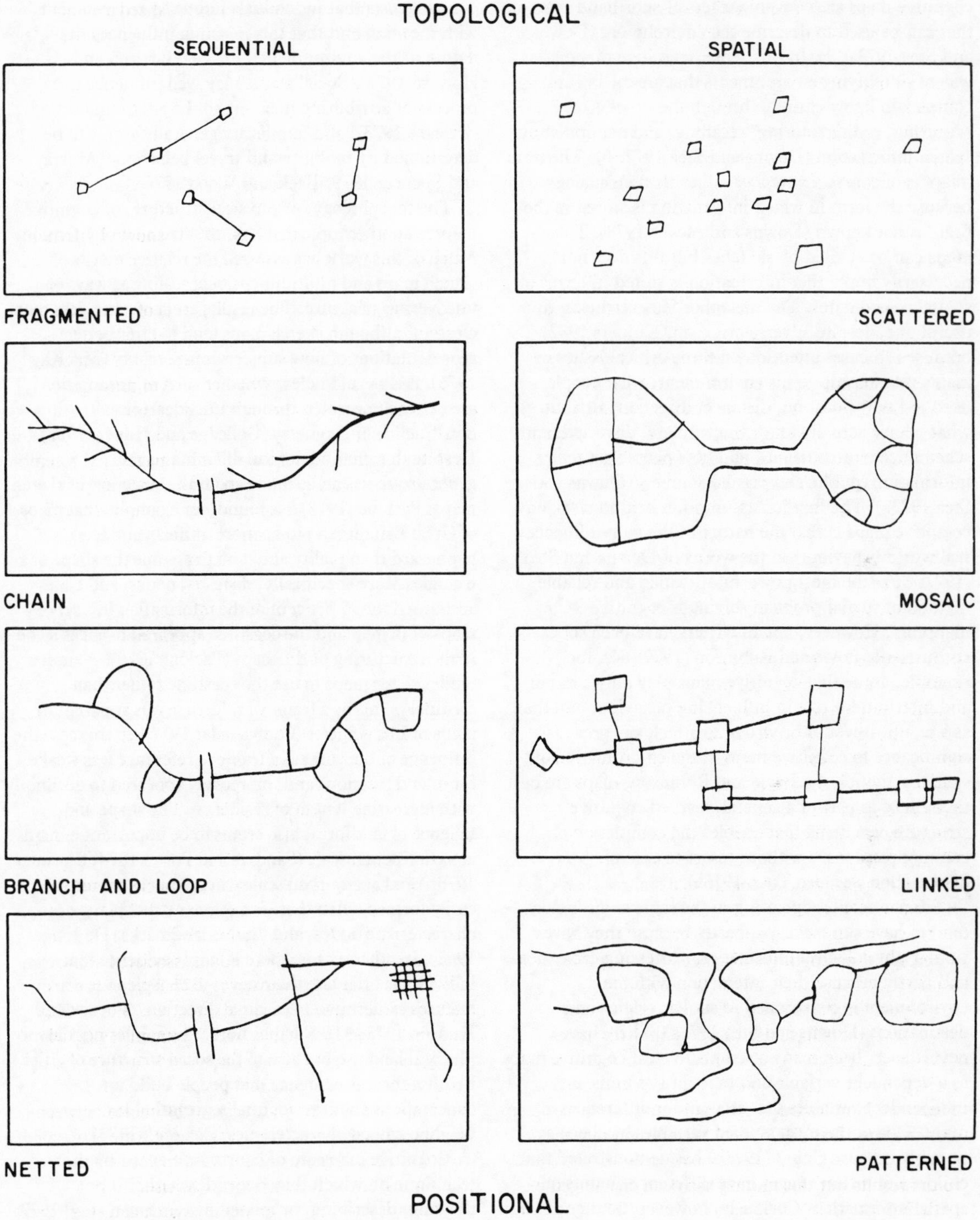

Fig. 7.4 Styles of cognitive mapping. *Source*: Appleyard (1969, 437).

cognitive maps are convenient sets of shorthand symbols that can be used to describe the environment (Downs and Stea 1973a: 9). In this sense, cognitive mapping is a way of simplifying environments that are too big and complex to know entirely through the process of acquiring, coding, storing, recalling, and manipulating spatial information (Downs and Stea 1977: 6). The term 'map' is of course a *metaphor* rather than an analogy because the form in which information is stored in the brain is not known (Downs and Meyer 1978). Thus maps can be elicited by sketches but this does not necessarily imply that information is stored in terms of spatial co-ordinates. The metaphor is nevertheless a useful one, despite adverse criticism (Kuipers 1982), because it focuses attention on three critical issues in man's relationship to his environment: what people need to know (location, distance, direction, attributes); what people actually know (incomplete, distorted, and schematized information); and how people get their information (public and private sources) (Downs and Stea 1973a). The implicit assumption behind work on cognitive maps is that the nature of the map influences real world behaviour: in the words of Downs and Stea (1977: 36), 'the most powerful, flexible, and reliable method of spatial problem solving is cognitive mapping'. However, not all writers have been so enthusiastic. Boyle and Robinson (1979: 64), for example, argue that cognitive maps play only a minor and intermittent role in influencing behaviour and that, as a result, it would be wrong to attach any great significance to cognitive maps in the co-ordination of spatial activities. To Boyle and Robinson, maps are best thought of as part of a general, learned cognitive structure or schema that enables the completion of commonplace tasks without resort to careful deliberation (see also Tuan 1975a).

Similar people, operating in the same environment, tend to have similar maps, partly because they have similar physiological information-processing capacities and partly because their interaction with the environment is constrained to similar origins and destinations (Downs and Stea 1973a). There have nevertheless been many attempts to treat cognitive maps as a dependent variable and to identify significant independent variables that account for differences in maps. One of the most studied variables has been age, possibly because Gould (1973b) has demonstrated that children of different ages have different amounts of spatial information. Curiously, however, neither age nor IQ has proved to be a significant variable in the analysis of children's maps (Maurer and Baxter 1972; Moore 1975). Instead the familiarity which individuals have with their environment seems to be the critical factor. This suggests that individuals imbue an environment with meaning and that this meaning influences the nature of the environmental image (Harrison and Howard 1972). Social status may well influence this process of attributing meaning to the environment (Orleans 1973), and familiarity generally seems to be determined by mobility and travel behaviour (Murray and Spencer 1979; Beck and Wood 1976).

The morphology, or physical structure, of cognitive maps is another topic that has attracted a lot of attention. Much of this work has assessed the relative merits of sketch maps and multidimensional scaling as ways of uncovering structure. The results are, however, less than clearcut: although sketch maps tend to offer better representations of how subjects image reality (MacKay 1976), it is as yet unclear whether such representations are better interpreted through Euclidean or non-Euclidean geometry (Golledge and Hubert 1982). Despite this methodological dilemma certain generalizations can be made about the structure of sketch maps. Pacione (1978) has found, for example, that maps of Great Britain tend to be more uniform and less haphazard than reality and tend to assume the shape of a triangle. More specifically, districts, nodes, and edges accounted for 95 per cent of the information in a set of maps of Britain and the coastline appeared to act as a cue in the structuring of the maps (Pacione 1976). A similar tendency for maps to use the coastline rather than cardinal points as a frame of reference was apparent in maps of Los Angeles (Cadwallader 1977). In this case the influence of the coast as a frame of reference was weakest for inland locations and, moreover, appeared to decline with increasing length of residence. The shape and salience of landforms also seems to be important in maps at a continental scale (Sanders and Porter 1974; Saarinen 1973b) and at an urban scale where images are most easily formed when there is a regular street plan, characteristic nodes, and unique landmarks (De Jonge 1962). In other words, there is ample evidence that individuals orientate themselves to conspicuous urban features rather than to cardinal directions (Pocock and Hudson 1978: 62). Furthermore, this applies not only to physical land use but also to the social structure of cities because there is evidence that people build up expectations about residential segregation and neighbourhood characteristics (Cox *et al.* 1979).

Cognitive maps are of course influenced by the technique on which they depend, whether it be drawing, describing, or modelling (Sherman *et al.* 1979; Pocock 1976a) and this presents problems in analysis. One way around these problems is to shift attention from getting subjects to *construct* a map to getting them to *complete* a map that has certain parts missing. Such completion tests are easy to analyse, comparable from person to person, and relatively unambiguous. The *cloze procedure* is one prominent technique. It derives from the Gestalt notion of 'clozure', that is, the tendency for a subject to go beyond a specific stimulus and to fill in missing information. It has been used in cognitive mapping by Robinson and Dicken (1979) in a study that imposed a grid over a map of Britain and then asked students to provide the name of a settlement in each of sixty-five grid squares for which information had been omitted at the rate of one in five. Three samples of students achieved success in between 15 and 30 per cent of cases. Obviously the grid size and omission frequency are critical in this sort of experiment. Moreover, the naming of a place does not necessarily imply knowledge of other characteristics of the place. The technique nevertheless offers an alternative to the more widely used constructive approaches, especially where the background information gives cues as to the positioning of localities (see Tversky 1981).

There is no doubt that, despite the lack of much really significant progress in the last decade, cognitive maps will continue to be studied, perhaps because of their 'lucky-dip' element and the genuine intellectual challenge of bringing order to the apparent chaos which they present (Boyle and Robinson, 1979: 73). Some authorities will continue to claim that cognitive maps are reflected in real world activities (e.g. Holahan and Dobrowolny 1978), whereas others will stress that images and maps do not play any essential role in spatial behaviour and will argue that attention needs to turn from maps to the schemata wherein public and private, specific and general information is organized (Tuan 1975a). In this sense, cognitive maps can be thought of as 'plans' (Canter 1977: 51), much in the same way that Miller, Galanter, and Pribam (1960) used the psychological concept of plan as a construct that helped structure behaviour. From this viewpoint, a cognitive map needs to be concerned not only with what is where in the environment (the designative element) but also with what emotions individuals feel towards the attributes of different locations (the appraisive element).

Appraisive images

The designative aspects of the image of an environment may be less important in contributing to the understanding of behaviour than are the *appraisive* aspects of the image, that is, the meanings evoked by the physical form (Pocock and Hudson 1978). This appraisive response can itself be differentiated into two components: the *evaluative* (concerned with the expression of an opinion) and the *affective* (concerned with the specification of a preference). The evaluative component is most clearly in evidence in verbal descriptions of environmental quality where an individual is required to state an opinion of a particular place by, for example, completing a semantic differential questionnaire. The difficulty with this approach is that the opinions offered tend to vary from case to case and it is therefore difficult to arrive at a common set of evaluative dimensions (see Kasmar 1970). In contrast, the affective component of appraisive images is more easily compared from case to case because it is possible to measure the response to stimuli on relatively straightforward ordinal or interval scales. For instance, people can be asked how much they would like to live in various regions within a country and their answers can be calibrated on a scale that ranges from a strong desire to live in a certain place through to absolute opposition to living in that place.

One of the first people to explore the affective component of appraisive images was Gould in a paper (1973a) concerned with residential desirability in the United States, Europe, and West Africa. This paper concluded that space preferences seem to be related to the information that people have about places which in turn seems to be related to the population size of the places in question. The methodology, whereby individuals score regions in terms of residential desirability to provide a data matrix which can be reduced by factor analysis to a component representing preference, has been applied widely (Gould and White 1974). The sort of picture of preference that emerges, with component scores standardized to a 100-point scale, is shown in Fig. 7.5.

The main problem with this approach is that it elicits preferences in a relatively unconstrained context. In other words, subjects state how much they want to live in an area irrespective of the real likelihood of living there. It is not surprising therefore that preferences vary widely in apparently homogeneous subject groups. Jackson and Johnston (1972) have illustrated this variability and have attributed it to the fact that individuals have different environmental images and different criteria for desirability. This suggests that personality variables may be important, thereby corroborating Proshansky's (1978) view that 'place identity' is a significant but much ignored component of overall self-identity. The evidence for the impact of personality is as yet limited although Walmsley (1982a) has shown how introverts and extroverts differ in residential preferences. Of course it may be that appraisive images will become more important as 'footloose' employment develops in the tertiary and

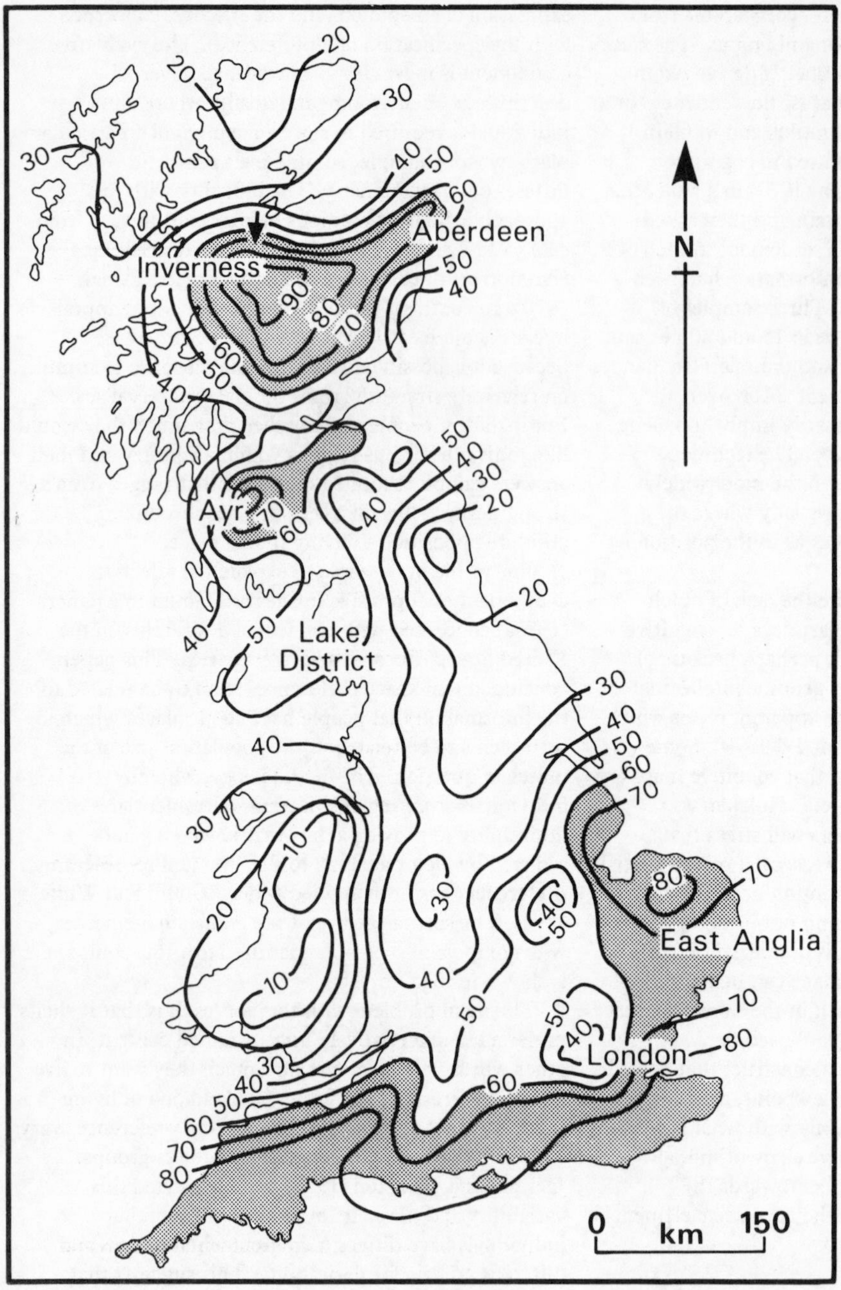

Fig. 7.5 The preference surface of Inverness school leavers. *Source*: Gould and White (1968, 170).

quaternary sectors of the economy (Pacione 1982) with the result that public authorities will have to place increasing emphasis on the manipulation, through advertising and promotion, of stereotyped images (Burgess 1982). For the moment, however, it is probably true to say that unconstrained choice has little bearing on real world behaviour (Massam and Bouchard 1976). It is important therefore to look specifically at overt behaviour.

Overt behaviour

There are two major methodological choices to be faced in any study of overt behaviour: whether to do experimental research with controlled variables or whether to conduct holistic research that looks at the real world environment and behaviour as a whole; and whether to rely on recall and self-report techniques or whether to adopt the logistically difficult approach of looking at behaviour as it happens (Ittelson *et al.* 1974: 208). In many ways these choices reflect what Craik (1968) believes are the key issues in the study of everyday environments: how to identify and present the pertinent characteristics of the environment; what behavioural reactions to record; and what groups to study.

Early research into overt behaviour by geographers was strongly inductive in approach in that it sought to generalize about observed empirical generalities. Thus Adams (1969) studied movement patterns within a city and concluded that individuals have wedge-shaped mental maps that take in both the central city and the individual's residence. From such empirical observations arose the concepts of *action space* (which refers to that part of the environment which has a place utility to the individual and with which the individual is therefore familiar) and *activity space* (which is that part of the action space with which an individual interacts on an everyday basis). Horton and Reynolds (1971) combined these concepts in an overall model that describes how social status, home location and length of residence, travel patterns, images, and the nature of the real world environment all interact (Fig. 7.6). The concept of action space has its antecedents in Kirk's (1963) distinction between the phenomenal (objective, physical) environment and the behavioural environment available for action and this, in turn, mirrors a similar distinction made by Koffka (1935). The concept has however been criticized because it combines the diverse element of perception, action, and preference into one elusive term (Higgs 1975). As a result the concept of activity space has perhaps proved more appealing than that of action space. For one thing it ties in with work done on *activity systems* (Chapin 1968; Chapin and Hightower 1965). The idea of an activity system is a simple one. Individual behaviour is comprised of episodes and if different people exhibit the same episode then that episode can be thought of as a class of activity (e.g. work-related activities, relaxation, shopping). An activity system is a sequence of such activities (Chapin and Brail 1969). In other words, an activity system has both a spatial component (the places visited) and a temporal component (the timing of visits), both of which are influenced by culturally defined constraints and the nature of the geographical environment (e.g. working hours and land use zoning determine the nature and timing of the journey-to-work). An activity system is, in this sense, a manifestation of a space–time budget (Anderson 1971).

There are a number of problems with activity systems research, notably how to get detailed records of behaviour, how to cope with multi-purpose activities, how to study socially unacceptable behaviour, and how to overcome the faulty recall of respondents. For the most part these problems are overcome by using either diaries or large samples at one point in time and these approaches have both yielded a great deal of descriptive data. For example, women have been shown to have different activity patterns from men (Hanson and Hanson 1980) and the elderly to have patterns that are not dissimilar from those of people in the workforce (P.

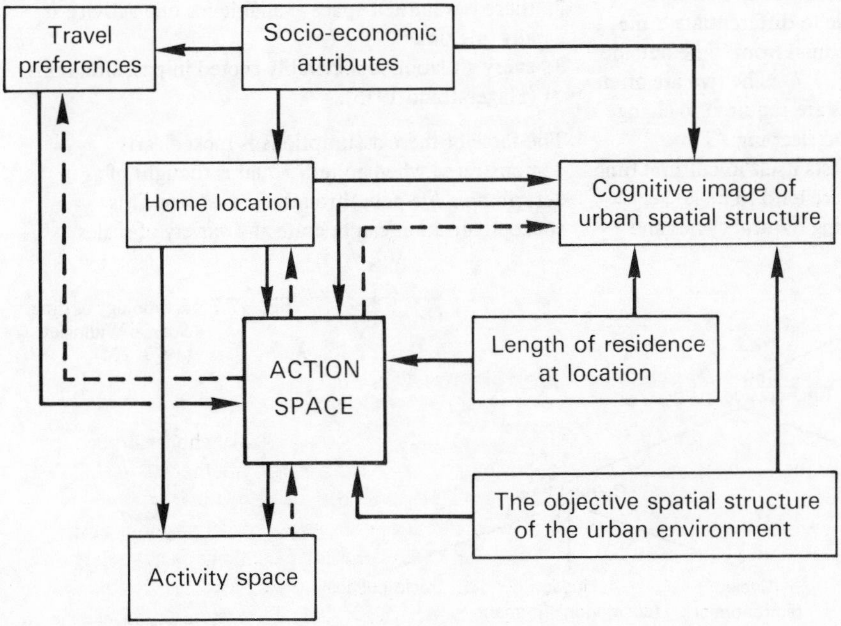

Fig. 7.6 Influences on action space. *Source*: Horton and Reynolds (1971, 41).

Hanson 1977). Such studies remain, however, essentially descriptive and activity systems research has made little progress towards the explanation and prediction of travel patterns.

Time and behaviour

One reason why studies of activity systems have not achieved as much as some researchers had hoped lies in the fact that they have sometimes tended to ignore time as a dimension of human behaviour. This is in fact a failing that is common to much social science: all too often time has been approached from the point of view of comparative statics, that is to say, behaviour has been compared at various points in time without due emphasis being given to consideration of what time means for the actors involved and to the way in which this meaning influences behaviour. Yet, in a very fundamental sense, space, time and place are irresolvably linked in experience (Tuan 1977). According to Lynch, what people think of time is crucial for their well-being and a desirable environmental image is 'one that celebrates and enlarges the present while making connections with past and future' (Lynch 1972: 1).

Recognition of the importance of time has led to pleas for a *chronogeographical* perspective in the study of human behaviour (Parkes and Thrift 1980). It has also generated a vast literature (see Carlstein *et al.* 1978a; 1978b; 1978c). Time is of course a multi-faceted concept and it is easy to identify many different meanings. For example, in addition to the personal images of time hinted at by Lynch, it is possible to differentiate 'time inside the body' (biological rhythms) from 'time outside the body' (Walmsley 1979) (Fig. 7.7). The two are often in conflict as when shift workers are required to change established patterns of eating and sleeping. 'Time outside the body' usually manifests itself in cultural time because human beings everywhere tend to make very similar temporal judgements using natural cycles and culturally determined social events (e.g. public holidays) (Doob 1978). This cultural time may be cyclical (e.g. lunar cycles), linear (birth to death), or imposed by the socio-political systems (e.g. daylight saving).

Just as it is possible to identify different types of time, so it is also possible to identify different approaches to the study of the importance of time. Three approaches are particularly relevant to human geography: the Lund School of time-geography; time budget analyses; and work on the sequencing of activities (Parkes and Wallis 1978).

The Lund School of *time-geography* began with the work of Hägerstrand in the mid-1960s but did not become widely known in the English-speaking world until much later (see Pred 1973b). Hägerstrand (1978: 123) has stated his value position very eloquently: 'we need a geography today which helps us to see ourselves, our fellow-passengers and our total environment in a more coherent way than we are presently capable of doing . . . the answer seems to lie in the study of the interwoven distribution of states and events in coherent blocks of space–time'. The development of time-geography is predicated on eight basic assumptions which state that:

1. the human being is indivisible;
2. the length of each human life is limited;
3. the ability of a human to undertake several tasks at once is limited;
4. every task has a duration;
5. movement between points in space consumes time;
6. there is a limit to the number of individuals that can be packed into one space;
7. there is a limited space available for one activity at any one time;
8. every situation is inevitably rooted in past situations (Hägerstrand 1975).

The force of these assumptions is most clearly demonstrated when an individual is thought of as describing a *life-path* through *time–space*. This conceptualization can operate at a variety of scales

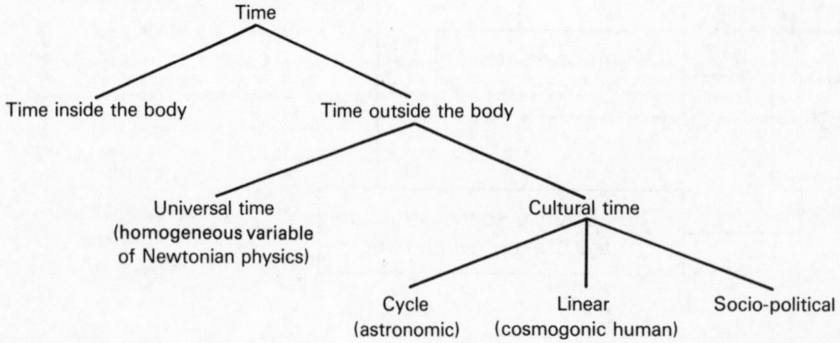

Fig. 7.7 A typology of time. *Source*: Walmsley (1979, 224).

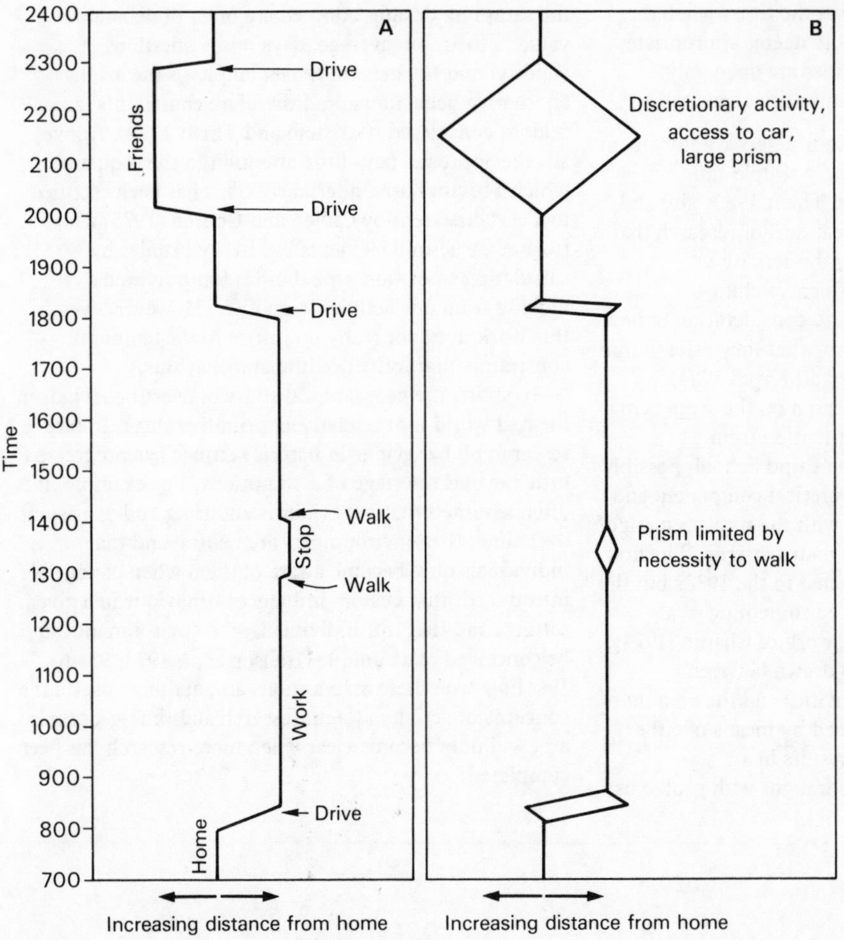

Fig. 7.8 A one day life-path in time-space.

(day-path, year-path, etc.). For example, Fig. 7.8A shows the day-path of the author of this chapter on the day that the chapter was completed. Places (work, home) that are essentially points (in that movement within them is inconsequential) are usually termed *stations* and are displayed as vertical lines (Lenntorp 1978). Travel is displayed as a diagonal line because it consumes both time and space.

In addition to describing what actually happens, time-geography can be used to investigate *possible* behaviours. It does this by introducing the idea of a *time–space prism* to delineate the scope of activity open to an individual. What this means can be illustrated by returning to Fig. 7.8B. If it is assumed that the author cannot leave home before 0800 hours and must return by 1815 hours and that work commitments demand his attention between 0815 and 1800 hours (except for a one-hour lunch break), then some indication of his scope for other activities can be gained by drawing prisms to indicate how far and how long he can go between prearranged commitments. Clearly, the range of behaviour is more restricted at lunch-time when the author must travel on foot than in the evening when he may travel by car. In other words, the size of the prism (and therefore the scope of activity) is limited by a variety of *constraints* which reflect such things as social considerations, environmental opportunities, and the attitudes of the individual concerned (Parkes and Thrift 1978). According to Hägerstrand (1970), these constraints can be differentiated into three types:

1. *Capability constraints* limit an individual's activities because of his biological make-up (and hence the need for sleep and food) and through restrictions on the facilities at his disposal, such as limited transport networks and limited access to cars.
2. *Coupling constraints*, which are often determined by a clock, refer to the need for individuals to be at the same place at the same time as other individuals (as, for instance, when school teachers and pupils need to coincide).
3. *Authority constraints* relate to the tendency for some

activities to be available only at the times when the person in charge of that activity deems appropriate (for example, child care facilities are open only during those hours that the authorities specify).

These and other ideas inherent in time-geography are, at one and the same time, disarmingly simple and inspiringly powerful (Parkes and Thrift 1980: xiv) and the approach has generated a great deal of research that ranges from the question of how the activity organization of a community influences child development (Martensson 1977) to consideration of how neighbourhoods differ in terms of what they offer within given time–space prisms (Forer and Kivell 1981).

Time budget studies and research on the sequencing of activities have attracted less attention from geographers than the work of the Lund School, possibly because they lack any major theoretical component and at times seem overly concerned with the measurement of actual rather than possible behaviour patterns. The first time budget studies were conducted in the 1930s but the approach has recently experienced something of a revival, largely as a result of the work of Chapin (1974; 1978). Generally a distinction is drawn between obligatory and discretionary activities and the amount of time devoted to each is ascertained by means of either diaries or questionnaires. This results in a methodological approach that is fraught with problems: the sampling designs adopted are often of debatable value; a focus on 'average' days raises questions of validity; and the general *ex post* emphasis means that alternative behaviours (and therefore constraints) are seldom considered (Carlstein and Thrift 1978). Above all, the approach pays little attention to the sequence in which activities are undertaken. This has been rectified to a certain extent by Cullen and Godsen (1975) who isolated structural elements in activity profiles by calculating transition probabilities for individuals moving from one activity to another. However, even this work does not really do justice to the temporal constraints that influence human behaviour.

In short, the geographical study of overt behaviour in the real world is at a relatively primitive stage. In fact research on behaviour in natural settings has progressed little beyond the stage of assumptions. For example, it is often assumed that behaviour is enduring and consistent over time, that environments are neutral and that individuals only become aware of them when change is introduced, that custom influences behaviour in a given setting, and that, for individuals, the environment can be conceived of as unique (Ittelson *et al.* 1974: 95–6). Just how true these assumptions are, and how useful the concepts of activity system research and time-geography are, will only become clear when more research has been completed.

Part Four

CASE STUDIES OF MICRO-SCALE BEHAVIOURAL APPROACHES

Much behavioural research in human geography, such as that reviewed in Part Three, has been concerned with building up a general understanding of how man interacts with his environment. Not surprisingly, there have been many attempts to apply this general knowledge to the examination of specific types of behaviour. The scope for such applied research is in fact enormous because, as has been pointed out throughout this book, behavioural approaches in geography have sought to complement rather than displace existing approaches. Nevertheless there is no one common theme in applied behavioural research just as there is no one model of how man processes and uses environmental information. Indeed it is a little artificial to make a distinction between the build-up of general understanding and the application of that understanding. In reality, knowledge of how man interacts with his environment has developed from both types of research: the general has been noted in the particular just as often as the particular has been derived from the general.

Part Four illustrates the way in which behavioural research has contributed to increased understanding of specific forms of man–environment interaction. Although the choice of case studies is to some extent eclectic, it does reflect the range of issues that have been studied by geographers. For example, the case studies differ in terms of whether they involve obligatory or discretionary behaviour, in terms of whether the behaviour under study is of high or low periodicity, and in the extent to which they emphasize overt or covert behaviour. Consumer behaviour (Ch. 8), for instance, differs from recreation behaviour (Ch. 12) in that the former is more or less obligatory whereas the latter is largely discretionary. Both involve frequent behaviour, certainly in comparison to migration (Ch. 14) and industrial location (Ch. 10) that are characterized by low periodicity activity. Moreover, all these forms of behaviour emphasize movement. They therefore differ from studies of orientation within cities (Ch. 9), hazard perception (Ch. 11), adjustment to stress (Ch. 13), and voting (Ch. 15) which highlight what goes on in the mind just as much as resultant behaviour.

Of course distinctions between obligatory and discretionary activity, between high and low periodicity, and between covert and overt behaviour represent continua rather than dichotomies. The placement of specific forms of behaviour on these continua is therefore a subjective matter: for example, in some circumstances migration may be 'obligatory' and shopping 'discretionary'. Consideration of these dimensions does nonetheless illustrate the breadth of issues covered in Part Four. The list of case studies is not of course fully illustrative of the range of issues to which behavioural research in geography has been directed. The coverage is however sufficient to reveal many of the general features of that research.

Chapter 8

CONSUMER BEHAVIOUR

The study of consumer behaviour has generated a vast literature, both in business (e.g. Foxall 1980) and in geography (e.g. Shepherd and Thomas 1980), despite the fact that shopping accounts on average for less than 1 per cent of an individual's time (Chapin and Brail 1969). Early studies focused on the relationship between consumer travel and central place theory (Berry 1967). Application of the theoretical ideal of rational economic man to the journey-to-shop led to the proposition that consumers *minimize travel* and therefore patronize the nearest shopping centre offering whatever goods are required. This proposition ignores the fact that rational economic man is sensitive to price and so may choose to patronize centres other than the nearest one if the price of the goods on offer is suitably low. It is, moreover, a proposition that is greatly at odds with real world behaviour. Studies in a number of places have shown that only a proportion of consumers minimize travel (see Thomas 1976: 37) and that many consumers do not use the central place hierarchy as 'rationally' as they should (Johnston and Rimmer 1967). There are several reasons for this: there is evidence that some consumers like to vary their shopping behaviour; factors like quality, service, and friendliness can outweigh economic considerations; and a great deal of shopping is undertaken on multipurpose trips, or in such a way as to fit in with the management of a consumer's other travel commitments.

The major weakness with the proposition of distance minimization is that it is deterministic: it reduces the complexity of the real world to only one variable which consumers treat in a specified way. In reality, of course, a decision as to which shopping centre to visit is often reached only after a trade-off between considerations like size, attractiveness, and distance. The nature of this trade-off has been studied in the approach usually referred to as *spatial interaction theory* (see Ch. 2). In this approach consumer travel is usually interpreted in terms of probabilistic gravity models (see Shepherd and Thomas, 1980). One of the first and best known of these models is the one developed by Huff (1963) and based on floor space and travel time:

$$P(C_{ij}) = \frac{\dfrac{S_j}{T_{ij}\lambda}}{\displaystyle\sum_{j=1}^{n} \left[\frac{S_j}{T_{ij}\lambda}\right]}$$

where $P(C_{ij})$ = the probability of a consumer at i going to j

S_j = square footage of space devoted to a particular class of good at j

T_{ij} = travel time

λ = a parameter to be estimated empirically to reflect the effect of travel time on various kinds of shopping trips

There are several problems with this type of approach. First, it does not do justice to the host of different factors that influence how a consumer evaluates a shopping centre. Second, there are very great problems involved in calculating parameter values for both distance (travel time) and attractiveness (square footage) (Openshaw 1973). Third, the approach lacks any sound theoretical underpinning (Jensen-Butler 1972) and violates certain technical aspects of neoclassical economic theory (Hubbard and Thompson 1981). Above all, the approach tends to produce descriptions of behaviour as it occurs in specific situations and it is not always clear whether the findings are applicable beyond the specific situation.

One attempt to model consumer behaviour in a way that enables consumer choice to be generalized beyond a specific situation is the *revealed space preference* approach developed by Rushton (1969a; 1976). This approach proposes that consumers rank all alternative shopping centres on a scale of preferredness, that consumers patronize the most preferred centre, and that overt behaviour can therefore be predicted from a knowledge

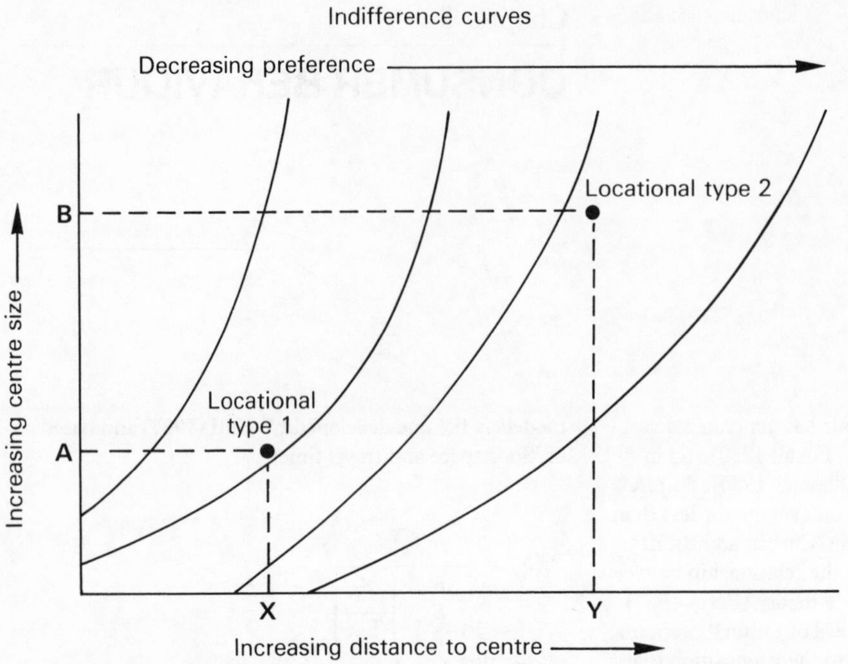

Fig. 8.1 Revealed space preference.

of preferences. Rushton believed that preferences were capable of measurement by means of non-metric multidimensional scaling of pairwise comparison data and he introduced generality to his model by discussing 'locational types' (various combinations of size and distance) rather than specific shopping centres. Computationally, the procedure is complex and it is not surprising to find that most studies have simplified the problem and considered only the two variables of size/attractiveness and distance. Figure 8.1 shows what the approach does: pairwise comparison of a large number of locational types produces indifference curves such that it is possible to see that a small centre (A) at a short distance (X) (locational type 1) is preferred to (and therefore used more than) a large centre (B) at a great distance (Y) (locational type 2).

Rushton's model was developed for inter-urban travel but has been adapted to intra-urban consumer behaviour by Timmermans (1979) in a paper that defined locational types on the basis of number of employees (cf. size) and 'reasonable travel time' (cf. distance). In other words, Timmermans, unlike Rushton, made the distance limit endogenous to the model. Instead of specifying distance constraints in the definition of locational types he permitted respondents to define for themselves what they considered to be a 'reasonable' amount of travelling time. Despite this refinement, the revealed space preference approach is open to many criticisms (Pirie 1976): locational types tend to be defined on only two variables in order to keep the number of alternatives to manageable proportions for inclusion in the time-consuming paired-comparison methodology; there is no real evidence that consumers use locational types in their evaluation of shopping centres; the approach can only really be applied to known and experienced situations and hence the findings cannot be extrapolated to the hypothetical situations encountered in planning; indifference curves represent only the average preference of the respondent group and so are of little use in predicting individual behaviour; and, perhaps more fundamentally, space and distance are not a dimension of choice but rather a constraint on choice (MacLennan and Williams 1979). The defence against these criticisms has been spirited. Timmermans (1981), for example, has attempted to show how preferences can be transferred from one context to another and has suggested that size and accessibility are the aspects of shopping centres that individuals consider most often (Timmermans *et al.* 1982). It remains true nonetheless that the revealed space preference approach fails to take stock of influences on consumers other than those related to the shopping centre. Huff (1960) has expressed some of these influences diagrammatically (Fig. 8.2) and has emphasized geographical location, social differentiation, and personal mobility. Geographical location was considered in rather more detail by Cadwallader (1975) who emphasized three variables: the attractiveness of stores (as reflected in the range, quality, and price of goods); the distance of a consumer from a store in both

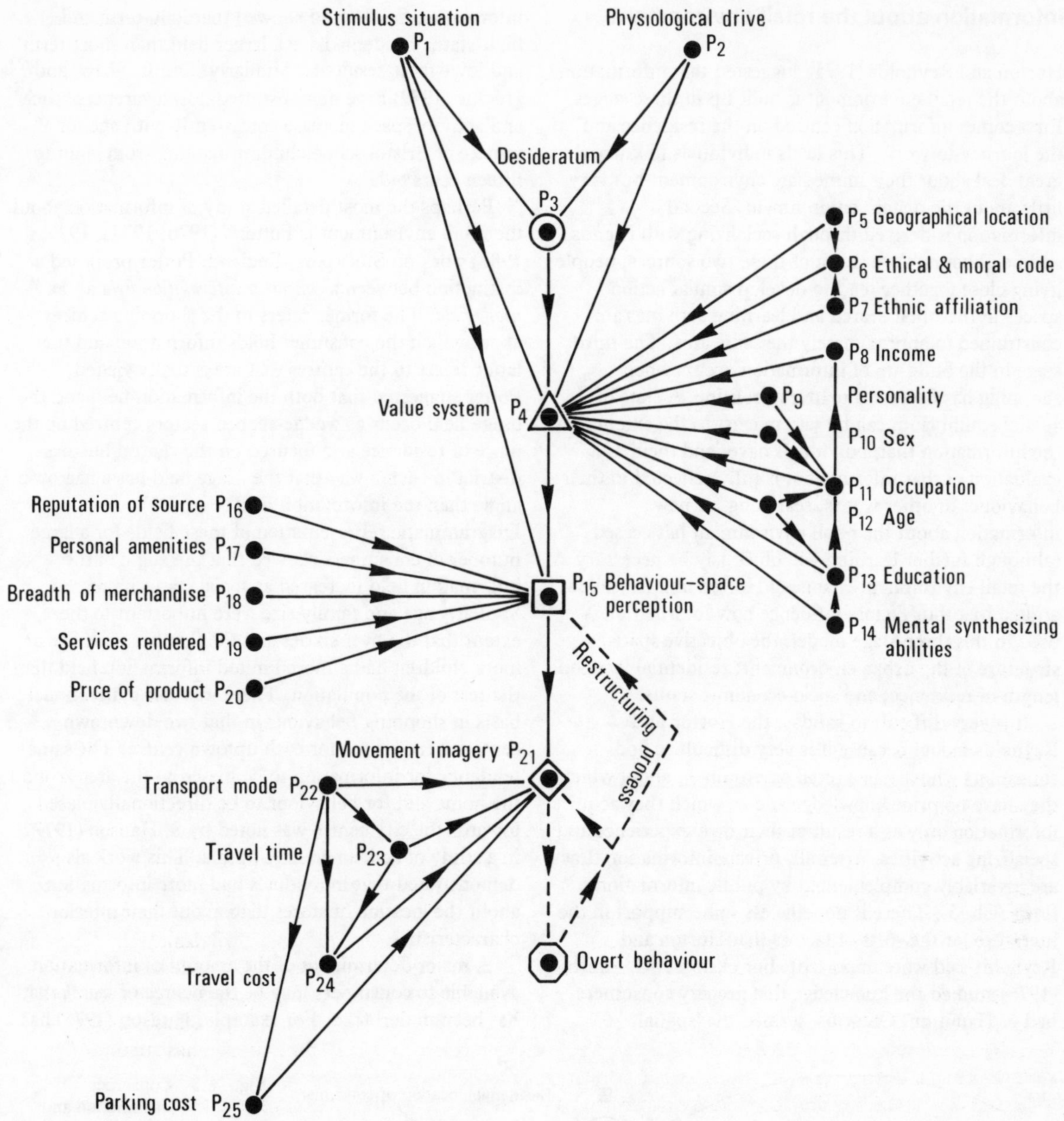

Fig. 8.2 Influences on consumer behaviour. *Source*: (Huff 1960, 165).

real and estimated terms; and the amount of information that consumers have about a store. More specifically, Cadwallader argued that

$$P_i = \left[\frac{A_i}{D_i}\right] I_i$$

where P_i = the proportion of consumers patronizing store i

A_i = the attractiveness of store i

D_i = the distance to store i

I_i = the amount of information consumers have about store i.

When attractiveness was evaluated by means of a semantic differential question, distance by means of subjective estimates, and information in terms of dichotomous yes/no categories, the model was found to provide a good description of consumer behaviour in Los Angeles. Certainly the model performed better than gravity models based on size and distance alone. This implies that *information* may be an important variable.

Information about the retail environment

Horton and Reynolds (1971) suggested that information about the retail environment is built up in three stages. First comes information centred on the residence and the journey-to-work. This leads individuals to know a great deal about their immediate environment but very little about the distant environment. Second, information is derived through socializing with friends and neighbours. As a result of these two sources, people living close together tend to develop similar action spaces in that their search and learning activities are constrained to approximately the same area. The third stage in the build-up of information occurs when shopping has become a matter of routine. A state of spatial equilibrium can be said to exist to the extent that the information that individuals have, and their evaluation of that information, is fully reflected in their behaviour. In other words, searching for new information about the retail environment has ceased (although further learning will obviously be necessary as the retail environment changes). Horton and Reynolds argued that four factors influence how information is used in this three-stage model: the objective spatial structure of the urban environment; residential location; length of residence; and socio-economic status.

It is very difficult to validate the Horton and Reynolds model because it is very difficult to find consumers who are in a retail environment about which they have no prior knowledge and in which they acquire information only as a result of their own experience and socializing activities. After all, private information flows are invariably complemented by public information flows (Ch. 5). There is nonetheless some support in the literature for the sorts of factors that Horton and Reynolds said were important. For example, G. Smith (1976) studied the knowledge that grocery consumers had of Hamilton, Ontario – termed the 'spatial information field' – and showed that long-term and high-status residents have a larger field than short-term and low-status residents. Similarly, Smith, Shaw, and Huckle (1979) have demonstrated how awareness space and activity space increase consistently with age for a sample of Bristol schoolchildren ranging from eight to fifteen years old.

Perhaps the most detailed study of information about the retail environment is Potter's (1976; 1977a; 1979; 1982) work on Stockport, England. Potter proposed a distinction between a *consumer information field* and a *usage field*. The former refers to the shopping centres about which the consumer holds information and the latter refers to the centres that are actually visited. Potter suggested that both the information field and the usage field occur as wedge-shaped sectors centred on the place of residence and focused on the central business district in such a way that the usage field has a narrower angle than the information field (Fig. 8.3). Diagrammatic representation of these fields for a large number of consumers showed that the angle of the information field increased as social status increased. Similarly age and family size were important to the extent that the over sixties and the families with five or more children had a more limited information field than the rest of the population. There was also a directional basis in shopping behaviour in that two downtown centres were visited for each uptown centre. The same tendency for information to be biased to the area around the home and for behaviour to be directionally biased towards the city centre was noted by S. Hanson (1977) in a study of consumers in Uppsala. This work also demonstrated that individuals had more information about the location of stores than about their interior characteristics.

A major determinant of the amount of information available to consumers may be the degree of *search* that has been undertaken. For example, Hudson (1975) has

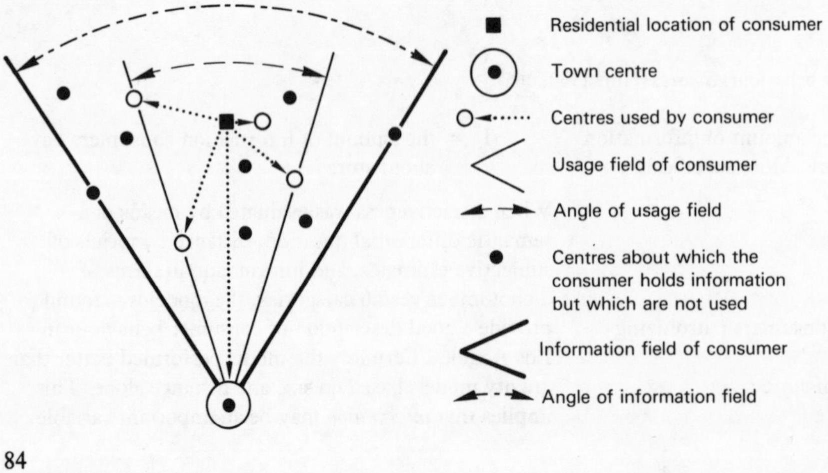

Fig. 8.3 Consumer information and usage fields. *Source*: Potter (1979, 21).

taken the view that, as search proceeds, consumers shift attention from simple factual knowledge to what they consider to be positive features of shopping centres (e.g. price, service). Of course, searching is by no means a simple process and market researchers have differentiated different types of search behaviour. Bucklin (1967), for example, distinguished between 'full search' involving visits to many stores, 'directed search' where some search is warranted, especially in relation to price, but full search is not worthwhile, and 'casual search' where information is gained in a non-purposeful manner. Moreover, the type of searching undertaken can be influenced by the type of good required: a consumer may treat the purchase of a costly item as an exercise in problem-solving but may adopt 'routinized response behaviour' in relation to more familiar items (Howard and Sheth 1969). And, of course, information about the retail environment is not something that is lying around waiting to be gathered. In many cases it is something actively promoted by retailers in the hope of influencing the images that consumers hold in their minds.

Images of the retail environment

The image of any environment represents 'stored information' (Downs, 1970a). It follows from this that work on images focuses on three issues: the way in which information contributes to the development of images; the nature of images; and the relationship between image and overt behaviour. The first of these issues has been largely ignored in the field of consumer behaviour, possibly because the link between information and image is extremely complex. Cadwallader (1978) has shown, for instance, that the information surfaces and preference surface of Los Angeles consumers are convoluted and only very weakly related to each other. It is not surprising, therefore, that behavioural geographers have directed most attention to the nature of the image of the retail environment and its relationship to shopping behaviour.

The seminal work on the nature of the image of shopping centres was produced by Downs (1970b). This study was concerned with the perception of the internal characteristics of the downtown shopping centre of Broadmead in Bristol. Downs hypothesized that there would be nine elements to the image of the centre: price, structure and design, ease of internal movement and parking, visual appearance, reputation, range of shops, quality of service, shopping hours, and atmosphere. Four semantic differential questions for each of these nine elements were presented to a sample of women. The wealth of data that was generated was reduced by subjecting the responses to a factor analysis which identified eight components of the image of the centre. Of the original nine elements, reputation and atmosphere did not prove to be significant. In contrast, ease of internal movement and parking was separated into two separate components: internal pedestrian circulation, and traffic conditions. In short, Downs showed that the image of a shopping centre is very complex. It covers both the retail establishments themselves (particularly considerations of service, price, hours, and range) and the structure and function of the centre as a whole (incorporating structure and design, pedestrian movement, appearance, and traffic conditions). This distinction is important because retailers can influence to a large extent the image of their own establishment (although the image that they hold may be rather different from that held by consumers (Bloomestein, Nijkamp, and Van Veenendaal 1980)) but they can do little about the image of the centre as a whole. Some types of shopping centre may in fact have poor images and this poor image may well influence consumer behaviour. For example, Potter (1977b: 352) has drawn attention to the 'poor imageability' of arterial shopping centres that results from 'their specialized functional character, linear morphology, fabric discontinuity and low qualitative tone' relative to nuclear shopping centres. In a similar vein, Walmsley (1972b) has shown how consumers travel further to patronize a planned centre than an unplanned centre.

It is one thing to suggest that particular types of shopping centres have favourable or unfavourable images but it is altogether a different problem to explain how the image of the retail environment as a whole may influence the way consumers choose between competing centres. At an aggregate level it is possible to show that consumer spatial behaviour is related more closely to a cognitive map than to a 'real' map (Mackay, Olshavsky, and Sentell 1975) but it is difficult to translate this into predictions about individual behaviour because of the very formidable methodological problems that surround the definition and measurement of images (Hudson 1974). One way of overcoming these difficulties may be to adopt the repertory grid methodology approach to personal construct theory (Ch. 5). Certainly, use of personal construct theory helped Hudson (1976a) to design an interesting model of how consumers decide which shop to patronize. A three-stage process is involved. First, consumers build up knowledge and preferences over time. That is to say, consumers learn about shops and develop constructs for evaluating these to the point where there emerges the notion of an 'ideal shop'. Second, specific needs arise and this leads to an evaluation of a sub-set of the shops known to the individual, possibly using a sub-set of the evaluative constructs. In other words, the basic image of the environment is transformed to give one relevant to the particular need. Third, an actual choice is made of one shop from within this simplified image, the shop selected being that which is most similar to the 'ideal shop'. Although Hudson's study of student shopping behaviour in Bristol lent some support to the model, its general applicability is limited because it focuses on very simple situations (the choice of a single shop) and because it has not been related closely to work on consumer learning and decision-making.

Consumer learning and decision-making

Shopping is a form of recursive behaviour. It can be presumed therefore that the genuine decision-making of a consumer when first placed in a new environment becomes routinized as behaviour is repeated. In other words, behaviour changes over time as learning occurs. According to Hudson (1970), four factors can influence this learning process: the nature of the retail environment; the nature of individual behaviour spaces; variations in individual evaluation of elements within behaviour spaces; and random fluctuations in behaviour. Moreover, learning itself can be conceptualized as either a change in behaviour or a change in cognitive structure. Hudson saw in this distinction a parallel with the difference between stimulus-response learning theories and cognitive learning theories. In Hudson's view, the former are based largely on need reduction, are derived from experimental psychology, and are of little value in the study of consumer behaviour despite their translation by Bush and Mosteller (1955) into Markov-based linear operator models. By way of contrast, cognitive theories are much more realistic in that they emphasize behaviour space and allow for changing expectations of behavioural outcomes. Elements of both approaches were combined by Hudson into a model based on the idea that social, psychological and physiological needs give rise to a motivational drive which is satisfied by selecting a shop to patronize from those shops in the individual's mental map. Confirmation or non-confirmation of the expectations surrounding that shop serves as feedback (Hudson 1970). The main problem with this model is that of measuring the impact of feedback on cognitive structures. Hudson suggested that personal construct theory provides the answer but other researchers have been less enthusiastic and many have preferred to look to mathematical learning theory.

Golledge has probably done more than anyone else to popularize geographical studies of learning (Golledge 1967; 1969; Golledge and Brown 1967). He argued that models of 'place loyalty', whereby individuals patronize a particular centre, represent only one of a number of solutions produced by the learning process. It is just as easy to see consumer behaviour as a market-sharing activity that is amenable to mathematical modelling. Specifically, Golledge drew attention to four types of learning model: 'concept identification' models simulate the trial and error process whereby consumers move from initial search through to routinized behaviour; 'paired associate' models use scaling to describe how consumers select between alternative shopping centres; 'interactance-process' models focus on the establishment of probabilities in competitive choice situations; and 'avoidance conditioning' models employ linear difference equations to account for the rewards and penalties involved in using different shopping centres. Each of these types of model was developed largely from laboratory experiments. Their application to the real world is therefore problematical. Burnett (1973), for example, argued against models that simply emphasize changing behavioural probabilities and in favour of a greater emphasis on the attributes that are used to differentiate between alternative shops and shopping centres. She also maintained that the attributes that consumers consider cannot be specified as *a priori* because they are subjective and can only be revealed by direct interrogation. In this context she was able to show, in a study of comparison goods shopping for two samples of women in Sydney, that consumers in the same sample use the same dimensions to discriminate between alternative shopping centres (although the dimensions produced by multidimensional scaling were complex and did not correspond closely to the objective retail environment). She also demonstrated that verifiable mathematical relationships exist between the probability of choosing each alternative centre and the decision-maker's subjective assessment of that centre in terms of the dimensions used to discriminate between centres. Furthermore, a difference emerged between the two samples and, because these groups differed in terms of their length of residence, this difference was interpreted in terms of learning.

Burnett's paper brought stern criticism from Louviere (1973) in a commentary that highlights many of the problems encountered in the modelling of consumer learning. To begin with, Louviere argued that Burnett failed to take account of existing theory in psychology and that the Markov approach, which Burnett had advocated, is conceptually inadequate in that it assumes a static environment whereas the retail environment is always changing. He went on to criticize the view that the dimensions used to discriminate between shops can be revealed *a posteriori* by multidimensional scaling. He also contended that learning cannot be inferred from cross-sectional data because there is no evidence that choice proportions become asymptotic over time. His point of view was expressed clearly when he claimed that 'models of human information processing, learning, choice, and the like, are similar to equivalent models in the physical sciences: they are "as if" models. Their builders use them to describe the behaviour of people "as if" these people (subjects) obeyed the rules expressed by the mathematics' (Louviere 1973: 322). Clearly, Louviere's view is that consumers do not behave in the way specified by the mathematics. Undeterred, Burnett (1977) proposed a linear learning model for household grocery shopping in Uppsala and used Bayesian probability theory to derive predictions about successive destination choices. This study represents an attempt to develop testable statements about heterogeneous population aggregates from assumptions about individual behaviour. In other words, an attempt is made to integrate the micro- and macro-scales of inquiry. A similar motivation led Wrigley (1980) to advocate a *stationary purchasing behaviour model* of shopping activity. This type of model focuses on *how* consumers behave not *why* they behave as they do. It allows for individual variability in purchasing while coping with the fact the overall aggregate purchasing pattern may be unchanged. It does this by assuming that purchase frequencies follow a Poisson distribution (i.e. that purchases are independent random events), that overall purchasing patterns follow a Gamma distribution, and that the resultant distribution of purchases at any point in time follows a negative binomial distribution. The model was originally devised for application to product purchasing but was applied successfully by Wrigley (1980) to shopping centre choice in Bradford. Unfortunately, however, the model copes with only one retail outlet at a time and Wrigley's suggestion that it be generalized to produce a stochastic model of multi-outlet purchasing behaviour has not yet been followed, largely because little is known about how consumers evaluate multi-dimensional alternatives.

Shopping centres vary in many ways – size, price, quality, layout – and it may be that consumers, in making comparisons, evaluate different centres on different dimensions. Thus consumers may not be able to order competing centres into a transitive preference structure since the same centre is frequently not the most preferred on all dimensions. Indeed, there is some evidence for this (Root 1975). In contrast, Walmsley (1977) has shown that 88 per cent of housewives in an area of Sydney could order major suburban centres (with more than sixty shops) into transitive preferences and that 67 per cent of the sample had overt behaviour that was congruent with their preferences. Of course, simple observation of transitive preferences leaves unanswered the question of how those preferences were arrived at or, in other words, how the many dimensions of each centre were combined to give an overall preference score. The answer to this question may lie in some sort of *conjoint analysis*. Schuler (1979) used this technique to model supermarket choice in Bloomington in a paper which suggested that consumers decide what attributes of a store are important, weight those attributes, calculate a summary score for each store based on the weighted attributes, and then maximize utility by patronizing the store with the highest score. This approach has been given some theoretical backing by Timmermans (1980) who has demonstrated that conjoint analysis is basically a method of measuring the joint effect of two or more independent variables (e.g. attributes of shopping centres) on the ordering of a dependent variable (e.g. a preference ranking of shopping centres). According to Timmermans, there are several composition rules whereby independent variables are combined. Most studies have assumed an additive rule which is compensatory in that a low value on one attribute is made up for by a high value on some other attribute. Timmermans suggested, however, that the best fit with his experimental data was achieved by a multiplicative composition rule which is non-compensatory in that a low value on one attribute tends to be compounded into a low overall utility. The corollary to this is that varying opinions as to the salience of attributes are likely to be reflected in varied behaviour patterns.

Variability in overt behaviour

A large number of factors have been found to influence consumer spatial behaviour: income, sex, age, occupation, ethnic affiliation, geographical location, mobility, culture, attitude, and personality (Williams 1981; Shepherd and Thomas 1980; Gayler 1980; Lloyd and Jennings 1978; Kassarjian 1971; Ray 1967). As a result overt behaviour patterns are very varied and generalizations hard to make. It does seem however that consumers often divide their purchases of particular commodities between a number of shopping centres. On the face of it this appears to be sub-optimal behaviour because it seems to violate the principle of distance minimization and the idea of transitive preferences. In practice, however, such behaviour may be a rational response to either the varying utility offered by shopping centres or to the costs involved in searching for information about centres (Hay and Johnston 1979).

Because search is costly, it tends to be constrained in both distance and directional terms to a relatively small geographical area. For example, other things being equal consumers are more likely to visit centres that lie between their home and the central business district than centres that lie in the direction away from the town centre (Lee 1962; Potter 1977b). This tendency is probably related to distance perception. Thompson (1963) was the first researcher to point out that subjective distance differed significantly from objective distance and, since his work appeared, several people have demonstrated that distances along familiar and preferred routes tend to be underestimated relative to distances along unfamiliar and disliked routes, both at the urban scale (Pacione 1975) and the scale of individual streets (Meyer 1977). Of course it would be wrong to overemphasize the importance of distance perception because its influence on travel behaviour is still unclear. Some of the differences that have been observed in journeys-to-shop may in fact be more apparent than real. For example, the apparent tendency for consumers to travel further for high-order goods than for low-order goods may be no more than an artefact of the denser 'packing' of low-order goods outlets because there is evidence that the amount of excess travel is very similar for different commodities (Walmsley 1975).

Observation of variability in overt behaviour has led some researchers to propose that there are different types of consumer. One of the first to do this was Stone (1954) who identified four sorts of consumers: price-conscious individuals for whom economic considerations are paramount; individuals who are bound by habit and who emphasize personal contacts; individuals who adopt an 'ethical' position such as supporting 'the little man'; and apathetic individuals who do not care which shop they visit. What this typology does, in other words, is highlight the social and psychological influences acting upon consumers. This point was taken up by Brooker-Gross (1981) who argued that 'outshopping' (inter-urban consumer spatial behaviour) should be interpreted as a social group activity. A more explicitly behaviourist typology of consumers was developed by Williams (1979). He proposed that individuals could be differentiated according to mode of travel (walk, bus, car), frequency of trip (frequent, infrequent), and size of centre visited (small, medium, large), and he went on to identify seven types of consumer in Birmingham.

The idea behind the development of typologies of consumers is that the classificatory technique on which it is based provides a way of linking micro- and macro-scale studies, that is to say a way of relating descriptions of individual behaviour to descriptions of the behaviour of aggregate populations. Critics of the revealed space preference approach have shown that it is impossible to work from the macro-scale to the micro-scale and to make assertions about individuals on the basis of groups. Typologies represent an attempt to go the other way, from the micro-scale to the macro-scale, by grouping together individuals whose behaviour is similar. A similar goal motivated Hudson (1976b) to use individual mental models of the retail environment (personal constructs) as the input for multiple regression models of aggregate behaviour. His hope was that the resultant aggregate models would be 'behaviourally more realistic and descriptively more accurate'. Unfortunately his hope was not realized. This is possibly because Hudson's work, like the overwhelming majority of studies of consumer spatial behaviour, adopted the standpoint of *consumer sovereignty*. Implicit in many studies has been the idea that consumers make free choices and that they go to whatever shopping centres they wish. In reality, of course, decisions by consumers are very highly constrained. In many instances overt behaviour may reflect the dictates of transport availability and time just as much as it reflects a rational evaluation of the centres 'on offer'. It is questionable therefore whether geographical studies of consumer behaviour will make great strides until these constraints are taken into account. Basically the constraints are of two sorts: those associated with the environment (poor shops, restricted trading hours, poor transport) and those associated with the consumer (lack of mobility, poverty, age) (Shepherd and Thomas 1980: 47–8). In this sense, therefore, it is incumbent upon students of consumer behaviour to look at developments within the retail environment as well as the constraints acting upon consumers. For example, the manner in which retailers influence the nature and amount of information available to consumers has not yet received the attention it deserves. Nor have geographical studies of consumer behaviour really begun to take stock of the changes that are underway in retailing generally (see Davies and Kirby 1980).

Chapter 9

URBAN LIVING

During the past three decades geographers have become very concerned with the study of urban life (Carter 1972; Herbert 1972; Knox 1982). The prime focus has been upon objective phenomena, emphasizing the 'mosaic of social worlds' and their associated pathologies (Herbert and Smith 1979). Much of this work was derived from the inter-war Chicago School of Urban Ecologists (Park *et al.* 1925) who viewed the city as a system which illustrated both the interdependent, co-operative working of nature, and its predatory and competitive aspects (Timms 1971; Robson 1969) (see Ch. 3). Yet over thirty years ago Robinson (1950) warned that such an aggregate approach to the city fails to account for much of the small group phenomena that characterise urban living. Even the application of sophisticated multivariate techniques did not overcome this weakness because variables were usually based on areal characteristics and were seldom predictive of individual behaviour. Moreover, much of the analysis has been correlative rather than causal. In other words, to know that a part of a city is occupied by a particular group does not allow prediction of how any individual or group will react to any changes which might affect their neighbourhood. This sort of understanding can only be achieved if attention is directed to the ways in which the urban environment is 'known' by its residents and has 'meaning' to them (Krampen 1981). Knowing and meaning are, in other words, crucial mediating factors in the interaction between individuals and the built environment (Mercer 1975; McGill and Korn 1982). An understanding of such covert behaviour is therefore necessary if the massive re-shaping of the urban environment, which is made possible by modern technology and planning, is to be a success.

Identity and belonging

Although cities are often thought of as urbane and civilized, the significance of urban living has been a source of considerable debate (Dyos and Wolf 1973; Burke 1975). Some believe that city life is inherently beneficial whilst others view it with suspicion (Williams 1973). Much of this controversy may be due to the fact that the modern industrial city is both environmentally and qualitatively different from the mercantile city of earlier times (Vance 1977). The larger and more complex city of today provides stimuli unknown to our ancestors and, therefore, requires new and different modes of adaptation and behaviour (P. Smith 1976). For example, in his classic paper on urbanism as a way of life, Wirth (1938: 11) argued that the 'bonds of kinship, of neighbourliness, and the sentiments arising out of living together for generations under a common folk tradition are likely to be absent, or at best, relatively weak' in a city whose residents have diverse origins and backgrounds. Although this view overlooks the possibility of a co-existence of different societal elements within the same community, it does highlight the complexity of modern cities. Pahl (1966: 322) has even gone so far as to argue that the city is so complex that 'any attempt to tie the patterns of social relationships to specific geographical milieux is a singularly fruitless exercise'. This view, in turn, has a certain appeal but fails to emphasize that modern city man is not simply attached to a certain area but rather interacts with a wide environment thereby building up an understanding of how places are related to each other. Places, in other words, are the locales of different activities and therefore become associated with, and symbolic of, those activities. This view is very much in line with Mumford's (1961) argument that the city is not mere bricks and mortar but rather is a tangible expression of man's beliefs and ideals and the supreme manifestation of civilization. The advent of the railway, the motor car, mass media, and mass culture has, of course, led to a lessening of the salience of place. According to Laslett (1968), in the 'world we have lost' everything physical was on a human scale and everything temporal was tied to the human life span,

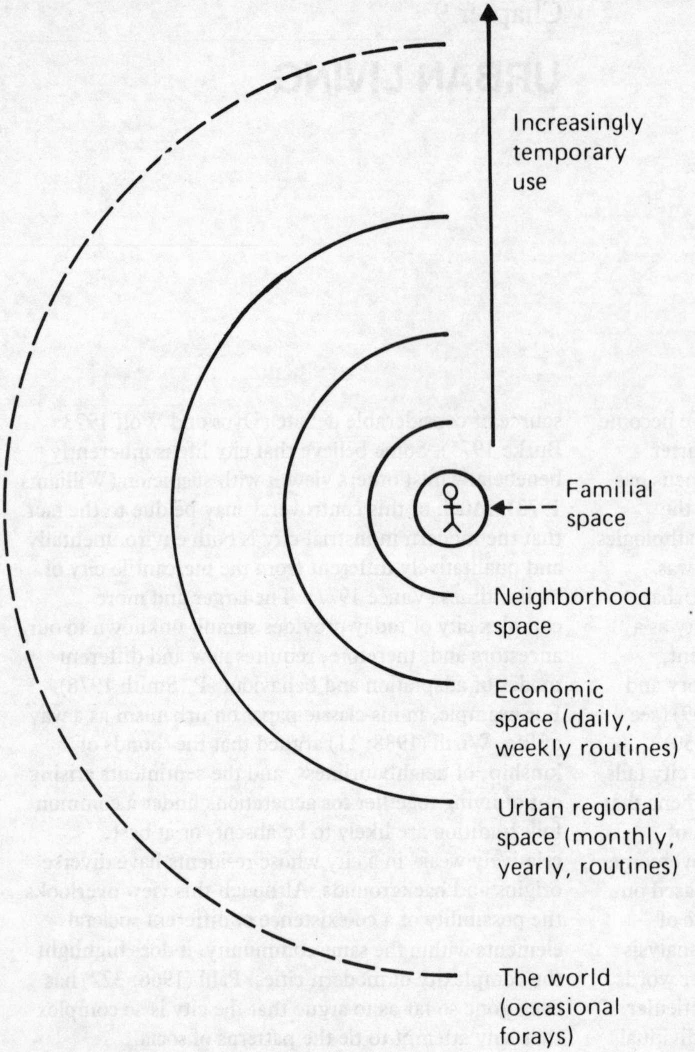

Fig. 9.1 A hierarchy of social spaces. *Source*: Porteous (1977, 92).

resulting in all communities being highly localized in their structure and activities (Lewis 1979). In contrast, the 'world we have gained' is distinguished by a widening of spatial horizons, which has led the planner Webber (1964a: 116) to suggest that 'it is interaction, not place, that is the essence of the city and city life'. From this perspective, modern urban living is characterized by interest-based community rather than community based on propinquity (McClenahan 1945; Webber 1964b). Of course not all researchers accept this perspective and many have questioned the validity of Webber's thesis. For example, even in a highly mobile society, there are large sections of the population, such as the elderly, the poor, and the young, who are still highly place-bound. Likewise, social heterogeneity can inhibit travel within cities. Nowhere is the importance of place better seen than in childhood where the immediate locality, both in a physical and social sense, is of utmost significance in the development of the individual. Moreover, even mobile individuals retain a strong feeling for their homeland and birthplaces, as exemplified by the growing number of 'return' migrants in North America and Western Europe (Lewis 1982). Similarly, much of the recent boom in locality-based interest groups, whether opposing new housing developments or motorway construction, or demanding improved social services or recreational facilities, is a reflection of middle-class desires for place identity (Proshansky 1978). At a larger scale, the growth in regional consciousness, whether it be the Welsh or the Scots, and the emergence of environmental consciousness, demonstrated in architectural and countryside conservation (Shoard 1980), is further evidence of man's feeling for place. What this illustrates is the continuing significance of place in the everyday life of all urban residents and the view that 'mobility will never destroy the importance of locality' (Pahl 1968: 48).

In the context of a mobile society, places may be regarded as 'foci where we experience the meaningful events of our existence . . . [and] . . . points of departure from which we orient ourselves and take possession of the environment' (Norberg-Schulz 1971:19). They are not therefore analogous to places in the animal world (see Dyson-Hudson and Smith 1978) but rather can be viewed, in De Lauwe's (1975) terms, as involving a hierarchy of social spaces each reflecting increasingly temporary use of the urban environment (Fig. 9.1). Despite this people appear to know and use only limited parts of the city; other segments may be totally unknown or vaguely and erroneously conceived (Buttimer 1969; Gold 1982). Such a geographically limited approach to urban living immediately raises several issues: How significant is the local neighbourhood for the modern urbanite? How much of the city does the individual use? How does the individual structure the city so as to find his way about?

The local neighbourhood

Recent studies on urban residential development have emphasized the continuing significance of the neighbourhood in city life (see Herbert and Johnston 1976a; 1976b). However, despite the detail and diversity of this research, there remains little agreement as to a neighbourhood's true nature and definition (Blowers 1973; Thorns 1976). Much of this confusion results from the fact that the terms 'neighbouring' and 'neighbourhood' involve a whole series of dimensions which are independent of each other in certain situations while being highly inter-related in other situations (Hunter 1979). Geographically, it is evident that a neighbourhood fulfils at least four roles:

1. It provides a means of translating social distance into geographical distance.
2. It affords a convenient unit for the provision of goods and services.
3. It gives identity to what might otherwise be anonymous residential suburbs.
4. It forms 'a territorial group the members of which meet on common ground for spontaneous and organised social contacts' (Glass 1948: 124).

Beyond this, the significance of neighbourhood in everyday life is unclear. Several sociologists have questioned its relevance in determining behaviour (Pahl 1966) whilst others have been highly critical of its political overtones (Dennis 1958). These differences of opinion might well be regarded as purely academic were it not for the fact that planners and architects use the neighbourhood concept as the basis for the development of the modern city (Gans 1968). Although the nature of the application varies a good deal, most planning uses of the neighbourhood concept derive from Perry's (1929) original six principles:

1. The neighbourhood unit should contain between 3,000 and 6,000 people, in order that one elementary school can be sustained.
2. The neighbourhood should have distinct boundaries, so that residents can visualize it as a distinct entity.
3. There should be a system of parks and recreation spaces.
4. The school, and other services, should be located at the centre of the neighbourhood.
5. The shopping district should be located on the periphery so that several neighbourhoods may be served and traffic will be able to avoid the residential areas.
6. The streets of the neighbourhood should be proportionate to their traffic load.

Inevitably the indiscriminate application of these principles by planners in North America and Western Europe during the post-war era has led to considerable criticism particularly of the ethics and utility of the neighbourhood concept. For example, Isaacs (1948: 20) saw the neighbourhood unit acting 'as an instrument for implementing segregation of racial and cultural groups', whilst Herbert (1963–64: 171) argued that the concept was based on a misconception of what constituted a primary group since basically 'people are not contained, or constrained in their behaviour by the planner's imposition of a territory based community'.

Despite definitional difficulties, as well as continuing controversy over its use for planning purposes, urban residents readily recognize the significance of neighbourhoods in their daily lives. Individuals and families still have neighbours, and live in neighbourhoods. Over the years research in Britain and the United States has shown that residents invariably have a sense of local spatial identity that encompasses both local social relationships and local places (Miller *et al*. 1980; Greenbaum and Greenbaum 1981). In other words, despite increased mobility, there are contexts where there is considerable attachment to the local neighbourhood. This is particularly true of those areas where a common bond of deprivation can lead to community action (Ley and Cybriwsky 1974a; Cox and McCarthy 1980). However, in a comparative study of two neighbourhoods in Leicester, one deprived and the other prestigious, Lewis (1981a) concluded that

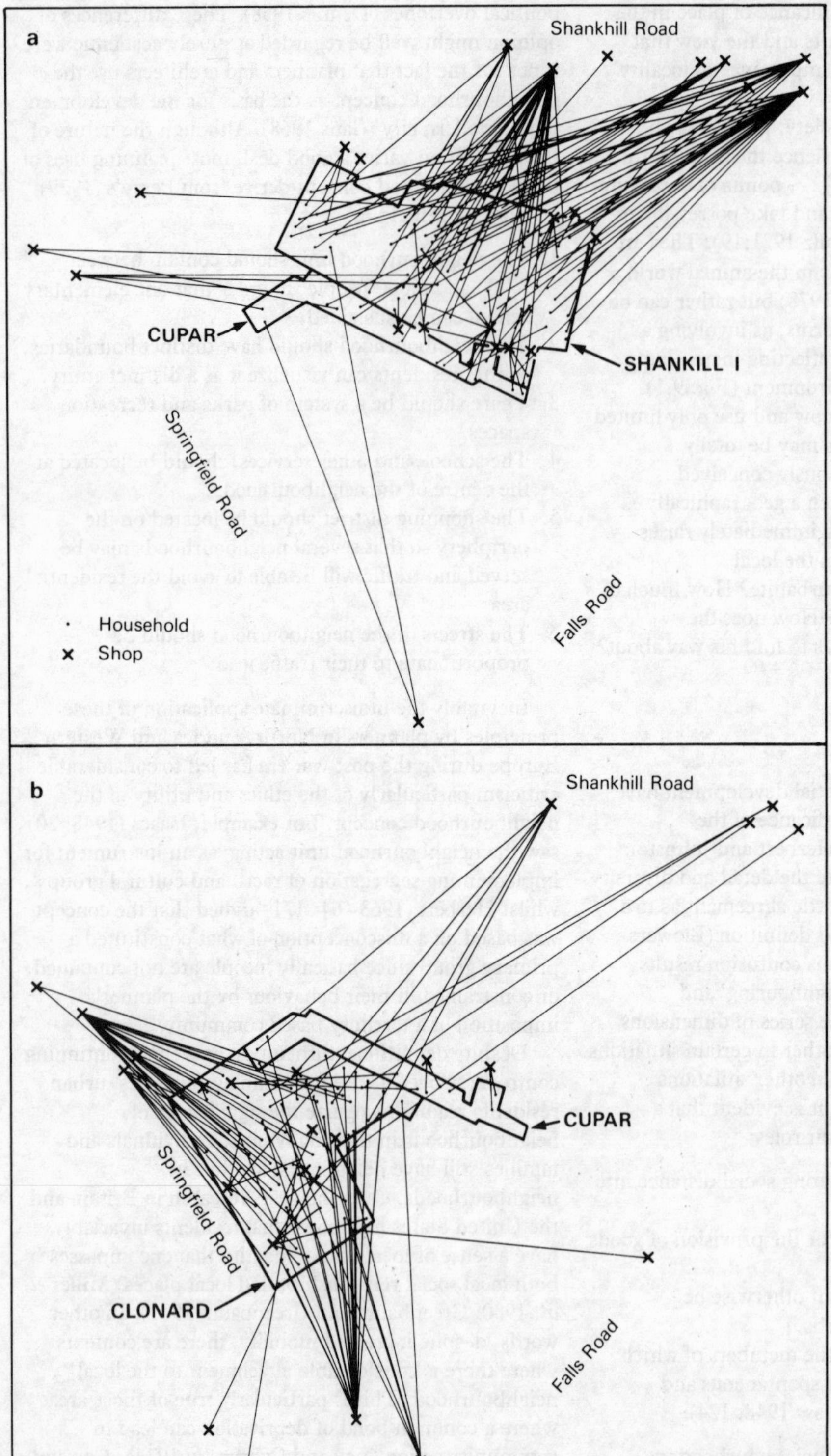

Fig. 9.2 **Activity patterns for the purchase of groceries in Belfast. a. Protestants, b. Roman Catholics.** ***Source*****: Boal (1969, 41 and 42).**

community feeling is so multi-faceted that the deprivation argument for community bonding has to be tempered with other evidence. When neighbourhoods were compared in terms of knowledge, overt behaviour, and satisfaction, it was only the latter which distinguished prestigious from poor. Moreover, the basis of the higher degree of satisfaction with the more prestigious area was not as a place to make friends or rear children but rather as a place to live. In other words, the widespread dissatisfaction with the deprived neighbourhood stemmed from deficiencies in its housing stock and a general lack of amenities rather than from any failings of neighbourliness (cf. Fried and Gleicher 1961; Duncan 1982).

In addition to serving as residential units neighbourhoods can also serve as a repository of social traditions or as a haven in an uncertain world. In such cases there emerges what has been described as *defended space*, where ethnic, religious, or socio-economic groups cluster together and actively discourage the intrusion of outsiders (Newman 1972; Mawby 1977). According to Suttles (1972: 21) such neighbourhoods may be identified by 'the residential group which seals itself off through the efforts of the delinquent gang, by restrictive covenant, by sharp boundaries, or by forbidding reputation'. In other words, these neighbourhoods can develop not only in the inner city but also in more prestigious districts, as exemplified by the so-called 'gilded' ghettoes of exclusive housing (Baltzel 1958; Kramer and Leventman 1961; Fainstein and Martin 1978). The means by which a neighbourhood can be defended is clearly demonstrated in Firey's (1945) classic study of Beacon Hill in Boston where restrictive covenants and a neighbourhood association successfully defended a prestigious residential area from encroachment by commercial interests for 150 years. The isolation of such 'defended' neighbourhoods is vividly illustrated in a series of papers by Boal (1969; 1971) on the activity patterns of the Catholic and Protestant population of Belfast where, even before the recent troubles, activity segregation was so marked that the main criterion in mobility appeared to be the desire to avoid crossing alien territory (Fig. 9.2).

In short, the available evidence suggests that the neighbourhood concept remains significant for urban living despite its weaknesses (Wolpert, Mumphrey and Seley 1972). Much of the controversy surrounding its use appears to result from terminological confusion, differing assumptions, and a lack of comparability of research findings (Gusfield 1977). As Stein (1960), a major proponent of neighbourhood theory, has suggested, this controversy and confusion can only be resolved after a more rigorous analysis of human behaviour at a local level. Following Keller (1968) and Lewis (1979) it can also be suggested that there are at least two approaches for ascertaining the presence of neighbourhoods within cities: assessment of the degree of localization of individual activities and examination of the degree of agreement in the identification of local residential environments.

Neighbouring and the perceived neighbourhood

The localization of social interaction as a basis of neighbourhood identification has been a source of considerable research, particularly by sociologists. Much of this research has however been weakened by problems of measurement and definition (Irving 1978). Nevertheless, following Bott's (1957) lead, some success has been achieved in conceptualizing social interaction in terms of a network (Mitchell 1969; Duncan and Duncan 1976; Wellman 1979; Wellman and Crump 1978; Wellman and Leighton 1979). Basically, *social network analysis* identifies the structure of social interaction by treating persons as points and relationships as connecting lines (Granovetter 1976), thus allowing the researcher to 'map out the complex reality of the interpersonal worlds surrounding specific individuals' (Smith 1978: 108). This procedure has the advantage of not being confined to any level of analysis. It also measures the connectedness, centrality, proximity, and range of social interaction (Irving 1977). In application of the technique a distinction is usually drawn between primary relationships (such as those involving kinsfolk and friends) and the more purposive secondary relationships, including those within voluntary associations (*expressive interaction*) and those associated with work, trade unions, political parties, and pressure groups (*instrumental interaction*) (Irving and Davidson 1973).

Of particular interest in neighbourhood studies is the role of distance and space in stimulating or retarding social interaction (Irving 1975; Smith and Smith 1978). Early work suggested that friendship patterns within housing projects appear to be governed by 'the mere physical arrangement of the houses' (Festinger, Schacter and Bach 1950: 10) but more recent research has shown that propinquity can initiate friendship and maintain less intense relationships but is not a sufficient basis of itself for creating intense or deeper relationships (Darke and Darke 1969). Likewise, length of residence is an important factor in increasing the circle of acquaintanceship, if not the intensity of relationship (Lipman and Russell-Lacy 1974). In addition, certain stages in the life cycle are marked by an increase in dependence upon the local community for social interaction (Carey and Mapes 1971). For example, propinquity is crucial for the development of social relationships among mothers with young children (Tivers 1977; Pred and Palm 1978) and among the elderly (Allon-Smith 1978). For more mobile sections of society a mixture of social distance and communality of values are probably the overriding determinants of friendship formation (Gans 1962a). Certainly evidence for this is to be seen in the highly localized 'urban village' social relationships of the working classes in western cities (Gans 1962b; Connell 1973). Of course, such 'villages' reflect not only limited spatial mobility but also the continuing significance of the extended family in working class social life (Young and Willmott 1962). There are therefore predictable differences between various sections of working class communities. For instance, among the diverse residents of the St Paul's district of Bristol, Richmond (1973) found that the Asians and the West Indians had greater levels of 'local' interaction than the Irish and the native population. Obviously, 'defensive' and 'cultural' forces contributed to this greater degree of localization in social relationships.

In contrast a number of early studies of the middle classes suggested that their 'local' friendship networks were more loosely knit since their greater social skills, greater diversity of interests, and greater social mobility resulted in their maintaining relationships over wider spatial areas (Lynd and Lynd 1956; Stein 1960). Subsequent investigation, however, has shown the need to revise this view since it has become clear that, even though lacking the feelings of mutuality of inner city residents, suburbanites are also involved in high levels of social interaction (Willmott and Young 1960; Gans 1967; Everitt 1976; Herbert and Emmison 1977). In particular in American suburbs Muller (1976) has suggested that social cohesion results from two complementary trends: first, constrained by income and life cycle, suburbs emerge that are based on life style; and second, a tendency to withdraw into a 'defended' enclave is sometimes apparent. Although these trends are less significant in European suburbs where housing is more diverse, social cohension is often as intense as in American suburbs, thus suggesting the operation of forces which characterize all suburbanites: their homogeneity, their self-selection, their eagerness to make friends, and even their physical isolation from previous social contacts (Fischer 1976).

Class differences in the localization of social contact can only really be uncovered through comparative study. In one such study Athanasiou and Yoshioka (1973) found that most individuals, irrespective of class, tended to have a high proportion of their more intense relationships in the immediate vicinity of their home. Support for this claim was forthcoming from a study of neighbour relations in Leicester, where 69 per cent of the respondents' 'best' friends resided within a half-mile of their home address (Lewis 1981a). Social class, life cycle, and length of residence were not significant discriminating variables in this pattern. However, when less intense relationships (such as knowing, naming, and speaking to neighbours) were analysed it was found that low-income areas around the city centre scored highly whereas the wealthier south-east sector and post-war suburbia scored lowly (Fig. 9.3). This suggests that, contrary to the popular view, the 'close' friendships of the wealthy classes are highly localized and it is their less intense relationships which are widely spaced. This, in turn, lends credence to the argument that suburban relationships are neither more or less superficial than those found in inner city areas (Baldassare and Fischer 1975; Fischer and Jackson 1976). In other words, to dichotomize urban residents into *localites* with restricted 'urban realms' and *cosmopolites* for whom distance is elastic is much too simplified and naïve. A great amount of research in different neighbourhoods will in fact be required before it will be possible to 'write the equation which specifies the probability that A and B are friends based on the distance between A and B and similarity of A and B' (Athanasiou and Yoshioka 1973: 63).

The considerable degree of localization of social activities which exists within cities might be expected to yield some agreement in the identification of the extent of neighbourhoods (Knowles 1972; Winters 1979). A major contribution on this theme was the Royal Commission on Local Government in England's (1969) survey of what 2,000 residents thought was the most appropriate size for local government units. Over 80 per cent of the respondents claimed to possess some feelings of attachment to a 'home' community area, and this tended to increase with length of residence. Several other studies have also revealed considerable agreement in the extent of 'perceived' neighbourhoods (see Maurer and Baxter 1972; Haney and Knowles 1978). For example, Eyles (1968) confirmed the significance of home, location, and physical landmarks in the determination of the 'perceived' Highgate village, whilst Herbert (1975) emphasized the compactness of working-class neighbourhoods in Adamsdown, Cardiff (Fig. 9.4). However, in a study of the working-class terraced housing district of Selly Oak, Birmingham, Spencer (1973) argued that the size of the neighbourhood varied according to the method employed in its delimitation. Notably, the graphic method produced much larger 'neighbourhood' maps than the verbal since respondents tended to draw a boundary around an area which often included housing

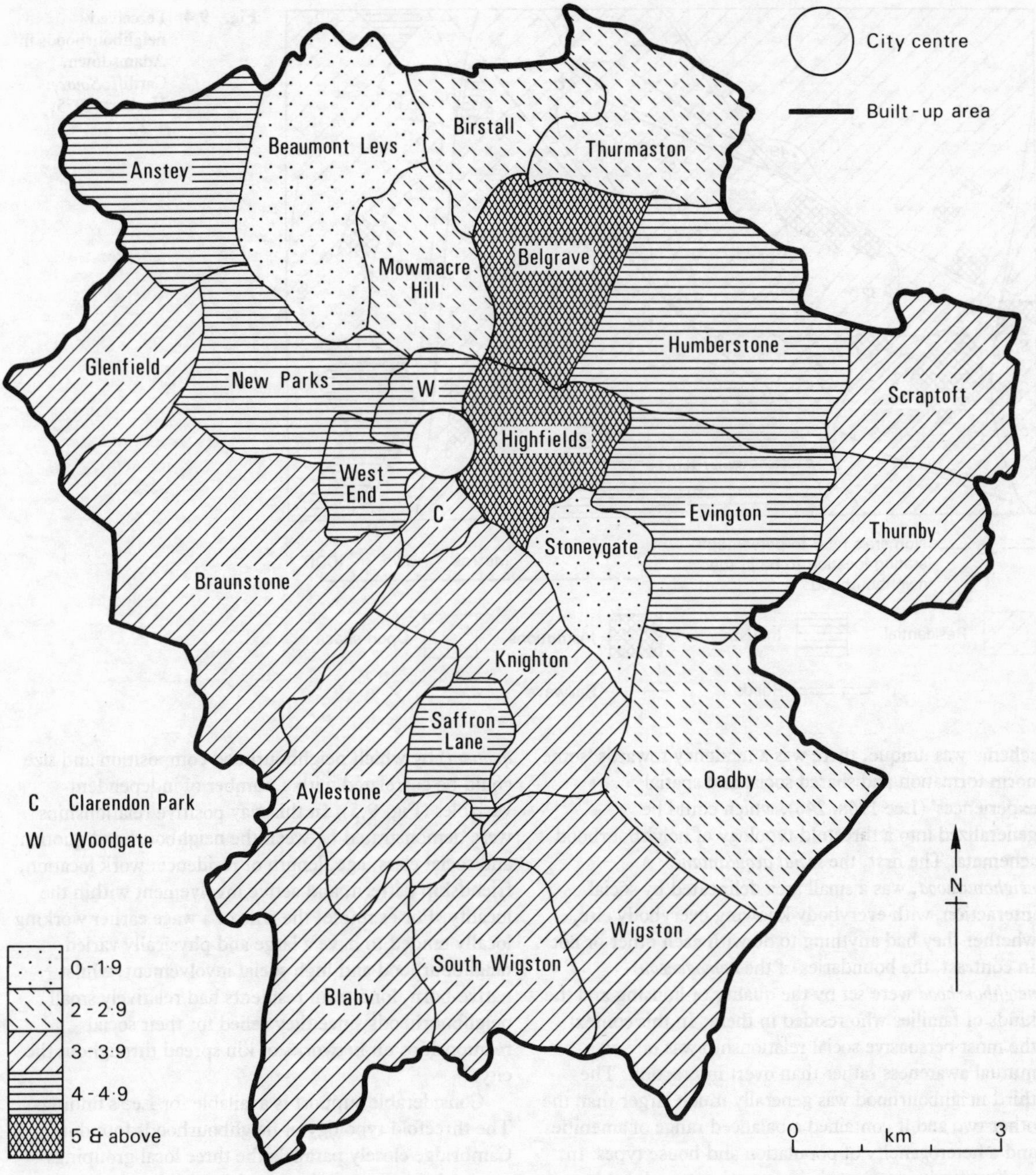

Fig. 9.3 Local intimacy scores in Leicester. *Source*: Lewis (1981a, 46).

and shops which had little significance to them. Only when the right questions were asked did respondents delimit neighbourhoods with the size and form that reflected spatial behaviour. This variability serves to emphasize the fact that an individual's own conception of his neighbourhood may be very different from what is officially designated as a neighbourhood (Lee 1976).

One of the pioneering studies of the difference between 'perceived' and 'real' neighbourhoods is to be found in Lee's (1968) examination of how 219 middle-class Cambridge housewives mapped the extent of their neighbourhood and recorded details of friendship, club membership, and shopping activity in the immediate locality. Although each 'socio-spatial'

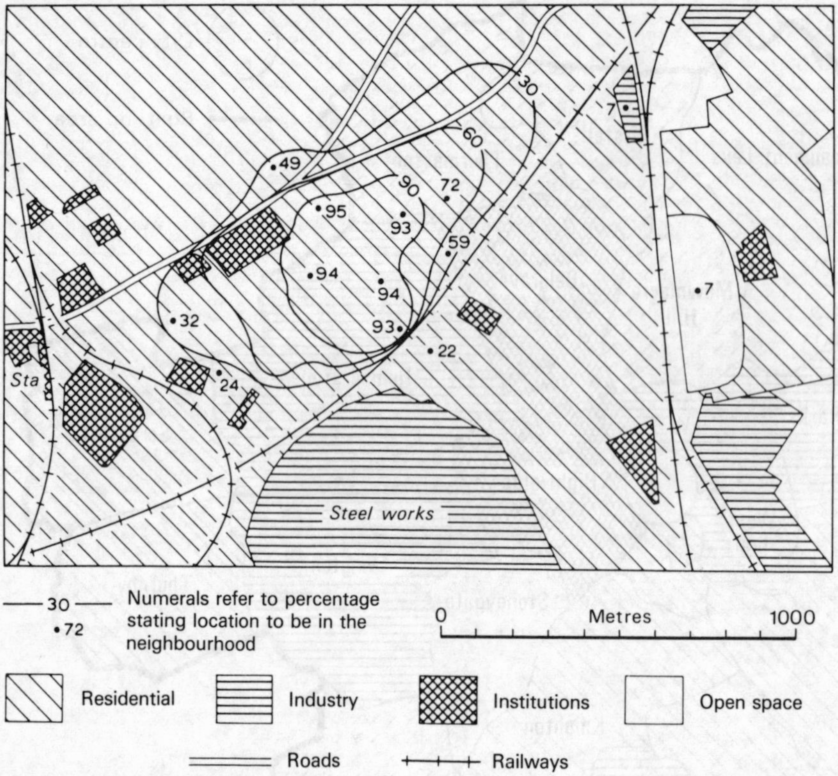

Fig. 9.4 Perceived neighbourhoods in Adamsdown, Cardiff. *Source*: Herbert (1975, 472).

schema was unique, there was a tendency towards 'some norm formation and shared social and spatial experiences' (Lee 1968: 246), which could be generalized into a threefold typology of neighbourhood schemata. The first, the *social acquaintance neighbourhood*, was a small area delineated by social interaction, with everybody knowing everybody else, whether they had anything to do with each other or not. In contrast, the boundaries of the *homogeneous neighbourhood* were set by the quality of housing and the kinds of families who resided in them. In this context the most persuasive social relationship was one of mutual awareness rather than overt interaction. The third neighbourhood was generally much larger than the other two and it contained a balanced range of amenities and a heterogeneity of population and house types. In many ways it corresponded most closely to the planner's conception of a neighbourhood and hence was termed the *unit neighbourhood*.

On the basis of the Cambridge maps Lee developed the argument that a neighbourhood is an amalgam of physical and social factors. By expressing the content (number of houses, shops, and amenity buildings) of neighbourhood maps relative to the content of a locality of half-mile radius from the respondent's house, it was possible to devise a measure (termed a *neighbourhood quotient*) by which neighbourhood composition and size could be correlated with a number of independent variables (Fig. 9.5). In this way positive relationships were demonstrated between the neighbourhood quotient and social class, age, length of residence, work location, friendship pattern, and active involvement within the locality. For example, the wife of a wage earner working locally tended to have a large and physically varied neighbourhood and high social involvement, whilst native-born, long-term residents had relatively small neighbourhoods since they relied for their social relationships on networks of kin spread throughout the city.

Considerable support is available for Lee's findings. The threefold typology of neighbourhoods found in Cambridge closely parallels the three local groupings – patriarchal, domestic, and parish echelons – distinguished by Bardet (1961) in a previous study of sixty rural and urban places in Europe and Africa. Similarly, Golledge and Zannaras (1973: 85) concluded their study of suburban neighbourhoods in Columbus, Ohio with the observation that physical and social space overlap so much 'that the two are very closely linked in the mind of the urban dweller'. Again class, length of residence, club membership, local friendships and shopping activities were the major factors which

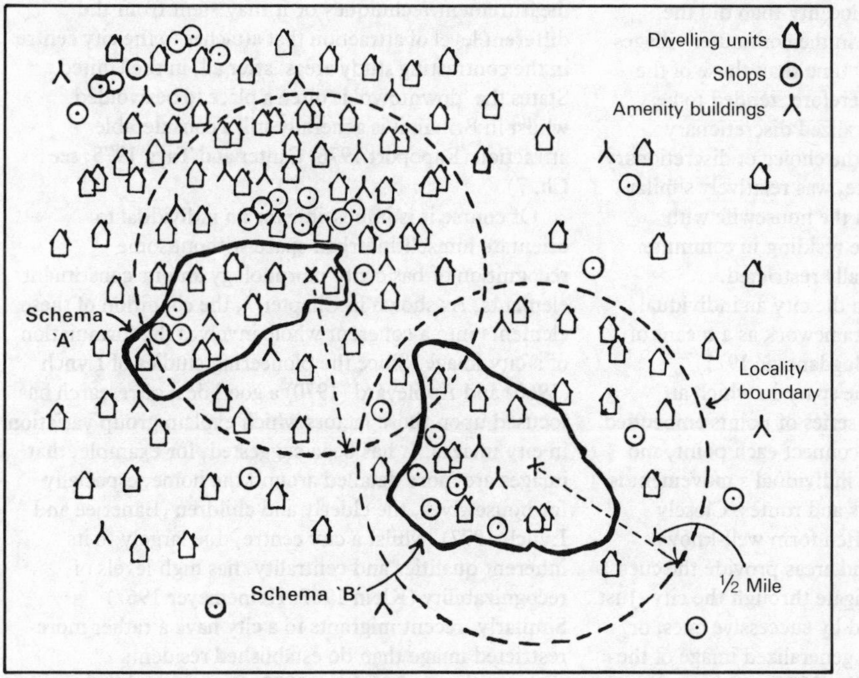

Fig. 9.5 The neighbourhood quotient. Schema 'A' illustrates an average Nh. Q. subject from a high density locality and 'B' a high Nh.Q. subject from a low density locality. *Source*: Lee (1968, 257).

differentiated those with large neighbourhoods from those with small. Everitt (1976) has also revealed a broad congruence between the perceived home area of a sample of residents in Los Angeles and their movements to work-place, friends' residences, and clubs and, in an interesting reanalysis of the Royal Commission data, Berry and Kasarda (1977) reaffirmed that community sentiment, including neighbourhood perception, is influenced by the degree of local participation, and length of residence. Even when such factors as population size, density, socio-economic status, and life cycle were held constant, this relationship held true. In short, activity patterns help to determine the extent of perceived neighbourhoods, as was clearly demonstrated in Everitt and Cadwallader's (1972; 1977; 1981) examination of how wives had greater 'perceived' neighbourhoods than husbands on account of greater local involvement.

Beyond the locality

In a recent survey in Leicester it was found that an average urban resident spends nearly 85 per cent of his time at home or in the local neighbourhood. Despite this localization of individual activity systems, most urban residents are also involved in a whole series of activities beyond the locality. Some of these activities are obligatory, others discretionary. Many are routine (Hägerstrand 1970). With the growth of interest in leisure activities and the quality of life in general, the way in which time has acted as a constraint on non-local activities within activity systems has become a focus of interest (Szalai 1966; Chapin 1965). What has been revealed is that the most time-consuming activity beyond the home is, predictably, work. For example, from a sample of nearly 1,500 respondents in over forty United States metropolitan cities, Chapin and Brail (1969) found that only about 5 hours of a typical adult's day were available for discretionary activity. Of this 80 per cent was usually spent at home (although this proportion increased for the retired, the unemployed, and those in the child-rearing stage of the life cycle). The most significant predictors of activity patterns were in fact sex, socio-economic status (income and education), and stage in the life cycle (age and household size). More recently these ideas have been taken a stage further by conceiving of an individual's activity system within a time–space framework (Thrift 1977; Carlstein, Parkes and Thrift 1978b; Parkes and Thrift 1980) (see Ch. 7). For example, an analysis of a sample of residents in Leicester's inner and suburban neighbourhoods, as well as the surrounding commuter villages, found that space played a significant role in determining the time allocation of activities. Not only did those on low income have less discretionary time at their disposal than did high-income residents, but also the former spent a greater part of their time between 7 a.m. and 11 p.m. within their locality than did the latter. Likewise those residing in the commuter villages had less available discretionary time than those of the suburbs and inner city and, therefore, tended to be involved in fewer and more localized discretionary activities. On the other hand, the choice of discretionary *activities*, irrespective of income, was relatively similar for the elderly, the young, and the housewife with young children, although those residing in commuter villages were particularly spatially restricted.

In his daily activities within the city an individual obviously uses some guiding framework as a means of moving from point-to-point (Bogdanovic 1975). According to Kaplan (1973) the space in which an individual moves consists of a series of points embedded in a network of routes, which connect each point, and pass through other points. An individual's movement is therefore determined by points and routes. Closely associated points and routes often form well-known areas. These routes, points, and areas provide the cues which help the individual navigate through the city. Just whether individuals are guided by successive cues, or whether individuals develop a generalized image of the environment, is unclear (see Clay 1973).

Both the established urban resident and the first-time visitor need to find their way between origins and destinations in a manner that meets their individual needs. Basically, this involves orientating themselves in relation to points and routes and in terms of perceived direction and distance. Nearly twenty years ago Thompson (1963) found that, within urban areas, both time and distance estimates to retail locations were significantly overestimated, with the greatest exaggeration being towards places not often frequented. Since that date a number of studies have been concerned with what has become known as 'subjective distance', although their general applicability is limited because most have involved student samples (Cadwallader 1976). Also there exists a degree of disquiet as to the extent to which an individual's cognition of distance is independent of the technique or unit of measurement used to obtain the estimate (Cadwallader 1973; 1979; Day 1976; see Ch. 7). Some studies, for example, have requested subjects to estimate route distance (Lee 1970), others straightline distances (Lowrey 1973), and some shortest travel distance (Briggs 1973b). Despite these difficulties a number of generalizations can be made to the extent that 'subjective' distance is invariably overestimated relative to 'objective' distance. In addition 'downtown' distances have been found to be exaggerated relative to 'uptown' distances in North American cities (Golledge, Briggs, and Demko 1969; Briggs 1973a). In Britain the opposite has been found to be the case (Lee 1962). This anomaly may result from various measurement techniques or it may stem from the different level of attraction that attaches to the city centre in the contrasting study areas: after all, in the United States the 'downtown' is often a place to be avoided whilst in Britain it is generally still a considerable attraction (Rapoport 1976; Canter and Tagg 1975; see Ch. 7).

Of course it is impossible for an individual to orientate himself in urban space without some recognition of basic city morphology and its constituent elements. As shown in Chapter 7, the cognition of these elements into a coherent whole involves the formulation of a city image. Since the pioneering studies of Lynch (1960) and Appleyard (1970) a good deal of research has focused upon those factors which explain group variation in city images. It has been suggested, for example, that images are more detailed around the home, especially for housewives, the elderly and children (Banerjee and Lynch 1977), whilst a city centre, due largely to its inherent qualities and centrality, has high levels of recognizability (Klein 1967; Heinemeyer 1967) Similarly, recent migrants to a city have a rather more restricted image than do established residents (Francescato and Mebane 1973; Spencer and Weetman 1981). It has also been demonstrated that the image of wealthy city residents may be several times more extensive than that of the residents of poor neighbourhoods (Budd 1979). Perhaps this simply means that the middle classes are able to conceptualize the city in a coherent and more concise manner than the working classes (Murray and Spencer 1979). After all, Lowenthal (1972b) and Lowenthal and Riel (1972b) have found class differences in urban images in several American cities; for example, the middle classes seem more inclined to attach significance to landmarks of historic interest, whilst the working classes are more concerned with places of work, shopping, and recreation.

Despite these class variations in urban images, it must not be forgotten that perception and memory of the city seem to be determined to a large extent by the form of the environment itself (Carr and Schissler 1969: 33). There is, after all, a considerable amount of research which provides evidence that the physical layout of the city is of utmost significance in determining the nature of an individual's image. For example, De Jonge (1962), in a comparative study of Dutch cities, showed that image formation was easiest, irrespective of the characteristics of the individual respondent, in cities with a regular street pattern, a dominant path, unique landmarks, and easily recognizable nodes. Of course it would be wrong of researchers to devote too much attetntion to the morphology of images. A much more worthy focus of attention is the degree of congruence between an individual's activity space and his image of the city. Lee's (1968) neighbourhood schemata revealed an element of congruence within the context of the home range. Beyond the local area, Milgram (1970) has stated explicitly that a relationship also exists; for example, the housewife with young children (who travels very little) is more familiar with the neighbourhood, but less familiar with the city as a whole, than her husband (who travels daily). The precise nature of the interaction between activity systems and images remains, however, a topic that has not attracted the attention it deserves.

Chapter 10

INDUSTRIAL LOCATION

Location theory has traditionally been the cornerstone of geography's respectability as a social science in so far as its nomothetic emphasis stood out for many years in stark contrast to the rest of an essentially descriptive discipline. Predictably, models of location have taken many forms that vary from the least transport cost solution advocated by Weber (1929) and subsequently elaborated upon by Hoover (1937), to the market area models of Lösch (1954), the locational interdependence emphasis of Hotelling (1929), and a number of linear programming techniques (see Cooper 1975). In essence all these models are normative and draw on the neoclassical micro-economic theory of the firm (Pocock and Hudson 1978: 11). Indeed, Moses (1958) and Smith (1971) did much to integrate location theory with marginalist economics.

Central to all these economic models has been the notion of profit maximization: to Weber maximum profit could be equated with minimum cost while to Hotelling and Lösch maximum profit equalled maximum sales. However, a major problem in applying the models occurs whenever an attempt is made to transpose the theoretical ideal of profit maximization to some real world profit function. This is because some firms do not appear to attempt to maximize (see Wolpert 1964) while others consider non-economic factors such as technological supremacy (see Thomas 1980) and, in any case, make mistakes (Webber 1969). In other words there is a great gulf between the theoretical ideal of location models and the variety of real world conditions. Location theory models, for instance, tend to overlook a number of major developments that characterize the present-day world economy: the adoption of mass production and the consequent expansion in the scale of plant; the increase in the capitalization of industry; the great growth in the size of firms; the evolution of multi-plant, multi-functional and often multi-national corporations; the agglomeration of industry in major city systems; inflation; technological advance; and international trading agreements (Hamilton 1974; 1978). Additionally, traditional models make the unreal assumption that spatial behaviour can be differentiated from general economic behaviour. Coupled with this disquiet about the lack of reality of traditional location theory has been a concern with whether or not the theory is internally consistent and with the fundamental epistemological problem of whether human behaviour can be reduced to the form of an abstract model (Massey 1979). It is not surprising therefore that calls have been made for a new form of location theory that emphasizes real behaviour, decision-making, and the organization of business enterprises (Hamilton 1974).

Behavioural approaches

One of the earliest and most cogent criticisms of normative location theory came from Pred (1967) who disputed the logical consistency of the assumptions involved in traditional formulations, questioned the motives of optimizing behaviour, and rejected the knowledge levels and mental acumen attributed to economic man. In particular, Pred argued that the concept of rational economic man ignores satisficing behaviour and non-economic considerations. He also demonstrated that the requirement that firms outguess competitors but not be outguessed is unworkable under conditions of imperfect competition because, under such conditions, what is optimal for one firm depends on the actions of other firms. Likewise, other writers have suggested that, instead of maximizing profits, firms may tend to minimize uncertainty by repeating previous behaviour, by locating in areas with which they are familiar, and by imitating the behaviour of competitors (Lloyd and Dicken 1972: 157). All this implies that firms should be viewed as organizations existing in, and adapting to, economic and socio-political environments from which they derive information (Gold 1980: 219–20). Thus in Pred's view every decision-making unit concerned with economic activity can be placed conceptually within a *behavioural matrix*, the axes of which measure the quality and quantity of information available to the decision-maker and that decision-maker's ability to handle information. Within such a matrix, traditional economic rationality represents but one out of a wide range of positions (see Fig. 6.4).

Of course not all authorities subscribe to the view that a new behavioural location theory is needed. Some support modifications of the classical approach. For example, Webber (1971; 1972) has argued that much criticism of location theory is unfairly harsh because traditional formulations like central place theory have never been tested empirically in that no attempt has ever been made to control the environmental assumptions of the theory. Similarly, Dicken (1977) has pointed out that least-cost location is still important for large multi-plant business enterprises, albeit on a much enlarged geographical and organizational scale. In a somewhat different vein, Smith (1979a: 54) has suggested that a proper perspective on industrial location requires 'a broad view of the production process that stresses the satisfaction of human needs in a broad societal context and recognizes the distribution of those things on which human well-being or ill-being depends'. Despite such initiatives it remains true that traditional approaches ignore the way firms interact with their uncertain environment, overlook considerations of information availability, and neglect the fact that organizational goals are many and varied (Keeble 1976: 3). Indeed, in the view of Townroe (1975: 33), the neoclassical value tradition in economics, on which much location theory is based, has afforded researchers 'with opportunities for both increasing abstraction and mathematical elegance as well as for increasing irrelevance and a widening gulf between theoretical reasoning and empirical progress'. To Townroe, the alternatives to traditional theory appear to lie in the use of operational research techniques that rely on optimizing procedures like linear programming, a managerial approach that emphasizes organizational structure and good management practice, and a behavioural approach that highlights the theory of the firm, information processing, decision-making, and perception. The last two of these alternatives have attracted the greatest attention, no doubt reflecting the fact that the majority of industrial location decisions are both planned and non-optimal (Stafford 1972: 205). However, for the most part empirical investigations of real world decisions have taken place after the event and have been structured around standard economic variables. Only recently has attention turned to the simulation of location decisions (see Hart 1980) and to in-depth interviews designed to uncover decision processes (Stafford 1972).

The plea for 'a geography of enterprises' and an emphasis on the power relations between large and small firms (Taylor and Thrift 1979) as an alternative to traditional industrial location theory draws from much earlier economic work on the theory of the firm (see Cyert and March 1963) and non-optimal behaviour (see Simon 1957; Katona 1975). In fact, by the time that geographers turned to location theory in the 1950s, economists were already arguing for a more behavioural approach (Pocock and Hudson 1978: 11). To geographers the behavioural approach offers a number of attractions: it is more flexible than the traditional approach and it is process-oriented (Leigh and North 1975); it considers both explicit spatial behaviour (e.g. opening a new plant) and implicit spatial behaviour (e.g. altering the scale of existing plant) (Hamilton 1978); it is dynamic and holistic and focuses on organizational adaptation to different environments (Wood 1975); and it highlights the importance of risk and uncertainty, internally generated constraints on growth and performance, information availability, and images and perception. As against this a behavioural approach to the study of industrial location poses important sampling problems in relation to obtaining representative data and runs the risk of substituting description for explanation (Leigh and North 1975). More fundamentally, the behavioural approach still holds to the view that highly complex human behaviour can be represented by an abstract model at the level of the individual decision-maker (Massey 1975a). Despite these problems, the behavioural approach dominates new work in industrial geography (Martin 1981).

Organization theory

Within the behavioural approach, organization theory appears to offer a means of understanding non-normative decision-making and learning by firms (Britton 1974). This is because organization theory focuses attention on the very issues that classical location theory has failed to accommodate: the persistent growth of large corporations; imperfect competition, monopoly, and oligopoly; the fact that corporate strategy reacts to things other than the external environment; and the fact that much economic behaviour is non-spatial (Hamilton 1978). In this sense a focus on organizations draws attention to the power and dependence relations *within* as well as *between* firms (Fredriksson and Lindmark 1979) and therefore goes some way to answering the pleas of those writers who have argued that a full understanding of industrial location can only be achieved if attention is paid to the structure of the political economy within which firms operate (Massey 1975a; 1979). What is required, then, from an organizational perspective is 'analysis of the evolution, structure, adjustment and goals of organizations engaged in industrial activities to establish how these elements affect perception of the spatial variable in location decisions of any kind and how that spatial dimension has a feedback effect upon organizational structures and their functioning' (Hamilton 1978: 12). In the eyes of many, this end is best achieved through the adoption of a systems theory framework (Hamilton and Linge 1979) because such a framework enables a number of important questions to be asked about organizational behaviour: How and why did the system emerge? Why did it grow more in some directions than in others? What holds it together? And what tension and conflict is there within the system? (McNee 1974: 49.)

An organization, viewed as a system, can be examined from the three perspectives of *structure* (based on information processing and decision-making), *function* (the response to environmental conditions), and *evolution* (McNee 1974). These perspectives correspond to Rapoport's (1968) systems concepts of 'being', 'acting', and 'becoming'. The fruitfulness of this systems

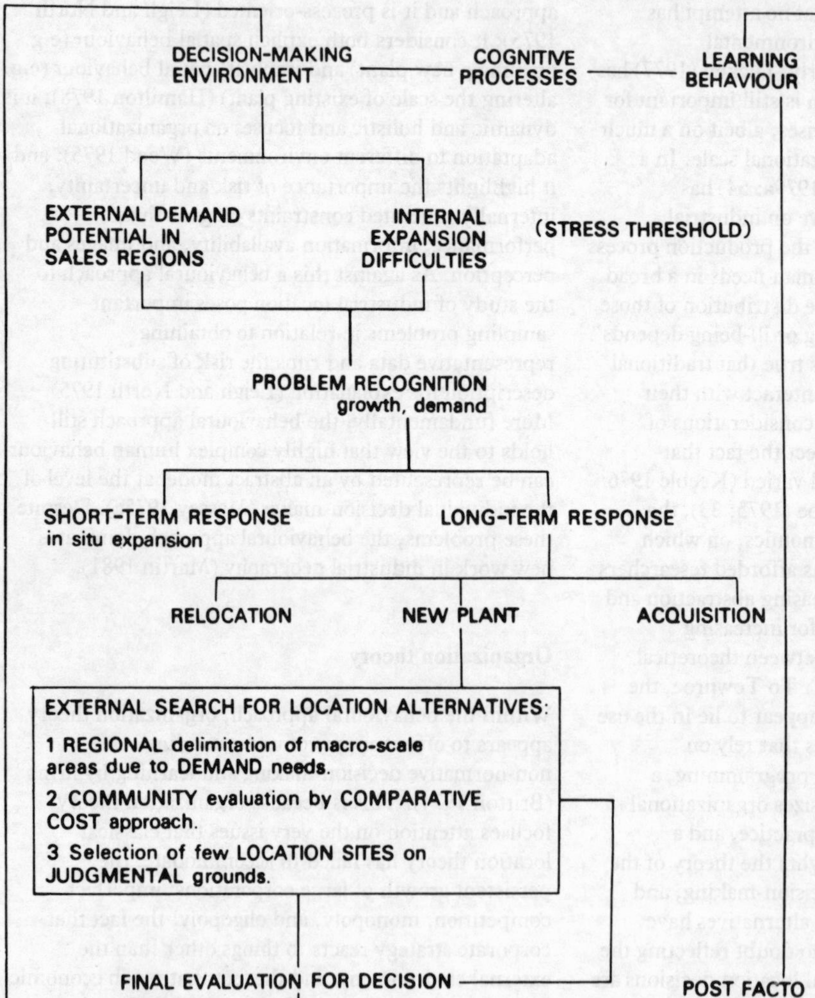

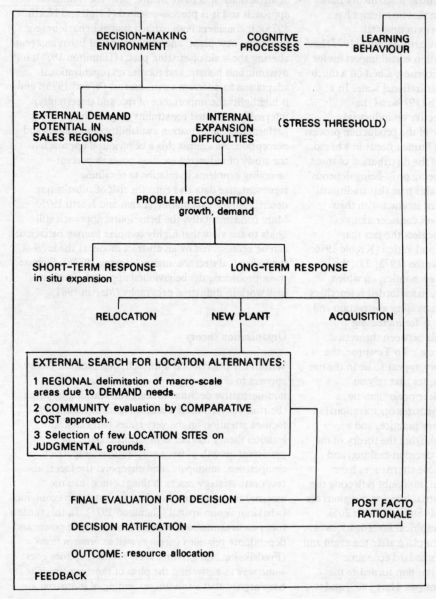

Fig. 10.1 A model of industrial location decision-making. *Source*: Rees (1974, 191).

framework has been demonstrated both in relation to hypothetical organizations like 'International Gismo, Inc.' (McNee 1974) and in relation to the harshly real world of the British plastics industry (North 1974). The latter study showed how locational decisions range across *in situ* expansion, complete transfer, the establishment of branches, acquisition or take-over, and even closure, thereby corroborating a behavioural pattern that has been found elsewhere (Fig. 10.1) (see Rees 1974). The study also showed how the type of decision made tends to reflect the stresses impinging on the organization: for example, unplanned growth tends to lead to relocation, planned growth to the opening of branches, and diversification to acquisition and take-over.

A major influence on what type of locational decision a firm takes in response to stress is the type of linkage that the firm has with other firms within its environment. Basically such linkages reflect economic considerations such as the type of product, the size of the production centre, the size of the market, the distance between producers and consumers, variations in pricing strategies, ownership ties, and the availability of local external economies (M. J. Taylor 1973). However, often overriding these monetary considerations are the behavioural benefits to be gained from the agglomeration of production units, notably the reduction in risk and uncertainty (Taylor 1978a). Likewise, the growth of the firm, the share of the market, the diversification of interests, entrepreneurial satisfaction, and perhaps even simple survival are behavioural considerations that may weigh just as heavily in decision-makers' minds as more conventional economic considerations. Indeed, locational decisions may be just as much a response to short-term stress as a part of a long-term economic plan (Hamilton 1974). Growth is, after all, both a way of achieving a further utilization of resources and a way of reducing uncertainty and mitigating the managerial, financial, and locational restraints that influence a firm's behaviour (Håkanson 1979). As a result, an organization theory perspective on industrial location needs to consider the organizational forms which shape the perception, images and actions of decision-makers, and the interpretation of organizational goals and functions by key individuals within the firm's management structure (Hamilton 1978: 13).

Decision processes

Rees (1974) has suggested that the process by which firms arrive at locational decisions can be reduced to a number of generalizations. For example, it seems that a firm's first action in accommodating stress at a particular location is to consider *in situ* adjustment. If a move is inevitable, alternatives are narrowed down by a cost analysis of specific sites, although the final decision usually combines both economic and intangible considerations. In this context a decision to set up a new plant is invariably a long-term investment solution to corporate growth and planning problems. Predictably, such decisions are more common in large organizations than in small ones. Of course, in addition to moving, firms can reduce the uncertainty and stress of their current situation by repeating past behaviour or by imitating competitors. Not all researchers agree, however, that behaviour can be simplified to such rational terms. Stafford (1972: 210–1), for example, has argued that decision-makers within business enterprises very rapidly and very drastically transform the infinite complexity of the optimal location problem to simple, intellectually manageable proportions by not indulging in difficult modes of analysis and, whenever possible, by avoiding arduous negotiation with groups such as unions and governmental regulatory agencies. Stafford has in fact suggested that the techniques used and the location principles applied in locational decision-making vary with the stage of locational choice from a simple emphasis on economies of scale through to the maximization of 'psychic' income (Table 10.1). A

Table 10.1 Location principles

Stage		*Appropriate techniques (*most commonly used)*	*Location principle*
I	In situ expansion	—	Economies of scale
II	Delimitation of region for location of new production facility	Regional demand projections*; regional and inter-regional input-output tables; linear programming	Maximum demand
III	Selection of finite number of feasible sites	Comparative costs*; linear programming; extrapolation from past experience*	Least cost
IV	Final site selection	Comparative costs; judgmental integration of data and attitudes*	Maximize 'psychic' income; minimize 'difficulties' (e.g. unions, governmental regulatory agencies, etc.)

Source: Stafford (1972, 212).

similar observation that decision-makers are aware of neither the full extent of the relevant information field nor the applicability of criteria for choice has been made by Townroe (1974) who concluded that, although large investments tend towards economic rationality, most firms choose a feasible rather than the optimal alternative out of the choices with which they are confronted. Knowledge and perception of the environment does not seem to be influenced, however, by the size of a firm (Barr and Fairbairn 1978), possibly because small firms can get to know their limited environments very well while big firms can often internalize much of their environment (e.g. having their own research and transport facilities) and thereby reduce uncertainty (Hamilton 1974).

Information flows

Environments change. The goals of firms change. As a result knowledge of the environment can never be complete and comprehensive. New information continually becomes available. Information flows, and communication generally, are in fact central to modern economies (McDaniel 1975). Törnqvist (1977), for example, has suggested that the present-day economy comprises three communications planes: first, the transport of goods; second, face-to-face communications; and third, telecommunications. The current prominence of the second and third communications planes diminishes the utility of classical location theory and highlights the need for an understanding of information sources and information flows in relation to the location of economic activity.

There are a number of reasons why information is an important consideration in locational decision-making: it is costly to obtain; it is costly to transfer both within and between firms, primarily because its transference requires highly skilled (and therefore highly paid) contact-intensive employees; and it is spatially biased in the sense that there occur locational variations in its availability. In addition, information circulation patterns and organizational locational patterns interact with each other, and feed back upon one another, to influence the nature of urban and economic growth through the creation of non-local multipliers in economic activity and the determination of diffusion paths for growth-inducing innovations (Pred 1973a). As a result, information is important not only in relation to *explicit locational decisions* regarding the setting up of new plant but also in relation to the sort of *implicit locational decisions* that are exemplified by such routine tasks as re-ordering materials when stocks are low. However, it is in relation to explicit decisions that the importance of information is most evident because place-to-place variations in the availability and accessibility of information are increasingly considered as a critical factor of location for administrative headquarters, banks, financial institutions, consultants, and data processing centres (Pred 1977a: 24).

Törnqvist (1968) was one of the first geographers to stress the importance of information when he drew attention to the significance of contacts between expert personnel in general problem-solving, planning, and reconnaissance. To Törnqvist, many business organizations can be differentiated into operating units (e.g. manufacturing plant) and administrative units (e.g. offices) with the latter being responsible for both routine and non-routine decisions. A somewhat more detailed classification of the work of such administrative units was provided by Thorngren (1970; 1973) who argued that all organizations operate in a knowledge environment and a values environment and that they come to terms with each of these environments by considering three time horizons:

1. *Orientation activities* deal with the furthest time horizon, focus on things like changing ideologies and possible scientific advances, and usually involve face-to-face, prearranged meetings between key personnel. (Class 1 in Fig. 10.2).
2. *Planning activities* are concerned with a medium term time span, and involve middle management in relatively frequent contact (often by telecommunication) in regard to such matters as potential technological innovations, administration, production, and sales. (Class 3).
3. *Programming activities* centre around the most immediate time-span and encompass largely routine tasks concerned with the day-to-day running of business organizations (see Frey 1981). (Class 2).

Empirical support for this threefold classification has come from Goddard's (1978) study of the external contacts of employees in a sample of central London offices (Fig. 10.2). Clearly, then, information processing is fundamental to the functioning and survival of business organizations. Moreover, the conceptualization of information, employed by Thorngren, Törnqvist and others, adopts an open systems perspective (whereby there is a continuous input of new information) rather than the closed system perspective of classical location theory. It is important therefore that research focus on how information is handled and specifically on how the environment is perceived, on how information is learned and evaluated, and on the nature of the resultant image.

Unfortunately very few studies have enquired into how organizations perceive their environment, no doubt

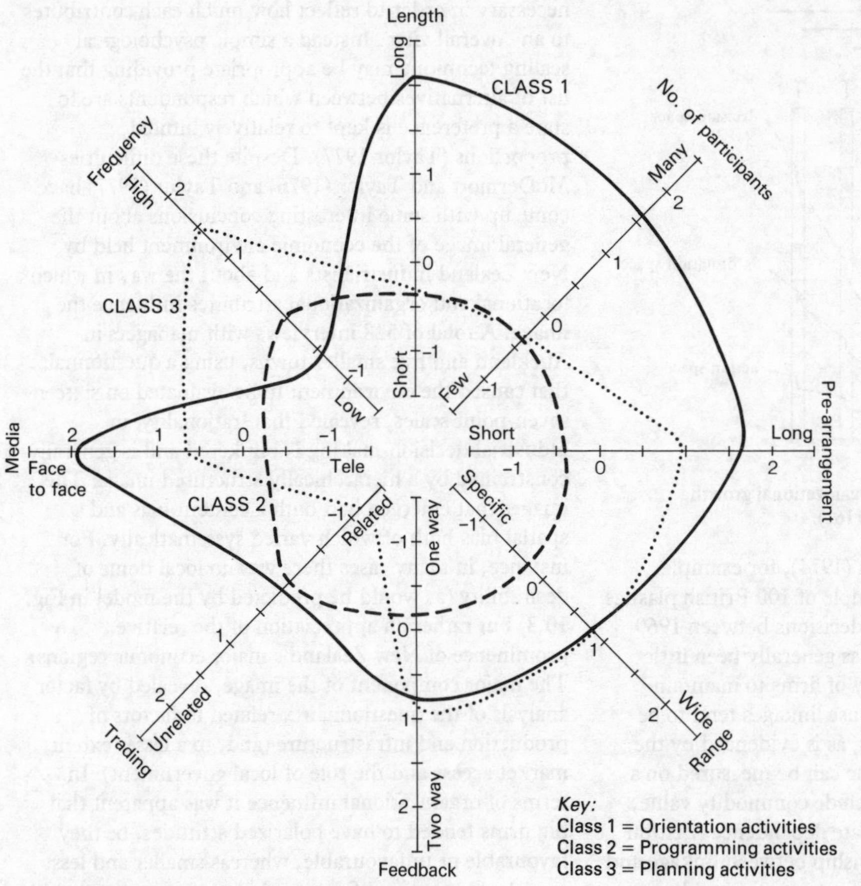

Fig. 10.2 External contacts of central London offices. *Source*: Goddard (1978, 79).

because of the enormous methodological problems encountered in trying to assess whose opinions within an organization are the ones to be noted. One exception is Taylor's (1978b) study of Auckland manufacturers which showed that the use of behavioural, non-Euclidean space, based on the 'hierarchic' distance between the major functional economic regions of New Zealand, provides a better prediction of Auckland manufacturers' sales linkages than do models based on either a cost-distance or a Euclidean metric. To give a simple example, Taylor's study shows that, from a behavioural point of view, Christchurch is nearer to Auckland than is the geographically closer city of Wellington.

The behavioural impact of a firm's linkages with its environment, and therefore with other firms, has been used as the basis for a model of locational decision-making (Taylor 1975). This model, derived from a study of the British West Midlands, suggests that *industrial linkages* define the geographical context within which a firm operates and thus the area within which locational decisions are made. Specifically, an *action space* can be identified on the basis of the firm's material (i.e. input and output) linkages, an *information space* can be defined in terms of the flows of information which the firm receives from sources within its environment, and a *decision space* can be specified such that it reflects the information evaluated by the firm as a basis for action. These three conceptual spaces are nested within each other in the manner described in Fig. 10.3. Each of the spaces expands over time as a result of organizational growth. Such expansion is often discontinuous as a result of organizational metamorphosis causing performance thresholds to be passed. Clearly the model implies that locational decision-making can be interpreted in the same way as general investment decision-making to the extent that both are determined by the pattern of linkages. In this sense the model complements earlier descriptions of location decisions that emphasized dissatisfaction with current performance as a basis for action, and stress reduction as a motive in the search for alternative locations (see Dicken 1971), in that it highlights ongoing environmental interaction and the importance of local scale linkages in search procedures.

The sort of explicit location decisions to which Taylor's model is relevant may be quite common events

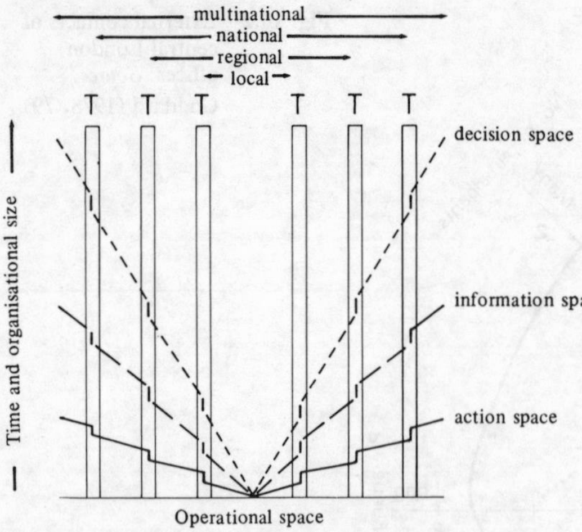

Fig. 10.3 Spatial learning and organizational growth.
Source: Taylor (1977, 1161).

in advanced economies. North (1974), for example, found that 70 per cent of a sample of 100 British plastics firms made explicit locational decisions between 1960 and 1971. Despite this there has generally been little consideration of the propensity of firms to maintain linkages. This is possibly because linkages tend to be complex and difficult to assess, as is evidenced by the fact that material linkages alone can be measured on a number of dimensions that include commodity value, linkage frequency, and corporate dependence (Britton 1978). In addition, the relationship between linkage and information in the decision process remains unclear: after all, despite Taylor's (1975; 1980) model, information flows may precede material linkages, information may be given to a firm rather than sought out by that firm, and linkages may well be a consequence rather than a cause of the decisions that are made (Harrison, Bull, and Hart, 1979).

Perhaps the true significance of information in locational decision-making lies not in its relation to a firm's linkages but in the contribution it makes to the development of a general image of the environment. Such images undoubtedly exist and may even be strongly structured despite the fact that they only partially reflect reality. Certainly this was the case in Taylor and McDermott's (1977) analysis of New Zealand manufacturing and Green's (1977) examination of images and attitudes towards Development Areas in Britain. There are however very great problems in trying to elicit such images from firms. The principal components methodology that works so well in the description of individual preference surfaces (see Gould and White 1974) is not truly applicable to the delimitation of organizational images because it does not really allow for the weighting of responses that is necessary in order to reflect how much each contributes to any overall view. Instead a simple psychological scaling technique may be appropriate providing that the list of alternatives between which respondents are to state a preference is kept to relatively limited proportions (Taylor 1977). Despite these difficulties McDermott and Taylor (1976) and Taylor (1977) have come up with some interesting conclusions about the general image of the economic environment held by New Zealand industrialists and about the way in which locational and organizational attributes influence the image. A total of 528 interviews with managers in Auckland and five smaller towns, using a questionnaire that caused the environment to be evaluated on sixteen seven-point scales, revealed that 'rationality' in industrial decision-making is blinkered and is generally constrained by a hierarchically structured image. The images that emerged had both a content bias and a spatial bias both of which varied systematically. For instance, in many cases there was no local dome of desirability (as would be predicted by the model in Fig. 10.3) but rather an appreciation of the relative prominence of New Zealand's major economic regions. The major component of the image, revealed by factor analysis of the questionnaire, related to factors of production and infrastructure (and, to a lesser extent, market access and the role of local government). In terms of organizational influence it was apparent that big firms tended to have polarized attitudes, be they favourable or unfavourable, whereas smaller and less complexly organized firms tended to have more weakly developed and less extreme opinions. To some extent these organizational influences compounded the locational influences, rendering it difficult to identify the latter. However, it did appear that Auckland managers differed from those in the smaller centres and that Auckland itself was perceived as having marketing and transport advantages while the smaller centres had land and labour cost advantages.

Specialised information and contact surfaces

Information flows are of such importance to modern business enterprises that most organizations set up specific departments to handle information. The departments concerned are invariably offices of one sort or another and, as such, they have come under increasing geographical attention (see Goddard 1973; Alexander 1979). To date, however, most work has looked at headquarters offices or at individual firms in preference to looking at offices within the overall spatial structure of corporate organizations (Goddard 1975a: 11). Yet offices are vitally important in that they represent the base for those contact-intensive employees engaged in information exchange. The location of offices is therefore highly significant, particularly because it is not unusual for 70–80 per cent of office contacts to be within 30 minutes' travel time (Goddard 1975a: 16). Of course, what contact intensive office employees handle is not information in general so much as *specialized information*. The essence of specialized information is that it is private information (see Walmsley 1982b). It is therefore not uniformly available but rather is spatially biased in that it reflects the action space and contact patterns of the firm concerned. Predictably, the greatest number of office-orientated contacts occur in metropolitan areas. Such areas also have advantages, or positive spatial biases, in accessibility to *non-local* specialized information because of their dominance of transport and communications networks (Pred 1973a: 43).

Contact-intensive employees are an important part of the workforce. Not only are they high income earners, and therefore presumably high spenders, but they also tend to attract other personnel and business services (Törnqvist 1978). As a result there have been a number of attempts to measure the information flows, contact patterns, and awareness levels of these employees. For example, Pred (1977a) has looked from an historical perspective at *public information accessibility* and has shown how the spatial information content of newspapers in the United States increased dramatically throughout the early nineteenth century. However, of greater interest is the work done explicitly on specialized information flows, notably in Sweden (see Pred 1973b). Törnqvist (1970), for instance, has stressed the importance of contact-intensive, face-to-face information exchange in post-industrial economies and has noted how the need for such exchanges encourages urbanization and metropolitan growth. In an attempt to illustrate the nature of the interdependence between information flows and city growth, attention was focused on the Swedish *contact landscape* (Törnqvist 1973). Given that there are groups within many business enterprises that are engaged in extensive contact activity, Törnqvist argued that it is possible to depict a contact landscape that assesses the contact potential of a given set of points. Values in the contact surface reflect the balance between the contact possibilities available at a point and the time and cost constraints involved in visiting that point. A sample contact landscape for Sweden in 1970, standardized at a 0–100 scale, is given in Fig. 10.4. Clearly the Stockholm region dominates the contact surface.

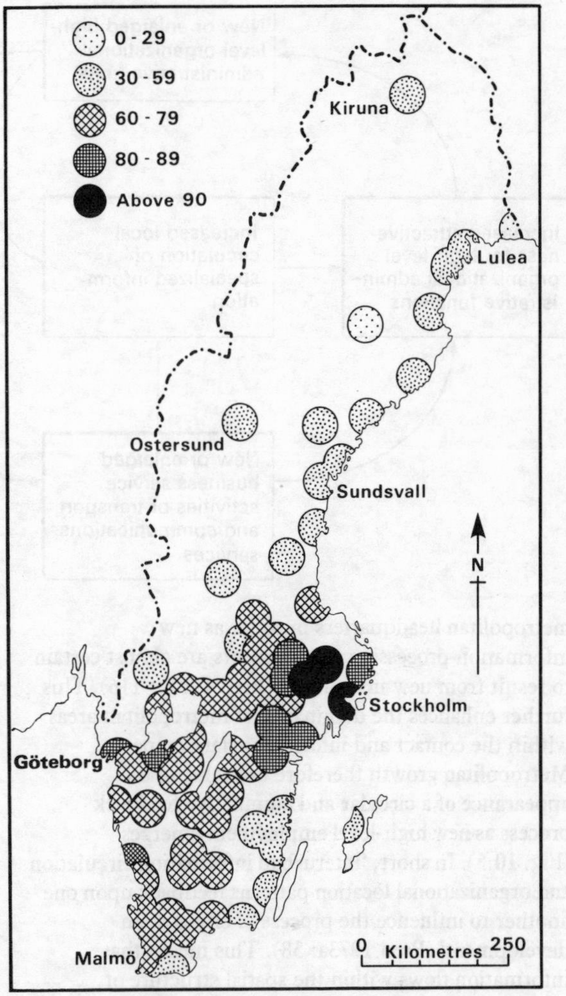

Fig. 10.4 The Swedish contact surface in 1970.
Source: Törnqvist (1973, 97).

The point of reference for contact surfaces is of course the region rather than the firm and their significance lies in their ability to model different transport and mobility constraints at a time when the circulation and availability of specialized information is mounting on account of ongoing structural shifts in the occupational composition of the workforce (Pred 1977a: 25). Of particular importance in this context is the increasing prominence of multilocational organizations, often resulting from mergers, in post-industrial societies (Pred 1977a: 99). This importance derives from the fact that the flow of information between the headquarters of such organizations and their subordinate units has a major impact on the pattern of interdependence that develops between cities. For example, because headquarters are invariably in metropolitan areas, and because these headquarters dominate specialized information flows, then it follows that, regardless of where it occurs within a system of cities, investment by a firm is likely to cause a multiplier effect at the firm's

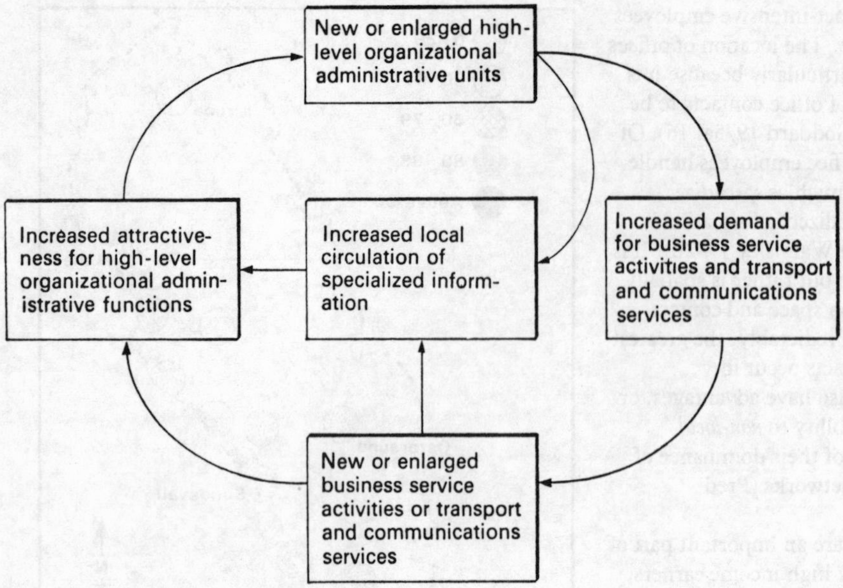

Fig. 10.5 The multiplier effect of specialized information. *Source:* Pred (1977, 117).

metropolitan headquarters in so far as new information-processing requirements are almost certain to result from new investment (Pred 1977a: 116). This further enhances the dominance of metropolitan areas within the contact and information landscape. Metropolitan growth therefore can take on the appearance of a circular and cumulative feedback process as new high-level employment emerges (Fig. 10.5). In short, 'interurban information circulation and organizational location patterns feedback upon one another to influence the process of city-system development' (Pred 1973a: 58). This means that information flows within the spatial structure of corporate organizations underlie and steer such urban and regional development processes as the spatial diffusion of innovation and the development of regional external economies (Goddard 1975b: 88). This has obvious implications for regional policy in general, and for the elimination of interregional inequalities in employment in particular. As yet, however, there has been little research into the perceptions and images that industrialists have of this growth transmission process. It may well be that managerial attitudes are both malleable (Taylor and Neville, 1980) and based on very limited information (Green 1977). It may even be that such images are grossly distorted and derive from stereotype, prejudice and myth. Whether these misperceptions and misconceptions can be remedied by advertising and public relations exercises remains a vexed question (see Pocock and Hudson 1978: 120–2).

Chapter 11
ADAPTATION TO HAZARDS

The study of natural hazards, and of how people perceive and adjust to environmental stress, is of central and traditional concern to the discipline of geography (see Parker and Harding 1979). The investigation of natural hazards has in fact been dominated by geographers. Moreover, the work that has been done has been characterized by a unified paradigm which provides a remarkable degree of coherence and integration (Gold 1980: 202). This paradigm, which had its origins in White's (1945) pioneering work on human adjustments to floods, views the human response to hazards from a systems perspective and focuses on the interaction between human use of the environment and natural events within the environment (Fig. 11.1). Clearly work done within the ambit of this paradigm is designed to be of value to resource managers in hazard-prone environments in so far as it seeks to emphasize and evaluate adjustment decision strategies in order to arrive at policy recommendations as to the cost-effectiveness of alternative hazard prevention and mitigation techniques (Kates 1971). In this sense the work reflects the spirit of an early study by White *et al.* (1958) which showed that increased spending on flood prevention in the United States (as a result of the Flood Control Act of 1936) was actually paralleled by greater losses from flood damage, possibly because people modify their attitude to flood plain occupance in the light of changing beliefs as to the power of available technology. Applied natural hazard research geared to the needs of resource managers also reflects the fact that losses from hazards can be severe and therefore demand attention and action. For example, between 1947 and 1967 at least 440,000 lives were lost as a result of natural disasters (Sheehan and Hewitt 1969).

Early research into the human response to natural hazards was dominated by the University of Chicago where White's pioneering work was followed by a number of studies, prominent among which were those by Kates (1962) and Saarinen (1966). Kates's examination of flood plain management corroborated the earlier finding that flood control can actually encourage an increase in damage potential. The study also highlighted the behavioural basis for decision-making and, in doing so, drew attention to three critical issues: the question of whether man is fully or boundedly rational; the types of decision processes which characterize human behaviour; and the way in which man comes to terms with risk and uncertainty (see Jackson 1981). Saarinen considered similar issues but shifted the research focus from floods to droughts in a study of the Great Plains which made interesting use of projective techniques (notably photographs around which respondents had to construct a story). To Saarinen, the perception of drought was a function not merely of a stimulus that was present (i.e. current water supply) but also of past learning and motivation. In fact, Saarinen suggested that farmers tend to take an optimistic stance and underestimate the frequency of drought. Generalizations are however difficult to make because the perception of drought, and of all hazards, tends to vary from individual to individual, partly as a result of the degree to which the hazard impinges on the livelihood of the individual concerned, partly as a result of the frequency of the hazard in question, and partly as a result of variations in personal experience (Burton and Kates 1964a).

In 1967 researchers at the University of Chicago, Clark University, and the University of Toronto began a collaborative programme to extend the early work of White and his colleagues to a wider range of hazards and to environments other than those found in North America. The research strategy was very simple (White 1974: 4):

1. Estimate the extent of human occupance in areas subject to extreme events in nature.
2. Determine the range of possible adjustments by social groups to those extreme events.
3. Examine how people perceive the extreme events and resultant hazards.

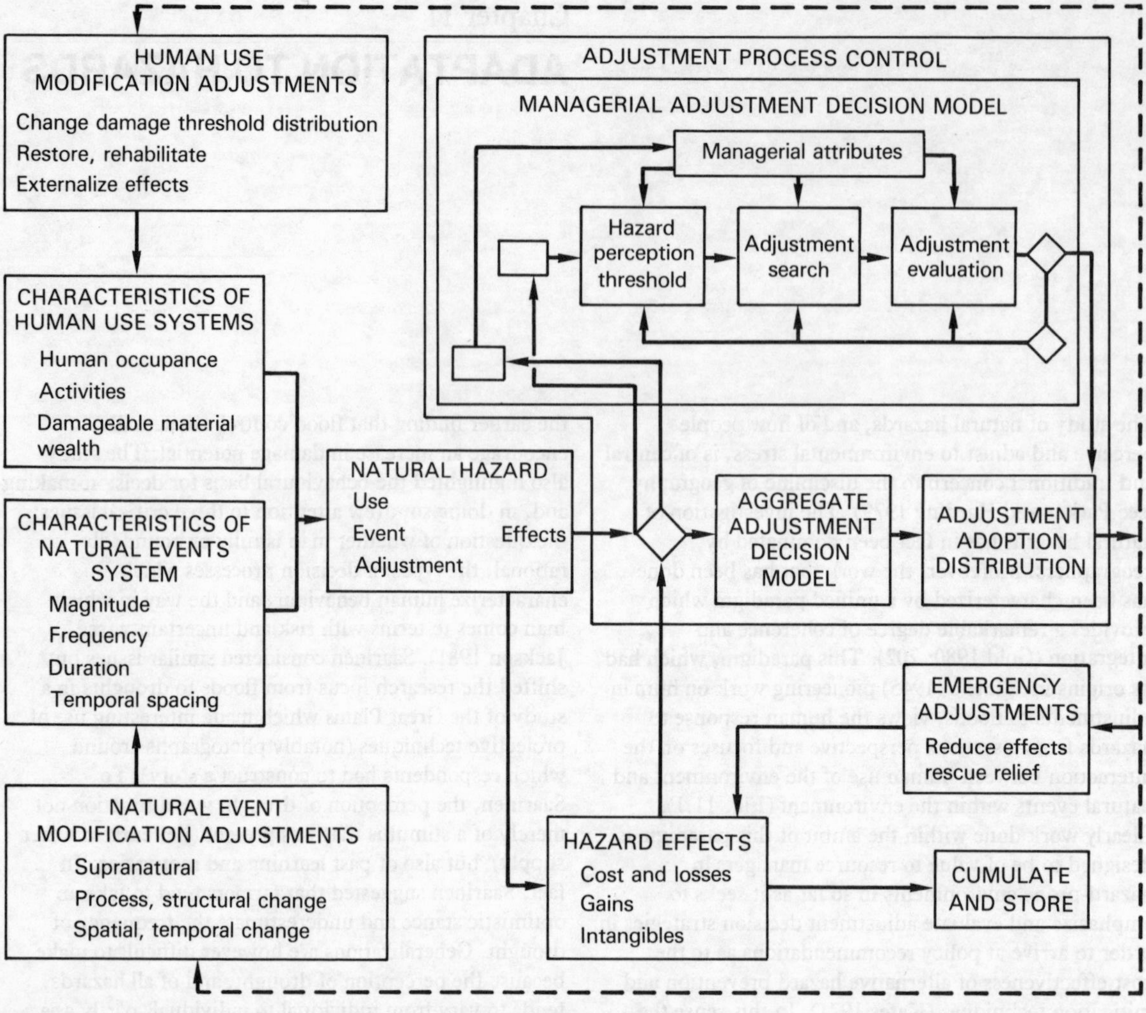

Fig. 11.1 Human adjustment to natural hazards. *Source*: Kates (1971, 444).

4. Examine the process of choosing damage-reducing adjustments.
5. Estimate what would be the effects of varying public policy upon that set of human responses.

In other words, attention was directed at three key questions: Why do people locate in areas prone to natural hazards? What do people know about these hazards? How does this compare with what they might know if they had the most up-to-date scientific and technological knowledge? (Burton, Kates, and Snead 1969). In answering these questions it became apparent that very often individuals react to uncertainty in one of two very different ways: some people attempt to change the unpredictable into the knowable by imposing order where none really exists (e.g. resorting to folk sayings about climatic variations) whereas other people deny all knowability and regard natural hazards as unique, unpredictable events (i.e. acts of God).

The research strategy developed jointly at Chicago, Clark, and Toronto has determined the direction of a great deal of work on hazards. It is not, however, a strategy that has escaped criticism. For example, Waddell (1977) has argued that the strategy is not, despite its claims, 'ecological' in the sense of seeing man *interacting* with biological and physical systems so as to arrive at a harmonious balance. Rather, in Waddell's (1977: 69) view, the research strategy is 'a resolutely deterministic one where the active forces are vested in nature and the passive in man'. In other words, the approach ignores man's efforts to devise land management systems that accommodate hazard and uncertainty in favour of a view which sees man as simply responding to environmental stimuli. Its widespread adoption therefore smacks of that blend of scientism where the dictates of the overall paradigm transcend those of reality to the point where naïve and banal conclusions can result, particularly when the approach is applied beyond the realm of advanced, western societies (Waddell 1977: 73). Despite this strident criticism, the research strategy advocated by White and others has proved very popular and, for the most part, research has focused on hazards in the sense of extreme geophysical events which greatly exceed normal human expectations in terms of magnitude or frequency and which cause major human hardship with possible loss of life (Oliver 1975: 99). Only occasionally have biological phenomena been included within the definition of hazards (see Burton and Kates 1964b).

The range of geophysical events studied in hazard research is broad: cyclones, tornados, storms, drought, frost, snow, hail, landslides, avalanches, tidal waves, earthquakes, heatwaves, fog, and dust storms (see Saarinen 1976: 151–2). Generally a distinction has been drawn between *adaptation* to a hazard and *adjustment* to a hazard. The former refers to the long-term arrangement of activity to take account of extreme events (e.g. the development of a farming system to accommodate drought) while the latter refers to specific acts undertaken in the hope of coping with risk and uncertainty (White and Haas 1975). Adjustment has attracted more attention than adaptation and three types of adjustment strategy have been commonly identified: attempts to modify natural events; attempts to modify the vulnerability of man to natural events; and attempts to distribute losses (Burton, Kates, and White 1978).

Table 11.1 Types of adjustment to natural hazards

	Types of adjustment		
Types of hazards	*Modify event*	*Modify vulnerability*	*Distribute losses*
Avalanche	Artificial release	Snow shields	Emergency relief
Coastal erosion	Beach nourishment	Beach groynes	Flood insurance
Drought	Cloud seeding	Cropping pattern	Crop insurance
Earthquake	Earthquake reduction (theoretical)	Earthquake-resistant buildings	Emergency relief
Flood	Upstream water control	Flood-proofing	SBA loans
Frost	Orchard heating	Warning network	Crop insurance
Hail	Cloud seeding	Plant selection	Hail insurance
Hurricane	Cloud seeding	Land use pattern	Emergency relief
Landslide	—	Land use regulation	—
Lightning	Cloud seeding	Lightning conductors	Homeowners insurance
Tornado	—	Warning network	Emergency relief
Tsunami	—	Warning network	Emergency relief
Urban Snow	—	Snow removal preparations	Taxation for snow removal
Volcano	—	Land use regulations	Emergency relief
Windstorms	—	Mobile home design	Property insurance

Source: White and Haas (1975, 86).

An illustration of these strategies is provided in Table 11.1.

The list of geophysical hazards contained in Table 11.1 is not an exhaustive one. Moreover it is becoming increasingly accepted that geophysical events are not the only environmental hazards of concern to humans. Phenomena like air and water pollution, which are caused by man rather than by natural forces, are also important although such phenomena of course differ from geophysical events in that they are probably more predictable, and possibly more complex in their origins, as is suggested in Fig. 11.2. Nevertheless, in a fundamental sense, soil erosion (Williams 1979) and roadside lead (Hunter 1976) are just as much hazards as are floods and droughts. The distinction between man-made hazards and natural hazards is in fact blurred: the Aberfan tip-slide involved natural processes operating on a man-made mountain and, likewise, bushfires are often started, albeit inadvertently, by man. As a result, some writers talk of natural disasters rather than natural hazards (see Whittow 1980). In this sense a disaster is something which 'affects the system of *biological survival* (subsistence, shelter, health, reproduction), the system of *order* (division of labour, authority patterns, cultural norms, social roles), the system of *meaning* (values, shared definitions of reality, communication mechanisms), and the *motivation* of the actors within all of these systems' (Fritz 1961: 655). Given that such disasters vary in their predictability, in their speed of onset, and in their scope and effects (Fritz 1968), it is perhaps not unreasonable to view hazards, which vary in a similar manner, from this perspective.

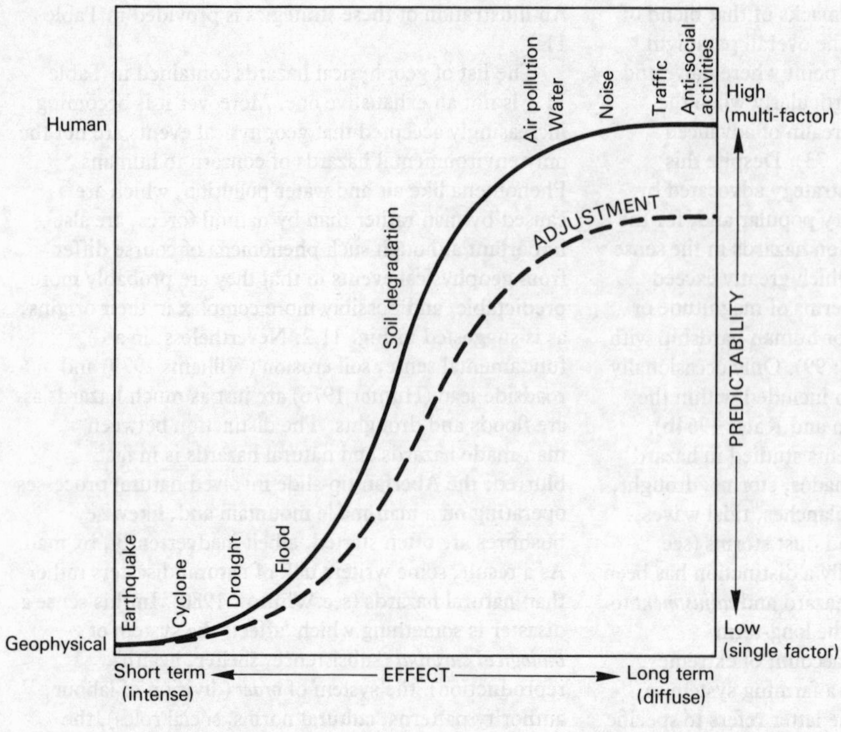

Fig. 11.2 Natural and humanly induced hazards. *Source*: Williams (1979, 276).

However, any attempt to view the human response to hazards as a special type of disaster behaviour must take stock of the methodological problems encountered in the study of hazards.

Methodological problems in hazard studies

The study of natural hazards is different from much of social science in that it is a field of enquiry that does not lend itself to traditional notions of sampling. Events can only be studied as they happen or, more usually, after they have happened. And because social scientists are seldom in attendance as hazards unfold, they have often to rely on journalistic accounts of post-impact behaviour. There are a number of pitfalls in this strategy, not the least of which is the fact that the media tend to report only major and remarkable events (see Sheehan and Hewitt 1969). It may be, for example, that newspaper accounts of post-hazard behaviour overemphasize the unusual and underemphasize the commonplace thereby giving a distorted impression of how people actually behave.

The lack of predictability of hazards means that there can be no before and after studies. The behavioural investigations that have taken place have therefore been retrospective and have asked people to recall and explain past behaviour. This approach runs the risk of encouraging *post hoc rationalization* if respondents are given time to ponder over their actions. This is especially true of residents of hazard-prone environments who tend to be a self-selected group with their own views on the frequency and severity of hazards. However, if respondents are not given time to rationalize their actions, or if an interviewer approaches victims too soon after a hazard, then the researcher can be placed in a highly reactive environment where responses are given as much to the presence of an intruder as to the questions asked. Compounding this consideration of the ethics and reliability of studies conducted immediately after the onset of a hazard is the fact that both the hazard and the resultant behaviour are complex in nature. Exactly what a hazard means to the people it affects is unclear (Saarinen 1974). Any improved understanding and improved prediction of human behaviour in hazard situations will therefore depend in part on social scientists 'devoting more research effort to exploring the preconceived ideas and feelings held by individuals concerning potential hazards' (Golant and Burton 1976: 364). One possible way of uncovering these preconceived ideas is to be found in the use of the psychological technique known as semantic differential analysis whereby phenomena like hazards can be evaluated in terms of bipolar adjectival scales (see Osgood *et al*. 1957). To date, however, the technique has been used for little more than grouping hazards into man-made, natural, and quasi-natural categories (see Golant and Burton 1976).

Human responses to hazards

The popular image of a hazard, derived largely from the media, highlights such features as panic, evacuation, helpless victims, looting, emotional disturbance, and the mobilization of rescue and recovery teams. Although this image contains an element of truth, it is overdrawn. In fact the human responses to hazards vary so widely that generalizations are sometimes very difficult to make. Nevertheless, White (1974: 5) has suggested that such responses can be grouped into three main types:

1. *Folk, or pre-industrial, adjustments* that are flexible, small scale, low in capital requirements, and easily abandoned in so far as they rest on behavioural rather than major physical developments.
2. *Technological, or industrial, adjustments* that are heavily reliant on technological actions to control nature and are high in both capital requirements and organizational demands.
3. *Comprehensive or post-industrial adjustments* that combine both folk and technological adjustments thereby providing a flexible range of responses and a variety of organizational strategies.

In some senses these three groupings reflect what Kluckhohn (1959) has argued are three fundamental attitudes to nature: man as subject to nature; man dominating nature; and man existing in harmony with nature. It would be wrong however to infer that people's attitudes and responses to hazards vary automatically with either their stage of economic development or with culture (see Brooks 1973). Rather the variation is often on an individual basis. There are a number of reasons for this: hazards are infrequent events and hence perception of them tends to be distorted according to personal experience; what is deemed possible by way of response varies from person to person; and information about hazards is often vague, ambiguous, uncertain and liable to misinterpretation (Ittelson *et al.* 1974: 310). Despite this, a certain degree of common ground exists in the specific responses to hazards that have been adopted, at least in advanced western economies. For example, Hewitt and Burton (1971) have suggested that man may try to affect the cause of a hazard (e.g. cloud seeding to dissipate storms), man may attempt to modify a hazard (e.g. build dams to control floods), man may modify the loss potential (e.g. develop warning systems), man may spread the losses resulting from the hazard (e.g. government aid from consolidated revenue transfers the cost to the community at large), man may plan for losses (e.g. insurance policies), or man may bear losses (e.g. stoically accept that life is made up of good and bad years). These alternatives have been the focus of a good deal of research largely because they fit comfortably into the applied, resource management-orientated mould of North American hazard research. However, such a focus overlooks the fact that premeditated hazard adjustment is but one element of the total human response to hazards. In order to gain some appreciation of this overall response it is probably necessary to turn to studies of disasters in general rather than hazards in particular despite the fact that some authorities have claimed, without very strong supporting evidence, that natural hazards are different in kind from social or physical hazards (Burton, Kates, and White 1968; Golant and Burton 1969). One very stimulating introduction to disaster behaviour is Fritz and Williams's (1957) description of a seven-stage response sequence involving disaster warnings, survival behaviour, convergence behaviour, co-ordination and control, hostility and blame, emotional aftermath, and social solidarity. Some of these stages are interdependent and they are perhaps better discussed in relation to information about hazards, the immediate response, the role of government, and the aftermath of hazards.

Information about hazards

In terms of hazard warnings, three things are critical: the scientific and technological accuracy of the information relating to the hazard; the media through which the information is relayed; and the receptiveness of the population to warning. Generally speaking the scientific and technological accuracy of disaster warnings is increasing as a result of improved surveillance and improved data handling (e.g. the development of satellite climatology). At the same time public information flows are improving with better broadcast and reception facilities (again often linked to satellites). Despite this, rumours tend to spread very quickly in disaster situations (Larson 1954), partly because formal communications channels sometimes break down, and partly because the population at risk is receptive to rumour. Indeed the receptiveness of the population to different types of information is a central issue in behavioural studies of the human response to hazards. There is in fact some evidence that prior warning can increase the stress effects of hazards (Hansson *et al.* 1982).

A descriptive model of how information about hazards is processed, from the point of view of resource management, is given in Fig. 11.3 which is derived from

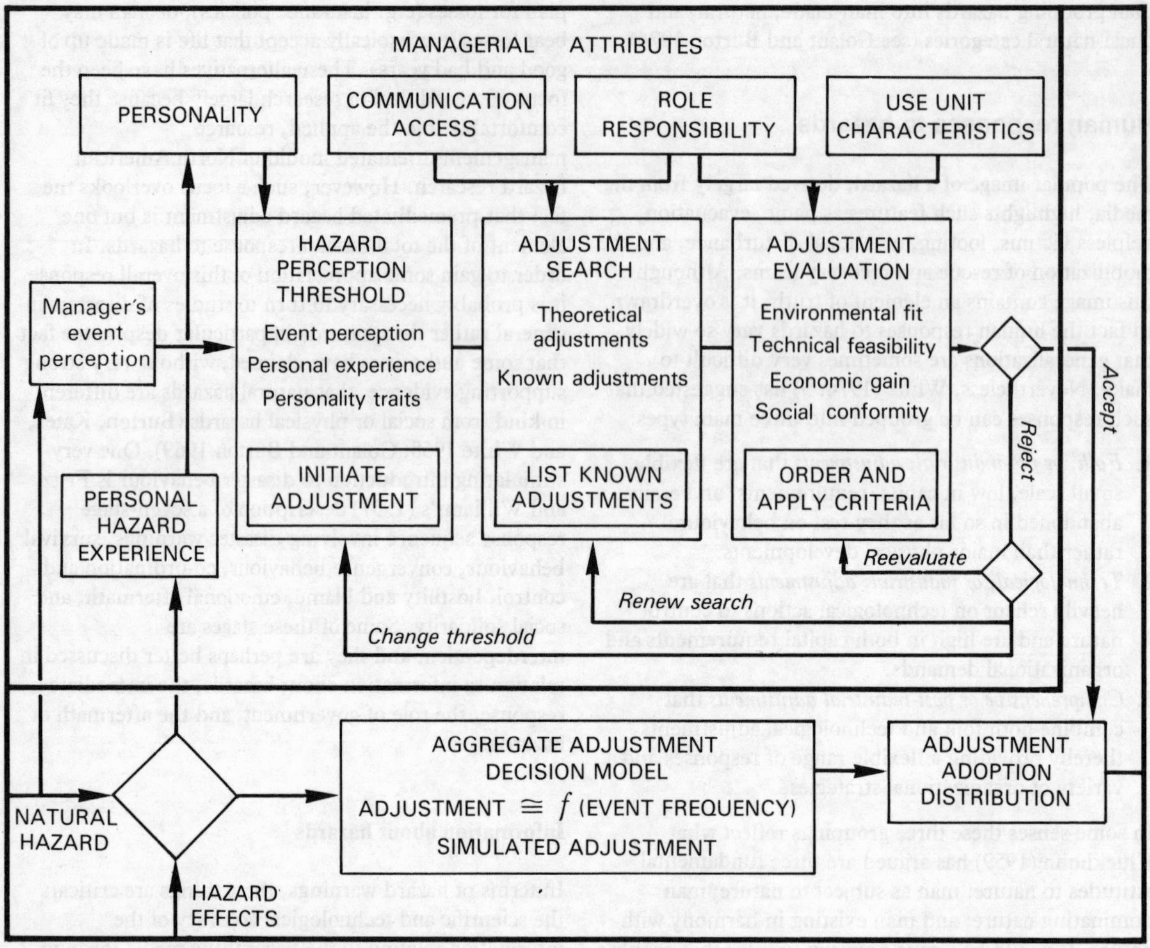

Fig. 11.3 The processing of information about hazards. *Source*: Kates (1971, 447).

Kates's (1971) rudimentary model of the short-run process of adjustment to natural hazards. This flow chart is open to criticism on a number of grounds, prominent among which is the fact that the model emphasizes rational decision-making and thus overlooks the tendency for individuals in hazard situations to misperceive risks and to replace known probabilities with intuitively derived laws of chance (Slovic *et al.* 1974). The model does nevertheless highlight the *perception of events*, *experience*, and *personality* as key issues. To these, in terms of influence on hazard adjustment strategies, can be added material wealth and *social status* (Burton, Kates, and White 1978).

The *perception of hazard events*, in the sense of man's immediate (cf. cognitive) encountering of those events, has been studied a good deal and, in simple terms, the main features of such perception can be stated as a number of generalizations (see Kilpatrick 1957). To begin with there is a tendency for people who are confronting a hazard directly to establish a dominant and familiar percept and to assimilate all happenings to it; for example, the sound of tornadoes is sometimes mistaken for the sound of trains. The importance of this lies in the fact that actions are undertaken by affected individuals that are appropriate to the situation as perceived even though they may seem inappropriate to the true nature of events as viewed by observers. Moreover, given that the perception of hazards involves the unfamiliar, there is both a tendency for suggestibility to be high (and hence for individuals to follow group leaders) and for people to isolate themselves from happenings around them and to fall back on familiar and well-tried behaviours. Frequently, perceptual cues are conflicting (as when individuals cannot decide whether to flee or fight hazards like floods) and prolonged exposure to this sort of situation can foster emotional disturbance. Just how well individuals cope with these problems of perception depends on their prior experience of similar situations.

It is part of the conventional wisdom of hazard studies that *experience* of an event heightens awareness of future similar events. After all, such a conclusion sounds entirely plausible and is supported by a wide body of evidence: on the one hand Williams (1957) has shown that information about a possible threat which has not been previously experienced tends to have low value, while on the other hand McDonald (1979) and Irish and Falconer (1979) have demonstrated how experience of drought and floods respectively makes people more aware of possible future hazards. It may in fact be that awareness rather than experience is the critical variable. Certainly this appeared to be the case in a study by Hanson *et al.* (1979) which suggested that awareness of a previous tornado, not necessarily direct experience, predisposed people to action. Unfortunately, however, the evidence for the importance of experience and awareness is less than overwhelming. For one thing, Kates (1967) has shown that people might be aware of a hazard but have different interpretations of the nature of that hazard. Likewise some individuals are well aware of the possibility of hazards but regard the potential danger as less significant than their attachment to the place under threat, as seems to be the case with earthquakes in San Francisco (Jackson and Mukerjee 1974). Information about hazards, in other words, is sometimes simply ignored (Palm 1981). Moreover, the recall of past experiences may be less than perfect: Kirkby (1974), for instance, has shown that the memory of farmers for specific rainfall events tends to be limited in duration and is mainly restricted to the largest falls. In short, there seems to be evidence that some individuals adopt the attitude that 'it couldn't happen here'. This was clearly demonstrated when a tsunami hit Hilo in Hawaii in May 1960: although 95 per cent of a study area population heard the warning siren, only 41 per cent decided to evacuate (Lachman *et al.* 1961). Such rejection of warnings is not uncommon but it is difficult to investigate because of the tendency for victims of hazards who have ignored a warning to deny all knowledge of that warning, possibly because they want to project the image of a self-reliant, commanding personality and possibly because of feelings of guilt (Irish and Falconer 1979). This tendency to rationalize behaviour can be explained by *cognitive dissonance theory* which holds that individuals reject information and suppress facts that might be damaging to their prevailing value system (Festinger 1957). The theory also goes some way to explaining why hazards are often ignored by people living in a threatened area (a 'threat denial response' to information) but exaggerated by individuals in neighbouring but as yet unaffected areas (a 'threat enhancement response') (Shippee *et al.* 1980). Both groups simply use information about hazards to justify their own residential choice.

In terms of *personality*, the trait most closely related to hazard response seems to be *locus of control* which is a measure that assesses people according to whether they see events as contingent upon their own behaviour or resulting from forces beyond their control. Those believing in the power of their own actions seem more favourably disposed to preventative action, whereas those who see events as beyond their control tend to favour reparative action once a hazard has occurred (Simpson-Housley and Bradshaw 1978). Other personality measures, such as introversion – extroversion, seem to have no discernible effect on risk avoidance (Golant and Burton 1969). In contrast, religious beliefs may be important in that devout Catholics have been shown to be likely to view hazards as acts of God and therefore beyond the realm of political action (Abney and Hill 1966).

Among the *socio-economic variables* related to hazard response, age seems to be the most important in that individual sensitivity to hazards seems to increase with age (Saarinen 1966; Harvey *et al.* 1979) and with length of residence in a given location (Auliciems and Dick 1976). High status groups and the better educated tend to be similarly sensitive and likely to take preventative action (Baker and Patton 1974). Of course, in addition to these socio-economic variables, the frequency, magnitude, and suddenness of onset of a hazard can have a major influence on the human response, as can the degree of personal vulnerability and consideration of whether the hazard is part and parcel of the environment (in the sense of being a recurrent event like a flood), or unpredictable (as with infrequent events such as earthquakes) (Kates 1971).

Immediate response to hazards

There has been very little study by geographers of the immediate response to hazards. However, work elsewhere in social science suggests that such responses usually follow a temporal sequence that begins with a choice between *fight* (combat the hazard) and *flight* (which can take the form of uncontrolled panic or controlled evacuation). This gives way to rescue and relief which are often sporadic and poorly organized, particularly if the victims are in a state of shock and unable to engage in self help (Wallace 1957). Eventually help arrives. Personnel, material, and food converge on the disaster area leading to what has been described as the 'Cornucopia phenomenon' (Wettenhall 1975), that is to say, a state where there is such an abundance of aid that it presents problems of distribution. This 'convergence behaviour', which is far greater in volume than the movement out of the disaster area, seems to occur world-wide. It presents a dilemma for those in authority not least because the needs of 'helpers' as well as of 'victims' have to be satisfied (Short 1979).

The role of government

'Natural disasters seriously challenge the established framework of government and social organization in all communities where they are liable to occur' (Wettenhall 1975: 16). This is because natural hazards present a stressful situation to which a response has to be made very quickly. Such a situation contrasts markedly with the gradual evolution of policy responses to which government bureaucracies are accustomed. Moreover, bureaucracies tend to operate largely on the basis of precedence and yet in most hazard situations there is a marked lack of precedents. In fact, in the absence of guidelines as to what should be done, governments tend to fall back on a popular image of disasters and hazards and act accordingly. Quarantelli and Dynes (1972) have outlined the nature of this response:

1. A fear that people will panic leads to cautiousness in issuing hazard warnings.
2. A suspicion that victims are immobilized by fear leads to immediate assistance.
3. A belief that organizations cannot handle the situation, given the magnitude of the damage, results in outside personnel being mobilized on a massive scale.
4. A fear of antisocial behaviour and looting leads to an emphasis on security.
5. A belief that community morale is low in stricken areas leads to visits by prominent public officials.
6. A fear that stricken communities descend into social chaos leads to an emphasis on developing strong leadership.

Although each element of this image of a disaster may be largely untrue, the responses do seem to be common. Of course, on top of these immediate initiatives, governments take responsibility in the longer term for what are usually referred to as 'remedy', 'recovery', and 'response' (Wettenhall and Power 1969; Power and Wettenhall 1970). Douglas (1979), for example, has shown how the government response to flooding in Australia usually involves emergency assistance, flood relief grants and loans, the establishment of interdepartmental committees, consultation with local government, and the preparation of a report on water management. Despite this sort of action, there do occur

	TASKS	
	REGULAR	NON-REGULAR
ESTABLISHED	Established Groups City police directing traffic after hazard	Extending Groups Construction companies using earth moving equipment to clear wreckage
EMERGENT	Expanding Groups Red Cross providing relief	Emergent Groups Ad hoc committees

Fig. 11.4 A typology of groups in post-hazard situations. *Source*: Quarntelli (1966, 39).

authority vacuums, particularly in the short term after a hazard has struck an area. These vacuums tend to be filled by the emergence of *ad hoc groups*.

Post-hazard group emergence has been studied extensively and Quarantelli (1966) has devised a fourfold typology according to whether the groups are *established* or *emergent* and whether they are doing *regular* or *non-regular tasks* (Fig. 11.4). Type 1 (established) and Type 3 (extending) groups are already in existence when a hazard strikes. Type 2 (expanding) groups do not exist in a permanent and full-time capacity but are capable of being organized when the need arises. Perhaps the most interesting groups are the Type 4 (emergent) ones. These generally come into being when the co-ordination between existing organizations breaks down, when an organizational authority structure crumbles, or when the demands placed on existing organizations are in excess of their response capability (Parr 1970). They have been observed in a great many situations and they tend to be *ad hoc*, local, and to survive only until the crisis has passed.

The aftermath of hazards

After a hazard it is relatively common to witness hostility on the part of the victims and attempts to find someone to blame for the damage that was done. To a large extent this attitude results from the emotional upset caused by the hazard. Janis (1954) has suggested that there are five sorts of emotional response to stressful situations: apprehensive avoidance (flight, shelter); stunned immobility; apathy and depression; docile dependency on others; and aggressive irritability. Whilst not all of these are evident in all hazard disasters, some of them certainly are. For example, headaches, irritability, nervous tension, depression, digestive disturbances, and shortness of breath have been found to be more common in flood victims than in control groups (Raphael 1979).

Perhaps the two disasters that have been most carefully studied in terms of their emotional aftermath are the surge of sludge that hit the American settlement of Buffalo Creek following a dam collapse in 1972 and the devastation caused by Cyclone Tracy on the Australian city of Darwin in 1974. In the former case 80 per cent of survivors exhibited traumatic or neurotic reactions compounded by unresolved grief and feelings of impotent rage and hopelessness. These symptoms and associated disorientation persisted for two years (Erickson 1976; Titchener and Kapp 1976). In the Darwin case the trauma was too much for many people: for example, shock, apathy, psychosomatic reactions, anxiety, and panic were common even among those residents who had been away at the time of the cyclone (Webber 1976). Over 35,000 people were evacuated from the city and a study of a sample of these one week after the event suggested that 58 per cent were probably psychiatric cases, with the aged and females faring worse than the rest of the population (G. Parker 1975). Severe stress was in fact much more common among evacuees than among those who stayed in Darwin, and returned evacuees had lower incidences of severe stress than non-returned evacuees (Milne 1977a; 1977b). This suggests that the mass evacuation may have caused more problems than it solved (Western and Milne 1979) and that hazards generally may be regarded by governments as too much of a physical crisis and not enough of a social crisis (Webber 1976).

Emotional disturbance decreases in severity and incidence with time. Societal norms re-establish themselves. However, no community reverts precisely to its pre-existing state. The social system that was disrupted by the hazard is changed irreversibly as a result of the stress of the disaster impact and the strain of the rehabilitation process (Bates *et al.* 1963). Very often this change takes the form of increased social cohesiveness. Fritz and Williams (1957: 48), for example, have claimed that the net result of many disasters is a dramatic increase in social solidarity and altruism, at least during the emergency and post-emergency periods. This raises the question of whether hazards are entirely detrimental in their effects. Some authorities have argued, for instance, that natural hazards can do some good to the extent that there are windfall profits to businesses involved in emergency activities and rehabilitation, there is a net inflow of public funds into stricken areas that might not otherwise attract funds, and there is a stimulus to counter disaster research and to disaster planning (Heathcote 1979). In addition, insurance payments may provide much needed capital and urban renewal may be forced on a community with a result that new and better buildings replace old ones (Oliver 1978). Thus, although individual victims may suffer as a result of hazards, it is possible that in some cases the community at large reaps certain benefits.

Chapter 12

LEISURE AND RECREATION

In recent years all developed economies have experienced a significant growth in leisure-time activities, which can be related to the rapid increase in most people's disposable incomes, mobility levels, and available discretionary time (Patmore 1970; Patmore and Collins 1980). In this sense leisure encompasses activities in which an individual 'may indulge of his own free will either to rest, amuse himself, to add to his knowledge and improve his skills disinterestedly and to increase his voluntary participation in the life of the community after discharging his professional, family and social duties' (Appleton 1974: 63). This trend of increasing leisure time can be related to the progression of society from pre-industrial and feudal status toward industrial and eventually post-industrial status (Roberts 1978). As illustrated in Table 12.1, this progression involves an increasing separation of work and leisure in time and space, so making leisure the vacuum between work periods. In the nineteenth century the distinction between work and leisure was the preserve of the wealthy but today it has filtered down to all income groups (Bailey 1978; Lowerson and Myerscough 1977). Moreover, as leisure time has increased for more people, a whole commercial entertainment business has developed (Kando 1975). Thus, according to Burns (1973: 46), 'social life outside the work situation . . . has been created afresh, in forms which are themselves the creation of industrialization, which derive from it and which contribute to its development, growth and further articulation'. For example, as discretionary time expands further and a post-industrial society emerges, then greater choice lends itself to

Table 12.1 The emergence of a society of leisure

	Society			
Ways of living	*Folk*	*Feudal*	*Industrial*	*Post-industrial*
Work	Entirely food producing, no surplus. Little labour specialization	Greater occupational diversity, such as trading and craft specialization	Marked division of labour as a result of occupational specialization. Factory mode of production.	Technological-based employment for the majority; re-emergence of craft specialization. An economy of plenty
Community	Small, homogeneous communities with strong sense of solidarity and cohesion. Low mobility. Little class distinction	Small aristocracy and large peasantry. Greater heterogeneity and stratification	Large communities of heterogeneous people and cultures. Impersonal relationships dominate. A fluid class system	Emergence of more pluralistic co-operative relationships. Often shared community decisions
Leisure	Little distinction between work and leisure. Sacred prevails over secular	Again little distinction between work and leisure for peasantry. Aristocracy involved in leisure pursuits	Leisure for the masses, now defined as a specific time earned from work	Greater time for leisure and fusion of work and leisure. Diversity of leisure based on individual needs.

Source: based on material in Murphy (1974, 181)

involvement in an even greater variety of leisure activities, leading to a fusion of work–leisure relationships (Cheek *et al.* 1978). In view of these trends, it is not surprising that the provision and use of leisure facilities has become the focus of a good deal of research. After all, leisure is now deemed vital for the maintenance of a reasonable quality of life (Hookway and Davidson 1970). As a result, researchers from several disciplines, including geography (Patmore 1970; Cosgrove and Jackson 1972; Lavery 1974; Simmons 1975; Coppock 1980), sociology (S. Parker 1975; 1976; Smith *et al.* 1973), and economics (Clawson and Knetsch 1966; Vickerman 1975), as well as multi-disciplinary researchers (Mercer, 1977: 1981; Johnson 1977; Dunn 1980), have investigated the nature of leisure time behaviour and thereby provided the basis for policy initiatives and land-use management strategies (see Appleton 1974; Kaplan 1975; Travis et *al.* 1981; Heeley 1981).

Table 12.2 The use of time

	Fully committed	*Highly committed*	*Leisure*
Sleeping	Essential sleep		Relaxing
Exercise	Health		Sport
Eating	Eating		Dining
Shopping	Essential	Optional	—
Work	Primary	Overtime	—
Housework	Cooking	Repairs	Gardening
Education	Schooling	Further Education	—
Culture	—	—	Reading, TV, Radio, hobbies and passive play
Travel	To work/school	—	Working/driving for pleasure

Source: After Cosgrove and Jackson (1972)

Leisure time activities

According to Young and Willmott (1973) any attempt to describe and measure leisure activities is like attempting to grab a jellyfish with bare hands because leisure has many meanings in different societies and to different people. Indeed, in some instances it is difficult to demarcate leisure from work and other forms of human behaviour; for example, the growing popularity of 'hobby' farming among the middle class is essentially a leisure activity, yet farming is a means of livelihood for millions and a source of income even for hobby farmers. This is demonstrated in Table 12.2, which emphasizes that, for any individual, depending on circumstances, the same activity can be considered as an essential or a leisure act. This has led Clawson and Knetsch (1966: 6) to suggest that 'the distinguishing characteristic of recreation is not the activity itself but the attitude with which it is undertaken'. Therefore, leisure can be conceived singly, or in combination, either as a period of time, as a certain activity, or an attitude of mind. (Tinsley and Kass 1979).

Once a pursuit has been defined as a leisure activity it then becomes necessary to distinguish the nature of that activity and its significance to the individual (Pierce 1980). Broadly, a leisure activity can be classified, on the basis of individual involvement, into *passive* and *active*, and on the basis of whether it takes place in the home, local neighbourhood or distant region (Fig. 12.1 (a)). A further complication is provided by the frequency of involvement in a particular activity and the length of time that the pursuit may involve, whether it be hours, days, or weeks (Wilman 1980). Figure 12.1(a) illustrates three very different leisure time activities: an individual who reads every evening for a couple of hours at home, an individual who spends an evening at a city centre cinema once a month, an individual who goes hiking once a year in a distant mountainous region for

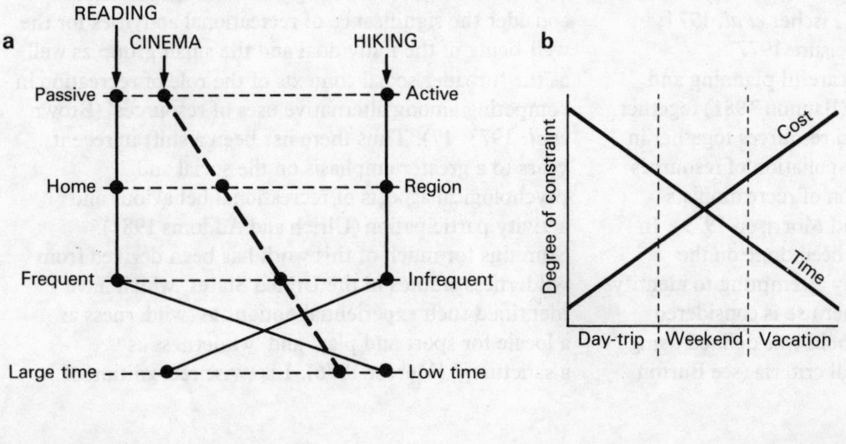

Fig. 12.1 Leisure-time activities. **a** individual involvement, **b** time – cost constraints.

three weeks. Likely participation in such alternatives is, of course, constrained by the availability of leisure opportunities within a time-cost framework. (Fig. 12.1(b)).

Despite the development of a vast commercial entertainment industry, the focus for most leisure time activities in the western world is still the home which may provide the venue for something like three-quarters of all leisure time pursuits (Mercer 1980). Such a fact provides support for Wingo's (1964: 138) view that 'the popularity of the low density suburban dwelling probably reflects the surging demands for more private forms of recreation among middle-class, child-oriented families, suggesting that metropolitan scatteration is as much a recreation as a housing phenomenon'.

Recreational behaviour

Leisure time activities that involve travel beyond the home are often thought of as *recreation*. Such activities encompass both passive pursuits (like pleasure driving) and active pursuits (like mountain walking) and since the 1950s a great deal of research has looked at the planning, provision, use, and impact of recreation facilities (Coppock and Duffield 1975; Mercer 1981). On the supply side extensive investment in recreation facilities has been undertaken by both the public and private sectors on both sides of the Atlantic (Vickerman 1975). Much research, particularly in the United States, has therefore been concerned with the cost-effectiveness of such investments and the economic benefits accruing from recreation (Clawson 1972). Marketing has also been identified in the United States as an important way of promoting recreational facilities to the public (La Page 1979). Similar work in the United Kingdom, by contrast, has been largely confined to the related area of tourism (Sillitoe 1969). Inventories of the number, size, and location of recreation sites, and studies of managerial and planning problems associated with recreational pressures and land use conflicts, have also been common in the literature (Fischer *et al.* 1974; Ontario Research Council on Leisure 1977). Increasingly the importance of careful planning and management has been stressed (Bannon 1981) together with the need to bring users and resources together in such a way as to prevent the despoilation of resources while maximizing the satisfaction of recreationists (Bosselman 1978; Brockman and Morrison 1979). In particular, important work has been done on the carrying capacity of resources by attempting to identify a threshold beyond which further use is considered undesirable. Initially this threshold was defined using physical, economic, or ecological criteria (see Burton 1971) but, of late, psychological thresholds have been introduced into the evaluation (Becker 1978). Generally, a greater number of users leads to a reduction in the satisfaction which individuals derive from the recreational experience, although the degree of sensitivity to, or tolerance of, crowding varies between different groups of recreationists (Cesano 1980). For example, canoeing in a wilderness area can have a low tolerance threshold compared to motorboating at the seaside.

On the demand side, research emphasis has been largely on observed usage patterns at different facilities within a given time–space framework (Davidson 1970; Outdoor Recreation Resources Review Commission 1962). This has involved sophisticated surveys, designed to identify participation rates in various activities, the trends in participation, and the factors influencing recreation behaviour. At an early stage it was found, for example, that age, education, and income were major factors influencing recreational activity (Rodgers 1969; Dottavio *et al.* 1980) and special attention has been given to the effect of transport availability and distance in determining recreational travel (Baxter 1979; Smith and Kopp 1980; Cooper 1981). These types of survey have often shown remarkable levels of recreational activity. For example, in New South Wales, which has a population of less than 6 million, there were, in 1979–80, no fewer than 68 million nights spent by individuals at locations more than 40 km from their home. This recreation involved 16 million trips (New South Wales State Pollution Control Commission 1978). Obviously such surveys involve large statistical aggregates and focus on what might be called 'average' behaviour. Such information has been useful for managing and marketing recreational facilities, and provides some indication of the significance of tourism in a national economy. However, many researchers have been sceptical as to the relevance of user surveys since 'most recreation research to date cannot stand the question, "So what?"' (Brown *et al.* 1973: 16). These sceptics have gone on to suggest that research should consider the significance of recreational activities for the well-being of the individual and the small group as well as the 'broader social contexts of the role of recreation in competing among alternative uses of resources' (Brown *et al.* 1973: 17). Thus there has been a shift in recent years to a greater emphasis on the social and psychological aspects of recreational behaviour and activity participation (Ulrich and Addoms 1981). Stimulus for much of this work has been derived from wilderness studies in the United States, which have identified such experiential notions as 'wilderness as a locale for sport and play' and 'wilderness as a sanctuary' (Mercer 1976). Likewise recognition of

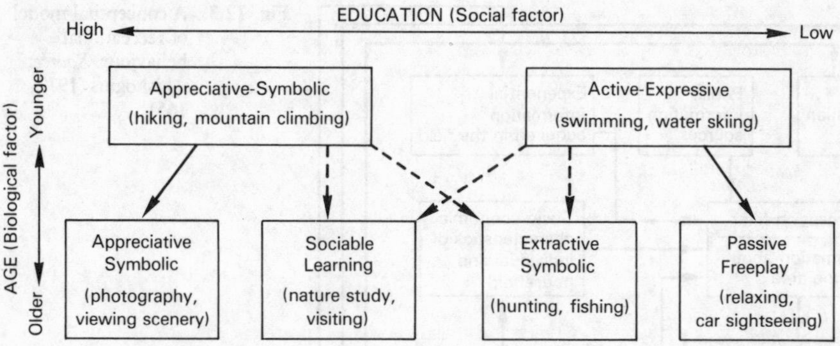

Fig. 12.2 Hypothetical changes in activity preferences with age and education. *Source*: Hendee, Gale and Catton (1971, 29).

varying sensitivity to crowding and wilderness intrusions has emphasized the need for more flexible management in order to maintain satisfaction for all groups of users. Precisely what comprises a group of users is of course difficult to define (Womble and Studebaker 1981). One interesting approach to grouping recreationists is that developed by Hendee *et al.* (1971) based on the perceived similarities in the underlying meanings of activities to participants (Fig. 12.2). Such a classification allows researchers to examine psychological, sociological, or environmental/situational effects on each grouping, and it has been employed as an initial framework in several contexts which have generally revealed that different localities can provide different experiences for recreationists, even though sometimes the same activity may be involved (Cool 1979; Warburton 1981). In a similar vein the United States National Advisory Council on Regional Recreation Planning has used information on recreational dimensions and related it to the planning process by advocating the classification of people into 'user-groups' based on the values – physical, emotional, aesthetic, educational, social, and intellectual – which people place on different leisure and recreational experience. Despite this shift towards an analysis of recreational experience as a key component of recreational behaviour, the vast majority of studies approach behaviour in the aggregate and therefore contribute little to an understanding of the underlying motives involved in the decision to recreate.

Recreational decision-making

According to Warburton (1981), recreational behaviour can be conceptualized as a system of five inter-related components: background variables; individual aspirations; intervening variables; individual satisfaction; and individual benefits. Essentially, the idea is that the level of benefit will, with the benefit of experience, either heighten or dampen recreational activity within the context of an individual's needs and opportunities. In other words decisions are made about whether or not to recreate, and where to go, on the basis of individual perceptions, needs, and opportunities (Iso-Ahela 1980). A similar interpretation is provided by Aldskogius's (1977) decision-making model of recreational-trip behaviour in Sweden, which distinguishes, on the one hand, the underlying motives of the individual from, on the other hand, the recreational resource endowment of an area, within the context of an individual's mobility potential, 'real' income, and time availability (Fig. 12.3). The central core of the model is the individual's cognitive image of recreational opportunities, within which information is integrated through a process of selection, transformation, and evaluation. In this information processing phase, an important part is played by the individual's social environment in general, and his socio-economic and household characteristics in particular. Two factors are of specific interest. First, there is the residential history of the individual. This is likely to have influenced the diversity of recreational experience and familiarity with different environments as well as contributing to preferences and attitudes with respect to different activities and resources. Second, it seems reasonable to assume that the greater the length of residence of an individual in an area, the greater will be that individual's knowledge of available recreational opportunities.

Motivation and preference

In any consideration of why individuals differ in their choice of recreational activity some attention must be paid to the underlying motives for recreation in general (Crandall 1980). In this context it is important to realize that individuals have a series of needs which they strive to fulfil. These needs can be thought of in terms of a hierarchy and only when low order physiological needs (e.g. shelter) have been met will higher order needs such

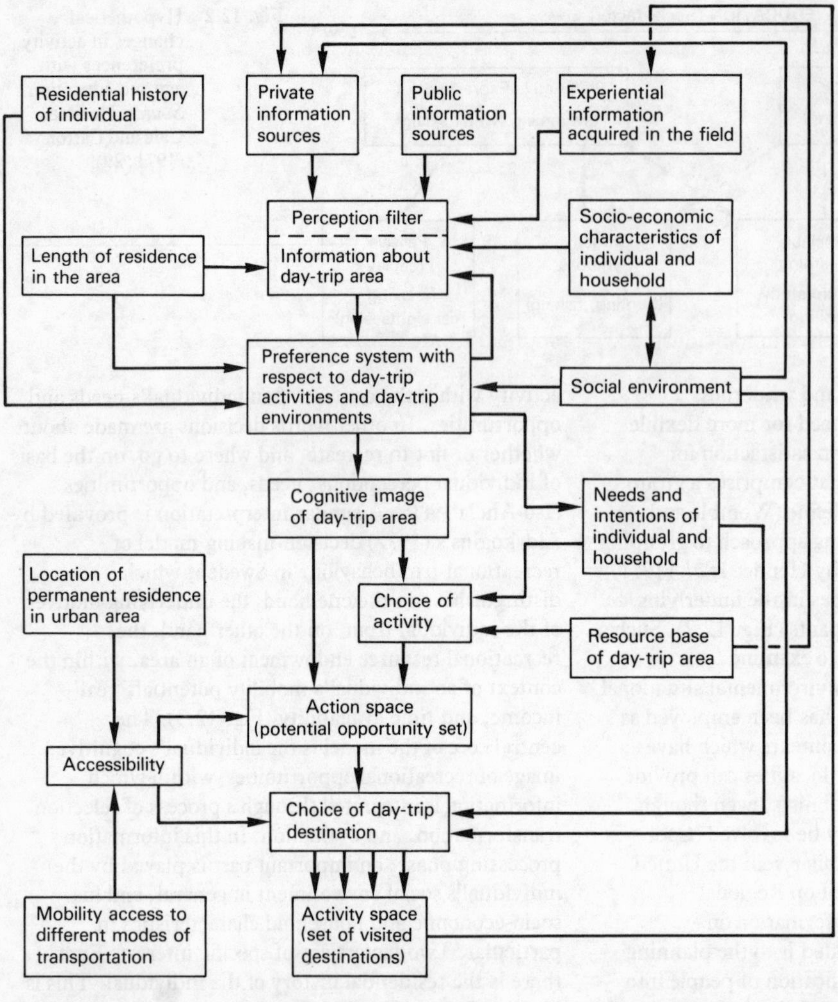

Fig. 12.3 A conceptual model of recreational behaviour. *Source*: Aldskogius (1977, 165).

as recreation play a significant role in an individual's life style (Maslow 1954; Glyptis 1981). Such higher order needs can be characterized by two opposite forces – tension-seeking and tension-reducing – between which a balance is struck. For example, recreation can serve both to ameliorate tension and also at times to actually increase it (Iso-Ahela 1980). However, it is extremely difficult for a researcher to identify whether an activity is fulfilling a tension-reducing or tension-seeking function. This is partly because needs and tensions are socially and culturally, as well as personally, defined, with a result that the researcher needs to consider the personality, experience, aspirations, and work situation of the individual recreationist.

Tension-seeking and tension-reducing perspectives underlie many general theories that have been advanced to explain choice behaviour. For example, *compensatory theory* hypothesizes that, whenever a person has the chance to avoid regular routine, that person will tend to choose a directly opposite activity. In the context of recreation this means that a person will form a leisure style that is opposite to his occupational life style. Evidence for this has come from Hendee (1969) who has illustrated that urban dwellers tend to develop an appreciative rather than a utilitarian attitude toward nature whilst rural dwellers are more inclined to seek out the 'busy and exciting' activities of the towns and cities. In contrast, *familiarity theory* claims that individuals seek out recreational activities which are not markedly different from their everyday occupational life style. Again Hendee (1969) found support for this to the extent that farmers are often involved in such activities as hunting and fishing. Very little research, however, has assessed the relative significance of these contradictory theories, no doubt due to the inherent difficulties involved in determining what is 'opposite' or 'familiar'. It may even be that recreational experiences for the majority of people are both familiar and compensatory.

After all, such a situation fits experimental evidence that individuals require a continually varied sensory input. Given this conflict, it is not surprising that most recent research on recreational choice has focused on an alternative, namely *personal community theory*, which argues that an individual's preference is affected by those with whom he is in regular contact (e.g. family, friends and work associates). One implication of this theory is that a recreational activity learned in childhood can often be carried into adulthood.

The underlying motives that are postulated by the different theories manifest themselves in individual preferences for different recreational activities, although these preferences need not necessarily translate into action or behaviour because of the fact that access to recreational opportunities is often highly constrained by time and cost (Beard and Ragheb 1980). There are nonetheless occasions on which behaviour seems to match preferences, as in Shafer and Mietz's (1968) study of campers. More recently, however, Warburton (1981) identified the role of water-based activities in the recreational preference structure of urban residents, and argued that the relationship between preference and behaviour was not really significant. It was suggested, for example, that for the majority of the respondents a number of constraints precluded their preferences becoming operative. Given this rather tenuous link between preferences and behaviour it is perhaps best to view actual recreational behaviour patterns as arising from a decision-making process that is characterized by uncertainty, limited awareness, and limited opportunity (Chase and Cheek 1979). Such a perspective is central to Maw and Cosgrove's (1972) model of recreational choice (Fig. 12.4). At the scale of the individual day-trip this model suggests that quite often the choice of activity and location is not clearly planned when the trip begins (as in behavioural categories 2, 3 and 4 of Fig. 12.4). As a result recreational behaviour needs to be seen as a continually unfolding learning process rather than an event or series of events isolated in time and space (Murphy and Rosenblood 1974). This is especially true of an individual or a family moving to a new residential location; in such cases recreational behaviour begins as a kind of random search process but with time becomes more habitual (Elson 1974). Learning is not, however, a simple function of personal experience because recreational behaviour patterns are at all times influenced by the social context in which they occur (Mercer 1976). As a result any attempt to explain recreational preferences needs to go beyond personality and gender, income and class, and time-space factors to consider the role of family life cycle, residential history, and information availability (Witt and Bishop 1970).

Category		Description	Diagrammatic representation
1	PRIMARY	Precise activity 'A' and precise location 'L' of destination decided (at place of origin 'O')	O → AL
2 A	SECONDARY	Precise activity decided, location uncertain	O — A → L_1 / - - L_2 / - - L_3
L		Activity uncertain, precise location decided	O — L → A_1 / - - A_2 / - - A_3
3 A	TERTIARY	Precise activity and location uncertain, subsequent decision about activity, and then about location	O — Lg — A → L_1 / - - L_2 / - - L_3
L		Precise activity and location uncertain, subsequent decision about location, and then about activity	O — Lg — L → A_1 / - - A_2 / - - A_3
AL		Precise activity and location uncertain, subsequent decision about both activity and location	O — Lg → AL
4	IMPULSE	Decision about either activity or location changed 'on impulse' i.e. by being made 'aware'	O - - - A_1L_1 ↓ A_2L_2

Fig. 12.4 The linkage between location and awareness. *Source*: Maw and Cosgrove (1972, 8).

Life cycle and role change

Personal community theory hypothesizes that individual recreational preferences are influenced by those around them (especially relatives, friends, and peer groups) and that a preferred activity developed in childhood is often maintained into adulthood. However, it is evident even to the casual observer that different groups influence individuals at different stages in their life cycle; for example, during infancy parents are dominant whereas during schooldays teachers and schoolmates become important. These developmental life events or transition parts have been incorporated by Rapoport and Rapoport (1975) into a simplified model of life-time influences on recreational choice (Fig. 12.5). The model highlights the changing influences acting upon an individual throughout a lifetime and the way in which different roles – dependent child, college student, breadwinner – are adopted. Each stage brings with it drives towards, and constraints on, different types of recreational behaviour.

Of course, at several stages of the life cycle an individual may be subject to a number of different roles with which are associated various social influences and recreational pursuits (Preston and Taylor 1981). In fact a constellation of roles can result in a diversity of recreational pursuits being carried on at the same stage of the life cycle as, for example, when a businessman pursues some activities with his family, some with friends, some with workmates, and some with business associates. However, each life cycle stage also involves a multitude of constraints which inhibit more active recreational involvement. In summary form these include such things as relative poverty (as in youth, retirement, or the early years of family formation), relative immobility (as when young children restrict the movements of other family members or when access to private or public transport is difficult or impossible), and lack of time (arising from the competing demands of work-related activities such as commuting) (Unkel 1981). In addition, recreational activities during child-rearing often revolve around the preferences of the children and are frequently centred on easily accessible activities. This may have the effect of increasing family cohesiveness, which is especially significant if one or both of the parents are in full-time employment (West and Merriam 1970). This, of course, introduces the idea of *preference subordination*, that is the extent to which the preference of an individual is subordinated to the needs and preferences of others.

Knowledge of life cycle changes and role changes is crucial in any attempt to determine the preference structure of individual recreational behaviour, not least because it draws attention to the difference between real

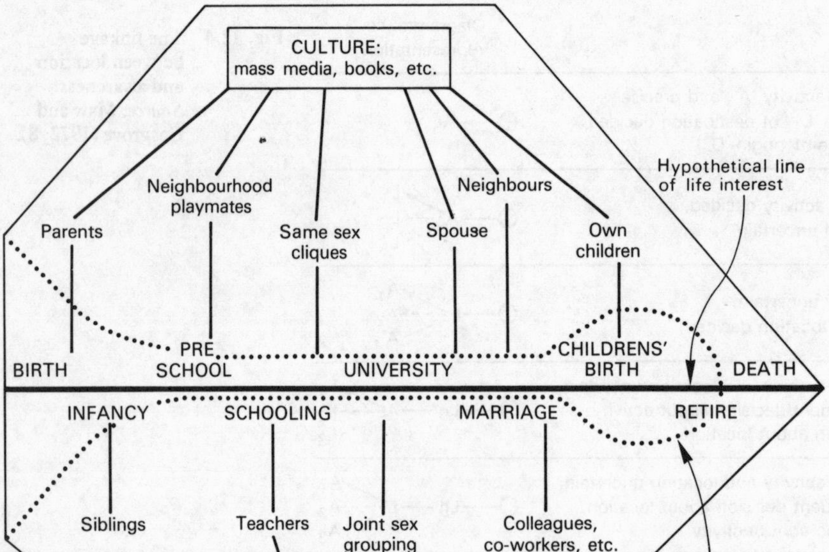

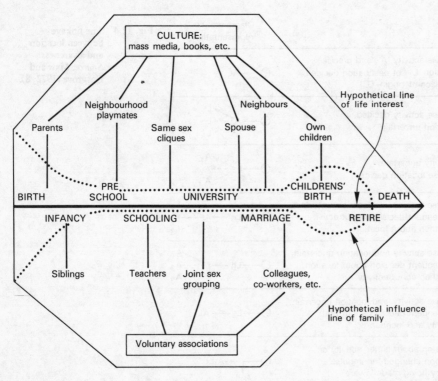

Fig. 12.5 Life cycle influences on recreational behaviour. *Source*: R. and R. Rapoport (1975, 22).

and professed motives for involvement in many recreational pursuits. Such motives are often highly complex and obscure. It may be, for example, that many motives are so deep-seated as not to be uncovered in the standard questionnaire schedule which might explain therefore why apparently different 'reasons' may be given by similar people to participation in the same activities (Murphy 1975). There is, in other words, a great need to consider the meaning of recreational pursuits for individuals, particularly in view of Kelly's (1974: 192) observation that 'the same activity may have differing social meanings and role relations at different times'. This, in turn, means that it might be useful to explore the suggestion that leisure is more identity-seeking for youth, more role-related for parents, more work and community-related in later years, and more interpersonal or solitary in retirement (Kelly 1974: 192). After all, such changes form the basis of the Hendee *et al.* (1971) typology of recreational activities (see Fig. 12.2).

Residential history and information access

It is almost axiomatic that the values and customs of an individual's locality and region will strongly influence and limit his choice of leisure pursuits. Different areas, in other words, have different recreational endowments which can have a direct impact on the manifest recreational behaviour of the population. For example, Knetsch (1974) found that people make greater use of water recreation facilities *per capita* in the Maritimes than they do in the Prairies, the differences having more to do with the availability of water than with differences in income, education or age distribution between the two populations. Of course with the absence of a particular recreational activity, the individual recreationist has either to substitute another available activity for the unavailable desired activity or enlarge his recreational 'space' by travelling further if recreational need is to be fulfilled (Smith 1980). The degree to which preferences are substituted is difficult to determine, partly because of the problems of forming suitable questions and partly because the substitute activity can become, over a period of time, the desired activity. Enlargement of recreational awareness space is more readily assessed. However, use of this enlarged space is not automatic but depends on the mobility potential of the individual (Harrison and Stabler 1981). Overall, though, an individual's action space plays a crucial role in determining recreational choices; for example, the recreational activity of slum-dwellers differs markedly from that of middle-class cosmopolites. Further, the residential history of an individual is an immensely important factor influencing recreational preferences and needs. An individual who has lived in a number of different places has probably had the opportunity to engage in a variety of recreational pursuits, is therefore aware of different recreational possibilities, and, inevitably, becomes sensitized to differences between the environments with which he comes into contact. Despite this, many individuals have recreation patterns that become habituated with regard to favoured activities and location. For these individuals a change in behaviour only comes about as a consequence of life cycle changes and/or changes in the availability of information.

An individual's choice of recreational pursuit is influenced markedly by the information available about likely recreational opportunities. All the various forms of media, as well as friends and relatives, provide details on places to visit and societies to join. Moreover a number of specialized magazines are devoted to providing information related to hundreds of individual recreational pursuits. Of course, advertising has over the years become strongly associated with leisure and recreation since it not only encourages people to participate in certain activities but also frequently uses a variety of recreational settings as a background for its general promotional activities. However, the effect of this information on recreational behaviour has yet to be analysed in any detail (see Larrabee and Meyerjohn 1960).

Whatever the source of an individual's information, recreation and tourism were generally regarded until relatively recently as beneficial both for individual well-being and for those organizations involved in providing recreational facilities. For example, great emphasis has been placed by planners on the regional multiplier effect and the way in which investment in tourism is supposed to trickle through to the local community (Archer 1973; Smith and Wilde 1977). However, of late, some attention has been drawn to issues of environmental quality and social justice (Cushman and Hamilton-Smith 1980). For the most part, this attention has focused on land use pressures and land management policies (Cheng 1980; Turner 1981; Bosselman 1978), and only rarely has there been any appreciation of the social costs of tourism in advanced western economies (Birrell and Silverwood 1981). This is perhaps changing. One of the earliest authors to sound a cautionary note in respect to the side-effects of tourism was Young (1973) who drew attention to the regional and local disbenefits of tourist development. More recently, Walmsley, Boskovic and Pigram (1981) have shown how increasing tourism is related to higher crime rates on the north coast of New South Wales. Looking into the future, the advancement of the microchip technology will almost certainly result in people working less and retiring earlier. This will mean a dramatic increase in leisure time (Seltzer and Wilson 1980). According to Jenkins and Sherman (1979; 1981), this may ultimately lead to the obliteration of the distinction between work and leisure. However in the intervening period, and whilst the work ethic still holds sway, leisure will continue to compete with work for both time and resources.

Chapter 13

STRESS AND PATHOLOGY

It is generally agreed that cities have proportionately higher rates of so-called pathological indicators – social disorganization, physical and mental illness, delinquent and criminal behaviour – than small towns and rural areas and the past two decades have seen numerous attempts at, and considerable success in, delineating the patterns of these pathologies (see Ch. 3). Attempts at explanation have been less satisfactory. This is partly because many of the aggregate relationships identified are in themselves not 'real' explanations of the pathologies. For example, correlations between aggregate indicators of pathology and areal structural characteristics (such as housing density) reveal little or nothing about what actually causes pathological behaviour. Several researchers have, therefore, argued in favour of a more behavioural approach to analysis while others have advocated a radical reinterpretation of the causes of phenomena like crime (see Peet 1975; 1976; Dear 1981). Of course, advocacy of a behavioural emphasis does not mean that the aggregate analyses of the urban ecologists are useless; rather the argument is that this type of structural macro-scale study needs to be complemented by micro-scale inquiry into individual case studies if the causal links between environment and pathology are ever to be uncovered. A more behavioural analysis also involves a shift of emphasis from environmental determinism, so beloved of the urban ecologist, to the problems actually experienced by individuals in coping with urban living. Appreciation of these problems involves an understanding of the concept of stress.

Environmental stress

Urban life is an endless round of conflicts, inconveniences, frustrations, and difficulties posed by phenomena such as noise, pollution, overcrowding, and congestion. The effect of these is to create *stress*, which, in general, may be defined as the affective behavioural and physiological response to aversive stimuli (Lazarus and Cohen 1977). According to Simmel (1957) and Plant (1957), stress is a personal state which is produced by certain agents, or *stressors*, in the environment. A failure to adapt to stressful conditions may result in a behavioural response that can adversely affect an individual's well-being (Glass and Singer 1972).

The extent to which some situations arouse stress, and the degree to which individuals can reduce this stress, is influenced by both the psychological structure of the individual and the cognitive features of the stimulus situation (Lazarus 1966). In simple terms, stress is aroused by stimuli from the environment. If the level of stress exceeds an individual's capacity to cope, then there sometimes results a condition of *cognitive overload*, that is to say, the individual may feel too pressurized to behave normally (Miller 1961; Milgram 1970). In such circumstances, the individual has to adopt coping strategies, with the purpose of eliminating or at least reducing the pressure. Continued exposure to pressure can produce cumulative effects which may lead to psychological problems. Despite the adoption of coping strategies, the effects of the stressful conditions can reappear after stimulation has terminated, possibly in a form that leaves the individual less capable of coping with subsequent emotional demands. Cognitive overload is not of course the only source of pressure. Stress may also be created by a deprivation of stimuli; for example, individuals undergoing prolonged isolation generally experience many of the symptoms of the mentally ill. Thus, according to Wohlwill (1970), individuals need some degree of stimulation for the development and maintenance of normal behaviour. There may exist, in other words, an optimal level of stimulation (Fig. 13.1).

The identification of the stressors which lead to individual or group sensory overload has been a focus of considerable research (McCarthy and Saegert 1978) and the legacy of urban ecology has encouraged many to seek the causes of stress in the fabric of the urban environment (Schmitt 1966; Fischer 1973). For example, much emphasis has been placed upon the role

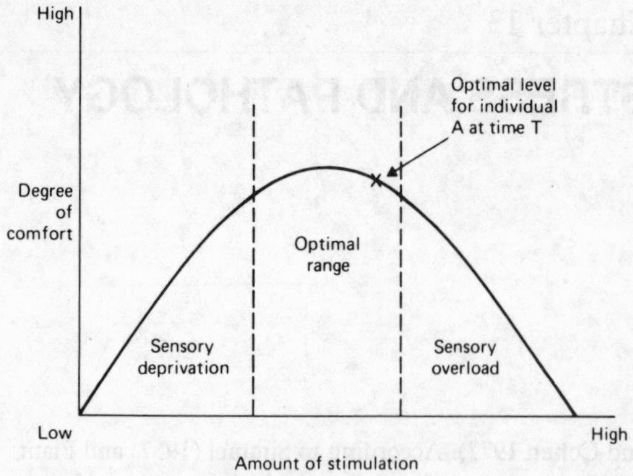

Fig. 13.1 The optimal level of stimulation. *Source*: Porteous (1977, 153).

of such physical stressors as mechanical vibration, noise, dirt, and other forms of pollution. Despite their likely harmful effects, there is, however, little detailed evidence as to how they affect behaviour and the quality of life. The reason for this may be attributed not only to the deficiency of research methodology but also to the fact that several of these stressors may occur together and may, in any case, reach their full impact only after a long period of time. Paralleling this line of argument is that which suggests that deviant behaviour and ill-health may be related to the layout and design of the urban environment. Largely derived from the work of the American architect Newman (1972), and focusing predominantly on high-rise living, this form of architectural determinism has, of late, gained considerable publicity. In particular, control of crime has been related to the concept of *defensible space*. In such a space, latent territoriality and a sense of community is translated into responsibility for ensuring a safe and well-maintained living environment (Merry 1981). In other words, public space is designed in such a way as to make it the responsibility of local residents. The potential criminal perceives such a space as being controlled by the residents and therefore avoids the area for fear of being recognized as an intruder.

Another source of stress in the city, and one which has wide-spread currency in the social science literature, is *crowding* (Collette and Webb 1976; Zlutnick and Altman 1972; Boots 1979). For example, a popular image has been created of the dark and overcrowded conditions of the urban slum being the breeding ground for deviant behaviour and ill-health. According to this perspective, the feelings of crowding, and the conditions associated with it, create tension which modifies behaviour to the extent that physical and social pathologies may result (Kirmeyer 1978). The main basis of this model is, however, research carried out with animals, where the links between crowding, stress, and abnormal behaviour have been established under laboratory conditions (Esser 1976; Edney 1977). For example, in a study of the effects of overcrowding on rats, Calhoun (1962; 1966) found that a point was reached in population increase at which the rats' social and territorial organization collapsed. This point, called the *behavioural sink*, resulted in disorganization and pathology, and was rapidly followed by a decline in the rat population as the rats became so deranged that normal reproduction proved difficult. Predictably this crowding theory has come in for stern criticism: the parallels between the animal laboratory and the large city are not close, and the influence that crowding might have is in any case masked by social and cultural variables (Baldassare and Fischer 1976). Despite these problems, the concept of crowding has been extensively used as a means of interpreting urban pathologies (Gad 1973). The line of argument generally used in such analyses may be outlined briefly. High urban densities are thought to make individuals feel crowded. The resultant overload of stimuli from the environment leads to overstimulation which can cause physiological and psychological stress. In an attempt to reduce the overstimulation associated with crowding, individuals often withdraw from society. In turn, that withdrawal can result in stimulus deprivation, which is also stressful. Moreover, withdrawal from society can bring with it rejection of society's norms, values, and modes. The resultant lack of pressure towards social conformity, coupled with the absence of traditional social support (family, neighbours), may lead to the adoption of antisocial behaviour or simply unacceptable levels of pressure. Therefore, stress, whether from stimulus overload or deprivation, may lead to pathologies such as physical illness, mental illness, and deviant behaviour (Freedman 1975; Verbrugge and Taylor 1980).

Patterns of pathology

When deviant behaviour and ill-health in the city are mapped, the revealed patterns are rarely random, but rather take the form of readily identifiable clusters. For example, McHarg (1969), in an extensive study of pathologies in Philadelphia, found that the incidences of a whole series of physical and mental illnesses, as well as a number of crimes and delinquencies, were concentrated in the centre of the city, with a gradual reduction toward the suburban periphery. Using a large number of territorial indicators of pathologies, in conjunction with social and environmental variables, later researchers such as Smith (1973) and Boal *et al.* (1978) identified similar statistically significant clusterings. Some researchers have labelled these clusters as *pathogenic areas*, thereby suggesting that some peculiarity of the area in question actually gives rise to pathology.

An important early attempt to explain these patterns of urban pathologies was that made by Schmitt (1966) in Honolulu. The prime object of this study was to discover which was most relevant – high density or household overcrowding – in generating pathologies. When the density of persons per acre was held constant, the degree of crowding within living quarters showed virtually no relation to the incidence of pathology. On the other hand, population per acre (a density measure) correlated significantly with such measures as family disorganization, juvenile delinquency, adult crime, high rates of physical illness, and mental breakdown. Any suggestion that density is a cause of pathology runs counter, however, to Winsborough's (1965) study of Chicago which found that density was actually associated with lower levels of morbidity, disease, and the need for public assistance. Winsborough also found, in contrast to Schmitt (1966), that his index of overcrowding – seven persons per room – correlated positively with pathology. The whole issue is complicated further by Schmitt's (1963) own study of Hong Kong, one of the world's most densely populated territories, and therefore an area where high rates of death, disease, and social disorganization might be expected. Even though the rates for maternal deaths and infant deaths in Hong Kong exceed those for American cities, the overall rates for mental illness and crime were considerably lower. Schmitt attempted to explain these differences in cultural terms, which, along with Winsborough's evidence, suggests that social structure is a crucial factor mediating people's behaviour under high-density conditions.

More recent studies of urban pathology and population density have gone a stage further and concluded that there is no convincing evidence that density causes or is related to pathology, mental disorder, or social disorganization (Fischer 1975; 1976). Thus, even though a few studies have revealed a relationship between crowding and pathology (see Carstairs 1960; Sharrod and Davis 1974), the majority report contradictory evidence (see Levy and Herzog 1974; Gillis 1977; Freedman *et al.* 1975; Snow and Han 1981). However, a number do suggest that density affects certain population groups, such as the young, old, and those under other forms of stress. For example, a major survey for the Canadian Government has concluded that population density and crowding are only modestly, if at all, related but that household crowding can have an adverse effect on the health and intellectual development of children. Likewise crowded conditions occasionally have greater adverse effects when people are already under stress due to low income or other problems (see Booth 1976; Booth and Johnson 1975; Booth and Edwards 1976; Booth *et al.* 1976). This survey is important because it deals with individual rather than aggregate data and so avoids the problems involved in interpreting ecological correlations (Fischer 1975). Moreover, from this kind of evidence, as well as Schmitt's earlier studies, it would appear that certain groups are more affected than others by high levels of density and household crowding (Schmidt *et al.* 1979). Therefore, for certain susceptible populations, and when in combination with other stressors, density may have deleterious effects on mental and physical health. However, it is important to distinguish between pathologies because different stressors may have different effects on different individuals (Sadalla 1978).

Physical pathology

The distribution of physical ill-health has been of interest to geographers for a considerable time (see Howe 1976; 1977; Learmonth 1978; McGlashan 1972; Hunter 1975; Phillips 1981). For example, major studies such as Howe's (1970) *National Atlas of Disease Mortality*, have emphasized regional variation in the incidence of diseases such as lung cancer, bronchitis, and tuberculosis whilst others have been concerned with the way in which contagious diseases spread through a population (Hunter and Young 1971). From these regional studies it has been established that cities in general are less healthy than rural areas. Intra-city variation in disease has therefore become a major focus of interest (Giggs 1979; Pyle 1979).

Evidence from the growing industrial cities in the nineteenth century Britain suggested that much physical ill-health was concentrated in localities with poor housing conditions (Rosen 1973). This was most convincingly illustrated in Snow's famous map linking the outbreak of cholera in London in the early 1850s with the distribution of polluted public water pumps (Stamp 1964). By today, however, advances in medical science have virtually eliminated a whole range of diseases and have reduced the effects of others. Yet recent researchers have suggested that certain forms of ill-health are still concentrated in particular urban neighbourhoods. For example, by adopting a factor analytic approach in a study of Chicago, Pyle and Rees (1971) were able to identify a typology of diseases and their social environmental correlates (Fig. 13.2). A

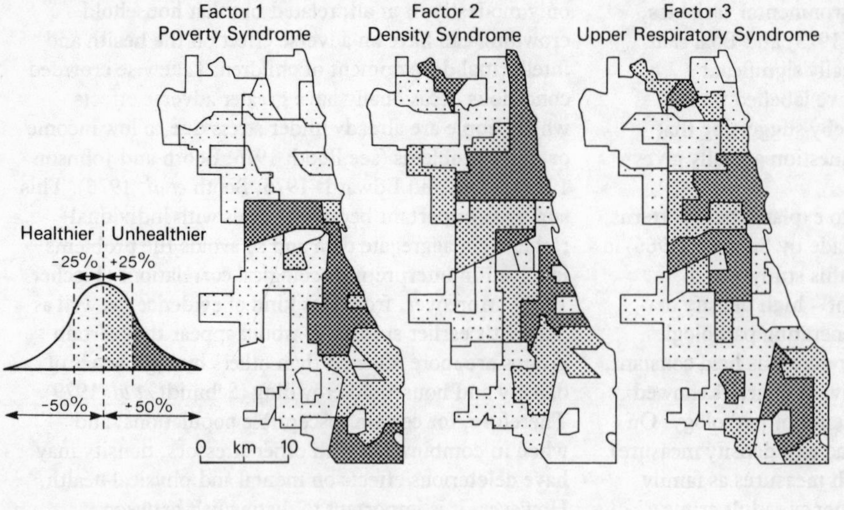

Fig. 13.2 Physical pathology in Chicago. *Source*: Pyle and Rees (1971, 477).

range of health measures, including infant mortality and tuberculosis, were linked with indices of poverty, and concentrated in the city's poorest neighbourhoods. Similarly, infectious diseases such as mumps and whooping cough occurred in overcrowded districts and infectious hepatitis revealed spatial correspondence with stretches of open water. This variability in the incidence of disease in the modern city has been replicated in a number of subsequent studies (see Castle and Gittus 1957; Griffiths 1971; Girt 1972).

Although intrinsically interesting, studies of the distribution of diseases are essentially macro-scale in emphasis and hence reveal little about why individuals in one area are more prone to fall sick than individuals in another area (King 1979). Even with increasingly sophisticated means of analysis, causal links between disease and environmental conditions are still difficult to establish, as was clearly illustrated by Dever's (1972) study of the incidence of leukaemia at four geographical scales in Buffalo. At the two intermediate scales, block and census tract, no relationship existed between measures of the local environment and leukaemia. However, at the macro-scale (the tax district) a relationship with population density was evident, and at the micro-scale (the housing unit) there existed a clear correlation with levels of overcrowding. This confused picture clearly demonstrates that causation can only be determined at the individual scale since the areal scale is only capable of revealing general associations. Giggs *et al*. (1980) came to a similar conclusion when analysing the incidence of primary acute pancreatitis in Nottingham where detailed local knowledge suggested a relationship between illness and a particular water supply source. Of course as the incidence of diseases declines, and their association with the environment becomes less evident, then behavioural factors such as access to, and use of, medical facilities play an increasingly significant role in further alleviating ill-health and reducing mortality (Shannon 1977; Mayer 1982). Despite the development of sophisticated health delivery systems in most western countries access to medical care still appears to vary inversely with that of need (Hart 1971). For example, in Britain and New Zealand, where a nationalized health service provides for the whole population, several maldistributions such as that of general practitioners are evident (Knox, 1978). In the use of primary care it has been found that distance has a marked negative effect upon consultancy rates (Phillips 1979) as has the influence of neighbours and friends (Knox and Paccoine 1980). In the United States the poor, the elderly, and the blacks visit physicians much less frequently than the higher income groups (Dutton 1978). In fact, they tend to make use of medical services only when they are chronically ill, usually the hospital emergency service, so it is little wonder that the mortality rates are high (de Vise 1973). Pyle (1973) has revealed in a study of the diffusion of measles in Akron that patterns of re-infection could only be interpreted in terms of health-care policy and behavioural response (Fig. 13.3). The appropriate vaccine was relatively expensive, and so cost became a barrier to innoculation for large numbers of low-income residents. Even physicians' referral practices can have an effect upon the health of patients; for example, in Oxford the rates of perinatal mortality were significantly higher among women who had not been referred to consultants' care, and especially so among high-risk women who lived a long way from consultants (Hobbs and Acheson 1966). The development of preventive medicine is also of significance, for instance, in Britain the policies of the Health Education Council have been found to have an effect upon the actions of

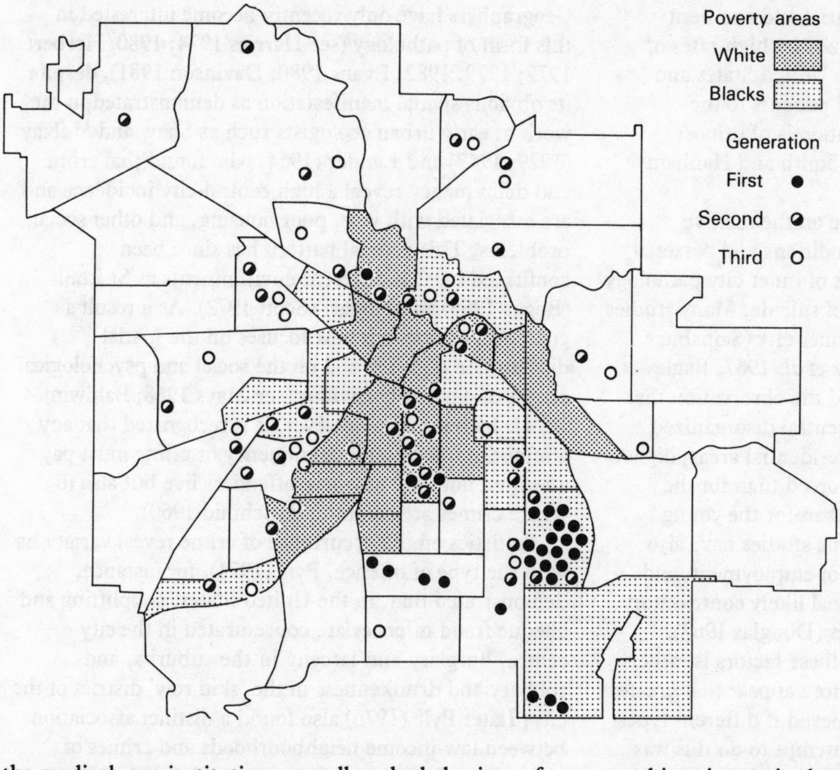

Fig. 13.3 The diffusion of measles in Akron. *Source*: based on Pyle (1973, 351–3).

the medical care institutions as well as the behaviour of the target populations (Budd and Budd 1981). This sort of behavioural interpretation of urban physical pathologies must not however be overemphasized; it may be important in western cities but in much of the third world physical environmental factors are still paramount (Learmonth 1975).

Mental pathology

Early studies of mental disorders within cities revealed high incidences in the city centre and progressively lower incidences in the suburbs (Faris and Dunham 1939; Bagley *et al.* 1973) (see Ch. 3.) More recently this general picture has been found to be more apparent than real to the extent that some types of mental illness display very distinctive spatial characteristics whilst others appear to be aspatial (Giggs 1979). For example, Mintz and Schwarz (1964) found that in North America schizophrenia was concentrated in underprivileged and sub-standard districts of the city, whilst manic depression had no such spatial pattern and was more explicable in terms of personality and psychological factors. Similarly, Giggs (1973) found that nearly 70 per cent of schizophrenics in Nottingham lived within 4 kilometres of the city centre, yet suggested that many of these were psychologically vulnerable persons who had moved into inner city locations. In other words, central city areas do not cause schizophrenia so much as attract schizophrenics. A similar suggestion that the mentally ill are mobile was made by Timms (1965) on the strength of his finding that mental illness in Luton was closely associated with municipal housing. There is, then, a degree of confusion as to whether residence in a given area is a cause or a symptom of mental illness. The increasing use of case-histories has, in part, allowed some of this confusion to be resolved. An important study which illustrates the use of case-histories was that by Bagley (1974) in three contrasting wards in Brighton. By collecting information on migration, housing, and psychiatric admissions he was able to test the relative significance of local housing conditions and selective migration as explanations of inner city mental illness. However, from the time that had elapsed since migration and the appearance of symptoms, Bagley concluded that both housing and selection were at work in the emergence of mental illness. Other studies generally concur with this but suggest that the relative significance of the two explanations varies both between cities and over time (Moos 1976; Deans and James 1981). In this context it is important to note an experiment by C. Smith (1976) who found that certain neighbourhoods were more supportive of former mental patients than others and were, therefore, associated with lower rates of recidivism, or return to hospital. Conversely, other areas, notably commercial-industrial and transient neighbourhoods, were characterized by high rates of recidivism. With the move in the United States and Britain towards returning mental patients to the community, this kind of information is of utmost significance (see C. Smith 1977; Smith and Hanham 1981; Dear and Taylor 1982).

The most convincing evidence on the relative significance of environmental conditions and personal migratory history as explanations of inner city pathology has come from the examination of suicide. Many studies have highlighted suicide in the inner city (Sainsbury 1955; Whitlock 1973; McCullock *et al.* 1967; Bagley *et al.* 1976) and generally confirmed the observation that the suicide rate is higher in the central disorganized sector of cities than in outlying residential areas, higher for the single, widowed, and divorced than for the married, and higher for the old than for the young (Henry and Short 1957: 63). Some studies have also argued that a loss of status, loss of employment, and increasing isolation were additional likely contributory factors towards high suicide rates (Douglas 1967). However, the universality of all these factors is rather inconclusive, and it would therefore appear that greater levels of explanation may be achieved if different types of suicide are considered. One attempt to do this was Bagley and Jacobson's (1976) test of the hypothesis that four types of suicide (depressive, socio-pathic, physical illness, and 'residual') vary significantly in prevalence between three contrasting parts of Brighton: the central wards of the city, which were characterized by poor housing and high rates of social disorganization; a group of middle-class wards; and a series of intermediate wards. The results revealed that two of the four types of suicide varied significantly between the three areas: 'socio-pathic' suicide occurred predominantly in the central wards, and 'physical illness' suicide in the middle-class wards. From this evidence it is apparent that any significant advances in causal research in relation to suicide, and possibly in relation to pathology generally, will depend upon carefully devised longitudinal analysis of individual life-histories for only in this way will it be possible to identify the different stresses that operate. Such 'life-event' research on mental illness is of course fraught with difficulties (see Dear 1981).

Social pathology

Crime and delinquency may be considered as examples of social pathology in that they represent a form of deviant behaviour which disregards a set of rules of behaviour which society as a whole has determined. Geographers have only recently become interested in this form of pathology (see Harries 1974; 1980; Herbert 1977; 1979; 1982; Evans 1980; Davidson 1981), despite its obvious spatial manifestation as demonstrated in the work of early urban ecologists such as Shaw and McKay (1929; 1942) and Lander (1954) who found that crime and delinquency reveal a high central-city incidence and are associated with vice, poor housing, and other social problems. This general pattern has since been confirmed in such different environments as St Louis (Boggs 1965) and Hobart (Scott 1972). As a result a good deal of research now focuses on the spatial distribution of crime and on the social and psychological causes of deviant behaviour (see Mays 1968; Baldwin 1974). Increasingly, however, it is recognized that any attempt to understand delinquency or crime must pay attention not only to where offenders live but also to where crimes are committed (Schmid 1960).

Statistics on the occurrence of crime reveal variations with the type of offence. Pyle (1974), for instance, demonstrated that, in the United States, shoplifting and cheque fraud offences are concentrated in the city centre, burglary and larceny in the suburbs, and robbery and drunkenness in the 'skid row' district of the city. Later Pyle (1976) also found a distinct association between low-income neighbourhoods and crimes of violence (including murder, rape, and assault) and between the 'transitional' areas of the city, characterized by a decaying physical environment and a concentration of manufacturing and wholesaling, and offences such as robbery, larceny and car theft (as well as assault and murder). In contrast, the middle to upper income suburban neighbourhoods were associated with property crimes such as burglary, larceny, and car theft. This pattern suggests that there might be marked spatial variations in opportunities for crime, particularly in large cities (see Corsi and Harvey 1975; Baldwin and Bottoms 1976).

The manner in which different parts of the city provide opportunities for crime has been analysed in several detailed micro-scale studies. For example, Ley and Cybriwsky (1974b) found that the occurrence of abandoned and stripped cars in Philadelphia, which appeared to have a random distribution, in fact was closely related to vacant land, doorless sides of buildings, and institutional land use. Herbert (1976) went further than this and, on the basis of the pattern of juvenile delinquency in Cardiff, argued that the incidence of deviance was related not only to detailed land use but also to the design of the built environment. Several studies have in fact found that high-rise housing projects have much higher rates of crime than low-rise housing, despite similarities in population size and social composition (Tata *et al.* 1975; Mawby 1977).

Similarly, Brantingham and Brantingham (1975) showed that the incidence of burglary in Tallahassee was highest in peripheral blocks of housing estates, where burglars could benefit from the weaker social control of anonymous boundary areas. Carter and Hill (1976) have even suggested that the offender's image of the attractiveness and vulnerability of particular neighbourhoods, streets, and buildings may be very significant. Certainly, low school vandalism rates seem to typify school buildings with high levels of aesthetic appeal, good maintenance, visible sites, and active neighbourhoods (Pablan and Baxter 1975). On balance, then, local environmental factors may be more important than the broader framework of societal structure in determining the locations at which crime occurs.

Societal forces are of course vitally important in predisposing an individual to crime. There is nevertheless an environmental influence to be determined even here in that the majority of criminals' home addresses are in central city areas. This pattern may however be changing. The regular gradient, with low rates of criminality in the suburbs and a peak in the inner city, is now less significant than it was as a result of the outward shift of offenders' residences caused by public housing policies and, more particularly, the tendency for public authorities to 'dump' offenders in 'problem' estates (Lambert 1970). The effect of these trends is to weaken the environmental argument that the central city in some way 'causes' criminal behaviour and to give greater emphasis to Schmid's (1960: 678) point that offenders, irrespective of where they live, 'are characterized by all or most of the following factors: low social cohesion, weak family life, low socio-economic status, physical deterioration, high rates of population mobility and personal disorganization'. However, Herbert (1976), in a more recent study of several delinquent and non-delinquent neighbourhoods in Cardiff, has re-emphasized the role of space by testing the hypothesis that the spatial order in the incidence of delinquency is underlain by systematic variations in related attitudes and behaviour. This study concluded that differences existed in the way residents labelled neighbourhoods as delinquent and non-delinquent. Geographical differences were also identified in residents' conception of what amounted to criminal behaviour; for example, residents of delinquent areas were less inclined to report petty theft and damage to property than were the residents of non-delinquent neighbourhoods. On the other hand, parents in delinquent areas tended to refer truancy to the schools whilst those from non-delinquent areas were more inclined to administer their own sanctions. In short, Herbert's study clearly illustrates the significance of geographical variations in attitudes and behaviour in any interpretation of deviant behaviour. However, many more studies along similar lines will be needed before the role of the social milieu can be more fully comprehended (see Taylor *et al.* 1973).

Stress reconsidered

The adoption of a more behavioural approach to the analysis of several types of pathologies has revealed that stress cannot be explained in terms of a single causal factor. Even when crowding is interpreted in its broadest sense it still fails to provide an adequate basis for explaining all pathologies in all contexts (Severy 1978). One common response to this dilemma has been to cite evidence in support of particular theories and concepts in specific situations, carefully overlooking the fact that it is possible to find support for quite different theories with the same evidence. A more sensible approach would be to look at multi-factor explanations of stress. Such an approach was developed by Herbert (1977) with reference to crime and delinquency (Fig. 13.4). The focus of the model is poverty, which is seen as the product of structural factors such as differential access to employment and educational opportunities. The net effect of these factors is to produce a number of 'losers', notably the unemployed, the aged, misfits, and members of minority groups (Schmitt *et al.* 1978).

The susceptibility of 'losers' to stressful conditions has recently been attributed to a perceived lack of control over the environment on the part of the individuals involved (Cohen and Sherrod 1978). In other words, it is becoming increasingly recognized that certain individuals have greater control over the environment than others. As a result several theories have been suggested to explain how perceived controllability influences human responses to stressful situations. For example, people who perceive themselves as effective manipulators of the environment develop a sense of personal causation and intrinsic motivation or self-efficacy (Bandura 1977). This increases their felt competence in the face of environmental stress. Conversely, people who experience inescapable environmental stress develop the expectancy that their own instrumental responses are ineffective in producing desirable outcomes. These feelings of 'helplessness' often become associated with defects in task performance (Seligman 1975) as well as with deteriorating health and well-being. This concept of control may be particularly important in understanding the effects of density on human behaviour because it has been argued that high-density

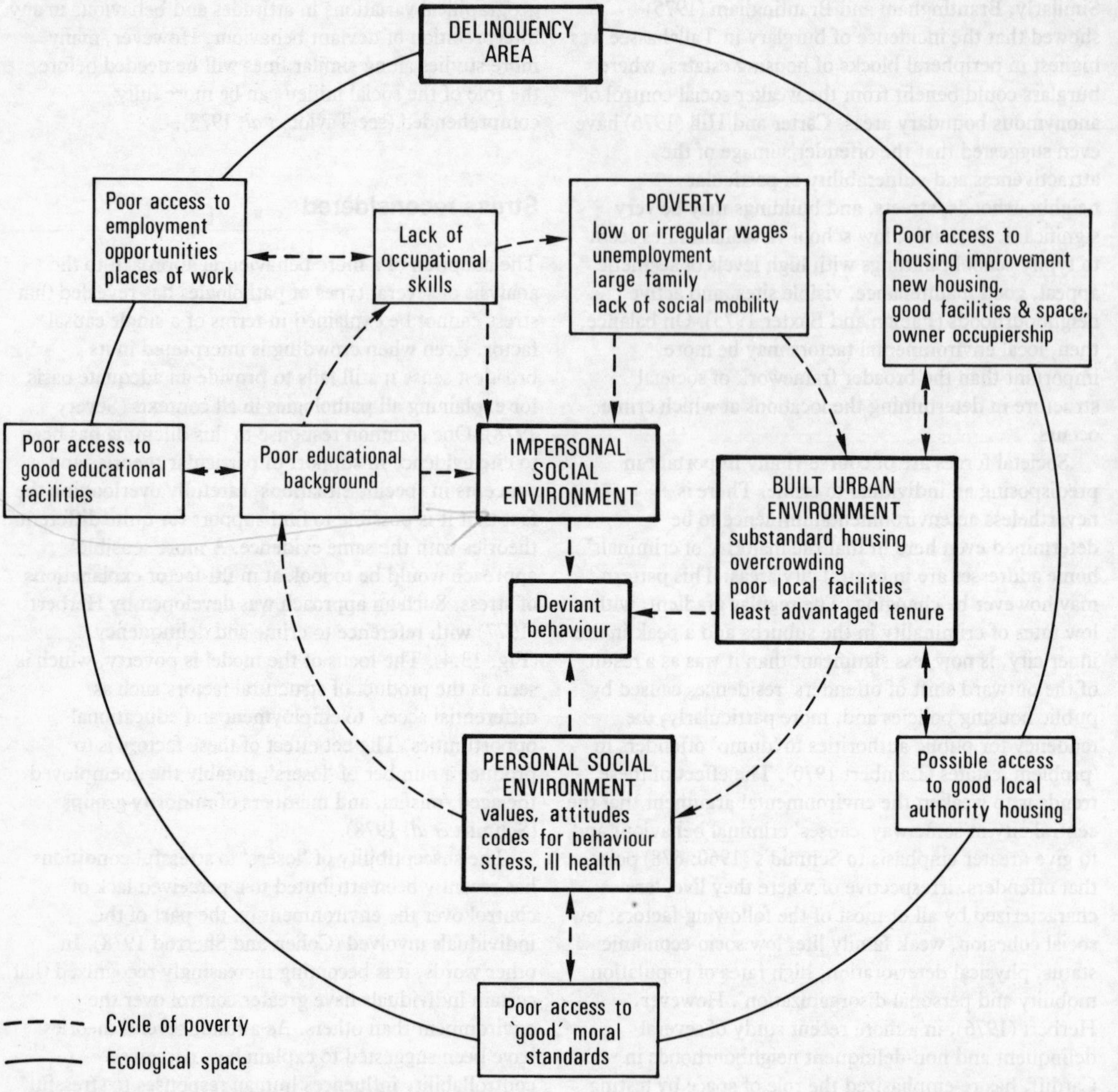

Fig. 13.4 The cycle of disadvantage. *Source*: Herbert (1977, 227).

environments are often uncontrollable environments (Stokols 1976). In particular, density may affect the perceived controllability of the environment in two ways: first, the close proximity of other individuals may restrict and interfere with the attainment of an individual's goals; and, second, high density may involve strangers, thereby rendering the environment not only restricting but also unpredictable, irritating, and hence potentially uncontrollable (Cohen and Sherrod 1978). Of course only certain types of density will deprive individuals of control over their environments and therefore not all situations will be equally threatening even to those groups who are susceptible to feelings of helplessness (Taylor 1981). Precisely what sorts of environments and what sorts of people are at risk has not yet been fully explored.

Chapter 14

MIGRATION AND RESIDENTIAL MOBILITY

Migration, or the movement of people from one home location to another, has been taking place since the origins of man. During recorded history it has not only increased in volume but has also involved steadily lengthening distances. With this increasing amount and diversity of migration has come a corresponding necessity to identify and explain such movements (Lewis 1974; Kosinski and Prothero 1975). Of course, this is not an entirely new development because, as long ago as the 1880s, Ravenstein (1885; 1889), using birthplace statistics contained in the 1881 census of England and Wales, suggested that migration could be generalized into seven 'laws':

1. The majority of migrants move only a short distance, and consequently there is a general displacement of persons producing currents of migration in the direction of the great centres of commerce and industry.
2. The process of absorption is created by movement from immediately around a great city, creating gaps which are filled from more remote areas. This also means that few migrants will be found in cities from areas progressively further away.
3. Dispersion has similar features and is the inverse of absorption.
4. Each main current of migration produces a compensating counter-current.
5. Long-distance migrants generally go to large cities.
6. Urban dwellers are less migratory than rural dwellers.
7. Females are more migratory than males.

Although this highly generalized framework refers very much to late Victorian Britain, it does emphasize that in any analysis of migration it is necessary to consider at least three inter-related elements: the place of migration; its causes; and its selective nature (Grigg 1977). Since the publication of Ravenstein's 'laws' no one researcher has attempted to produce such a comprehensive framework, although individual parts have been analysed in a more sophisticated manner (Lee, 1960).

For some time geographers were content with describing and explaining migratory flows in terms of distance decay, as expressed in the gravity model and its later derivative, the intervening opportunity model (see Ch. 2). However, even with the inclusion of additional socio-economic factors, usually within a regression equation, it was found that such formulations achieved a fair degree of prediction only at the aggregate level (Ter Heide 1963; Willis 1974). This caused disquiet. Hägerstrand (1970: 8), for example, claimed that nothing truly general can be said about aggregate regularities until it has been made clear how far they remain invariant with organizational differences at the micro-level. Comments such as this stimulated many researchers to conceptualize the migratory process in terms of 'push' and 'pull' forces and to seek information, in sample surveys, on what motivates individuals to resolve these contradictory forces in a particular way (Lewis 1982). Yet even this procedure fails to determine whether there are any systematic influences that condition migration decisions, and fails to suggest by what evaluative processes individuals arrive at decisions whether to migrate (Pryor 1975). What is evident is that people differently located in space and social structure have different degrees of knowledge about, different perceptions of, and are able to benefit to different extents from opportunities at places other than those in which they currently reside (Jones 1980). Given that this is so, then simply asking questions about motives reveals little about the mechanics of the migration process (Taylor 1969).

In response to these criticisms the last decade or so has witnessed the emergence of a more behavioural approach to the study of migration and, in particular, urban residential site selection (Adams and Gilder 1976; Michelson 1977; Clark 1981). Such an approach argues that migration occurs because individuals believe that they will be able to better satisfy their aspirations in a location other than the one at which they are resident. In other words, the decision to migrate is made on the basis of perceived opportunities (with different locations providing different levels of opportunities to different individuals and groups) (White and Wood 1980; Coupe and Morgan 1981). Essentially, it is these perceived differences in opportunities that are important rather than any response to some 'objective' factor such as economic wage-rate fluctuation, or even a simple 'push' or 'pull' mechanism. If such an argument is accepted, then a more detailed explanation of why migration occurs must be concerned with at least two aspects of household behaviour:

1. The decision to seek a new location.
2. The search for, and selection of, a new location.

Such a two-stage framework has been widely adopted. However, before looking at the decision to move it is important to consider the reasons for migrating and the way in which these reasons change with the life cycle of potential migrants.

Reasons for migrating

In any consideration of migration it is necessary to distinguish between voluntary and involuntary moves (Cebula 1980). Although the latter are more often than not associated with wars, famines, and persecutions, there is growing evidence to suggest that, even within a city, something like 15 per cent of all moves are of a 'forced' nature, mostly associated with property eviction and demolition, retirement, ill-health, and divorce (Lewis 1982). In terms of voluntary migrations, however, the literature suggests that long-distance moves are generally motivated by economic factors such as unemployment, income, and career advancement, whilst short-distance moves are motivated by more social forces such as neighbourhood change, investment, marriage, and dwelling space requirements (Shaw 1975; Lewis 1982).

Following Wolpert's (1965; 1966) introduction of the *place utility* concept, most attempts to determine the reasons for migrating have been conceptualized within a *stress–satisfaction formulation*. Briefly, this viewpoint argues that the basis of any decision to migrate is the household's belief that the level of satisfaction obtainable elsewhere is greater that the present level of satisfaction (Lieber 1978). The difference between the two levels can, therefore, be regarded as a measure of stress. Clark *et al.* (1979) have suggested that in such circumstances the probability (P) of someone migrating depends on the relative weight of the pros and cons of migration at the time (t) in question:

$$P(t) = c \text{ Stress } (t) - \text{Resistance}(t)$$

Therefore, the estimation per individual at time t of his or her social–spatial circumstances depends on weighing advantages and disadvantages and judging the results within a set of tolerance limits:

$$P(t) = c\, A(t) - D(t)$$

where A stands for advantages, D for disadvantages, and c is a correction factor which is specific for the person, time, and space.

Despite the simplicity of the stress–satisfaction formulation, it is extremely difficult to operationalize (Brummell 1981; Salling and Harvey 1981). This was shown in Brown and Longbrake's (1970) pioneering study of residential mobility between 1966 and 1967 in Cedar Rapids. A principal components analysis revealed that over 64 per cent of the migration could be explained in terms of family status, income levels, housing quality, residential density, and site quality, and from this it was inferred that place utilities leading to migration were most likely to occur in those districts which were 'deprived' in comparison to other examples of the same type of area. In other words, the precise nature of a district was less significant than how it related to the norm of other similar districts. Unfortunately, such a measure of stress reveals little as to its precise nature and the way in which it affects the migration decision. Clark and Cadwallader (1973) have however remedied this failing by attempting to consider how stressors affect the migration decision. At the outset five indicators of stress were chosen for analysis:

1. The size and facilities of the dwelling unit.
2. The kind of people living in the neighbourhood.
3. Proximity of friends and relations.
4. Proximity to work.
5. Levels of air pollution.

The significance of these indicators was then tested in Los Angeles where a sample of households was asked to rate, on the basis of the five indicators, how easy or difficult it would be to find a more desirable location elsewhere. They were also asked to evaluate their level of satisfaction with their present residence and neighbourhood. A highly significant correlation of 0.384 was achieved between a desire to move and locational stress. Therefore, it would appear that most stress was experienced by those households who thought they could find a better residence elsewhere and who were the least satisfied with their present location. Apart from the pollution stressors, each of the other four indicators was important in creating household stress, with the size and facilities of the dwelling unit the most significant and proximity to work the least significant. Similarly,

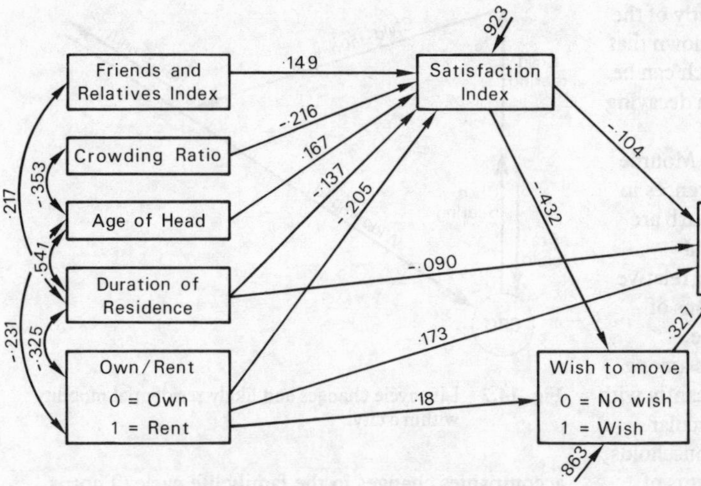

Fig. 14.1 Determinants of migration in Rhode Island, 1969. Included are all paths where the correlation coefficients are statistically significant at $p < .05$ based on two-tailed test. Intercorrelations of less than 0.2 between socio-economic variables are not shown. *Source*: Speare (1974, 181).

Speare (1974) developed an index of residential satisfaction based on housing and neighbourhood characteristics, and found, among a sample of households in Rhode Island, that it provided a meaningful measure of whether the households wished to migrate and whether they moved the following year. It was also found that individual attributes acted indirectly through the residential satisfaction index to affect mobility potential (Fig. 14.1). Clearly, both of these studies identified housing as the crucial variable in determining household stress and, therefore, corroborate findings of studies more directly concerned with the causes of residential mobility (Table 14.1).

The findings of Speare should not be overemphasized since there is more to residential satisfaction than housing and family requirements (Galster and Hesser 1982). Individuals identify with their residential location and endow it with social meaning. It therefore provides a base for social interaction as well as a symbol of social standing. In western society, for example, suburban residence appears to symbolize all the values of 'good' living as was found in Michelson's (1977) study of the way in which Toronto residents rated single-family dwellings as better than high-rise apartments. Likewise Zehner (1972) calculated that 86 per cent of the residents of four suburbs in New York State rated their neighbourhood as being excellent, with friendliness, safety, good schools, and a pleasant environment being the most significant attributes. Similar figures have been produced for middle-class suburbs in Cardiff (Herbert 1975). In contrast, it might be thought that inner city neighbourhoods with their decaying fabric, overcrowding and poor living conditions, often referred to by the media as 'slums', would be a source of considerable dissatisfaction. Surprisingly, this is not

Table 14.1 Causes of residential mobility

	Percentage of households in each sample	*Reason given*
Bedminster	70	Marriage/to own a house
(19th-century terraced dwellings, manual households, owner occupied)	13	Change in household size
St George	66	Marriage/to own a house
(Cheaper new owner-occupied housing)	12	Change in household size
	12	Troublesome neighbours
Westbury	28	Change in household size
(High status owner-occupied housing)	23	To own a house
	10	Previous residence was only temporary
St Pauls	21	Forced to move
(Mixed, run-down inner-city)	21	Setting up new household
	20	Changing space requirement
	12	Last place too expensive
	10	Poor physical condition of previous dwelling

Source: Short (1978a, 538).

always the case. For example, in his classic study of the Adam district in Chicago, Suttles (1972) has shown that the slum can generate its own subculture, which can be sufficient to offset the many disadvantages of a decaying fabric. Ley (1974) found a similar high level of satisfaction among the black population of the Monroe district of Philadelphia. This means that differences in the physical condition of the slum and the suburb are not always matched by differences in residential satisfaction levels because satisfaction is purely relative and varies according to the needs and aspirations of particular individuals and groups. For example, Onibokuw (1976) found that satisfaction levels among Canadian public housing estates varied significantly with the social attributes of the population. In particular residential satisfaction was low among large households, one-parent families, unemployed tenants, tenants of high socio-economic status, recent immigrants from Europe, tenants with lengthy residence in public housing, tenants who had moved from owner-occupied properties, tenants who had moved from town, semi-detached, or single family 'dwellings', tenants who perceived their neighbourhood as lower- or upper-class in status, and tenants who perceived themselves as lower- or upper-class in status. In summary, then, residential satisfaction is a multi-faceted concept, which means that in some social settings it might have the opposite effect to what it has in others (Preston and Taylor 1981).

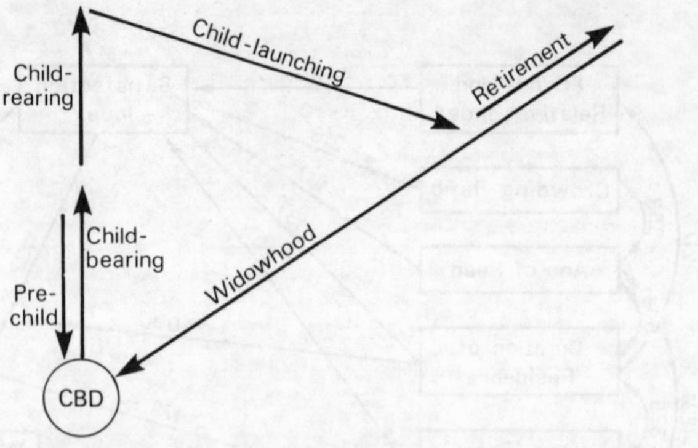

Fig. 14.2 Life cycle changes and likely residential mobility within a city.

Family life cycle and threshold formation

A major factor in determining residential mobility is the changing threshold of residential dissatisfaction that accompanies changes in the family life cycle (Thorns 1980b). From the formation to the dissolution of the cycle, critical events can be identified which increase or decrease the propensity to migrate (Table 14.2). Moreover, life cycle can affect the direction of migrant flows at an intra-urban scale: outward shifts of families predominate until old age is reached when a reversal in direction begins (Fig. 14.2). Marriage and child-bearing are among the critical events which commonly increase the probability of migration. In contrast, the birth of the last child may herald a phase of reduced mobility if suitable housing has been found to accommodate the family at its maximum size. This stability continues until the phase of family dissolution when the probability of migration increases again. Thus, as children leave home, parents begin to reconsider their residential needs. Retirement provides a further opportunity to re-evaluate not only housing but also environmental circumstances. Finally, infirmity caused

Table 14.2 The life cycle and residential mobility

Stage	*Access*	*Space*	*Median tenure*	*Housing age*	*Mobility*	*Locational preference*
Pre-child	Important	Unimportant	Rented flat	—	1 move to own home	Centre city
Child-bearing	Less important	Increasingly important	Rented house	Old	High 2–3 moves	Middle and outer rings of centre city
Child-rearing	Not important	Important	Owned	Relatively new	1 move to owned house	Periphery of city or suburbs
Child-launching	Not important	Very important	Owned	New	1 move to second home	—
Post-child	Not important	Unimportant	Owned	New when first bought	Unlikely to move	—
Later life	Not important	Unimportant	—	Widow leaves owned house to live with grown child		—

by age and the death of the spouse can precipitate moves as the home becomes more difficult to manage. The resultant migrant flows are of course complex. For example, according to Golant (1972) and Wiseman and Virden (1977) in their studies in Toronto and Kansas City respectively, the movement of the elderly towards the city centre was outweighed by movement into suburban areas.

The first, and most significant, interpretation of migration by means of the life cycle approach was Rossi's (1955) classic study of residential mobility in Philadelphia which concluded that the major function of mobility is the adjustment of the family housing needs generated by the shifts in family composition which accompany life cycle changes. Despite several later researchers confirming this (see Herbert 1973a; Simmons 1974), some writers have revealed that life cycle changes are never perfectly correlated with mobility levels, with a result that a question mark must be placed over the universality of life cycle as a differentiator in migrant potential (Lewis 1982). For example, on the evidence of residential mobility in Exeter, Morgan (1976) has argued that constraints of housing availability, access to mortgages, and provision of council housing were also significant predictors of migratory potential. In another context, Nalson's (1968) study of farmer mobility in Staffordshire suggested that the nature of the occupation, and the opportunities within it, were crucial differentiating factors. Clearly the evidence provided by these studies points out the necessity to consider the selectivity of the life cycle dimension within the broader context of social mobility and career patterns. Even Rossi (1955: 179) recognized this when he argued that 'families moving up the occupational "ladder" are particularly sensitive to the social aspects of location and use residential mobility to bring their residences into line with their prestige needs'. Despite this evidence, however, a number of other studies have suggested that the role of social mobility should not be overemphasized (Butler *et al.* 1969). For example, Lipset and Bendix (1952), using two class categories, found that only 30 per cent of North Americans leave the social class in which they were raised and hence residential relocation is required only once in the lifetime of a third of the population. Goldstein and Mayer (1963) also revealed that in Rhode Island over 60 per cent of all moves adjust housing within a neighbourhood of similar characteristics. More recently, McKay and Whitelaw (1977) have highlighted the significance of *organizations* in determining migratory flows in Australia. For example, those seeking career advancement and employed in health care, education, and local government bureaucracies were generally restricted to intra-state moves, whilst those involved in the private sector (especially manufacturing and financial institutions) generally moved between metropolitan centres. Essentially, such migrants are *spiralists*. An example is to be seen in 'a manager in a large corporation who moves around the country either at the corporation's bidding or while changing corporations . . . [and who] . . . is prepared to go anywhere to further his career' (Mann 1973: 11). Such individuals contrast markedly with *locals* who achieve career progression while staying within one particular locality.

A notable attempt to assess the relative significance of life cycle and career factors in determining differential propensity to migrate was Leslie and Richardson's (1961) pioneering study of residential mobility in Lafayette. For the purpose of analysis the life cycle dimension was identified by three variables (age of household head, household size, and tenure status) and the career dimension by five variables (years of formal education completed by head of household, respondent's estimate of own social class compared with neighbours, respondent's estimate of prospects for upward social mobility, respondent's attitude towards present housing, and respondent's attitude towards present neighbourhood). The results obtained suggested that, in general, the career variables were more highly correlated with residential mobility than life cycle ones. Of the individual variables, it was found that the respondent's estimation of his prospects for upward social mobility, in combination with years of formal education, were the most significant predictors of migration. However, as Adams and Gilder (1976: 165) have observed, 'households often undergo changes in their family status at the same time as they experience changes in income and social status', with a result that it is dangerous to explain mobility exclusively in terms of one or the other (Pickvance 1974). In fact Clark (1976) and Weinberg (1979) have argued that the real underlying motive of even intra-urban mobility may be essentially economic. After all, many households want to relocate because of housing needs but are prevented from doing so because suitable housing is not available at a price they can afford (Jones 1981).

The decision to move

Since the introduction of the concept of place utility there have been several attempts to model the migration process within a decision-making context (Roseman 1971; Brummell 1979; Lieber 1979). The most widely accepted model was that introduced by Brown and Moore (1970) in which mobility was conceived as a form of adaptation to stress in the environment (Fig. 14.3).

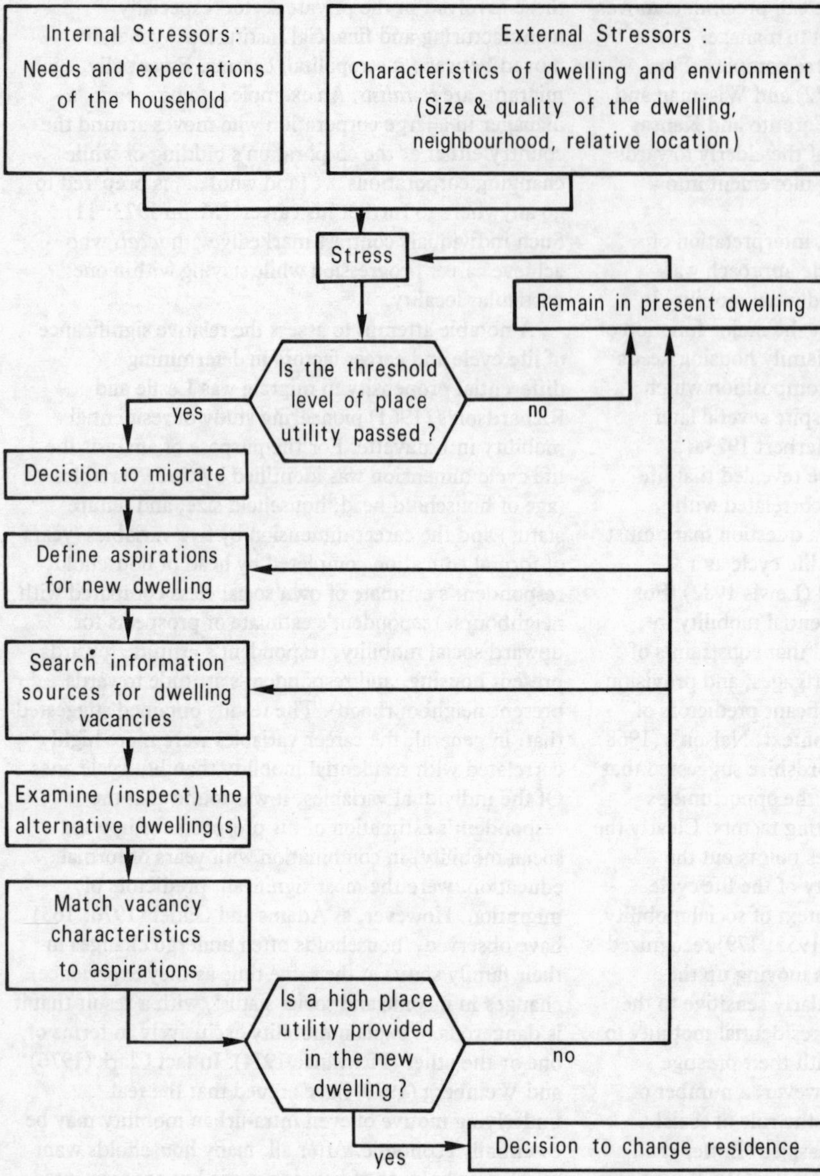

Fig. 14.3 A model of relocation decision-making. *Source*: based on Brown and Moore (1970, 1–13).

This model highlights changes in the needs and expectations of the household as well as changes in the characteristics of both the dwelling and the environment. Only when the place utility is reduced, either by internal or external sources of stress, or both, below a certain threshold level, will the household decide to move. Even this decision does not automatically entail migration because stress can sometimes be overcome by the household either reducing its aspirations or improving its existing circumstances. The decision where to move involves searching information sources about likely vacancies and matching these with the household's aspirations. If a high place utility is provided by the new location then there is a decision to migrate. If not, a decision to remain in the present location, or continue the search, is made.

The significance of the Brown and Moore model lies in its emphasis on the need to consider housing and environmental stress within the context of the needs, expectations, and aspirations of householders. For example, based on income, family status, religion, and ethnicity, the model suggests that each household has a frame of reference towards urban living in general and its housing situation in particular. Essentially, this manifests itself in a series of life styles, each with a distinctive set of orientations in relation to housing and residential location. Bell (1958b) has suggested the existence of at least three life styles (family-oriented, careerists, and consumerists) whilst Moore (1972) has added a fourth (community seekers). Such a typology can be criticized for its middle-class overtones, since it overlooks the 'life style' of those with little choice in society. However, the model allows for this to the extent that households with only modest incomes are expected to aspire only to housing which meets their minimum absolute needs.

In view of the fact that not all decisions are free, and the fact that a wide variety of constraints upon movement operate within all societies, many have suggested that the Brown and Moore model is rather unrealistic (Popp 1976; Thorns 1980a). Essentially these writers argue that the relocation decision process may not come to fruition because of the existence of a set of constraints on decision-making (Short 1978b). According to Murie (1975) these constraints include:

1. Household preferences (based on values, income, and occupation) which affect the interpretation of opportunities and their changing character.
2. Search and information-gathering restrictions, which influence a household's perception and awareness.
3. Access to housing, which affects the eventual outcome since both the public and private sector have 'rules' of access.
4. Limited availability of the type of dwelling required.

Clearly the first two of these form an integral part of the behavioural approach to locational decision-making (Smith and Clark 1982); on the other hand, the remaining two focus on the role of institutions (such as banks and bureaucracies) in restricting migration opportunities. In other words, what is being emphasized is that all households make decisions about migration within a set of individual and societal constraints which, in turn, lead to marked differences between migrants and non-migrants.

An interesting attempt to operationalize the Brown and Moore model within an actual migratory context was Gustavus and Brown's (1977) analysis of a sample of migrants into Columbus, Ohio. Using four different methodologies they confirmed the operation of a two-stage process. In the first stage, a set of alternative destinations was identified based on comparisons, over thirteen attributes, with the former place of residence. Although in the abstract all thirteen attributes were significant, in a trade-off situation, housing, jobs, schools, and health care facilities were particularly critical. The second stage of the process involved choosing from among the alternative destinations identified. The authors emphasized that it is an extremely complex process to measure accurately and objectively the suitability of one place against another. It is likely, then, that places are evaluated in terms of threshold levels rather than on a continuous scale. This would explain why Columbus and the second choice place were both perceived as dramatically different from the former place of residence but nearly identical to each other. Since all the respondents voluntarily chose to move to Columbus, it would appear that personal contacts, not isolated by the thirteen attributes used in the study, provided the migrant with accurate information and a means of adjusting relatively easily to a new environment.

Information and searching

The comparative evaluation of the present location and potential future locations is based upon the knowledge a migrant has concerning each alternative. The procedure by which an individual gathers such information is guided by the extent and content of his information field, or the set of places about which he has knowledge. Such a field can be divided into two: an activity space and an indirect contact space (see Ch. 7). An *activity space* is made up of all those locations with which an individual has regular, almost day-to-day contact. It comprises, therefore, a fairly well-known, albeit spatially restricted, area. In contrast, *indirect contact space* lies beyond the area of the individual's day-to-day contacts, and familiarity with it partly depends upon information from the mass media and other public information services. For both types of information field there tends to be a distance decay in the accuracy and content of the information an individual possesses. Within cities this bias is sectorally oriented, reflecting the regular movements of households from their home to the city centre. According to Adams (1969) this is why the majority of households move within sectors of the city (Simmons 1968).

The search for another house or a new job depends not only on the household's knowledge of alternative opportunities or locations but also on the type of available information (T. Smith *et al.* 1979). In a study of residential mobility in Baltimore, Rossi (1955) found that the most successfully used source was essentially *informal*. As a result, it seems that estate agents, who might be expected to be the main source of information, are often the least important as well as the least effective (Palm 1976b). Similar conclusions were reached by Herbert (1973b) in Swansea. For example, in the case of a high-cost neighbourhood 39 per cent of respondents discovered the required vacancy 'by looking around' while a further 25 per cent found what they wanted through family and friends; only 11 per cent found vacancies through newspapers and only 17 per cent through estate agents. The picture in a low-cost neighbourhood was even more striking in that the respective figures were 21 per cent and 58 per cent as against 13 per cent and 8 per cent. The importance which attaches to these casual information channels suggests that it is more than likely that households will first search areas with which they are already familiar and, if this is so, then the action space of households will play a not inconsiderable part in their selection of the area to which they eventually move.

Information about migration opportunities outside the 'local' environment tends to be provided from sources other than direct personal experience. One of the most significant of these channels is that formed by friends and relatives, who not only provide detailed information about their own location but also can assist the assimilation of the newcomer into a strange community. The effect of such information feedback is to create a distinctive migration stream between two places. For example, Hillery and Brown (1965: 47) have shown that southern Appalachia is not a region in the sense that its parts belong to the same migration system but rather is a collection of 'backyards' which are connected to non-Appalachian areas, often distant cities, through migration. As a result kinship structure provides a highly persuasive line of communication between kinsfolk and a type of linkage which tends to direct migrants to those areas where their groups are already established (Brown *et al.* 1963). However, there is a tendency within migration literature to overemphasize this type of kinship connection at the expense of other information channels. The dangers of this should be noted. In the Welsh Borderland, for instance, it has been shown that between 1968 and 1975 the information source upon which migrants relied varied with the type of migration (Lewis 1981b): in rural-to-rural migration, which was predominantly local, personal experience was the most significant source while in rural-to-urban migration information was overwhelmingly drawn from the mass media. In both cases the feedback of knowledge from friends and relatives was of little significance. In other words, the arrival of the mass media seems to have superseded traditional information sources, possibly because of its ability to disseminate greater and more detailed knowledge about locational opportunities. However, the mass media were not a particularly important information source in urban-to-rural migration in the Welsh Borderland. Instead the information used was determined by the purpose of the movement. Generally, those families who had settled in the region upon retirement based their decisions on knowledge derived either from previous residence or holiday visits, whilst those who moved out from the adjacent towns were guided by their personal knowledge. Clearly the manner in which a rural migrant chooses his new home location is as complex as that revealed for the intra-urban migrant (Adams and Gilder 1976).

Information flows are not of course static. Rather they change in time and space. For example, individual learning occurs as activity spaces and indirect contact spaces develop and as new information sources come into prominence. This learning, in turn, can be reinforced by searching the environment, particularly the sort of purposeful searching that occurs in the choice of a new residential location. Unfortunately, the nature of environmental learning and searching is poorly understood (Silk 1971). Of late, however, the changing information pattern of individuals as a result of purposeful search has become a source of investigation, particularly in relation to residential mobility and consumer behaviour within the city (Brown and Holmes 1971; Hudson 1976b). In this context Schneider (1975) and Flowerdew (1976) have considered the nature of search models and have suggested their applicability in a spatial context. Generally such models argue that the search for a new residence in the city will be concentrated near to the home, or in other accessible areas, simply because an individual's activity and awareness space are so highly localized (Barrett, 1973; 1976). Any extension of this search space will be attenuated by economic and psychological costs (Meyer 1980). Some models also conceptualize searching as a sequence of stages (Lewis 1982). In the first stage the search tends to be *space-covering* and generally involves a wide area, with the home area being the focal point. At the second stage, which is *space-organizing*, the search focuses on a small area where a satisfactory vacancy is likely to be found. If a suitable vacancy is not found then a third stage is initiated, in which the intensity of the search is increased and, possibly, widened. Finally, as time runs out and still no suitable vacancy has been found, households redefine their strategy, either by changing house and neighbourhood requirements or even reversing the decision to move.

The spatial bias in the process of house search has been analysed in detail in several studies (see Brown and Holmes 1971; Whitelaw and Gregson 1972). For example, by collecting information on respondents' previous places of residence, as well as information on the locations of all the houses which they inspect, it is possible to determine migrant search spaces. By then constructing standard ellipses which best fit the resulting aggregate distribution some spatial biases may

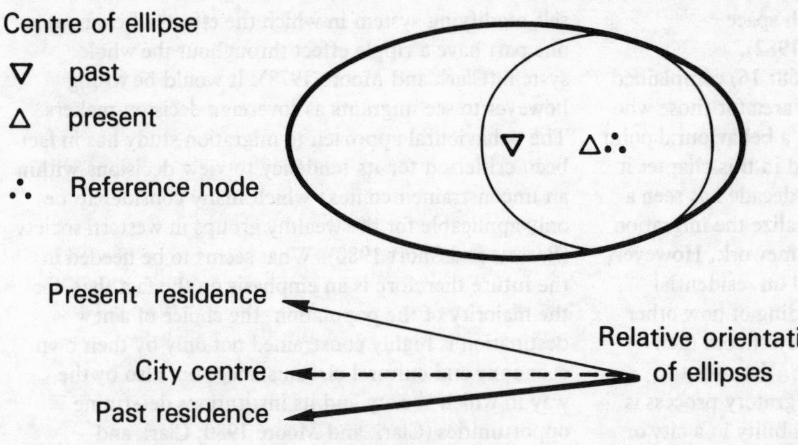

Fig. 14.4 Inspected residential vacancies in Leicester

be discerned. Figure 14.4 reveals the distribution of the inspected vacancies with reference to both past and present residence sites in Leicester. The distribution around the present site is both smaller and more circular than that around the past site. This indicates that households selected a relatively small area within that with which they were familiar and searched it for suitable vacancies. The site chosen was generally quite close to the centre of the area searched. The degree of ellipticity around the past home shows a directional bias in the search pattern and the orientation of the ellipse almost exactly towards the city centre shows that the bias is sectoral. Brown and Holmes (1971) found similar differences in the distribution of the search space of inner and outer city residents in Cedar Rapids. With reference to the home from which they had moved, inner city migrants searched an almost circular area whereas outer city migrants' search was sectorally biased. Of course the area from which migrants come may not be the only determinant of the shape of search space. Of crucial importance in a successful search for a house vacancy may be the length of residence; after all, the more accurate information available to long-term residents may shorten the length of the search (Whitelaw and Gregson 1972). Nevertheless, it remains true that information restriction of one sort or another prevents individuals from searching the whole area which is potentially available to them and results in a

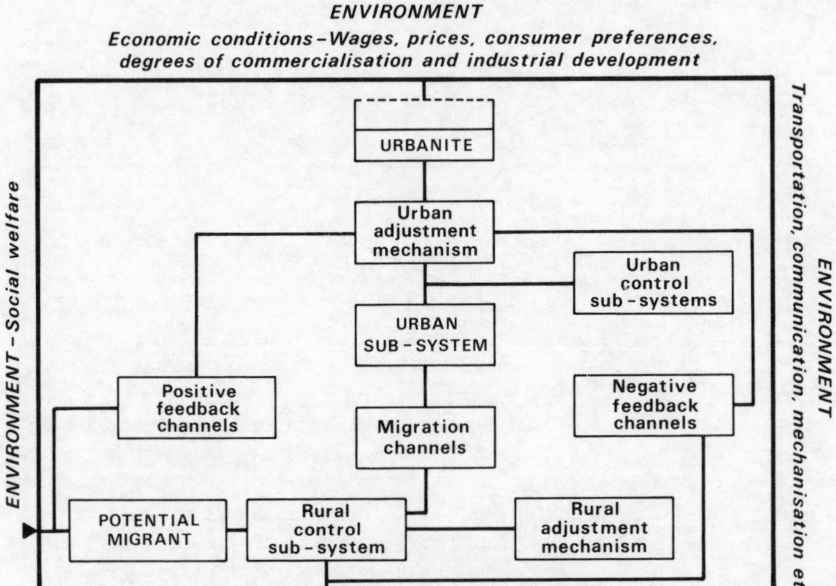

Fig. 14.5 A general model of migration. *Source*: Mabogunje (1970, 3).

distance and directional bias of search space (McCracken 1975; Clark and Smith 1982).

Over a decade ago Mangalam (1968: 16) complained that 'migration is practically a virgin area for those who want to study the phenomenon from a behavioural point of view'. From the evidence reviewed in this chapter it can be safely concluded that the last decade has seen a proliferation of attempts to conceptualize the migration process within a decision-making framework. However, much of this research has been based on residential mobility within cities and understanding of how other migrants decide to move and how they choose their destinations is still far from complete. Yet, what is evident from Fig. 14.5 is that the migratory process is the same whether it be residential mobility in a city or rural to urban movements in West Africa (Mabogunje 1970). Essentially, it is a circular, inter-dependent and self-modifying system in which the effects of changes in one part have a ripple effect throughout the whole system (Clark and Moore 1978). It would be wrong however to see migrants as sovereign decision-makers. The behavioural approach to migration study has in fact been criticized for its tendency to view decisions within an unconstrained context which many consider to be only applicable for the wealthy groups in western society (Bassett and Short 1980). What seems to be needed in the future therefore is an emphasis on the fact that, for the majority of the population, the choice of a new destination is highly constrained not only by their own economic and cultural circumstances but also by the way in which society and its institutions determine opportunities (Clark and Moore 1980; Clark and Everaers 1981).

Chapter 15

VOTING BEHAVIOUR

A great many electoral systems have a territorial basis in that individuals are elected to represent a given area. As a result, the study of electoral affairs has long been prominent in political geography where attention has focused on such issues as the geographical reasons that prompt a government to select a given electoral method or electoral boundaries, the geographical factors that contribute to electoral patterns, and the reasons why governments seek to change electoral procedures (Prescott 1969). This kind of research, which is very descriptive and largely idiographic, dominated the geographer's concern with elections until relatively recently when interest was awakened in the analysis of voting patterns themselves rather than in the systems through which votes are cast. This interest in voting behaviour has taken two forms: the *areal–structural* (or ecological) approach and the *behavioural* (process-orientated) approach (McPhail 1974). Areal–structural studies are concerned with aggregate data on how individuals vote in given spatial units such as electoral and census divisions. Basically, information on voting behaviour is correlated with social profile data in order to see what sort of people vote for what sort of candidate or party. Such an approach reveals nothing about the factors that motivate an individual voter although it is usually possible, with care, to draw some *general* inferences. In contrast, the behavioural approach looks at how individuals come to acquire and evaluate political information. Particular attention is paid to the tendency for political information to circulate within formal and informal social groups.

Areal–structural studies often rely on rather crude cartographic representation of voting patterns, as shown in Lewis's (1965) examination of the shift of Michigan negro voters to Democratic sympathies over the period 1932–62. They thereby differ markedly from behavioural studies which frequently use survey data and which emphasize the processes underlying a voting decision to the point where the electoral outcome of those decisions is virtually ignored. Great claims were made on behalf of such behavioural studies, particularly in the late 1960s and early 1970s. For example, in 1972 it was argued that 'the impact of the behavioural approach has been rapid and far reaching in political geography and this sector of the discipline can now be characterized as one of the main areas where insights into human spatial behaviour are being achieved' (Golledge, Brown and Williamson 1972: 72). Part of the appeal of the behavioural approach seems to have derived from the prominence of information flows and information processing in models of voting behaviour. Moreover, the fact that voting decisions appeared to be related to social and spatial processes operating on the individual seemed to hold out hope for the development of those branches of behavioural geography that are more concerned with movement and travel. Electoral studies, in other words, seemed to be giving a lead to behavioural geography generally. Unfortunately this early enthusiasm has not been sustained. In fact, recent commentaries have called for a redirection of political geography away from the study of voting behaviour and towards the crucial role of political decisions in structuring spatial systems (see Johnston 1978a). Just why the behavioural approach to electoral geography has failed to make the progress expected of it is an important question that must be addressed because the answer to the question throws light on methodological problems that are germane to behavioural research in geography generally. The nature of these problems can only be appreciated however by examining the work that has been done on voting patterns and voting decisions.

Voting patterns

Several researchers have looked at the geographical outcome of electoral processes. In so doing, they have summarized, in map form, who votes for what and where. Generally the goal of such research has been to relate the voting pattern to one or more independent variables, often through the use of multivariate statistics. A good example of this type of work is to be seen in Roberts and Rumage's (1965) examination of the left-wing vote in the British general election of 1951. Through use of multiple regression the authors were able to explain 81 per cent of the spatial variation in the Labour vote in terms of a positive association with variables measuring proximity to coalfields, mining and manufacturing employment, and low social status, and a negative association with variables measuring full-time education, females, and high social status.

Perhaps the most cited geographical investigation of voting patterns is Cox's (1968) inquiry into suburban voting behaviour in London. In this paper Cox attempted to find a link between suburban residence and voting preference for sixty-nine constituencies at the 1951 general election. The implicit assumption, derived from the experience of Eisenhower's campaign in the United States, was that suburban areas are intrinsically conservative. By reducing twenty-one variables through factor analysis to four components, and then applying Blalock's (1964) causal correlation model, this implicit assumption was vindicated. Suburban areas tended to be conservative although the pattern was less than clear-cut in that the influence of suburbanism was compounded by the influence of other socio-economic variables such as age, social class, and commuting. Cox (1968: 111) argued from these results that 'suburbanism probably affects party preference in two ways: conversion of erstwhile central city Labour party supporters and immigration of Conservatives from the central city'. This *conversion and transplantation* thesis has attracted stern criticism, notably from Kasperson (1969) who was very critical of electoral geography's tendency to indulge in non-cumulative research, its weak theoretical position, and its inclination to lag behind political science in its conceptual development. In specific terms, Kasperson criticized Cox on a number of grounds. First, he argued that the ecological correlation approach adopted by Cox does not allow the researcher to test the essentially behavioural nature of the conversion-transplantation thesis because it relies entirely on aggregate data that throws very little light on individual decisions and the influences (such as personality) that lead to these decisions. It does not, in other words, shed any light on the link between embourgoisement and conservatism (see Johnston 1981). Second, Kasperson stressed that the dichotomy between central city and suburb is questionable because the variability within each category is possibly as great as the variability between the categories. Different socio-economic groups live in different areas and as a result it is not possible to equate suburbanism with conservatism (Berger 1960). Third, Kasperson noted that Cox's conversion theory is at odds with the empirical finding that the Labour vote increased over time. Fourth, although the idea of communication between suburban housewives leading to political conversion is an attractive one (in that it opens the door to the role of local interaction in such areas as image formation and environmental cognition), it is an idea that is really without foundation. Little is known about the political content of neighbourhood conversation and about the way that such information is evaluated *vis-à-vis* media-based information. It may be, for example, that local interaction reinforces rather than converts political views. Fifth, the transplantation thesis tends to assume a unidirectional flow of people from central cities to suburbs that is very much at odds with the complex migratory patterns found in most cities (see Ch. 14). Finally, Kasperson made the point that many of Cox's key variables (e.g. social rank) are non-geographical. This in itself is a trifling criticism. However, there is undoubtedly a tendency, noted by Reynolds (1974), for some electoral research to treat social characteristics of areas as abstract punctiform data and thereby to overlook spatial interaction. A case in point is Kaufmann and Greer's (1959) interpretation of voting from the point of view of social area analysis.

Cox's (1969a) defence against Kasperson's criticism was a very reasonable one although he was forced into conceding many of the weaknesses of the areal – structural approach. This is not to say that the approach is moribund. It has been used with effect in several studies, most notably McPhail's (1971) analysis of the 1969 mayoral election in Los Angeles where a black candidate (Bradley), leading on the primary poll, was defeated by the incumbent (Yorty) in a run-off. What made this election particularly interesting was the fact that, like many local (cf. national) elections, it was dominated by personalities rather than issues. By factor analysing census tract and voting data (aggregated from precinct to tract level), McPhail was able to relate the structural characteristics of the population to voting preferences. His maps of factor scores and of voting patterns are examples of what can be achieved with the areal – structural approach.

Notwithstanding the contribution of McPhail, geographical studies of voting patterns have generally suffered from the lack of a clear theoretical framework. As a result there has been little or no connection between one study and the next. This situation may now be changing because Taylor and Johnston (1979) have argued that the work of Rokkan (1970) provides the foundation for a theoretical framework. In simple terms Rokkan argued that, in many countries, political parties are more important than candidates in so far as parties offer a package of responses to the issues of the day. Parties, in other words, develop as relatively stable groups of politicians. As time passes they develop an image. According to Rokkan, the variety of political parties existing at any point in time can only be understood by examining party evolution in the country concerned since modern political parties reflect the conflicts of the past (see Taylor and Johnston 1979: 111). In other words, *conflicts* create *cleavages* which are mirrored in *parties*. In Rokkan's view, the revolution of nationalism in European history produced cleavages between subject and dominant cultures and between churches and government while the Industrial Revolution produced cleavages between the primary and the secondary economy and between workers and employers. Most European political parties can be differentiated in terms of these four cleavages. The message in all this for electoral geographers is that such cleavages provide a foundation for the study of the social bases of voting (see Taylor and Johnston 1979: 164–218) and thereby provide a comparative framework that has been lacking to date. The extent to which Rokkan's ideas will stimulate progress in electoral geography depends ultimately of course on the degree to which his cleavages are congruent with the perceptions of individual voters. In other words, a comparative framework is only useful if it accurately reflects the many factors which impinge on individuals when deciding how to vote.

Voting decisions

How individuals vote can be influenced by the activities of the political parties desiring their support, by the degree to which individuals identify with the community within which they live, and by social interaction generally (Putnam 1966). Despite geographical variations in campaign strategies (see Rumley and Minghi 1977), the first of these influences tends to be weak, possibly because political parties are constrained in both financial terms (the funds they have at their disposal) and political terms (what consensus will allow them to offer to the electorate) (Johnston 1977a). The influence of the local community is stronger and more easily identified. After all, this is the focus of much of the areal–structural approach which highlights the relationship between social position and voting response. As a result, it is not difficult to identify a structural or class effect in most voting patterns (see Forrest and Johnston 1973). However, there is some evidence that class may be of diminishing significance as a determinant of voting behaviour in advanced, western societies (Kemp 1975). If this is so, the personal component of voting decisions may become of increasing importance and so researchers may no longer be able to treat it simply as a residual component left over after the influence of class has been taken into account.

Arguments that behavioural studies in electoral geography should focus on the individual have been around for some time (see Rowley 1969) and for the most part research has viewed the individual as one node in an information network. In this sense the individual voter is conceptualized as fitting into a series of overlapping social networks that can be formal or informal, frequent or infrequent, obligatory or discretionary (Johnston 1977a: 4). These networks provide the individual with a series of contacts, and interaction with these contacts promotes a socialization process whereby the individual can adopt or adapt to the views and attitudes of others. Many of these networks take a spatial form; prominent among them are homes, neighbourhoods, schools, workplaces, venues of leisure-time activities, and formal organizations (Taylor and Johnston 1979). Evidence of the significance of these networks is provided through either surveys of party preferences and voting behaviour or analyses of actual voting records. In both cases research aims to identify what is known as the *contextual effect* on voting, a concept that goes back to the work of Ennis (1962) (see Rumley 1975). Contextual influences on voting behaviour manifest themselves most commonly in the clustering of individuals and areas with similar voting preferences. This clustering can operate at a variety of levels from the regional scale (e.g. the traditional Democrat vote in the southern states of the USA) to the micro-scale (e.g. small pockets of party support). This clustering can be attributed to the clustering–segregation process that groups together individuals who are similar in terms of supposedly politically relevant characteristics like income, class, and race (Reynolds 1974). Alternatively, it can be interpreted in terms of information flows and spatial contagion where a predisposition to vote in a certain way passes from one individual to a neighbouring one. In such cases the focus of attention is either on electors and the way in which they acquire the voting characteristics of the neighbourhood in which they live or on candidates and the way in which they draw high levels of support, that are far greater than could be expected on the basis of party allegiance, from their home area. The former is often referred to as the *neighbourhood effect* and the latter as the *friends and neighbours effect* although there is a tendency for the terminology to be used loosely and interchangeably. In any case, both involve the spatial contagion of voting decisions.

The neighbourhood effect

Individuals can be conceptualized as points in an information network. An individual's connections with other points within the network provide him with an ever-changing flow of information that covers both public sources such as the mass media and private sources such as friends and neighbours. Some of these connections will be symmetrical in that they involve a two-way exchage of information but others, particularly those related to the mass media, will be asymmetrical in that information flows only *to* the individual voter. It is private information flows that have interested geographers most and a variety of spatial biasses have been noted in information emanating from these sources (Cox 1969b). To begin with there is the obvious distance decay bias arising from the fact that the probability of two individuals exchanging information decreases as the distance between the individuals increases (Olsson 1965). Additionally, there is an acquaintance circle bias stemming from the fact that members of a given group tend to communicate more with each other than with non-group members. This is closely related to the reciprocity bias that arises when individuals in close communication tend to end up with similar views. The significance to the geographer of these information flow biases lies in the fact that they often take a spatial form because of the tendency for groups to operate and interact on a local basis. Thus, in general terms, the people with whom an individual interacts most will be those to whom he is geographically closest and it is not surprising therefore that neighbours tend to adopt similar attitudes, views, and behaviours.

One of the most obvious ways of examining the influence of information flows as a determinant of voting behaviour is to look at what happens when information flows change. This has been done by Cox (1970) in a study of how in-migrants to a residential neighbourhood of Columbus, Ohio, receive and adopt partisan political viewpoints. Basically, Cox developed a conceptual model to take stock of the fact that residential relocation often leads to a discontinuity in information flows and the concomitant elimination of reference groups. This discontinuity means that the new information to which a migrant is subjected may be inconsistent with the information remembered from the previous residence. Cox argues that this conflict situation results in the migrant being significantly affected by personal and relatively ephemeral factors which allow him to escape from conflict by arriving at a relatively hasty voting decision. Migrants may therefore exhibit a voting pattern which is more unstable from election to election than that of the rest of the population. However, as the migrant assimilates, a new set of information sources and loyalties emerges and conflict declines. In this way, a new local contextual effect appears (although its influence might be masked by the transferral of some affiliations, such as union or church membership, from the previous location). Although Cox's model is very general it does have support in the work of Campbell *et al.* (1960) and in Cox's own survey which showed that recent residents in Columbus had more volatile voting patterns than long-term residents and were less likely to exhibit voting preferences that were consistent with the local climate of political opinion.

Adjustments in voting behaviour after residential relocation are of course only a special case of local environmental influence in general. If voting can be interpreted as an expression of self-interest (and the assumption that class interests influence voting patterns is central to the areal–structural approach in electoral geography), then it can be hypothesized that there are many occasions when it is in a voter's self-interest to vote in the same way as his neighbours (perhaps in the hope of stimulating action in relation to a local problem). In such cases a process of conversion may take place as a local consensus emerges. Geographers have devoted a good deal of attention to this spatial contagion of voting decisions. Johnston (1977b), for instance, has argued that repeated contact in a local area with people of different attitudes can lead to pressure on an individual to change his views so as to conform to group norms. This contagion can take two forms: at an individual level conversion can come about if a supporter of Party X has more contacts with supporters of Party Y than with supporters of Party X, and at a group level conversion can come about when a minority of group members find themselves at odds with overall group views. In both cases the result is the same in that contagion produces an *amplification* of the majority viewpoint. This means that the greater the percentage of an area's population supporting a particular political party, the greater will be the likelihood of conversion from the minority view (Johnston 1977b: 18) (Fig. 15.1). There is a good deal of empirical support in the literature for this amplification thesis. For example, Rumley (1981) has shown that the percentage of West Australian manual workers who vote Labour in a given area increases as the percentage of manual workers in that area increases. Likewise, Orbell (1970) has noted a tendency for majorities for a party to be enhanced in areas where that party is dominant rather than in areas where it has only a slender lead over its opponents, and Johnston (1977b) himself found evidence of contagion taking place between the 1969 and 1972 elections in Christchurch, New Zealand. Cox (1969c), using the same survey data for Columbus, Ohio, as did Orbell

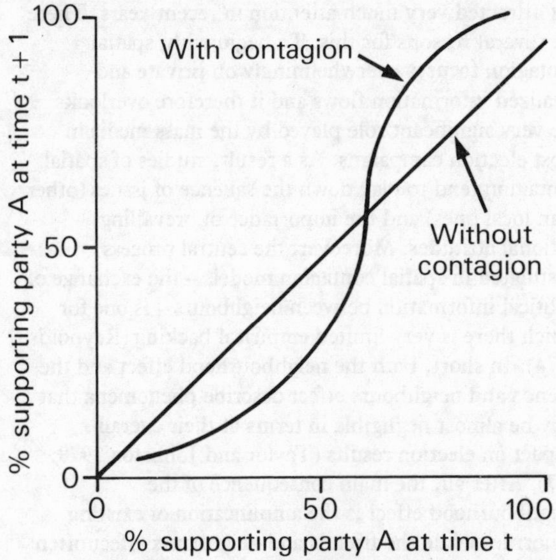

Fig. 15.1 The amplification of majority voting through contagion. *Source*: Taylor and Johnston (1979, 260).

(1970), suggested that the sort of people most open to the *neighbourhood effect* were those whose informal contacts took place mainly around the home and whose formal social contacts were mainly local. He also reasoned that committed party supporters are unlikely to be converted, that apathetic electors vote in a random fashion, and that, as a result, those most open to conversion are those in the middle of a scale of political involvement. Whether these individuals are the ones who join local social groups, and then adjust to group norms, is of course difficult to establish because there have been extremely few detailed case studies of the flow of political information at the micro-scale. However, Fitton's (1973) examination of an area of terraced housing in Manchester does lend some support in so far as he found that, when a change occurs in voting behaviour, it is predominantly in the direction of the street sub-group to which the swinging voter is attached.

Further evidence of the neighbourhood effect has come from Butler and Stokes's (1974) observation that, in a time of electoral reversals, there is much less loss of party support in an area where the party is strong and where individual voters get most political information from local interaction than where electors rely on the mass media. Generally speaking, then, the neighbourhood effect seems to be greatest where classes are segregated and where, as a result, there is a high degree of cohesion within classes (Almy 1973). Of course not all neighbourhoods are uniform: there are always individuals who deviate from group norms; there are voters whose ties with a previous residence are stronger than their ties with the local environment; and there are individuals who join in neighbourhood affairs *(localites)* and those whose frame of reference is spatially more extensive *(cosmopolites)* (Taylor and Johnston 1979: 234). Obviously, the relative mix of these different categories can influence the strength of neighbourhood allegiance. The existence of a neighbourhood effect is, in other words, predicated on the existence of an appropriate areal unit with which people identify and within which they interact (Reynolds 1974). If such neighbourhoods cannot be identified, it is hardly likely that voting patterns will be influenced by spatial contagion.

The friends and neighbours effect

The neighbourhood effect in voting patterns seems to be an indisputable fact of political life in that there is ample evidence of individuals voting in the same way as those people who live close to them. A local consensus opinion has been observed in a variety of areas. Development of the idea of a neighbourhood effect, and discussion of the idea so far in this chapter, has focused on a community's reaction to political information that is not *directly* connected with the community. However, in many cases a community or neighbourhood has a direct stake in an election, as when a member of the neighbourhood is standing as a candidate. In such cases a good deal of research has looked at the extent to which the local candidate gets support at the local level that is over and above that which could be attributed to party or class effects. This 'home area' vote was first noticed by Key (1949) in Democratic primaries in the south of the United States. It has been more adequately described as a *friends and neighbours* effect because the increased vote that has been found to accrue to local candidates can be attributed to (a) the high probability of a voter having personal contact with a local candidate or with the candidate's key supporters, and (b) the candidate's identification with politically influential local groups and politically significant local issues (McPhail 1974).

In most elections it is very difficult to identify a friends and neighbours effect because of the tendency for such an effect to be swamped by other influences such as class and party allegiance (Johnston 1974). Even at local elections it is not unusual for the party effect to account for up to 80 per cent of the variance in voting patterns (Forrest *et al*. 1977). There are nonetheless certain conditions under which a friends and neighbours effect is generally identifiable. For example, the effect is very pronounced in intra-party elections (such as the primaries held in the United States), in cases where candidates do not have strong party loyalties, and where candidates are seeking major political office for the first time and hence are generally unknown to the electorate (Reynolds 1969). Similarly, a friends and neighbours effect can generally be isolated if there are many candidates and if they live well away from each other (Tatalovich 1975). On the other hand, the alignment of a candidate with national as opposed to local issues, and the use of extensive advertising, can all but obliterate local effects.

Notwithstanding these difficulties, Reynolds (1969; 1974) has developed a model to describe the friends and neighbours effect. The model allows for two types of voting behaviour: (1) voting for a candidate on a friends and neighbours basis (in other words, because the candidate or his key supporters are known personally or because the candidate identifies with local issues); and (2) voting for a candidate on some other basis. Transition from type (2) to type (1) voting is conceptualized as coming about through random shocks associated with variables that are not included in the model. In contrast, transition from type (1) to type (2) voting is viewed as resulting from a linear function that describes the impediment to interpersonal interaction posed by both the distance of a voter from the candidate's home and the number of other voters who live closer to the candidate. Drawing on the work of Coleman (1964: 217–77), Reynolds (1974: 238–9) set out the model as follows:

$$P_x - t = \frac{\varepsilon_1}{\alpha} \frac{D_x}{N_x} + \frac{\varepsilon_1}{\varepsilon_1 + \varepsilon_2}$$

where Px = the proportion of voters living within x miles voting for the candidate; t = the proportion of the total electorate voting for the candidate; D_x = the distance from the centre of an areally defined voting group to the boundary of the group; N_x = the population of the group with diameter x; ε_1/α = rate of increase with increasing '*per capita* communicating distance' (D/N) in the mean tendency to vote on a friends-and-neighbours basis (ε_1) relative to the mean tendency to vote on some other basis; and $\varepsilon_1/(\varepsilon_1 + \varepsilon_2)$ = initial average tendency to vote on a friends and neighbours basis (D/N = 0).

The significance of voting

Both the neighbourhood effect and the friends and neighbours effect come about as a result of spatial contagion and both are therefore intrinsically interesting to geographers. However, despite Reynolds's (1974) attempts to express the friends and neighbours effect formally in terms of an equation, spatial contagion has not attracted very much attention in recent years. There are several reasons for this. To begin with, spatial contagion focuses overwhelmingly on private and localized information flows and it therefore overlooks the very significant role played by the mass media in most election campaigns. As a result, studies of spatial contagion tend to play down the salience of issues (other than local ones) and the importance of prevailing national attitudes. Moreover, the central process postulated in spatial contagion models – the exchange of political information between neighbours – is one for which there is very limited empirical backing (Reynolds 1974). In short, both the neighbourhood effect and the friends and neighbours effect describe phenomena that may be almost negligible in terms of their overall impact on election results (Taylor and Johnston 1979: 267). After all, the main consequence of the neighbourhood effect is the amplification of existing majorities while the friends and neighbours effect often only becomes really apparent in the unusual event of there being no major issues, no parties, and no well-known candidates. Where these conditions are not met, local contextual influences are likely to be swamped by considerations of party affiliation and media exposure (Johnston 1972).

The behavioural approach adopted by geographers in the study of elections has, in other words, a number of shortcomings in that it focuses on issues that are somewhat ephemeral relative to the overall condition and well-being of society. The same cannot be said of the areal–structural approach because this attaches far greater importance to considerations of party and class. Areal–structural studies are however bedevilled by methodological problems that stem from a reliance on ecological correlations. It is not surprising therefore that geographers have begun to ask themselves whether the analysis of voting patterns can provide the insights into human spatial behaviour that were hoped for even a decade ago. Nor is it surprising that geographers have turned their attention to the question of how electoral support is translated into political representation (P. J. Taylor 1973). The *geography of representation* has in fact emerged as a distinct field of study that focuses on the way in which constituency sizes can be varied to favour some electors at the expense of others (*malapportionment*) and the way in which electoral boundaries can be drawn so as to maximize party support (*gerrymander*) (Taylor and Johnston 1979: 335–434). To some geographers this sort of *districting problem* diverts attention from yet more basic issues. Thus, several authorities have argued that geographers should turn their attention to questions of inequality and social justice (see Coates *et al.* 1977; D. M. Smith 1977; 1979b) and to questions of resource allocation and locational conflict (Cox *et al.* 1974). This in turn has led to consideration of political economy (Dear and Clark 1978; Eyles 1978). In some cases this implies concern for the sort of structural marxism that was outlined in Chapter 2, whereas in other cases it involves advocacy of the sort of humanistic perspective dealt with in Part Five (see Eyles 1981). In any event the retreat from models of individual voting behaviour is an important development and its significance should not go unnoticed in behavioural geography.

Part Five

HUMANISTIC APPROACHES

Micro-scale behavioural approaches have contributed a great deal to the understanding of man–environment interaction by emphasizing the processing and use of environmental information. This means that such approaches complement macro-scale approaches: for example, studies of consumer decision-making add to the understanding of consumer mobility derived from gravity models, and, likewise, the examination of voting decisions provides insights into the structure of voting patterns. Micro-scale behavioural approaches do however have certain weaknesses: they tend to assume a congruence between cognition and behaviour that is at times unwarranted; they frequently treat the mind as no more than a 'black box'; they tend to under-emphasize constraints on behaviour; and they are based in large measure on enthusiastic rather than significant ties with allied disciplines. As a result of these weaknesses some writers have suggested that research should be directed away from micro-scale behavioural approaches and into areas such as the aggregate and structural approaches discussed in Part Two. A less extreme view holds that a focus on the micro-scale of the individual can still provide insights into man–environment providing that the methods used take full account of how man experiences the world about him. This has become known as the 'humanistic' perspective.

A focus on experiential environments highlights the meaning which man ascribes to his surroundings and the extent to which this meaning is intersubjective, that is to say, shared by a group of people. It also highlights the values and intentions of the actors under study. It therefore entails a holistic perspective that views man in his entirety rather than as a bundle of fragmented responses to diverse stimuli. The term 'humanistic' is commonly applied to this sort of approach. This is because such approaches emphasize distinctly human characteristics and therefore break away from a positivistic, scientific view of man. In no way does the term imply strict adherence to the philosophical position of humanism.

Chapter 16 outlines the major criticisms levelled at micro-scale behavioural approaches in geography and presents the rationale for a humanistic perspective. Particular attention is paid to the phenomenological, existential, and idealist philosophies on which many humanistic approaches have been based. The potentialities of the humanistic perspective are explored in relation to the interpretation of landscape, man's sense of place, and the taken-for-granted world before an assessment is made of the general strengths and weaknesses of humanistic approaches.

CHAPTER 16

EXPERIENTIAL ENVIRONMENTS

Despite generating a vast literature behavioural geography has also generated some important criticisms. For example, many researchers have noted both the methodological difficulties involved in studying how man comes to know an environment and the problem of validating findings concerning the degree to which cognition influences overt behaviour (Cullen 1976; Bunting and Guelke 1979). Others have stressed that behavioural research so far in geography has concentrated on individual behaviour at the expense of group behaviour and has tended to ignore the fact that behaviour takes place in time as well as space (Cullen 1978). On a more fundamental level it has been argued that behavioural geography over-emphasizes choice and under-emphasizes constraints on behaviour and thereby overlooks the fact that behaviour is, to a very significant degree, produced by the social structure in which it occurs (Rieser 1973; Massey 1975b). One corollary to this criticism is that researchers should pay just as much attention to repressed behaviour as to acted-out behaviour (Eyles 1971). Another corollary suggests that the goal of a value-free scientific geography is both undesirable and unrealistic (N. Smith 1979).

The force of these arguments has caused some individuals to reject behavioural geography: it is seen as no more than a prop to the *status quo* that, by focusing on incremental amelioration of the human condition, serves to divert attention away from the true causes of pressing social problems. Others have argued that an understanding of human spatial behaviour can be better advanced by reworking macro-scale models along the lines of statistical mechanics. Both of these groups deserve attention (see Ch. 2). Another alternative approach that claims to overcome many of the problems of mainstream behavioural geography is the subject of attention in this chapter. This approach, which has parallels in other social sciences such as psychology (Armistead 1974) and sociology (Lally and Preston 1973), adopts a *hermeneutic* perspective and argues that man – environment interaction is best understood by focusing on the way in which humans experience and interpret their surroundings. Because this approach rests on a non-positivist philosophical framework that encourages a holistic, experiential view of man–environment interaction, it has frequently been labelled 'humanistic' (see Buttimer and Seamon 1980).

There is nothing devastatingly new in the point of view that human geographers should adopt a humanistic approach. After all, such an idea was implicit in the work of De la Blache and in much French human geography (Buttimer 1978). What is new is a willingness on the part of geographers to confront the philosophical basis of humanistic thinking directly rather than merely by implication. Thus in the 1960s human geographers, like other social scientists, began to become aware of the strengths and weaknesses of humanistic principles over and against the prevailing preoccupation with techniques of scientific rationality (Ley and Samuels 1978a: 1). In simple terms, humanism in its broadest sense offers a critique of scientific method that stresses that man must be viewed as a complete being with due emphasis given to his creativity, individuality, and to the subjective way in which he interprets the world around him. To persist with a fragmented view of man that highlights particular reactions to particular environmental stimuli (e.g. distance cognition experiments) is, it is argued, dehumanizing. In the view of Ley (1980), a geography that fails to give adequate attention to man as a complete human being has four significant shortcomings: first, it suppresses the issue of *subjectivity* and hence glosses over the subjectivity of the researcher; second, it overlooks *intentionality* in human behaviour and hence devalues the power of human consciousness and human action to redirect the course of events and to overcome constraints that would otherwise inhibit behaviour; third, it reduces questions of meaning to questions of technique and therefore runs the risk of prescribing inappropriate technical solutions for human problems; and finally, it lays altogther too much emphasis on human passivity.

A geography that adopts a humanistic perspective and does justice to man's distinctly human characteristics would emphasize that action is a response to the meanings that man attributes to the physical and social environment (Cullen 1976). Such a geography would therefore begin with the premise that the study of human spatial behaviour is different in kind from the sort of study conducted in the natural sciences in so far as man exhibits characteristics (creativity, individuality, human values) that are not generally evident in the sort of phenomenon studied in natural science. It follows from this that the techniques of natural science are inappropriate for the study of human behaviour and need to be replaced by an approach that gives much more attention to *values* (Buttimer 1974) and to man's day-to-day *experience* of the environment (Tuan 1976b). Of course it is one thing to advocate a new value-oriented, interpretative approach but quite another to spell out what is involved because the adoption of a humanistic perspective poses problems concerned with philosophy, methodology, and the degree to which different people share the same experience and attribute the same meaning to their surroundings (Ley and Samuels 1978a: 9).

To distinguish between philosophy (issues of belief) and methodology (a concern for logical procedures) in relation to humanism is however to extend a separation made in 'science', and exemplified in Harvey's (1969a) treatise on explanation in geography, to a field where it does not really apply. That is to say, advocates of a humanistic perspective contend that philosophy and methodology cannot be differentiated because the means of analysis are intimately related to the meaning of analysis (Ley and Samuels 1978c). To be specific, the philosophical stance associated with humanism stresses *anthropocentrism*, *holism*, and *intersubjectivity* and none of these can be investigated other than from the point of view of human experience. In short, there is no way that human experience can be studied other than through human experience (Ley and Samuels 1978c: 50–1).

Anthropocentric views of the environment have been recognized by geographers for a long time. For example, Lowenthal (1961) has stressed that everyone interacting with an environment builds up a geographical epistemology which is founded on personal geographies composed of direct experience, memory, and fantasy. This world view is influenced by both unique variables such as personality and social variables like culture. Moreover, although shared, this world view is transient: 'it is neither the world our parents knew nor the one our children will know' (Lowenthal 1961: 245). In a very fundamental sense these personal geographies are 'mirrors for man' in that they reflect and reveal human nature by emphasizing the way that man seeks order and meaning in his experiences of the world (Tuan 1971). It would be simplistic however to assume that it an easy matter to uncover these personal geographies. This is because man's attitudes towards the environment are sometimes ambivalent and ambiguous (and therefore difficult to interpret) (Tuan 1973) and because a researcher can only understand a subject's behaviour to the extent that they share common cognitive categories and conceptualizations of the environment (Ley and Samuels 1978b). Interpretative knowledge is, after all, 'mediated through the categories of the interpreter's pre-understanding' (Buttimer 1979: 22).

A further difficulty in interpreting the world as viewed by an individual stems from the fact that an individual's view is *holistic* and needs to be comprehended in its entirety. Furthermore, man continually interacts with his environment and is therefore continually confronted by new experiences that may necessitate changes in his world view. 'There is no room in a humanistic perspective for a passive concept of man dutifully acquiescing to an overbearing environment. But neither is man fully free, for he inherits given structural conditions and, indeed, may be unaware of the full extent of his bondage' (Ley and Samuels 1978a: 12). The holistic perspective characteristic of humanism is of course very different from the holism associated with systems theory: the synthesis of behaviour and environment to which humanists aspire is not functional but *dialectical*, and not abstract but *contextual* (Ley and Samuels, 1978a: 11). The need for humanistic geographers to appreciate the context of behaviour becomes particularly acute when it is realized that man operates to a very significant degree in a *symbolic* environment (see Tuan 1978b). Symbolism in this sense exists in the mind. It is an element of consciousness. To focus on symbolism is therefore to concentrate on consciousness and the world of ideas. Such a course of action may be intellectually fascinating but it runs the risk of diverting the humanist's interest from the world of experience and material conditions (Ley 1978: 45). After all, it is relatively easy to demonstrate *intersubjectivity* in the sense of shared experiences and conditions but much more difficult to reveal the extent to which consciousness is shared.

Although humanism puts great emphasis on the existence of intersubjectively shared experiences and meanings, it studiously rejects all types of aggregate, statistical measurement. Instead a more particularistic methodology is advocated whereby the meanings that individuals or groups attribute to an environment are uncovered through such techniques as participant observation, the use of unobtrusive measures, and various forms of encounter and in-depth interviewing

(Ley and Samuels 1978c: 121). In this way the humanistic perspective avoids the idealized and contrived laboratory conditions that are common in much of social science. After all, participant observation allows the researcher to become an involved insider rather than a detached outsider and thereby to gain an insight into the everyday world of his subjects, as was well illustrated in Symanski's (1979) study of hobos and freight trains. There are of course problems with this sort of interpretative approach. To begin with, it runs the risk of becoming preoccupied with the unique and the esoteric to the extent that description becomes an end in itself. Research, in such cases, becomes non-incremental (Ley and Samuels 1978c). Conversely, there is always the danger that the researcher will see order where none exists and will assume a concordance between mind and behaviour that is perhaps not justified (Tuan 1976b).

Humanism itself is an umbrella term that covers a wide variety of approaches. These approaches are perhaps best classified according to their underlying philosophy. In behavioural research in geography three philosophical positions have attracted special attention: phenomenology, existentialism, and idealism.

Phenomenology

Phenomenology is a philosophy developed largely in continental Europe and, as a result, it made very little impact until relatively recently on the world of English-speaking geographers. The philosophy is usually said to have begun with Husserl (1931) and his attempts to break away from an obsession with facts in the study of human behaviour. In its simplest form, it affords a radical method of enquiry that proceeds from pure consciousness without presupposing an existent world (Walmsley 1974b). Its focus of attention is the link between experience and meaning in man's interaction with his environment, and its underlying value position holds that the social scientist changes an object of study while he studies it and because he studies, with a result that he needs to know as much about the eye that sees as about the object that is seen (Strasser 1963). Phenomenologists argue that man cannot be independent of the world, that man comes to know the world through his own consciousness, and that social scientists must therefore study how man experiences the world. Thus 'if scientific method is a way of thinking that realises itself as a way of doing, phenomenology is a way of thinking that reveals itself in a *way of being*' (Relph 1981a: 101). In order to concentrate on 'being', phenomenologists focus on the lived-world or *Lebenswelt*. Their goal is to identify the essences (necessary and invariant features of objects) that provide the structure of being that underlies all relationships in this *Lebenswelt*. In simple terms this goal is achieved by adopting the method of *verstehen*, that is to say, the researcher attempts to understand the behaviour of the person under study by empathizing with that person and imagining himself in that person's position in order to comprehend the *intentions* that motivated the person in his behaviour.

There is no one brand of phenomenology; rather, the philosophy has changed and developed over time (Walmsley 1974b). For example, Husserl's emphasis on pure consciousness gave way to Heidegger's focus on man-in-the-world (see Warnock 1970). Although this formulation has appealed to some geographers (e.g. Tuan 1971) as a means of studying how man is implicated in and responds to his environment, its popularity has not been great. Instead it is the work of Schutz (1967) that has had the greatest impact on social science, largely because he developed phenomenology as an academic method rather than as pure philosophy. Schutz argued that 'phenomenology is empirical because it is based on observation, it is systematic because it is concerned with the organization of the phenomena of experience, and it is rigorous because it is reflexive, that is, it subjects its own procedures to critical appraisal' (Relph 1981a: 103). In this sense phenomenology redefines the subject matter of social inquiry and presents new issues for investigation. It is not however simply a new perspective on old problems. The new focus is on lived experience. In the words of Relph (1981a: 109): 'We live in a world of buildings, streets, sunshine and rainfall and other people with all their sufferings and joys, and we know intersubjectively the meanings of these things and events. This pre-intellectual world, or life-world, we experience not as a set of objects somehow apart from us and fixed in time and space, but as a set of meaningful and dynamic relations'. This pre-intellectual life-world manifests itself in a sense of belonging to a place, in landscape appreciation, and in the existence of a taken-for-granted world.

Existentialism

Existentialism and phenomenology are similar to the extent that both seek 'to define the relationship between *being* (existence, reality, and material condition) and *consciousness* (mind, idea, image)' (Samuels 1978: 23). Both philosophies are therefore anthropocentric and both offer a chance to break away from quantitative geography's emphasis on space and to look instead at the concept of *place*. In simple terms, as it has been interpreted by geographers, existentialism is a philosophy that is concerned with man's attachment to, and alienation from, place. Existentialism thus attempts to restore the concrete, immediate experience of existence to a position of prominence in the study of man–environment interaction. The philosophy begins with the subjective in the sense that the human subject is seen as firmly grounded in irreducibly concrete, historical and geographical facts of existence. From this point the philosophy argues that man sets himself apart from the space around him in order to enter into relations with the objects and phenomena in that environment (Samuels 1981: 117–19). In other words, man defines the environment as opposite to and separate from himself. This means that man sets the world at a distance, thereby *alienating* himself from it. This alienation, or setting apart of man and environment, is overcome by man developing *relationships* with objects within the environment. 'What distance necessitates (detachment), relation fulfils (belonging)' (Samuels 1981: 119). In short, relations with the environment give meaning to man's existence. Man's distancing of himself from his environment and his relations with that environment are therefore dialectical concomitants of one another.

Despite an attempt to look at such things as the 'uprootedness' of alcoholics from an existential viewpoint (Godkin 1980), the philosophy has had only a limited impact on geography. Samuels (1981: 129), the staunchest advocate of an existential viewpoint in geography, sees existential geography as 'a type of historical geography that endeavours to reconstruct a landscape in the eyes of its occupants, users, explorers and students in the light of historical situations that condition, modify, or change relationships'. Whether this is an attainable goal is open to debate. Many authorities still see existentialism as anti-intellectual philosophy on the grounds that one of its central tenets holds that reality and existence can only be experienced through living and cannot therefore be made the object of thought. Perhaps ultimately then the significance of existentialism to geographers is simply that it offers a perspective that stresses the quality and meaning of human life in the concrete everyday world (Buttimer 1979).

Idealism

The philosophical position of idealism holds that the activity of the mind is the foundation of human existence and knowledge. The world, in other words, can only be known indirectly through ideas (Guelke 1981: 133). There is no 'real' world that can be known independently of mind because each person acts on the world, and the 'world' is formed and structured through consciousness (Moore and Golledge 1976b: 13). The corollary to this is that the social sciences are necessarily different from the natural sciences: the former look at the world in the head and the latter at the world outside the head. The idealist thesis is that knowledge 'gives birth to a world which for us is the only world' (Moore and Golledge 1976b: 13). To strict idealists, nothing exists apart from what is in the mind and the contents of the mind therefore comprise reality. Order, in other words, is present in all rational action. From this point of view, a human action or its product is understood – that is to say, its rationality is discovered – by a scholar rethinking or reconstructing the thought contained in the action. The researcher has therefore no need of theories which impose order because order is already inherent in action. As a result, the key concern of the idealist geographer is not to provide a causal explanation of an event (in the sense of listing all the necessary and sufficient conditions for its occurrence) but rather to elucidate its meaning and significance (Guelke 1981: 134–6). This process of 'rethinking' is virtually identical with the *verstehen* of the phenomenologists. Idealism differs from phenomenology, however, in that it goes beyond an interest in the subjectively experienced life-world and seeks out verifiable knowledge (Guelke 1981). Idealists, for example, pay a great deal of attention to the concept of *culture* in so far as this comprises an idea in the mind of man which influences his behaviour and which is capable of verification by reference to shared meanings which are manifest in societal norms, institutions, and customs. However, as with so many interpretative approaches, idealism suffers from inherent weaknesses. There is, for instance, no way of knowing whether the 'rethinking' of two or more idealists would produce the same results. Nor is there any way that the process of 'rethinking' can take complete account of emotions and feelings without the researcher imputing his own values to the subject under study (Curry 1982). Above all, idealism as adopted by geographers tends to suffer from a rather cavalier use of language (Harrison and Livingstone 1979).

Interpretation of landscape

One of the fields of geographical enquiry where a humanistic perspective has been most prominent is the interpretation of landscape. Landscape is, however, an ambiguous term. It usually implies nature, scenery, environment, and place and yet it is not synonymous with any of these. Rather, landscape is best thought of as that continuous surface that we see all around us. It need not be spectacular and memorable; it may in fact be very ordinary and be taken for granted by most people (Meinig 1979b). In this sense a landscape is an artefact of man's use of the environment. However, although it results from a totality of human influences, landscape can be interpreted in an idiosyncratic way by individual human beings. For example, landscapes can be imbued with symbolic value which, in turn, can generate strong attachments. Likewise, how a landscape is interpreted can reflect the values and attitudes of the individuals concerned. Thus a capitalist may interpret a landscape in monetary terms, an artist in aesthetic terms, a scientist in ecological terms, and a social activist in terms of disorder and injustice (Meinig 1979c). Despite these differences most landscapes do have some intersubjectively shared meaning. In large measure this intersubjective meaning derives from the cultural nature of landscapes and, in this context, Lewis (1979) has suggested a series of axioms to guide the study and understanding of landscapes.

1. Landscapes are clues to culture in that they yield evidence as to the type of people that occupy them.
2. All elements in a landscape reflect culture and in this sense all are equally important.
3. Common landscapes that are often taken for granted are difficult to study by conventional academic means and therefore demand new approaches such as those offered by a humanistic perspective.
4. Consideration of the meaning of a landscape demands consideration of the history of that landscape.
5. Elements of a cultural landscape make little sense unless they are studied within their geographical context.
6. Because most cultural landscapes are intimately related to the physical environment, interpretation of landscape depends on a knowledge of that physical landscape.
7. Almost all objects in a landscape convey some sort of message, although not necessarily in any obvious way.

The development of axioms for landscape interpretation rests on the assumption that all men experience their surroundings in a similar way and that their response to their environment is mediated by the culture and society to which they belong. Shared images and shared experiences result, in other words, from shared social situations. Although this view on the development of attitudes to landscape may sound plausible, it is by no means the only one that has been suggested. Some writers have preferred to interpret man's response to landscape as reflecting innate properties of the human body and the human mind. Tuan (1979), for example, has argued that images of landscape are potentially infinite but that they tend to have a 'family likeness' that results from a common principle of organization. Thus the upright carriage of the human body lends itself to simple geometrical concepts like 'top', 'bottom', 'back', and 'front'. Likewise the development and increasing sophistication of children's minds results in landscapes being seen in an increasingly complex manner.

Appleton (1975) has gone even further and put forward the proposition that man's response to landscape is mainly a function of atavistic mechanisms that derive from the time when man had to use the landscape in an immediate sense for survival (Cosgrove 1978). This proposition finds expression in what is known as *habitat theory*. According to this theory, 'aesthetic satisfaction, experienced in the contemplation of landscape, stems from the immediate perception of landscape features which, in their shapes, colours, spatial arrangements and other visible attributes, act as sign-stimuli indicative of environmental conditions favourable to survival' (Appleton 1975: 2). The spontaneous, aesthetic response of man to a landscape is, in other words, conditioned by the survival mechanisms developed by his primitive ancestors. This type of reasoning has been refined even more in *prospect-refuge theory* which holds that the landscapes which appear most satisfying to man are those that provide an ability to see (prospect) without being seen (refuge) (Appleton 1975). Use of this theory has allowed different landscapes to be compared. It has also provided a basis for the evaluation of landscape painting, poetry, and literature (Gold 1980: 121). For example, both prospect and refuge can be characterized symbolically: the former by light, open areas (e.g. sea shores) and the latter by dark, impenetrable areas (e.g. woodland). In short, prospect-refuge theory argues that the sensitivity which man experiences towards a landscape, whether it be a painting or the real world, hinges on whether the landscape provides man with an ability to see without being seen and that this, in turn, derives from behaviour mechanisms which are innate (Appleton 1975: 11). This means that although landscape appreciation can be trained, it can never escape these innate mechanisms. Therefore, according to prospect-refuge theory, there is a limit to man's ability to replace natural surroundings with artificial surroundings without inhibiting the process of aesthetic enjoyment (Appleton 1975: 11). Predictably, this theory has come in for criticism (see Cosgrove 1978), not least because it rests on an assumption that many archaeologists would now challenge, namely that primitive man was a hunter.

The number of landscapes that impinge upon man

directly is obviously limited. Yet man is aware of many landscapes that are beyond his direct experience. He encounters these landscapes through the medium of literature. A literary perspective has however been generally neglected in geography because the evidence it provides is not in a quantitative form and because the experiences described in literature have rarely thrown much light on the sorts of rational economic behaviour with which much of geography has been preoccupied for so long (Tuan 1976a: 271). Nevertheless, literary sources can be of value to the geographer in several ways: they provide clues as to how people value the environments about them by capturing the ambience of a setting (Salter and Lloyd 1976); they can articulate experience and can transpose inchoate feelings into comprehensible forms (Tuan 1976a: 263); they can reveal something of environmental perceptions and preferences; and, above all, the way that literature can balance the subjective and the objective may provide a more generally applicable model of geographic synthesis (Tuan 1978a). Perhaps the way in which literature blends the subjective and the objective and captures ambience is best shown in relation to how people develop a sense of place.

A sense of place

Profound psychological and emotional links develop between people and the place they live in and experience (Tuan 1977). For the most part, however, people's attachment to place has not attracted the attention it merits from geographers who have been very largely preoccupied with the abstract, geometrical, and objective concept of *space* (Tuan 1974b). Places are nonetheless important phenomena in the lived-world of everyday experience. In fact experience and consciousness of the world centres on places. Despite this, little is known about how places acquire meaning. In the words of Relph (1976: 6), 'we live, act and orient ourselves in a world that is richly and profoundly differentiated into places, yet at the same time we seem to have a meagre understanding of the constitution of places and the ways in which we experience them'.

Most of man's experience of the everyday world is unselfconscious and not clearly structured. The experiential concept of place is particularly difficult to grasp, largely because of its complexity (Relph 1976). The term 'place' implies a location and an integration of nature and culture. As a result, places are unique and yet they are connected together by man's circulation within the environment. In this sense places are localized in that they are part of larger areas. Moreover, the nature of places changes over time as the nature of culture and society changes. Above all, places have meanings. A place is in fact a centre of meaning and it ranges in size from a rocking chair, through an urban neighbourhood, to a nation-state. Similarly, experience of places can occur in different modes, from relatively passive ones like smell to active ones like seeing and thinking. Small places may be known directly and intimately through the senses whereas large places may be known as a result of indirect experiences gained through concepts and symbols (Tuan 1975b). And the net result of this process of getting to know place is often a strong sense of attachment which, in terms of its contribution to a person's well-being, may be every bit as important as close relationships with other people.

By conceptualizing place as a multifaceted phenomenon of experience and by examining properties of place such as location, landscape, and personal involvement, some assessment can be made of the extent to which these properties are essential to man's experience and sense of place (Relph 1976: 29). The task is not however an easy one. Although places usually have a fixed location and possess features which persist in an identifiable form, the meaning of a place comes neither from location, nor from the trivial function that places serve, nor from the community that occupies it, nor from superficial and mundane experiences (Relph 1976: 43). The meaning of places is far deeper and can only really be uncovered by studying the intentionality that underpins human behaviour. Gibson (1978) has suggested that the subjective meaning that attaches to place can be studied through a philosophy and methodology developed by Weber. In Gibson's view, geography has placed too much emphasis on Durkheim's concept of *social milieu* as a determinant of the human condition that stands somewhat apart from human will (see Ch. 3). In its place, Gibson advocates a focus on *human experience* rather than on the treatment of man as an object because in this way it becomes possible to understand how an individual's feelings and thoughts come to be associated with events, acts, and places. This process of understanding implies *verstehen*. It therefore presents problems of validity and verification. It should not be imagined, however, that these problems are any greater than those surrounding positivistic scientific method because quantitative, survey-based attempts to delimit a sense of place in north-east England have also met with methodological detractors (see Townsend and Taylor 1975; Taylor and Townsend 1976; Cornish *et al.* 1977).

At the centre of methodological debates about the measurement of a sense of place lies the question of the extent to which the meaning attached to a place is a shared one. This was a problem addressed by Tuan (1974a) when he used the term *topophilia* to refer to the affective bond that develops between people and place or setting. Topophilic sentiments range in variety and intensity and cover aesthetic and tactile responses as well as a sense of belonging. The development of these sentiments has, in Tuan's view, a lot to do with the role of groups in the transmission of culture. For example, Tuan argues that, although man is a biological organism with a number of senses, it is culture which tends to determine which sense is favoured (as in the case of vision being dominant in most western societies (Pocock 1981a)). Similarly, culture serves to encourage the development of symbols. It does this partly through the medium of literature which provides a means whereby shared meanings can be passed on from individual to individual. For example, the rise of the English regional novel in the nineteenth century (Pocock 1981b) did much to perpetuate the sense of place attached to areas such as Hardy's Wessex (Birch 1981) and geographers generally can learn a good deal about man and place through close scrutiny of how literary sources treat the environment (Pocock 1981c).

Much behavioural research into man–environment interaction avoids issues of symbolism and topophilia and simplifies the world into easily represented structures or models that ignore much of the subtlety and significance of everyday experience (Relph 1976). This is an unfortunate bias, not only because it means that a sense of place tends to be overlooked in academic research, but also because the simplified models often serve as a basis for the design of new environmental settings and the manipulation of people and places. Uniform planning and environmental design is in fact doing away with localism and creating homogeneous landscapes (clearly shown by the tendency for international hotels to look alike, irrespective of their location). Planners, in other words, are creating a placeless geography and fostering a sense of *placelessness*. Increasingly, man has no sense of awareness of the deep and symbolic significance of places and no appreciation of the role of places in his own identity (see Relph 1976; 1981b).

The taken-for-granted world

Attempts to identify a sense of place have met with criticism. All too often research has been cast in obscurantist terms, that either parrot the views of artists or rely on anecdotes which convey mood but little message (Ley 1978: 45). Too much attention has been devoted to cognitive processes and too little to concrete situations and too much research has focused on trivial subject matter (Ley 1981b). Ley (1977: 498–501) claims that these criticisms arise because behavioural geography has failed to draw upon an appropriate philosophical underpinning to engage the distinctive epistemological issues of subjectivity and has relied instead on the general positivist viewpoint that the subjective is metaphysical and therefore unknowable, irrational, private, and beyond the range of theory. In the view of Ley, the solution to this problem is for behavioural geography to break away from the type of *psychologism* that, in imitating the natural sciences, destroys the situational aspects which are integral to the meaning of experience. Instead researchers should recognize that man–environment interaction is characterized by relations which are fuzzy and ambiguous. In particular, Ley advocates a focus on the world of experience, and especially the *taken-for-granted-world*, as a means of developing a holistic view of the dialectical relations between man and his surroundings. Schutz's (1960) phenomenological theory of social action provides an appropriate philosophical underpinning for a focus on this taken-for-granted world in that it entails the researcher in asking the question 'What does this social world mean for the observed actor within this world and what did he mean by his acting within it?' (Ley 1977: 505). Obviously, such a question can be applied to individuals, to groups, and to organizations.

Ley's argument about the taken-for-granted world is closely related to Seamon's (1979) humanistic study of three key elements in man-environment interaction: *movement* (which varies in scale but is often habitual), *rest* (which involves belonging to somewhere where energies can be renewed), and *encounters* (situations of heightened consciousness when individuals are particularly aware of environments). It is also related to Buttimer's (1976) earlier plea for geographers to explore the concept of *lifeworld*. Buttimer argued that geographical studies of overt behaviour and its cognitive foundations often fail to speak in categories appropriate for the elucidation of lived experience to the extent that they make artificial distinctions between subjects and objects, people and environments. Buttimer (1976: 278) implies that phenomenology may provide a starting point for exploration of the lifeworld but cautions that the philosophy provides neither ready-made solutions to the epistemological problems facing science today nor clear operational procedures to guide the empirical investigator. However, in Buttimer's view, phenomenology and positivism are not opposing views, and she appeals for a dialogue between the two approaches. To date, little has come of whatever dialogue may have taken place. It may be however that a promising line of research is that associated with *symbolic interaction theory* (see Mead 1934). For example, Wilson (1980) has pointed out that, according to this theory, human actions are in part based on things that have shared meanings to the extent that the individual relies on interaction to develop a sense of his own being. It follows therefore that the spatial behaviour of an individual is partly a function of his interaction with members of specific reference groups and of his awareness of shared group meanings in relation to the environment. However, it is as yet unknown whether the concept of 'self', which is built up through group interaction and manifest in spatial behaviour, can help in the exploration of lifeworld.

A perspective on humanism

The term 'humanism' implies neither a single philosophical position nor a universally accepted methodology. Rather it is a label applied in geography to a wide variety of approaches that seek to break away from a preoccupation with scientific method and quantification and to study instead distinctly human traits such as meaning, feeling, and emotion. Each of the many humanistic approaches has its advocates and detractors. However, in addition to noting individual approaches, it is important to take an overview and to assess the contribution of the humanistic perspective as a whole. At the risk of glossing over subtle but significant differences between the various formulations, the main features of humanism can be summarized briefly: humanism is against the fragmentation of the totality of human behaviour in the interests of analytical convenience; it is against any attempt to reduce man to the status of a bundle of responses awaiting a stimulus; it is against the abstraction of behaviour from the context in which it occurs; and it is in favour of a much greater emphasis on subjectivity, intentions, values, meanings, and the affective bond that develops between man and the environment.

Phenomenology is probably the most cited humanistic approach, possibly because it incorporates a method – *verstehen* – that appears to provide a way whereby the researcher can come to terms with the subjective meanings that man attaches to his surroundings. The differences between phenomenology and other humanistic approaches such as existentialism are, however, not always clear (Entrikin 1976). Moreover, humanistic approaches in general have not stimulated the volume of research that might have been expected given their claim to being an alternative to scientific method. *Verstehen*, in particular, is alluded to more as a panacea for the methodological problems of interpretative social science than as a strict method of inquiry (Smith 1981). Some of this lack of research effort can probably be attributed to academic inertia and to the failure of geographers to master a new and unfamiliar vocabulary but much of it probably also derives from the fact that important criticisms have been made of the humanistic perspective. For example, Ley (1981a: 252) has criticized humanism for being overly concerned with the activities of the human mind and has argued that 'a preoccupation with perception and meaning rather than with contexts, both antecedents and effects, runs the risk of a fixation upon consciousness which eclipses equally relevant preconditions and consequences of thought and action'. A more fundamental criticism has come from Olsson (1978) who has suggested that the goals of humanism are not being achieved because the mental and linguistic categories which man uses in trying to understand behaviour are themselves dehumanizing in so far as there exists a gap between language and meaning. Olsson sees a surrealist attack on language as a way of liberating meaning but thereby runs foul of the fact that, in attacking form, he endangers communication because meaning itself is only articulated and communicable through formal expression (Ley and Samuels 1978a: 12).

Perhaps, in the final analysis, humanism is best seen as a theoretical perspective which emerged in a particular intellectual context as a reaction to a human geography which had been reduced to the abstract study of space and structures (Ley 1981a: 253). Certainly this is the view of Entrikin (1976) who has argued that humanism offers a form of criticism that helps to counter the excessive abstraction of scientific method. Moreover, in Entrikin's view, many of the humanist arguments about empathy, intuition, and introspection

Table 16.1 Gurvitch's levels of social reality

1. Morphological and ecological surfaces (such as easily observed geographic and demographic phenomena).
2. Social organizations with more-or-less regularized forms of behaviour.
3. Social patterns and models (including the signs, signals, and rules that give regularity to collective behaviour).
4. Regular collective behaviour not confined to social organizations (exemplified by moves and fashions).
5. The web of social roles that individuals play within groups.
6. Collective attitudes and dispositions which urge groups or even whole societies to act in common.
7. Social symbols.
8. Spontaneous, innovative, and creative collective behaviour that changes social patterns, models, and symbols (e.g. revolutions, discoveries).
9. Collective ideas and values that supply a fundamental orientation for higher levels of social reality.
10. Collective mentalities and collective consciousness (based on the intersubjectivity of intuition).

Source: based on material in Thompson (1971) and Tuan (1974c).

are in fact old geographical arguments in a new vocabulary. Above all, though, it is the failure of *verstehen* to produce verifiable results that has hampered humanism. As with all interpretation, there is no way for a researcher to know if he is viewing the same view as an actor and no guarantee that two independent researchers would themselves have the same view. Perhaps the way forward lies in a dialogue between the scientists and the humanists (Buttimer 1976). This may serve as a basis for a new critical theoretical geography which emphasizes the ideological bases of knowledge (see Gregory 1978) or it may serve to demonstrate that scientists and humanists study different levels of social reality, as has already been suggested by Gurvitch (see Thompson 1971) (Table 16.1).

BIBLIOGRAPHY

Abler, R. and **Falk, T.** (1981) Public information services and the changing role of distance in human affairs, *Economic Geography* 57, 10–22.

Abney, F. G. and **Hill, L. B.** (1966) Natural disasters as a political variable: the effect of a hurricane on an urban election, *American Political Science Review* **60**, 974–81.

Abu Lughod, J. L. (1969) Testing the theory of social area analysis: the ecology of Cairo, Egypt, *American Sociological Review* **34**, 198–212.

Ackoff, R. L. and **Emery, F. E.** (1972) *On Purposeful Systems*, Tavistock: London.

Acredolo, L. P., Pick, H. L. and **Olsen, M. G.** (1975) Environmental differentiation and familiarity as determinants of children's memory for spatial location, *Developmental Psychology* **11**, 494–501.

Adams, J. S. (1969) Directional bias in intra-urban migration *Economic Geography* **45**, 302–23.

Adams, J. S. and **Gilder, K. A.** (1976) Household location and intra-urban migration, in D. T. Herbert and R. J. Johnston (eds) *Social Areas in Cities. Vol. 1 Spatial Processes and Form*, Wiley, London, pp. 159–92.

Agnew, J. A. and **Duncan, J. S.** (1981) The transfer of ideas into Anglo-American human geography, *Progress in Human Geography* 5, 42–57.

Ajo, R. (1953) *Contributions to 'Social Physics': a programme sketch with special regard to national planning*, Lund Publications in Geography Series B No. 4.

Aldskogius, H. (1977) A conceptual framework and a Swedish case study of recreational behaviour and environmental cognition, *Economic Geography* **53**, 163–83.

Alexander, I. (1979) *Office Location and Public Policy*, Longman: London.

Allon-Smith, R. D. (1978) The migration of the elderly: a social geography, unpublished Ph.D thesis, University of Leicester.

Almy, T. A. (1973) Residential location and electoral cohesion: the pattern of urban political conflict, *American Political Science Review* **67**, 914–23.

Altman, I. (1975) *The Environment and Social Behaviour*, Brooks-Cole: Monterey.

Althusser, L. (1969) *For Marx*, Penguin: Harmondsworth.

Alwan, A. J. and **Parisi, D. G.** (1974), *Quantitative Methods for Decision-making*, Eurospan: New York.

Amedeo, D. and **Golledge, R. G.** (1975) *An Introduction to Scientific Reasoning in Geography*, Wiley: New York.

Anderson, J. (1971) 'Space-time budgets and activity studies in urban geography and planning', *Environment and Planning* 3, 353–68.

Anderson, T. R. and **Bean, L. L.** (1961) The Shevky-Bell areas: confirmation of results and reinterpretation, *Social Forces* **40**, 119–24.

Anderson, T. R. and **Egeland, J. A.** (1961) Spatial aspects of social area analysis, *American Sociological Review* **36**, 329–9.

Appleton, I. (ed.) (1974) *Leisure Research and Policy*, Scottish Academic Press: Edinburgh.

Appleton, J. (1975) *The Experience of Landscape*, Wiley: London.

Appleyard, D. (1969) City designers and the pluralistic city, in L. Rodwin (ed.) *Planning Urban Growth and Regional Development*, MIT Press: Cambridge, Mass., pp. 422–52.

Appleyard, D. (1970) Styles and methods of structuring a city, *Environment and Behaviour* 2, 100–17.

Appleyard, D. (1973) Notes on urban perception and knowledge, in R. M. Down and D. Stea (eds) *Image and Environment*, Aldine, Chicago, pp. 109–14.

Appleyard, D. (1978) The major published works of Kevin Lynch: an appraisal, *Town Planning Review* **49**, 551–7.

Appleyard, D., Lynch, K., and **Meyer, J.** (1964) *The View From the Road*, MIT Press: Cambridge, Mass.

Archer, B. (1973) *The impact of domestic tourism*, University of North Wales, Bangor Occasional Papers in Economics No. 2.

Ardrey, R. (1967) *The Territorial Imperative*, Fontana: London.

Armistead, N. (1974) Introduction, in N. Armistead (ed.) *Reconstructing Social Psychology*, Penguin, Harmondsworth, pp. 7–27.

Athanasiou, R. and **Yoshioka, G. A.** (1973) The spatial character of friendship formation, *Environment and Behaviour* 5, 43–65.

Auliciems, A. and **Dick, J. H. A.** (1976) Factors in environmental action: air pollution complaints in Brisbane, *Australian Geographical Studies* **14**, 59–67.

Bagley, C. (1974) The built environment as an influence on personality and social behaviour: a spatial study, in D. Canter and T. Lee (eds) *Psychology and the Built Environment*, Architectural Press, London, pp. 156–64.

Bagley, C. and **Jacobson, S.** (1976) Ecological variation in three types of suicide, *Psychological Medicine* **6**, 423–7.

Bagley, C., Jacobson, S. and **Palmer, C.** (1973) Social structure and the ecological distribution of mental illness, suicide, and delinquency, *Psychological Medicine* **3**, 177–82.

Bagley, C., Jacobson, S. and **Rehin, A.** (1976) Completed suicide: a taxonomic analysis of clinical and social data, *Psychological Medicine* **6**, 429–38.

Bailey, P. (1978) *Leisure and Class in Victorian Society*, Methuen: London.

Baker, E. J. and **Patton D. J.** (1974) Attitudes towards hurricane hazards on the Gulf Coast, in G. F. white (ed.) *Natural Hazards: local, national, global*, Oxford University Press, London, pp. 30–6.

Baldassare, M. and **Fischer, C. S.** (1975) Suburban life: powerlessness and need for affiliation, *Urban Affairs Quarterly* **10**, 314–26.

Baldassare, M. and **Fischer, C. S.** (1976) The relevance of crowding experiments to urban studies, in D. Stokols (ed.) *Psychological Perspectives on Environment and Behaviour*, Plenum, New York, pp. 85–99.

Baldwin, J. (1974) Social area analysis and studies of delinquency, *Social Science Research* **3**, 151–68.

Baldwin, J. and **Bottoms, A. E.** (1976) *The Urban Criminal*, London: Tavistock.

Baltzel, E. D. (1958) *Philadelphia Gentlemen: the making of a national upper class*, Free Press: New York.

Bandura, A. (1977) Self-efficacy: toward a unifying theory of behavioural change, *Psychological Review* **84**, 191–215.

Banerjee, T. and **Lynch, K.** (1977) On people and places: a comprehensive study of the spatial environment of adolescence, *Town Planning Review* **48**, 105–15.

Bannister, D. and **Fransella, F.** (1971) *Inquiring Man: the theory of personal constructs*, Penguin: Harmondsworth.

Bannon, J. J. (1981) *Problem Solving in Recreation and Parks*, Cliffs. Prentice-Hall: Englewood.

Bardet, G. (1961) Social topography: an analytic-synthetic understanding of the urban texture, in G. A. Theodorson (ed.) *Studies in Human Ecology*, Row, Peterson, Evanston, Ill., pp. 370–83.

Barker, R. G. (1965) Explorations in ecological psychology, *American Psychologist* **20**, 1–14.

Barker, R. G. (1968) *Ecological Psychology: concepts and methods for studying the environment and behaviour*, Stanford University Press: Stanford.

Barr, B. M. and **Fairbairn, K. J.** (1978) Linkages and manufacturer's perception of spatial economic opportunity, in F.E.I. Hamilton (ed.) *Contemporary Industrialization: spatial analysis and regional development*, Longman, London, pp. 122–43.

Barrett, F. A. (1973) *Residential search behaviour: a study of intra-urban relocation in Toronto*, Geographical Monographs No. 1, York University, Toronto.

Barrett, F. A. (1976) The search process in residential relocation, *Environment and Behaviour* **8**, 169–98.

Bartlett, F. C. (1932) *Remembering*, Cambridge University Press: Cambridge.

Bartlett, P. G. (1982) *Agricultural Decision Making*, Academic Press: New York.

Bassett, K. and **Short, J. R.** (1980) *Hoursing and Residential Structure*, Routledge and Kegan Paul: London.

Bates, F. L. *et al.* (1963) *The Social and Psychological Consequences of a Natural Disaster: a longitudinal study of Hurricane Audrey*, DRG Disaster Study No.18: Washington.

Batty, M. (1970a) An activity allocation model for the Nottingham-Derbyshire subregion, *Regional Studies* **4**, 307–32.

Batty, M. (1970b) Models and projections of the space economy: a subregional study in Northwest England, *Town Planning Review* **41**, 121–48.

Batty, M. (1976a) *Urban Modelling, Algorithms, Calibrations, Predictions*, Cambridge University Press: Cambridge.

Batty, M. (1976b) Reilly's challenge: new laws of retail gravitation which define systems of central places, *Environment and Planning A* **10**, 185–219.

Baxter, M. J. (1979) The interpretation of the distance and attractiveness components in models of recreational trips, *Geographical Analysis* **11**, 311–15.

Beard, J. B. and **Ragheb, M. G.** (1980) Measuring leisure satisfaction, *Journal of Leisure Research* **12**, 20–33.

Beck, R. J. and **Wood, D.** (1976) Cognitive transformation of information from urban geographical fields to mental maps, *Environment and Behaviour* **8**, 199–238.

Becker, R. H. (1978) Social carrying capacity and user satisfaction: an experimental function, *Leisure Sciences* **1**, 241–58.

Bell, W. (1958a) Economic, family and ethnic status: an empirical test, *American Sociological Review* **20**, 45–52.

Bell, W. (1958b) Social choice, life style and suburban residence, in W. Dobriner (ed.) *The Suburban Community*, Putnam, New York, pp. 225–47.

Bennett, R. J. and **Chorley, R. J.** (1978) *Environmental Systems: philosophy, analysis, and control*, Methuen: London.

Berger, B. M. (1960) *Working Class Suburbs*, University of California Press: Berkeley.

Berkman, H. G. (1965) The game theory of land use determination, *Land Economics* **41**, 11–19.

Berry, B. J. L. (1967) *Geography of Market Centres and Retail Distribution*, Prentice-Hall: Englewood Cliffs.

Berry, B. J. L. and **Kasarda, J. D.** (1977) *Contemporary Urban Ecology*, Macmillan: New York.

Birch, B. P. (1981) Wessex, Hardy and the nature novelists, *Transactions of the Institute of British Geographers* **6**, 348–58.

Birrell, R. and **Silverwood, R.** (1981) The social costs of environmental deterioration: the case of the Victorian coastline, in D. Mercer (ed.) *Outdoor Recreation: Australian perspectives*, Sorrett, Melbourne, pp. 118–24.

Blaikie, P. (1978) The theory of the spatial diffusion of innovations: a spacious cul-de-sac, *Progress in Human Geography* **2**, 268–95.

Blake, R. B., **Mouton, J. S.** and **Bidwell, A. C.** (1962) The managerial grid, *Advanced Managements Office Executive* **1**, 10–19.

Blakemore, M. (1981) From way-finding to map-making: the spatial information fields of aboriginal peoples, *Progress in Human Geography* **5**, 1–24.

Blalock, H. M. (1964) *Causal Inferences in Nonexperimental Research*, University of North Carolina Press: Chapel Hill.

Blaut J. M. (1977) Two views of diffusion, *Annals of the Association of American Geographers* **67**, 343–9.

Blaut, J. M. and **Stea, D.** (1971) Studies of geographic learning, *Annals of the Association of American Geographers* **61**, 387–93.

Bloomestein, H., **Nijkamp, P.** and **Van Veenendaal, W.** (1980) Shopping perceptions and preferences: a multi-dimensional attractiveness analysis of consumer and entrepreneurial attitudes, *Economic Geography* **56**, 155–74.

Blouet, B. W. and **Lawson, M. P.** (eds) (1975) *Images of the Plains: the role of human value in settlement*, University of Nebraska Press: Lincoln.

Blowers, A. (1973) The neighbourhood: exploration of a concept, in *The City as a Social System*, Open University, Milton Keynes, pp. 49–90.

Boal, F. W. (1969) Territoriality on the Shankill-Falls Divide, Belfast, *Irish Geography* **6**, 30–50.

Boal, F. W. (1971) Territory and class: a study of two residential areas in Belfast, *Irish Geography* **6**, 229–48.

Boal, F. W., **Doherty, P.** and **Pringle, D. G.** (1978) *Social problems in the Belfast urban area: an exploratory analysis*, Occasional Paper No. 12, Department of Geography, Queen Mary College, London.

Bogdanovic, B. (1975) Symbols in the city and the city as symbols, *Ekistics* **39**, 140–6.

Boggs, S. L (1965) Urban crime patterns, *American Sociological Review*, **30**, 899–908.

Booth, A. (1976) *Human Crowding and its Consequences*, Praeger: New York.

Booth, A. and **Johnson, D.R.** (1975) The effect of crowding on child health and development, *American Behavioural Scientist* **18**, 736–47.

Booth, A. and **Edwards, J. N.** (1976) Crowding and family relations, *American Sociological Review* **41**, 308–21.

Booth, A., Welch, S. and **Johnson, D. R.** (1976) Crowding and urban crime rates, *Urban Affairs Quarterly* **11**, 291–321.

Boots, B. N. (1979) Population density, crowding and human behaviour, *Progress in Human Geography* **3**, 13–64.

Bosselman, F. P. (1978) *In the Wake of the Tourist: managing special places in eight countries*, Conservation Foundation: Washington.

Bott, E. (1957) *Family and Social Networks*, Tavistock: London.

Boulding, K. E. (1956) *The Image: knowledge in life and society*, University of Michigan Press: Ann Arbor.

Boulding, K. E. (1959) National images and international systems, *Journal of Conflict Resolution* **3**, 120–31.

Boulding, K. E. (1973) Foreword, in R. M. Downs and D. Stea (eds) *Image and Environment*, Aldine, Chicago, pp. vii–xi.

Bowden, M. J. (1975) Desert wheat belt, plains corn belt: environmental cognition and behaviour of settlers in the plains margin, 1850–99, in B. W. Blouet and M. P. Lawson (eds) *Images of the Plains: the role of human value in settlement*, University of Nebraska Press, Lincoln, pp. 189–202.

Boyle, M. J. and **Robinson, M. E.** (1979) Cognitive mapping and understanding, in D. T. Herbert and R. J. Johnston (eds) *Geography and the Urban Environment: progress in research and application. Vol. II*, Wiley, London, pp. 59–82.

Brantingham, P. L. and **Brantingham, J.** (1975) Residential burglary and urban form, *Urban Studies* **12**, 273–84.

Briggs, R. (1973a) Urban cognitive distance, in R. M. Downs and D. Stea (eds) *Image and Environment* Aldine, Chicago, pp. 361–88.

Briggs, R. (1973b) On the relationship between cognitive and objective distance, in W. F. E. Preiser (ed.) *Environmental Design Research*, Dowden, Hutchinson, and Ross, Stroudsburg, pp. 186–99.

Briggs, R. (1976) Methodologies for the measurement of cognitive distance, in G. T. Moore and R. G. Golledge (eds) *Environmental Knowing*, Dowden, Hutchinson, and Ross, Stroudsburg, pp. 325–34.

Britton, J. N. H. (1974) Environmental adaptation of industrial plants: service linkages, locational environment and organization, in F. E. I. Hamilton (ed.) *Spatial Perspectives on Industrial Organization and Decision-Making*, Wiley, London, pp. 363–90.

Britton, J. N. H. (1978) Influences on the spatial behaviour of manufacturing firms in Southern Ontario, in F. E. I. Hamilton (ed.) *Contemporary Industrialization: spatial analysis and regional development*, Longman, London, pp. 110–21.

Brockman, C. F. and **Morrison, L. G.** (eds) (1979) *Recreational Use of Wild Lands*, McGraw-Hill: New York.

Brooker-Gross, S. R. (1981) Shopping behaviour in two sets of shopping destinations: an interactionist interpretation of outshopping, *Tijdschrift voor Economische en Sociale Geografie* **72**, 28–34.

Brookfield, H. C. (1964) Questions on the human frontiers of geography, *Economic Geography* **40**, 283–303.

Brookfield, H. C. (1969) On the environment as perceived, *Progress in Geography* **1**, 51–80.

Brooks, R. H. (1973) Differential perception of drought in north-eastern Brazil, *Proceedings of the Association of American Geographers* **5**, 31–4.

Brown, J. S., Schwarzweller, H. K. and **Mangalam J. J.** (1963) Kentucky Mountain migration and the Stem family: an American variation on the theme of Le Play, *Rural Sociology* **28**, 53–4.

Brown, L. A. (1982) *Innovation Diffusion: a new perspective*, Methuen: London.

Brown, L. A. and **Cox, K. R.** (1971) Empirical regularities in the diffusion of innovation, *Annals of the Association of American Geographers* **61**, 551–9.

Brown, L. A. and **Holmes, J.** (1971) Search behaviour in an intra-urban migration context: a spatial perspective, *Environment and Planning* **3**, 307–26.

Brown, L. A. and **Longbrake, D. B.** (1970) Migration flows in intraurban space: place-utility considerations, *Annals of the Association of American Geographers* **60**, 368–84.

Brown, L. A. and **Moore, E. G.** (1970) The intra-urban migration process: a perspective, *Geografiska Annaler* **52B**, 1–13.

Brown, M. A. (1981) Behavioural approaches to the geographic study of innovation diffusion: problems and prospects, in K. R. Cox and R. G. Golledge (eds) *Behavioural Problems in Geography Revisited*, Methuen, London, pp. 123–44.

Brown, P. J., Dyer, A. and **Whaley, R. S.** (1973) Recreation research – so what?, *Journal of Leisure Research* **5**, 16–24.

Brown, R. V., Kahr, A. S., and **Petersen, C.** (1974) *Decision Analysis for the Manager*, New York: Holt, Rinehart and Winston.

Brummell, A. C. (1979) A model of intra-urban mobility, *Economic Geography* **55**, 338–52.

Brummell, A. C. (1981) A method of measuring stress, *Geographical Analysis* **13**, 248–61.

Bruner, J. S., Olver R. R. and **Greenfield, P. M.** (eds) (1966) *Studies In Cognitive Growth*, Wiley: New York.

Brunswik, E. (1956) *Perception and the Representative Design of Psychological Experiments*, UCLA Press: Los Angeles.

Bucklin, L. P. (1967) The concept of mass in intra-urban shopping, *Journal of Marketing* **31**, 37–42.

Budd A. J. and **Budd J. L. S.** (1981) Politics, health and mass media: a geographical perspective from Leicestershire, in D. Turnock (ed.) *Leicester Geographical Studies*, Occasional Paper No. 1, Department of Geography, University of Leicester, pp. 19–36.

Budd, J. L. S. (1979) The cognition of residential districts in Leicester, Unpublished Ph.D thesis, University of Leicester.

Bunting, T. E. and **Guelke, L.** (1979) Behavioural and perception geography: a critical appraisal, *Annals of the Association of American Geographers* **69**, 448–62.

Burgess, E. W. (ed.) (1920) *The Urban Community*, University of Chicago Press: Chicago.

Burgess, J. A. (1982) Selling places: environmental images for the executive, *Regional Studies* **16**, 1–17.

Burke, G. L. (1975) *Towns in the Making*, Arnold: London.

Burnett, P. (1973) The dimensions of alternatives in spatial choice processes, *Geographical Analysis* **5**, 181–204.

Burnett, P. (1976) Behavioural geography and the philosophy of mind, in R. G. Golledge and G. Rushton (eds) *Spatial Choice and Spatial Behaviour*, Ohio State University Press, Columbus, pp. 23–48.

Burnett, P. (1977) Tests of a linear learning model of destination choice: applications to shopping travel by heterogeneous population groups, *Geografiska Annaler* **59B**, 95–108.

Burnett, P. (1978a) Time cognition and urban travel behaviour, *Geografiska Annaler* **60B**, 107–15.

Burnett, P. (1978b) Markovian models of movement within urban spatial structures, *Geographical Analysis* **10**, 142–53.

Burnett, P. (1981) Theoretical advances in modeling economic and social behaviours: applications to geographical policy-oriented models, *Economic Geography* **57**, 291–303.

Burns, T. (1973) Leisure in industrial society, in M. A. Smith, S. Parker, and C. S. Smith (eds) *Leisure and Society in Britain*, Allen Lane, London, pp. 40–55.

Burton, I. (1963) The quantitative revolution and theoretical geography, *Canadian Geographer* **7**, 151–62.

Burton, I. and **Kates, R. W.** (1964a) The perception of natural hazards in resource management, *Natural Resources Journal* **3**, 412–41.

Burton, I. and **Kates, R. W.** (1964b) The flood plain and the sea shore: a comparative analysis of hazard zone occupance, *Geographical Review* **54**, 366–85.

Burton, I., Kates, R. W. and **White, G. F.** (1968) *The human ecology of extreme geographical events*, Natural Hazard Research: Working Paper No. 1, Department of Geography, University of Toronto.

Burton, I., Kates, R. W. and **Snead, R. E.** (1969) *The human ecology of coastal flood hazard in megalopolis*, University of Chicago, Department of Geography Research Paper No. 115.

Burton, I., Kates, R. W. and **White, G. F.** (1978) *The Environment as Hazard*, Oxford University Press: New York.

Burton, T. L. (1971) *Experiments in Recreation Research*, Allen and Unwin: London.

Bush, R. R. and **Mosteller, F.** (1955) *Stochastic Models for Learning*, Wiley: New York.

Butler, D. E. and **Stokes, D. E.** (1974) *Political Change in Britain: forces shaping electoral choice*, Macmillan: London. (2nd edn).

Butler, E. W. *et al.* (1969) *Moving behaviour and residential choice: a national survey*, National Co-operative Research Program Report No. 81: Washington.

Buttimer, A. (1969) Social space in interdisciplinary perspective, *Geographical Review* **59**, 417–26.

Buttimer, A. (1974) *Values in geography*, Association of American Geographers Commission on College Geography, Resource Paper No. 24: Washington.

Buttimer, A. (1976) Grasping the dynamism of lifeworld, *Annals of the Association of American Geographers* **66**, 277–92.

Buttimer, A. (1978) Charism and context: the challenge of La Geographie Humaine, in D. Ley and M. S. Samuels (eds) *Humanistic Geography: prospects and problems*, Maaroufa Press, Chicago, pp. 58–76.

Buttimer, A. (1979) Erewhon or nowhere land, in S. Gale and G. Olsson (eds) *Philosophy in Geography*, Reidel, Dordrecht, pp. 9–37.

Buttimer, A. and **Seamon, D.** (eds) (1980) *The Human Experience of Space and Place*, Croom Helm: London.

Cadwallader, M. (1973) A methodological examination of cognitive distance, in W. F. E. Preiser (ed.) *Environmental Design Research*, Dowden, Hutchinson, and Ross, Stroudsburg, pp. 193–9.

Cadwallader, M. (1975) A behavioural model of consumer spatial decision making, *Economic Geography* **51**, 339–49.

Cadwallader, M. (1976) Cognitive distance in intraurban space, in G. T. Moore and R. G. Golledge (eds) *Environmental Knowing*, Dowden, Hutchinson, and Ross, Stroudsburg, pp. 316–24.

Cadwallader, M. (1977) Frame dependency in cognitive maps: an analysis using directional statistics, *Geographical Analysis* **9**, 284–92.

Cadwallader, M. (1978) Urban information and preference surfaces: their patterns, structures, and interrelationships, *Geografiska Annaler* **60B**, 97–106.

Cadwallader, M. (1979) Problems in cognitive distance: implications for cognitive mapping, *Environment and Behaviour* **11**, 559–76.

Cadwallader, M. (1981) Towards a cognitive gravity model: the case of consumer spatial behaviour, *Regional Studies* **15**, 275–84.

Calhoun, J. B. (1962) Population density and social pathology, *Scientific American* **206**, 139–48.

Calhoun, J. B. (1966) The role of space in animal sociology, *Journal of Social Issues* **22**, 46–58.

Cambell, A. *et al.* (1960) *The American Voter*, Wiley: New York.

Canter, D. V. (1977) *The Psychology of Place*, Architectural Press: London.

Canter, D. V. and **Tagg, S. K.** (1975) Distance estimation in cities, *Environment and Behaviour* **7**, 59–80.

Carey, H. C. (1858) *Principles of Social Science*, Lippincott: Philadelphia.

Carey, L. and **Mapes, R.** (1971) *The Sociology of Planning: a study of social activity on new housing estates*, Batsford: London

Carlstein, T., Parkes, D. and **Thrift, N.** (eds) (1978a) *Timing Space and Spacing Time. Vol. 1: Making sense of time*, Arnold: London.

Carlstein, T., Parkes, D. and **Thrift, N. J.** (1978b) *Timing Space and Spacing Time. Vol. 2: Human activity and time geography*, Arnold: London.

Carlstein, T., Parkes, D. and **Thrift, N. J.** (eds) (1978c) *Timing Space and Spacing Time. Vol. 3: Time and regional dynamics*, Arnold: London.

Carlstein, T. and **Thrift, N. J** (1978) Afterword: towards a time-space structured approach to society and environment, in T. Carlstein *et al.* (eds) *Timing Space and Spacing Time. Vol. 2: Human activity and time geography*, Arnold, London, pp. 235–63.

Carr, S. and **Schissler, D.** (1969) The city as trip, *Environment and Behaviour* **1**, 7–35.

Carroll, J. S. and **Payne, J. W.** (eds) (1976) *Cognition and Social Behaviour*, Erlbaum Associates: New York.

Carstairs, G. M. (1960) Overcrowding and human aggression, in H. D. Graham and T. R. Curr (eds) *Violence in America*, Bantam, New York, pp. 751–64.

Carter, H. (1972) *The Study of Urban Geography*, Arnold: London.

Carter, R. L. and **Hill, K.** (1976) The criminal's image of the city and urban crime patterns, *Social Science Quarterly* **57**, 597–607.

Castells, M. (1977) *The Urban Question*, Arnold: London.

Castells, M. (1978) *City, Class and Power*, Macmillan: London.

Castle, I. and **Gittus, E.** (1957) The distribution of social

defects in Liverpool, *Sociological Review* 5, 43–64.
Castles, F. G., **Murray, D. J.** and **Potter, D. C.** (1977) *Decisions, Organizations and Society*, Penguin: Harmondsworth.
Cebula, R. J. (1980) *The Determinants of Human Migration*, Lexington Books: Lexington, Mass.
Cesano, F. J. (1980) Congestion and the valuation of recreation benefits, *Land Economics* **56**, 329–38.
Chapin, F. S. (1965) *Urban Land Use Planning*, University of Illinois Press: Urbana.
Chapin, F. S. (1968) Activity systems and urban structure: a working schema, *Journal of the American Institute of Planners* **34**, 12–18.
Chapin, F. S. (1974) *Human Activity Patterns in the City: things people do in time and space*, Wiley: New York.
Chapin, F. S. (1978) Human time allocation in the city, in T. Carlstein *et al.* (eds) *Timing Space and Spacing Time. Vol. 2: Human activity and time geography*, Arnold, London, pp. 13–26.
Chapin, F. S. and **Brail, R. K.** (1969) Human activity systems in the metropolitan United States, *Environment and Behaviour* **1**, 107–30.
Chapin, F. S. and **Hightower, H. C.** (1965) Household activity patterns and land use, *Journal of the American Institute of Planners* **31**, 222–31.
Chapman, G. P. (1974) Perception and regulation: a case study of farmers in Bihar, *Transactions of the Institute of the British Geographers* **62**, 71–93.
Chase, D. R. and **Cheek, N. H.** (1979) Activity preferences and participation: conclusions from a factor analytic study, *Journal of Leisure Research* **11**, 92–101
Cheng, J. R. (1980) Tourism: how much is too much? Lessons for Canmore from Barff, *Canadian Geographer* **24**, 72–80.
Cheek, N. H., **Field, D. R.** and **Burdge, R. J.** (1978) *Leisure and Recreation Places*, Ann Arbor Science Publishers Inc.: Ann Arbor.
Clark, D. and **Unwin, K. I.** (1981) Telecommunications and travel: potential impact in rural areas, *Regional Studies* **15**, 47–56.
Clark, W. A. V. (1976) Migration in Milwaukee, *Economic Geography* **52**, 48–70.
Clark, W. A. V. (1981) Residential mobility and behavioural geography: parallelism and independence, in K. R. Cox and R. G. Golledge (eds) *Behavioural Problems in Geography Revisited*, Methuen, London, pp. 182–205.
Clark, W. A. V. and **Cadwallader, M.** (1973) Locational stress and residential mobility, *Environment and Behaviour* **5**, 29–41.
Clark, W. A. V. and **Everaers, P. C. J.** (1981) Public policy and residential mobility in Dutch cities, *Tijdschrift voor Economische en Sociale Geografie* **72**, 322–33.
Clark, W. A. V., **Huff, J. O.** and **Burt, J. E.** (1979) Calibrating a model of the decision to move, *Environment and Planning A* **11**, 689–704.
Clark, W. A. V. and **Moore, E. G.** (1978) *Population mobility and residential change*, Northwestern Studies in Geography No. 25: Evanston.
Clark, W. A. V. and **Moore, E. G.** (eds) (1980) *Residential Mobility and Public Policy*, Sage: New York.
Clark, W. A. V. and **Smith, T. R.** (1979) Modelling information uses in a spatial context, *Annals of the Association of American Geographers* **69**, 575–88.
Clark, W. A. V. and **Smith, T. R.** (1982) Housing market search behaviour and expected utility theory: 2 The process of search, *Environment and Planning A* **14**, 717–38.
Clawson, M. (1972) *Methods of Measuring the Demand For and Use of Outdoor Recreation*, Resources for the Future: Washington.
Clawson, M. and **Knetsch, J. L.** (1966) *Economics of Outdoor Recreation*, Johns Hopkins University Press: Baltimore.
Clay, G. (1973) *How to Read the American City*, Pall Mall: London.
Cliff, A. D. and **Ord, J. K.** (1973) *Spatial Autocorrelation*, Pion: London.
Coates, B. E., **Johnston, R. J.** and **Knox, P. L.** (1977) *Geography and Inequality*, Oxford University Press: London.
Cohen, R. *et al.* (1973) *Psych city: a simulated community*, Pergamon: Oxford.
Cohen, S. and **Sherrod, D. R.** (1978) When density matters: environmental control as a determinant of crowding effects in laboratory and residential settings, *Journal of Population* **1**, 189–202.
Coleman, J. S. (1964) *Introduction to Mathematical Sociology*, Free Press: New York.
Collette, J. and **Webb, S.** (1976) Urban density, household crowding and stress reactions, *Australian and New Zealand Journal of Sociology* **12**, 184–91.
Collingwood, R. G. (1956) *The Idea of History*, Oxford University Press: London.
Connell, J. (1973) Social networks in urban society, in *Social Patterns in Cities*, Institute or British Geographers Special Publication No. 5, London, pp. 41–52.
Cool, S. F. M. (1979) Recreation activity packages at water-based resources, in C. S. Van Doren *et al.* (eds) *Land and Leisure: concepts and methods in outdoor recreation*, Methuen, London, pp. 123–41.
Cooper, C. P. (1981) Spatial and temporal patterns of tourist behaviour, *Regional Studies* **15**, 359–71.
Cooper, M. J. M. (1975) *The industrial location decision making process*, University of Birmingham Centre for Urban and Regional Studies Research Paper No. 34.
Coppock, J. T. (1980) The geography of leisure and recreation, in E. H. Brown (ed.) *Geography Yesterday and Tomorrow*, Oxford University Press, London, pp. 263–79.
Coppock, J. T. and **Duffield, B.** (1975) *Recreation in the Countryside*, Macmillan: London.
Cordey Hayes, M. and **Wilson, A. G.** (1970) *Spatial interaction*, Centre for Environmental Studies Working Paper No. 57.
Cornish, M. *et al.* (1977) Regional culture and identity in industrialized societies: a critical comment, *Regional Studies* **11**, 113–16.
Corsi, T. and **Harvey, M. E.** (1975) The socio-economic determinants of crime in the city of Cleveland: the application of canonical scores to geographical problems, *Tijdschrift voor Economische en Sociale Geografie* **66**, 323–36.
Cosgrove, D. (1978) Place, landscape, and the dialectics of cultural geography, *Canadian Geographer* **22**, 66–72.
Cosgrove, I. and **Jackson, R.** (1972) *The Geography of Recreation and Leisure*, Hutchinson: London.
Coupe, R. T. and **Morgan, B. S.** (1981) Toward a fuller understanding of residential mobility: a case study in Northampton, *Environment and Planning A* **13**, 201–16.
Cox, K. R. (1968) Suburbia and voting behaviour in the London Metropolitan Area, *Annals of the Association of American Geographers* **58**, 111–27.
Cox, K. R. (1969a) Comment in reply, *Annals of the Association of American Geographers* **59**, 411–15.
Cox, K. R. (1969b) The voting decision in a spatial context, *Progress in Geography* **1**, 81–117.

Cox, K. R. (1969c) The spatial structuring of information flows and partisan attitudes, in M. Dogan and S. Rokkan (eds) *Quantitative Ecological Analysis in the Social Sciences*, MIT Press, Cambridge, Mass., pp. 157–86.

Cox, K. R. (1970) Residential relocation and political behaviour: conceptual model and empirical tests, *Acta Sociologica* **13**, 40–53.

Cox, K. R. (1981) Bourgeois thought and the behavioural geography debate, in K. R. Cox and R. G. Golledge (eds) *Behavioural Problems in Geography Revisited*, Methuen, London, pp. 256–79.

Cox, K. R. and **McCarthy, J. J.** (1980) Neighbourhood activism in the American city: behavioural relationships and evaluation, *Urban Geography* **1**, 22–38.

Cox, K. R., Reynolds, D. R. and **Rokkan, S.** (eds) (1974) *Locational Approaches to Power and Conflict*, Sage: Beverly Hills.

Cox, K. R., McCarthy, J. J. and **Nartowicz, F.** (1979) The cognitive organization of the North American city: empirical evidence, *Environment and Planning A* **11**, 327–34.

Craik, K. H. (1968) The comprehension of the everyday physical environment, *Journal of the American Institute of Planners* **34**, 29–37.

Craik, K. H. (1970) Environmental psychology, *New Directions in Psychology* **4**, 1–121.

Craik, K. H. (1973) Environmental psychology, *Annual Review of Psychology* **24**, 403–22.

Craik, K. H. (1977) Multiple scientific paradigms in environmental psychology, *International Journal of Psychology* **12**, 147–57.

Crandall, R. (1980) Motivations for leisure, *Journal of Leisure Research* **12**, 45–54.

Cullen, G. (1961) *Townscape*, Architectural Press: London.

Cullen, I. G. (1976) Human geography, regional science, and the study of individual behaviour, *Environment and Planning A* **8**, 397–409.

Cullen, I. G. (1978) The treatment of time in the explanation of spatial behaviour, in T. Carlstein *et al.* (eds) *Timing Space and Spacing Time. Vol. 2: Human activity and time geography*, Arnold, London, pp. 27–38.

Cullen, I. G. and **Godson, V.** (1975) Urban networks: the study of activity patterns, *Progress in Planning* **4**, 5–96.

Curry, M. (1982) The idealist dispute in Anglo-American geography, *Professional Geographer* **26**, 37–50.

Cushman, G. and **Hamilton-Smith, E.** (1980) Equity issues in urban recreational services, in D. Mercer and E. Hamilton-Smith (eds) *Recreation Planning and Social Change in Urban Australia*, Sorrett, Melbourne, pp. 167–78.

Cyert, R. M. and **March, J. G.** (1963) *A Behavioural Theory of the Firm*, Prentice Hall: Englewood Cliffs.

Darke, J. and **Darke, R.** (1969) *Physical and social factors in neighbourhood relations*, Centre for Environmental Studies Working Paper No. 41, London.

Davidson, J. (1970) *Outdoor Recreation Surveys: design and use of questionnaires for site surveys*, Countryside Commission: London.

Davidson, R. N. (1981) *Crime and Environment*, Croom Helm: London.

Davies, R. L. and **Kirby, D. A.** (1980) Retail organization, in J. A. Dawson (ed.) *Retail Geography*, Croom Helm, London, pp. 156–92.

Day, R. A. (1976) Urban distance cognition: review and contribution, *Australian Geographer* **13**, 193–200.

Deans, K. G. and **James, H. D.** (1981) Social factors and admission to psychiatric hospital: schizophrenia in Plymouth, *Transactions, Institute of British Geographers*, **6**, 39–52.

Dear, M. (1981) Social and spatial reproduction of the mentally ill, in M. Dear and A. J. Scott (eds) *Urbanization and Urban Planning in Capitalist Society*, Methuen, London, pp. 481–97.

Dear, M. and **Clark, G. L.** (1978) The state and geographic process: a critical review, *Environment and Planning A* **10**, 177–84.

Dear, M. J. and **Taylor, S. M.** (1982) *Not on Our Street: community attitudes to mental health care*, Pion: London.

De Jonge, D. (1962) Images of urban areas: their structure and psychological foundations, *Journal of the American Institute of Planners* **28**, 266–76.

De Lauwe, P-H. C. (1975) *Des hommes et des villes*, Payot: Paris.

Dennis, N. (1958) The popularity of the neighbourhood community idea, *Sociological Review* **6**, 191–208.

Dever, G. E. A. (1972) Leukaemia and housing: an intra-urban analysis, in N.D. McGlashan (ed.) *Medical Geography*, Methuen, London, pp. 233–46.

De Vise, P. (1973) *Misused and misplaced hospitals and doctors*, Resource Paper No 22, Commission on College Geography, Association of American Geographers, Washington, DC.

Dicken, P. (1971) Some aspects of the decision making behaviour of business organizations, *Economic Geography* **47**, 426–37.

Dicken, P. (1977) A note on location theory and the large business enterprise, *Area* **9**, 138–43.

Doob, L. W. (1978) Time: cultural and social anthropological aspects, in T. Carlstein *et al.* (eds) *Timing Space and Spacing Time. Vol. 1: Making sense of time*, Arnold, London, pp. 56–65.

Dottavio, F. D., O'Leary, J. T. and **Koth, B. A.** (1980) The social group variable in recreation studies, *Journal of Leisure Research* **12**, 357–67.

Douglas, I. (1979) Flooding in Australia: a review, in R. L. Heathcote and B. G. Thom (eds) *Natural Hazards in Australia*, Australian Academy of Sciences, Canberra, pp. 143–63.

Douglas, J. D. (1967) *The Social Meanings of Suicide*, Princeton University Press: Princeton.

Downs, R. M. (1970a) Geographic space perception: past approaches and future prospects, *Progress in Geography* **2**, 65–108.

Downs, R. M. (1970b) The cognitive structure of an urban shopping centre, *Environment and Behaviour* **2**, 13–39.

Downs, R. M. (1976) Personal constructions of personal construct theory, in G. T. Moore and R. G. Golledge (eds) *Environmental knowing*, Dowden, Hutchinson, and Ross, Stroudsburg, pp. 72–87.

Downs, R. M. (1979) Critical appraisal or determined philosophical skepticism?, *Annals of the Association of American Geographers* **69**, 468–71.

Downs, R. M. (1981) Cognitive mapping: a thematic analysis, in K. R. Cox and R. G. Golledge (eds) *Behavioural Problems in Geography Revisited*, Methuen, London, pp. 95–122.

Downs, R. M. and **Meyer, J.T.** (1978) Geography and the mind: an exploration of perceptual geography, *American Behavioural Scientist* **22**, 59–77.

Downs, R. M. and **Stea, D.** (1973a) Cognitive maps and spatial behaviours: processes and products, in R. M. Downs and D. Stea (eds) *Image and Environment*, Aldine,

Chicago, pp. 8–26.

Downs, R. M. and **Stea, D.** (1973b) Cognitive representations, in R. M. Downs and D. Stea (eds) *Image and Environment*, Aldine, Chicago, pp. 79–87.

Downs, R. M. and **Stea, D.** (1973c) Preface, in R. M. Downs and D. Stea (eds) *Image and Environment*, Aldine, Chicago, pp. xiii–xviii.

Downs, R. M. and **Stea, D.** (1977) *Maps in Minds: reflections on cognitive mapping*, Harper and Row: New York.

Duncan, J. S. (ed.) (1982) *Housing and Identity*, Croom Helm: London.

Duncan, J. S. and **Duncan, N. G.** (1976) Housing as presentation of self and the structure of social networks, in G. T. Moore and R. G. Golledge (eds) *Environmental Knowing*, Dowden, Hutchinson, and Ross, Stroudsburg, pp. 247–53.

Duncan, J. and **Ley, D.** (1982) Structural marxism and human geography: a critical assessment, *Annals of the Association of American Geographers* **72**, 30–59.

Dunham, H. W. (1937) The ecology of functional psychoses in Chicago, *American Sociological Review* **2**, 467–79.

Dunn, D. R. (1980) Urban recreation research: an overview, *Leisure Sciences* **3**, 25–58.

Dutton, D. (1978) Explaining the low use of health services by the poor: costs, attitudes or delivery systems?, *American Sociological Review* **43**, 348–68.

Dyos, H. J. and **Wolff, M.** (eds) (1973) *The Victorian City: images and realities*, Routledge and Kegan Paul: London.

Dyson-Hudson, R. and **Smith, E. A.** (1978) Human territoriality: an ecological reassessment, *American Anthropologist* **80**, 21–41.

Edney, J. J. (1976a) Human territories: comment of function properties, *Environment and Behaviour* **8**, 31–48.

Edney, J. J. (1976b) The psychological role of property rights in human behaviour, *Environment and Planning* **8**, 811–22.

Edney, J. J. (1977) Theories of human overcrowding: a review, *Environment and Planning* **9**, 1211–32.

Edwards, W. and **Tversky, A.** (eds) (1967) *Decision Making*, Penguin: Harmondsworth.

Ekman, G. and **Bratfisch, O.** (1965) Subjective distance and emotional involvement: a psychological mechanism, *Acta Psychologica* **24**, 430–7.

Elbing, A. (1978) *Behavioural Decisions in Organizations*, Scott, Foresman: Glenview, Ill.

Elson, M. J. (1974) *Activity spaces and recreation trip behaviour*, Oxford Polytechnic, Department of Town Planning Paper No. 19.

Ennis, P. H. (1962) The contextual dimension in voting, in W. N. McPhee and W. A. Glasser (eds) *Public Opinion and Congressional Elections*, Free Press, New York, pp. 180–211.

Entrikin, J. N. (1976) Contemporary humanism in geography, *Annals of the Association of American Geographers* **66**, 615–32.

Ericksen, R. H. (1975) *The effects of perceived place attributes on cognition of urban distance*, University of Iowa, Department of Geography Discussion Paper No. 23.

Erickson, K. T. (1976) Loss of community at Buffalo Creek, *American Journal of Psychiatry* **133**, 302–5.

Esser, A. H. (ed.) (1971) *Behaviour and Environment: the use of space by animals and man*, Plenum: New York.

Esser, A. H. (1976) Theoretical and empirical issues with regard to privacy, territoriality, personal space and crowding, *Environment and Behaviour* **8**, 117–24.

Evans, D. J. (1980) *Geographical Perspectives on Juvenile Delinquency*, Gower: Farnborough.

Everitt, J. C. (1976) Community and propinquity in a city, *Annals of the Association of American Geographers* **66**, 104–16.

Everitt, J. and **Cadwallader, M.** (1972) The home area concept in urban analysis, in W. J. Mitchell (ed), *Environmental Design: research and practice*, University of California Press: Los Angeles.

Everitt, J. C. and **Cadwallader, M.** (1977) Local area definition revisited, *Area* **9**, 175–6.

Everitt, J. C. and **Cadwallader, M. T.** (1981) Husband-wife role variation as a factor in home area definition, *Geografiska Annaler* **63**B, 23–34.

Eyles, J. (1968) *The inhabitants' images of Highgate village, London*, London School of Economics, Department of Geography Graduate Discussion Paper 15.

Eyles, J. (1971) Pouring new sentiments into old theories: how else can we look at behavioural patterns?, *Area* **3**, 242–50.

Eyles, J. (1978) Social geography and the study of the capitalist city: a review, *Tijdschrift voor Economische en Sociale Geografie* **69**, 296–305.

Eyles, J. (1981) Why geography cannot be Marxist: towards an understanding of lived experience, *Environment and Planning A* **13**, 1371–88.

Fainstein, M. J. and **Martin, M.** (1978) Support for community control among local urban elites, *Urban Affairs Quarterly* **13**, 443–68.

Falk, T. and **Abler, R.** (1980) Intercommunications, distance, and geographical theory, *Geografiska Annaler* **62B**, 59–67.

Faris, R. E. L. and **Dunham, H. W.** (1939) *Mental Disorders in Urban Areas*, University of Chicago Press: Chicago.

Festinger, L. (1957) *A Theory of Cognitive Dissonance*, Row Peterson: Evanston.

Festinger, L., Schacter, S. and **Bach, K.** (1950) *Social Pressures in Informal Groups*, Harper: New York.

Firey, W. (1945) Sentiment and symbolism as ecological variables, *American Sociological Review* **10**, 140–8.

Fischer, C. S. (1973) On urban alienation and anomie, *American Sociological Review* **38**, 311–26.

Fischer, C. S. (1975) Towards a subcultural theory of urbanism, *American Journal of Sociology* **80**, 1319–41.

Fischer, C. S. (1976) *The Urban Experience*, Harcourt, Brace Jovanovitch: New York.

Fischer, C. S. and **Jackson, R. M.** (1976) Suburbs, networks and attitudes, in B. Schwartz (ed.) *The Changing Face of the Suburbs*, University of Chicago Press, Chicago, pp. 279–307.

Fischer, D. W. Lewis, J. E. and **Priddle, G. B.** (eds) (1974) *Land and Leisure: concepts and methods in outdoor recreation*, Maaroufa Press: Chicago.

Fishbein, H. D. (1976) An epigenetic approach to learning theory: a commentary, in G. T. Moore and R. G. Golledge (eds) *Environmental Knowing*, Dowden, Hutchinson, and Ross, Stroudsburg, pp. 131–6.

Fitton, M. (1973) Neighbourhood and voting: a sociometric explanation, *British Journal of Political Science* **3**, 445–72.

Flowerdew, R. T. W. (1976) Search strategies and stopping rules in residential mobility, *Transactions of the Institute of British Geographers* **1**, 47–57.

Flowerdew, R. (ed.) (1982) *Institutions and Geographical Patterns*, Croom Helm: London.

Florence, P. S. (1964) *Economics and Sociology and Industry: a realistic analysis of development*, Watts: London.

Forer, P. C. and **Kivell, H.** (1981) Space-time budgets, public transport, and spatial choice, *Environment and Planning A* **13**, 497–509.

Forrest, J. and **Johnston, R. J.** (1973) Spatial aspects of voting in the Dunedin City Council elections of 1971, *New Zealand Geographer* **21**, 166–81.

Forrest, J., **Marjoribanks, E.** and **Johnston, R. J.** (1977) Local effects at New Zealand local elections, in R. J. Johnston (ed.) *People, places and votes: essays on the electoral geography of Australia and New Zealand*, Department of Geography, University of New England, Armidale, pp. 35–50.

Foxall, G. R. (1980) *Consumer Behaviour: a practical guide*, Croom Helm: London.

Francescato, D. and **Mebane, W.** (1973) How citizens view two great cities: Milan and Rome, in R. M. Downs and D. Stea (eds) *Image and Environment*, Aldine, Chicago, pp. 131–47.

Fransella, F. and **Bannister, D.** (1977) *A Manual For Repertory Grid Technique*, Academic Press: London.

Fredriksson, C. G. and **Lindmark, L. G.** (1979) From firms to systems of firms: a study of interregional dependence in a dynamic society, in F. E. I. Hamilton and G. J. R. Linge (eds) *Spatial Analysis, Industry and the Industrial Environment: progress in research and applications Vol. 1: Industrial systems*, Wiley, Chichester, pp. 155–86.

Freedman, J. L. (1975) *Crowding and Behaviour*, Freeman: San Francisco.

Freedman, J. L., **Heshua, S.** and **Levy, A.** (1975) Population density and pathology. Is there a relationship?, *Journal of Experimental Social Psychology* **11**, 539–52.

Frey, A. (1981) The geographer's burden of office, *Progress in Human Geography* **5**, 131–9.

Fried, M. and **Gleicher, P.** (1961) Some sources of residential satisfaction in an urban slum, *Journal of the American Institute of Planners* **27**, 305–15.

Fritz, C. E. (1961) Disaster, in R. K. Merton and R. A. Nisbet (eds) *Contemporary Social Problems*, Harcourt, Brace, Jovanovitch, New York, pp. 651–94.

Fritz, C. E. (1968) Disasters, *International Encyclopaedia of the Social Sciences* **4**, 202–7.

Fritz, C. E. and **Williams, H. B.** (1957) The human being in disasters: a research perspective, *Annals of the American Academy of Political and Social Science* **309**, 42–51.

Gad, G. H. N. (1973) Crowding and pathologies: some critical remarks, *Canadian Geographer* **17**, 373–90.

Galster, G. C. and **Hesser, G. W.** (1982) Residential satisfaction: compositional and contextual correlates, *Environment and Behaviour* **14**, 735–58.

Gans, H. J. (1962a) *The Urban Villagers: groups and class in the life of Italian-Americans*, Free Press: New York.

Gans, H. J. (1962b) Urbanism and suburbanism as ways of life, in A. M. Rose (ed.) *Human Behaviour and Social Processes*, Routledge and Kegan Paul, London, pp. 625–48.

Gans, H. J. (1967) *The Levittowners*, Pantheon: New York.

Gans, H. J. (1968) *People and Plans*, Basic Books: New York.

Gayler, H. J. (1980) Social class and consumer spatial behaviour: some aspects of variation in shopping patterns in metropolitan Vancouver, Canada, *Transactions of the Institute of British Geographers* **5**, 427–45.

Getis, A. and **Boots, B. N.** (1971) Spatial behaviour: rats and man, *Professional Geographer* **23**, 11–14.

Gibson, E. (1978) Understanding the subjective meaning of places, in D. Ley and M. S. Samuels (eds) *Humanistic Geography: prospects and problems*, Maaroufa Press, Chicago, pp. 138–54.

Giggs, J. A. (1973) The distribution of schizophrenics in Nottingham, *Transactions of the Institute of British Geographers* **51**, 55–76.

Giggs, J. A. (1979) Human health problems in urban areas, in D. T. Herbert and D. M. Smith (eds) *Social Problems and the City*, Oxford University Press, London, pp. 84–116.

Giggs, J. A., **Ebdon, D. S.** and **Bourke, J. O.** (1980) The epidemiology of primary acute pancreatitis in the Nottingham defined population area, *Transactions of the Institute of British Geographers* **5**, 229–42.

Gillis, A. R. (1977) High-rise housing and psychological strain, *Journal of Health and Social Behaviour* **18**, 418–32.

Girt, J. L. (1972) Simple chronic bronchitis and urban ecological structure, in N. D. McGlashan (ed.) *Medical Geography*, Methuen, London, pp. 211–33.

Gittus, E. (1964) The structure of urban areas, *Town Planning Review* **35**, 5–20.

Glacken, C. J. (1967) *Traces on the Rhodian Shore*, University of California Press: Berkeley.

Glass, R. (1948) *The Social Background of a Plan: a study of Middlesbrough*, Kegan Paul: London.

Glass, D. C. and **Singer, J. E.** (1972) *Urban Stress*, Academic Press: New York.

Glyptis, S. A. (1981) Leisure life styles, *Regional Studies* **15**, 311–26.

Goddard, J. B. (1973) *Office Linkages and Location*, Pergamon: Oxford.

Goddard, J. B. (1975a) *Office Location in Urban and Regional Development*, Oxford University Press: London.

Goddard, J. B. (1975b) Organizational information flows and the urban system, in D. Massey and W. I. Morrison (eds) *Industrial Location: alternative frameworks*, Centre for Environmental Studies Conference Paper 15, London, pp. 87–135.

Goddard, J. B. (1978) The location of non-manufacturing activities within manufacturing industries, in F. E. I. Hamilton (ed.) *Contemporary Industrialization: spatial analysis and regional development*, Longman, London, pp. 62–85.

Godkin, M. A. (1980) Identity and place: clinical applications based on notions of rootedness and uprootedness, in A. Buttimer and D. Seamon (eds) *The Human Experience of Space and Place*, Croom Helm, London, pp. 73–85.

Golant, S. M. (1972) *The residential location and spatial behaviour of the elderly: a Canadian example*, University of Chicago, Department of Geography Research Paper No. 143.

Golant, S. and **Burton, I.** (1969) *Avoidance – response to the risk environment*, University of Toronto, Natural Hazard Research Working Paper No. 6.

Golant, S. and **Burton, I.** (1976) A semantic differential experiment in the interpretation and grouping of environmental hazards, in G. T. Moore and R. G. Golledge (eds) *Environmental Knowing*, Dowden, Hutchinson, and Ross, Stroudsburg, pp. 364–74.

Gold, J. R. (1980) *An Introduction to Behavioural Geography*, Oxford University Press: London.

Gold, J. R. (1982) Territoriality and human spatial behaviour, *Progress in Human Geography* **6**, 44–67.

Goldstein, S. and **Mayer, K. B.** (1963) *Residential Mobility, Migration and Commuting in Rhode Island*, Rhode Island Development Council: Providence.

Golledge, R. G. (1967) Conceptualizing the market decision process, *Journal of Regional Science* **7**, 239–58.

Golledge, R. G. (1969) The geographical relevance of some learning theories, in K. R. Cox and R. G. Golledge (eds) *Behavioural problems in geography: a symposium*, Northwestern University Studies in Geography No. 17, pp. 101–45.

Golledge, R. G. (1976) Methods and methodological issues in environmental cognition research, in G. T. Moore and R. G. Golledge (eds) *Environmental Knowing*, Dowden, Hutchinson, and Ross, Stroudsburg, pp. 300–14.

Golledge, R. G. (1978) Learning about urban environments, in T. Carlstein *et al.* (eds) *Timing Space and Spacing Time. Vol. 1: Making sense of time*, Arnold, London, pp. 76–98.

Golledge, R. G. (1979) Reality, process, and the dialectical relation between man and environment, in S. Gale and G. Olsson (eds) *Philosophy in Geography*, Reidel, Dordrecht, pp. 109–20.

Golledge, R. G. (1981) Misconceptions, misinterpretations, and misrepresentations of behavioural approaches in human geography, *Environment and Planning A* **13**, 1325–44.

Golledge, R. G., **Briggs, R.** and **Demko, D.** (1969) The configuration of distances in intraurban space, *Proceedings of the Association of American Geographers* **1**, 60–5.

Golledge, R. G. and **Brown, L. A.** (1967) Search, learning and the market decision process, *Geografiska Annaler* **49B**, 116–24.

Golledge, R. G., **Brown, L. A.** and **Williamson, F.** (1972) Behavioural approaches in geography: an overview, *Australian Geographer* **12**, 59–79.

Golledge, R. G. and **Rushton, G.** (1976) Introduction, in R. G. Golledge and G. Rushton (eds) *Spatial Choice and Spatial Behaviour*, Ohio State University Press, Columbus, pp. 1–2.

Golledge, R. G and **Hubert, L. J.** (1982) Some comments on non-Euclidean mental maps, *Environment and Planning A* **14**, 107–18.

Golledge, R. G. and **Zannaras, G.** (1973) Cognitive approaches to the analysis of human spatial behaviour, in W. H. Ittelson (ed.) *Environment and Cognition*, Seminar Press, New York, pp. 59–94.

Gould, P. R. (1963) Man against his environment: a game theoretic framework, *Annals of the Association of American Geographers* **53**, 290–7.

Gould, P. (1969) Methodological developments since the fifties, *Progress in Geography* **1**, 1–49.

Gould, P. R. (1972) Pedagogic review: entropy in urban and regional modelling, *Annals of the Association of American Geographers* **62**, 689–700.

Gould, P. (1973a) On mental maps, in R. M. Downs and D. Stea (eds) *Image and Environment*, Aldine, Chicago, pp. 182–220.

Gould, P. (1973b) The black boxes of Jonkoping: spatial information and preference, in R. M. Downs and D. Stea (eds) *Image and Environment*, Aldine, Chicago, pp. 235–45.

Gould, P. (1975) Acquiring spatial information, *Economic Geography* **51**, 87–99.

Gould, P. and **Lafond, N.** (1979) Mental maps and information surfaces in Quebec and Ontario, *Cahiers de Geographie de Quebec* **23**, 371–98.

Gould, P. and **White, R.** (1968) The mental maps of British school-leavers, *Regional Studies*, **2**, 161–82.

Gould, P. and **White, R.** (1974) *Mental Maps*, Penguin: Harmondsworth.

Gouldner, A. (1980) *The Two Marxisms*, Seabury: New York.

Graham, E. (1976) What is a mental map?, *Area* **8**, 259–62.

Granovetter, M. S. (1976) Network sampling: some first steps, *American Journal of Sociology* **81**, 1287–303.

Graves, T. D. (1966) Alternative models for the study of urban migration, *Human Organization* **25**, 295–9.

Green, D. H. (1977) Industrialists' information levels and regional incentives, *Regional Studies* **11**, 7–18.

Greenbaum, D. E. and **Greenbaum, S. D.** (1981) Territorial personalization: group identity and social interaction in a Slavic-American neighbourhood, *Environment and Behaviour* **13**, 574–89.

Gregory, D. (1978) *Ideology, Science and Human Geography*, Hutchinson: London.

Griffiths, M. (1971) A geographical study of mortality in an urban area, *Urban Studies* **8**, 111–20.

Grigg, D. B. (1977) E. G. Ravenstein and the 'laws' of migration, *Journal of Historical Geography* **3**, 41–54.

Guelke, L. (1974) An idealist alternative in human geography, *Annals of the Association of American Geographers* **64**, 193–202.

Guelke, L. (1977) The role of laws in human geography, *Progress in Human Geography* **1**, 376–86.

Guelke, L. (1981) Idealism, in M. E. Harvey and B. P. Holly (eds) *Themes in Geographic Thought*, Croom Helm, London, pp. 133–47.

Gusfield, J. R. (1977) *Community: a critical response*, Blackwell: Oxford.

Gustavus, S. and **Brown, L. A.** (1977) Place attributes in a migration decision context, *Environment and Planning* **9**, 529–48.

Hägerstrand, T. (1952) *The propagation of innovation waves*, Lund studies in Geography, Series B, No. 4.

Hägerstrand, T. (1957) Migration and area, in D. Hannerberg *et al.* (eds) *Migration in Sweden*, Lund Studies in Geography 13B, 27–158.

Hägerstrand, T. (1970) What about people in regional science?, *Papers and Proceedings of the Regional Science Association* **24**, 7–21.

Hägerstrand, T. (1975) Time, space and human conditions, in A. Karlqvist *et al.* (eds) *Dynamic Allocation of Urban Space*, Saxon House, Farnborough, pp. 3–14.

Hägerstrand, T. (1978) Survival and arena, in T. Carlstein *et al.* (eds) *Timing Space and Spacing Time. Vol. 2: Human activity and time geography*, Arnold, London, pp. 122–45.

Haggett, P. (1965) *Locational Analysis in Human Geography*, Arnold: London.

Håkanson, L. (1979) Towards a theory of location and corporate growth, in F. E. I. Hamilton and G. J. R. Linge (eds) *Spatial Analysis, Industry and the Industrial Environment: progress in research and applications. Vol. 1: industrial systems*, Wiley, Chichester, pp. 115–38.

Hall, E. T. (1959) *The Silent Language*, Doubleday: New York.

Hall, E. T. (1966) *The Hidden Dimension*, Doubleday: New York.

Hamilton, F. E. I. (1974) A view of spatial behaviour, industrial organizations and decision-making, in F. E. I. Hamilton (ed.) *Spatial Perspectives on Industrial Organization and Decision Making*, Wiley, London, pp. 3–43.

Hamilton, F. E. I. (1978) The changing milieu of spatial industrial research, in F. E. I. Hamilton (ed.) *Comtemporary Industrialization: spatial analysis and regional development*, Longman, London, pp. 1–19.

Hamilton, F. E. I. and **Linge, G. J. R.** (1979) Industrial systems, in F. E. I. Hamilton and G. J. R. Linge (eds) *Spatial Analysis, Industry and the Industrial Environment: progress in research and applications. Vol. 1: Industrial* *systems*, Wiley, Chichester, pp. 1–23.

Hamnett. C. (1979) Area-based explanations: a critical appraisal, in D. T. Herbert and D. M. Smith (eds) *Social Problems and The City* Oxford University Press, London, pp. 244–60.

Haney, W. E. and **Knowles, E. S.** (1978) Perception of neighbourhoods by city and suburban residents, *Human Ecology* 6, 201–14.

Hanson, P. (1977) The activity patterns of elderly households, *Geografiska Annaler* **59**B, 109–24.

Hanson, S. (1976) Spatial variation in the cognitive levels of urban residents, in R. G. Golledge and G. Rushton (eds) *Spatial Choice and Spatial Behaviour*, Ohio State University Press, Columbus, pp. 157–88.

Hanson, S. (1977) Measuring the cognitive levels of urban residents, *Geografiska Annaler* **59**B, 67–81.

Hanson, S. and **Hanson, P.** (1980) Gender and urban activity patterns in Uppsala, Sweden, *Geographical Review* **70**, 291–9.

Hanson, S., Vitek, J. D. and **Hanson, P. O.** (1979) Natural disaster: long-range impact on human response to future disaster threats, *Environment and Behaviour* **11**, 268–84.

Hansson, R. O., Noulles, D. and **Bellovich, S. J.** (1982) Knowledge, warning, and stress: a study of comparative roles in an urban floodplain, *Environment and Behaviour* **14**, 171–85.

Harries, K. D. (1974) *The Geography of Crime and Justice*, McGraw-Hill: New York.

Harries, K. D. (1980) *Crime and the Urban Environment* Thomas: Springfield.

Harrison, A. J. M. and **Stabler, M. J.** (1981) An analysis of journeys for canal based recreation, *Regional Studies* **15**, 345–58.

Harrison, E. F. (1975) *Managerial Decision-Making Process*, Houghton Mifflin: Boston.

Harrison, J. and **Howard, W. A.** (1972) The role of meaning in the urban image, *Environment and Behaviour* **4**, 389–411.

Harrison, J. and **Sarre, P.** (1971) Personal construct theory in the measurement of environmental images: problems and methods, *Environment and Behaviour* **3**, 351–74.

Harrison, R. T., Bull, P. J. and **Hart, M.** (1979) Space and time in industrial linkage studies, *Area* **11**, 333–8.

Harrison, R. T. and **Livingstone, D. N.** (1979) There and back again – towards a critique of idealist human geography, *Area* **11**, 75–9.

Hart, J. T. (1971) The inverse care law, *Lancet*, **i**, 405–12

Hart, P. W. E. (1980) Problems and potentialities of the behavioural approach to agricultural location, *Geografiska Annaler* **62**B, 99–107.

Hart, R. A. and **Moore, G. T.** (1973) The development of spatial cognition: a review, in R. M. Downs and D. Stea (eds) *Image and Environment*, Aldine, Chicago, pp. 246–88.

Harvey, D. (1969a) *Explanation in Geography*, Arnold: London.

Harvey, D. (1969b) Conceptual and measurement problems in the cognitive–behavioural approach to location theory', in K. R. Cox and R. G. Golledge (eds) *Behavioural problems in geography: a symposium*, Northwestern University Studies in Geography No. 17, pp. 35–68.

Harvey, D. (1973) *Social Justice and the City*, Arnold: London.

Harvey, D. (1978) The urban process under capitalism: a framework for analysis, *International Journal of Urban and Regional Research* **2**, 101–31.

Harvey, D. and **Chatterjee, L.** (1974) Absolute rent and the structuring of space by government and financial institutions, *Antipode* **6**, 22–36.

Harvey, M. E., Frazier, J. W. and **Matulionis, M.** (1979) Cognition of a hazardous environment: reactions to Buffalo airport noise, *Economic Geography* **55**, 263–86.

Hawley, A. H. (1950) *Human Ecology: a theory of community structure*, Ronald Press: New York.

Hay, A. M. and **Johnston, R. J.** (1979) Search and the choice of shopping centre: two models of variability in destination selection, *Environment and Planning A* **11**, 791–804.

Heathcote, R. L. (1979) The threat from natural hazards in Australia, in R. L. Heathcote and B. G. Thom (eds) *Natural Hazards in Australia*, Australian Academy of Sciences, Canberra, pp. 3–12.

Hedb, D. O. (1949) *The Organization of Behaviour*, Wiley: New York.

Hedb, D. O. (1966) *A Textbook of Psychology*, Saunders: Philadelphia.

Heeley, J. (1981) Planning for tourism in Britain: an historical perspective, *Town Planning Review* **52**, 61–79.

Heinemeyer, W. F. (1967) The urban core as a centre of attraction, in *Urban Core and Inner City*, Bull, Leiden, pp. 82–99.

Hendee, J. C. (1969) Rural–urban differences reflected in outdoor recreation participation, *Journal of Leisure Research* **1**, 333–41.

Hendee, J. C. Gale, R. P. and **Catton, W. R.** (1971) Typology of outdoor recreation activity preferences, *Journal of Environmental Education* **3**, 28–34.

Henry, A. F. and **Short, J.** (1957) The sociology of suicide, in E. S. Schneidman and N. L. Farberow (eds) *Clues to Suicide*, McGraw-Hill, New York, pp. 58–69.

Herbert, D. T. (1972) *Urban Geography: A Social Perspective*, David and Charles, Newton Abbot.

Herbert, D. T. (1973a) Residental mobility and preference: a study of Swansea, in *Social Patterns in Cities*, Special Publication No. 5, Institute of British Geographers, pp. 103–21.

Herbert, D. T. (1973b) The residential mobility process: some empirical observations, *Area* **5**, 44–8.

Herbert, D. T. (1975) Urban neighbourhoods and social geographical research, in A. D. M. Phillips and B. J. Turton (eds) *Environment, Man and Economic Change*, Longman, London, pp. 459–78.

Herbert, D. T. (1976) The study of delinquency areas: a social geographical approach, *Transactions of the Institute of British Geographers* **1**, 472–92.

Herbert, D. T. (1977) Crime, delinquency and the urban environment, *Progress in Human Geography* **1**, 208–39.

Herbert D. T. (1979) Urban crime: a geographical perspective, in D. T. Herbert and D. M. Smith (eds) *Social Problems and the City*, Oxford University Press, London, pp. 117–38.

Herbert, D. T. (1982) *The Geography of Urban Crime*, Longman: London.

Herbert, D. T. and **Johnston, R. J.** (eds) (1976a) *Social Areas in Cities: spatial processes and form*, Wiley: Chichester.

Herbert, D. T. and **Johnston, R. J.** (eds) (1976b) *Social Areas in Cities: spatial perspectives on problems and policies*, Wiley: Chichester.

Herbert, D. T. and **Smith, D. M.** (eds) (1979) *Social Problems and the City*, Oxford University Press: London.

Herbert, G. (1963–64) The neighbourhood unit: principles and organic theory, *Sociological Review* **11–22**, 165–213.

Herbert, R. and **Emmison, B.** (1977) Social contact among surburban housewives, *Australian Journal of Social Issues* **12**, 307–15.

Herbst, P. G. (1964) Organisational commitment: a decision model, *Acta Sociologica* **7**, 34–45.

Hewitt, K. and **Burton, I.** (1971) *The hazardousness of a place: a regional ecology of damaging events*, University of Toronto, Department of Geography Research Paper No. 6.

Higgs, G. (1975) An assessment of the action component of action space, *Geographical Analysis* **7**, 35–50.

Hill, P. H. (ed.) (1979) *Making Decisions: a multidisciplinary introduction*, Addison–Wesley: Reading, Mass.

Hillery, G. A. and **Brown, J. S.** (1965) Migrational systems of the southern Appalachians: some demographic observations, *Rural Sociology* **30**, 3–48.

Hobbs, M. S. T. and **Acheson, E. D.** (1966) Perinatal mortality and the organization of obstetric services in the Oxford area in 1962, *British Medical Journal* **1**, 499–505.

Holahan, C. J. and **Dobrowolny, M. B.** (1978) Cognitive and behavioural correlates of the spatial environment: an interactional analysis, *Environment and Behaviour* **10**, 317–34.

Hookway, A. J. and **Davidson, J.** (1970) *Leisure: problems and prospects for the environment*, Countryside Commission: London.

Hoover, E. M. (1937) *Location Theory and the Shoe and Leather Industries*, Harvard University Press: Cambridge, Mass.

Horton, F. and **Reynolds, D. R.** (1971) Effects of urban spatial structure on individual behaviour, *Economic Geography* **47**, 36–48.

Hotelling, H. (1929) Stability in competition, *Economic Journal* **39**, 41–57.

Howard, J. A. and **Sheth, J. N.** (1969) *The Theory of Buyer Behaviour*, Wiley: New York.

Howe, G. M. (1970) *National Atlas of Disease Mortality in the United Kingdom*, Nelson: London.

Howe, G. M. (1976) *Man, Environment and Disease in Britain*, Penguin: Harmondsworth.

Howe, G. M. (ed.) (1977) *A World Geography of Human Diseases*, Academic Press: London.

Hubbard, R. and **Thompson, A. F.** (1981) Preference structures and consumer spatial indifference behaviour: some theoretical problems, *Tijdschrift voor Economische en Sociale Geografie* **72**, 35–9.

Huber, G. (1980) *Decision Making*, Scott Foreman: Glenview, Ill.

Hudson, R. (1970) *Personal construct theory, learning theories and consumer behaviour*, University of Bristol, Department of Geography Seminar Paper Series A No. 21.

Hudson, R. (1974) Images of the retailing environment: an example of the use of repertory grid methodology, *Environment and Behaviour* **6**, 470–94.

Hudson, R. (1975) Patterns of spatial search, *Transactions of the Institute of British Geographers* **65**, 141–54.

Hudson, R. (1976a) *Environmental images, spatial choice and consumer behaviour*, University of Durham, Department of Geography Occasional Paper No. 9.

Hudson, R. (1976b) Linking studies of the individual with models of aggregate behaviour: an empirical example, *Transactions of the Institute of British Geographers* **1**, 159–74.

Huff, D. L. (1960) A topographical model of consumer space preferences, *Papers and Proceedings of the Regional Science Association* **6**, 159–73.

Huff, D. L. (1963) A probabilistic analysis of shopping centre trade areas, *Land Economics* **39**, 81–90.

Hull, C. L. (1952) *A Behaviour System*, Yale University Press: New Haven.

Hunter, A. (1979) The urban neighbourhood: its analytical and social contexts, *Urban Affairs Quarterly* **14**, 267–88.

Hunter, J. M. (ed.) (1975) *The geography of health and disease*, University of North Carolina at Chapel Hill, Department of Geography, Study in Geography No. 6.

Hunter, J. M. (1976) Aerosol and roadside lead as environmental hazards, *Economic Geography* **52**, 147–60.

Hunter J. M. and **Young, J.** (1971) Diffusion of influenza in England and Wales, *Annals of the Association of American Geographers* **61**, 637–53.

Hurwicz, L. (1970) Optimality criteria for decision making under risk, Cowles Commission Paper, Statistics 350 (mimeo).

Husserl, E. (1931) (trans. W. R. B. Gibson) *Ideas: general introduction to pure phenomenology* Allen and Unwin: London.

Irish, J. L. and **Falconer, B.** (1979) Reaction to flood warning, in R. L. Heathcote and B. G. Thom (eds) *Natural Hazards in Australia*, Australian Academy of Science, Canberra, pp. 313–29.

Irving, H. (1975) Distance, intensity, kinship: key dimensions of social interaction, *Sociology and Social Research* **60**, 70–86.

Irving, H. (1977) Social networks in the modern city, *Social Forces* **55**, 867–80.

Irving, H. W. (1978) Space and environment in interpersonal relations, in D. T. Herbert and R. J. Johnston (eds) *Geography and the Urban Environment. Vol. 1*, Chichester, Wiley, pp. 249–84.

Irving, H. W. and **Davidson, R. N.** (1973) A working note on the measurement of social interaction, *Transactions of the Bartlett Society* **9**, 7–19.

Isaacs, R. R. (1948) The neighbourhood theory: an analysis of its adequacy, *Journal of the American Insitute of Planners* **14**, 15–23.

Iso – Ahela, S. E. (ed.) (1980) *Social Psychological Perspectives on Leisure and Recreation*, Thomas: Springfield, I11.

Ittelson, W. H. *et al.* (1974) *An Introduction to Environmental Psychology*, Holt, Rinehart and Winston: New York.

Ittelson, W. H. (1978) Environmental perception and urban experience, *Environment and Behaviour* **10**, 193–214.

Jackson, E. L. (1981) Response to earthquake hazard: the West Coast of North America, *Environment and Behaviour* **13**, 387–416.

Jackson, E. L. and **Mukerjee, T.** (1974) Human adjustment to the earthquake hazard of San Francisco, California, in G. F. White (ed.) *Natural hazards: local, national, global*, Oxford University Press, London, pp. 160–6.

Jackson, L. E. and **Johnston, R. J.** (1972) Structuring the image: an investigation of the elements of mental maps, *Environment and Planning* **4**, 415–27.

Jackson, R. H. (1978) Mormon perception and settlement, *Annals of the Association of American Geographers* **68**, 317–34.

Jakle, J. A., Brunn, S. and **Roseman, C. C.** (1976) Human *Spatial Behaviour: a social geography*, Duxbury: North Scituate.

Janis, I. L. (1954) Problems of theory in the analysis of stress behaviour, *Journal of Social Issues* **10**, 12–25.

Jarvis, I. and **Mann, L.** (1977) *Decision Making: a psychological analysis of conflict, choice and commitment*, Free Press: New York.

Jenkins, C. and **Sherman, B.** (1979) *The Collapse of Work*, Eyre Methuen: London.

Jenkins, C. and **Sherman, B** (1981) *The Leisure Shock*, Eyre Methuen: London.

Jensen-Butler, C. (1972) Gravity models as planning tools: a review of theoretical and operational problems, *Geografiska Annaler* **54B**, 68–78.

Jensen-Butler, C. (1981) *A critique of behavioural geography: an epistemological analysis of cognitive mapping and of Hägerstrand's time-space model*, Aarhus University Department of Geography Arbejdsrapport No. 12.

Johnson, C. R. (1977) *Leisure and Recreation: introduction and overview*, Lea and Febinger: Philadelphia.

Johnston, R. J. (1972) Spatial elements in voting patterns at the 1968 Christchurch City Council election, *Political Science* **24**, 49–61.

Johnston, R. J. (1974) Local effects in voting at a local election, *Annals of the Association of American Geographers* **64**, 418–29.

Johnston, R. J. (1976) Residential area characteristics: research methods for identifying urban sub-areas, in D. T. Herbert and R. J. Johnston (eds.) *Social Areas in Cities: spatial processes and form*, Chichester, Wiley, pp. 193–35.

Johnston, R. J. (1977a) People, places and votes: an introduction, in R. J. Johnston (ed.) *People, Places and Votes: essays on the electoral geography of Australia and New Zealand*, Department of Geography, University of New England, Armidale, pp. 1–9.

Johnston, R. J. (1977b) Contagious processes and voting patterns: Christchurch 1969–1972, in R. J. Johnston (ed.) *People, Places and Votes: essays on the electoral geography of Australia and New Zealand*, Department of Geography, University of New England, Armidale, pp. 11–33.

Johnston, R. J. (1978a) *Political, Electoral and Spatial Systems*, Oxford University Press: London.

Johnston, R. J. (1978b) *Multivariate Statistical Analysis in Geography*, Longman: London.

Johnston, R. J. (1979) *Geography and Geographers: Anglo-American human geography since 1945*, Arnold: London.

Johnston, R. J. (1980) On the nature of explanation in human geography, *Transactions of the Institute of British Geographers* **5**, 402–12.

Johnston, R. J. (1981) Embourgeoisement and voting: England, 1974, *Area* **13**, 345–51.

Johnston, R. J. and **Rimmer, P. J.** (1967) A note on consumer behaviour in an urban hierarchy, *Journal of Regional Science* **7**, 161–6.

Jones, C. (1981) Residential mobility: an economic model, *Scottish Journal of Political Economy* **28**, 62–75.

Jones, R. C. (1980) The role of perception in urban in-migration: a path analytic model, *Geographical Analysis* **12**, 98–108.

Jordan, T. G. (1978) Perceptual regions in Texas, *Geographical Review* **68**, 293–307.

Kando, T. M. (1975) *Leisure and Popular Culture in Transition*, Mosby: St Louis.

Kaplan, M. (1975) *Leisure: theory and policy*, Wiley: New York.

Kaplan, S. (1973) Cognitive maps in perception and thought, in R. M. Downs and D. Stea (eds) *Image and Environment*, Aldine, Chicago, pp. 63–78.

Kaplan, S. (1976) Adaptation, structure, and knowledge, in G. T. Moore and R. G. Golledge (eds) *Environmental Knowing*, Dowden, Hutchinson and Ross, Stroudsburg, pp. 32–45.

Kasmar, J. V. (1970) The development of a usable lexicon of environmental descriptors, *Environment and Behaviour* **2**, 153–69.

Kasperson, R. E. (1969) On suburbia and voting behaviour, *Annals of the Association of American Geographers* **59**, 405–11.

Kassarjian, H. H. (1971) Personality and consumer behaviour: a review, *Journal of Marketing Research* **8**, 409–18.

Kates, R. W. (1962) *Hazard and choice perception in flood plain management*, University of Chicago, Department of Geography Research Paper No. 78.

Kates, R. W. (1967) The perception of storm hazard on the shores of megalopolis, in D. Lowenthal (ed.) *Environmental Perception and Behaviour*, Research Paper No. 109, Department of Geography, University Chicago, pp. 60–74.

Kates, R. W. (1971) Natural hazards in human ecological perspective: hypotheses and models, *Economic Geography* **47**, 438–45.

Katona, G. (1975) *Psychological Economics*, Elsevier: New York.

Kaufmann, W. C. and **Greer, S.** (1959) Voting in a metropolitan community: an application of social area analysis, *Social Forces* **38**, 196–204.

Keeble, D, (1976) *Industrial Location and Planning in the United Kingdom*, Methuen: London.

Keller, S. (1968) *The Urban Neighbourhood: a sociological perspective*, Random House: New York.

Kelly, G. A. (1955) *The Psychology of Personal Constructs*, Norton: New York.

Kelly, J. R. (1974) Socialization toward leisure: a developmental approach, *Journal of Leisure Research* **6**, 181–93.

Kemp, D. (1975) Social change and the future of political parties: the Australian case, in L. Maisel and P. M. Sack (eds) *the Future of Political Parties*, Sage, Beverly Hills, pp. 124–64.

Key, V. O. Jr. (1949) *Southern Politics*, Alfred Knopf: New York.

Kilmartin, L. and **Thorns, D. C.** (1978) *Cities Unlimited*, Allen and Unwin: Sydney.

Kilpatrick, F. P. (1957) Problems of perception in extreme situations, *Human Organisation* **16**, 20–2.

King, L. J. and **Golledge, R. G.** (1978) *Cities, Space, and Behaviour: the elements of urban geography*, Prentice-Hill: Englewood Cliffs.

King, P. E. (1979) Problems of spatial analysis in geographical epidemiology, *Social Science and Medicine* **13** D, 249–52.

Kirk, W. (1952) Historical geography and the concept of the behavioural environment, *Indian Geographical Journal* **25**, 152–60.

Kirk, W. (1963) Problems of geography, *Geography* **48**, 357–71.

Kirkby, A. V. (1974) Individual and community responses to rainfall variability in Oaxaco, Mexico, in G. F. White (ed.) *Natural Hazards: local, national, global*, Oxford University Press, London, pp. 119–28.

Kirmeyer, S. (1978) Urban density and pathology: a review of research, *Environment and Behaviour* **10**, 247–70.

Klein, H. J. (1967) The delimitation of the town centre in the image of its citizens, in *Urban Core and Inner City*, Leiden, Brill, pp. 286–306.

Klingbeil, D. (1980) Concepts of geographical activity analysis: structures and problems, *Geografiska Annaler* **62B**, 49–58.

Kluckhohn, F. R. (1959) Dominant and variant value orientations, in C. Kluckhohn, H. A. Murray, and D. M. Schneider (eds) *Personality in Nature, Culture and Society*, Knopf, New York, pp. 342–57.

Knetsch, J. L. (1974) *Outdoor Recreation and Water Resources Planning*, American Geophysical Union: Washington.
Knowles, E. S. (1972) Boundaries around social space. *Environment and Behaviour* **4**, 437–45.
Knox, P. L. (1982) *Urban Social Geography: an introduction*, Longman: London.
Knox, P. L. (1978) The Intra-urban Ecology of primary medical care: patterns of accessibility and their policy implications, *Environment and Planning A* **10**, 415–35.
Knox, P. L. and **Pacione, M.** (1980) Localised behaviour, place preferences and the inverse care law in the distribution of primary medical care, *Geoforum*, **11**, 43–55
Koestler, A. (1967) *The Ghost in the Machine*, Pan: London.
Koffka, K. (1935) *Principles of Gestalt Psychology*, Harcourt-Brace: New York.
Koroscil, P. M. (1971) The behavioural environmental approach, *Area* **3**, 96–9.
Kosinski, L. A. and **Prothero, R. M.** (eds) (1975) *People on the Move: studies in internal migration*, Methuen: London.
Kramer, J. and **Leventman, S.** (1961) *Children of the Gilded Ghetto*, Yale University Press: New Haven.
Krampen, M. (1981) *Meaning in the Urban Environment*, Pion: London.
Kuipers, B. (1982) The 'map in the head' metaphor, *Environment and Behaviour* **14**, 202–20.
Lachman, R., Tatsuoka, M. and **Bonk, W. J.** (1961) Human behaviour during tsunami of May 1960, *Science* **33**, 1405–9.
Ladd, F. C. (1970) Black youths view their environment: neighbourhood maps, *Environment and Behaviour* **2**, 74–99.
Lally, J. and **Preston, D.** (1973) Anti-positivist movements in contemporary sociology, *Australian and New Zealand Journal of Sociology* **9**, 3–9.
Lambert, J. R. (1970) *Crime, Police and Race Relations: a study in Birmingham*, Oxford University Press: London.
Lander, B. (1954) *Towards an Understanding of Juvenile Delinquency*, Columbia University Press: New York.
La Page, W. F. (1979) Market analysis for recreation managers, in C. S. Van Doren, G. B. Priddle, and J. E. Lewis (eds) *Land and Leisure: concepts and methods in outdoor recreation*, Methuen, London, pp. 151–73.
Larrabee, E. and **Meyerjohn, R.** (1960) *Mass Leisure*, New York: Free Press.
Larson, O. N. (1954) Rumours in disaster, *Journal of Communication* **4**, 111–23.
Laslett, P. (1968) *The World We Have Lost*, Methuen: London.
Lavery, P. (ed.) (1974) *Recreational Geography*, David and Charles: Newton Abbott.
Lazarus, R. S. (1966) *Psychological Stress and the Coping Process*, McGraw-Hill: New York.
Lazarus, R. S. and **Cohen, J. B.** (1977) Environmental stress, in I. Altman and J. F. Wohlwill (eds) *Human Behaviour and Environment, Volume 2*, Plenum, New York, pp. 90–127.
Learmonth, A. T. A. (1975) Ecological medical geography, *Progress in Geography* 7, 202–20.
Learmonth, A. T. A. (1978) *Patterns of Disease and Hunger*, David and Charles: Newton Abbott.
Lee, E. S. (1960) A theory of migration, *Demography* **3**, 47–57.
Lee, T. R. (1962) 'Brennan's Law' of shopping behaviour. *Psychological Reports* **11**, 662.
Lee, T. (1968) Urban neighbourhood as a socio-spatial schema, *Human Relations* **21**, 241–67.
Lee, T. R. (1970) Perceived distance as a function of direction in the city, *Environment and Behaviour* **2**, 40–51.
Lee, T. R. (1971) Psychology of architectural determinism, *Architectural Journal* **154**, 253–61, 475–83, 651–9.
Lee, T. R. (1976) *Psychology and the Environment*, Methuen: London.
Leff, H. L. and **Gordon, L. R.** (1979) Environmental cognitive sets: a longitudinal study, *Environment and Behaviour* **11**, 291–327.
Leff, H. L., Gordon, L. R. and **Ferguson, J. G.** (1974) Cognitive set and environmental awareness, *Environment and Behaviour* **6**, 395–447.
Leigh, R. and **North, D.** (1975) A framework for the study of the spatial aspects of acquisition activity in manufacturing industry, in D. Massey and W. I. Morrison (eds) *Industrial location: alternative frameworks*, Centre for Environmental Studies Conference Paper No. 15, London, 49–78.
Lenntorp, B. (1978) A time-geographic simulation model of individual activity programmes, in T. Carlstein *et al.* (eds) *Timing Space and Spacing Time. Vol. 2. Human Activity and time geography*, Arnold, London, pp. 162–80.
Leslie, G. R. and **Richardson, A. H.** (1961) Life cycle career pattern and the decision to move, *American Sociological Review* **26**, 894–902.
Levi-Strauss, C. (1966) *Structural Anthropology*, Basic Books: New York.
Levy, L. and **Herzog, A. N.** (1974) Effects of population density and crowding on health and social adaptation in the Netherlands, *Journal of Health and Social Behaviour* **15**, 228–40.
Lewin, K. (1936) *Principles of Topological Psychology*, McGraw-Hill: New York.
Lewin, K. (1951) *Field Theory in Social Science: selected theoretical papers* (ed. D. Cartwright) Harper: New York.
Lewis, G. J. (1974) *Human Migration*, Open University Press, Regional Analysis and Development Unit 9: Milton Keynes.
Lewis, G. J. (1979) *Rural Communities: a social geography*, David and Charles: Newton Abbot.
Lewis, G. J. (1981a) Urban neighbourhood and community: exploratory studies in Leicester, in D. Turnock (ed.) *Leicester Geographical Studies*, Occasional Paper No. 1, Department of Geography, University of Leicester, 37–52.
Lewis, G. J. (1981b) Rural migration: a study of the Welsh Borderlands, unpublished paper, Department of Geography, University of Leicester.
Lewis, G. J. (1982) *Human Migration: a geographical perspective*, Croom Helm: London.
Lewis, G. J. and **Davies, W. K. D.** (1974) The social patterning of a British city: the case of Leicester, *Tijdschrift voor Economische en Sociale Geographie* **65**, 194–207.
Lewis, P. F. (1965) Impact of negro migration on the electoral geography of Flint, Michigan, 1932–1962: a cartographic analysis, *Annals of the Association of American Geographers* **55**, 1–25.
Lewis, P. F. (1979) Axioms for reading the landscape: some guides to the American scene, in D. W. Meinig (ed.) *The Interpretation of Ordinary Landscapes*, Oxford University Press, New York, pp. 11–32.
Ley, D. (1974) *The Black Inner City as Frontier Outpost: images and behaviour of a Philadelphia neighbourhood*, Association of American Geographers Monograph Series No. 7: Washington.
Ley, D. (1977) Social geography and the taken-for-granted world, *Transactions of the Institute of British Geographers* **2**, 498–512.

Ley, D. (1978) Social geography and social action, in Ley D. and M. S. Samuels (eds) *Humanistic Geography: prospects and problems*, Maaroufa Press, Chicago, pp. 41–57.

Ley, D. (1980) *Geography without man: a humanistic critique*, Oxford University, Department of Geography Research Paper No. 24.

Ley, D. (1981a) Cultural/humanistic geography, *Progress in Human Geography* 5, 249–57.

Ley, D. (1981b) Behavioural geography and the philosophies of meaning, in K. R. Cox and R. G. Golledge (eds) *Behavioural Problems in Geography Revisited* , Methuen, London, pp. 209–30.

Ley, D. and **Cybriwsky, R.** (1974a) The spatial ecology of stripped cars, *Environment and Behaviour* **6**, 63–7.

Ley, D. and **Cybriwsky, R.** (1974b) Urban graffiti as territorial markers, *Annals of the Association of American Geographers* **64**, 491–505.

Ley, D. and **Samuels, M. S.** (1978a) Introduction: contexts of modern humanism in geography, in D. Ley and M. S. Samuels (eds) *Humanistic Geography: prospects and problems*, Maaroufa Press, Chicago, pp. 1–17.

Ley, D. and **Samuels, M. S.** (1978b) Epistemological orientations, in D. Ley and M. S. Samuels (eds) *Humanistic Geography: prospects and problems*, Maaroufa Press, Chicago, pp. 19–21.

Ley, D. and **Samuels, M. S.** (1978c) Methodological implications, in D. Ley and M. S. Samuels (eds) *Humanistic Geography: prospects and problems*, Maaroufa Press, Chicago, pp. 121–2.

Lieber, S. R. (1976) A comparison of metric and nonmetric scaling models in preference research, in R. G. Golledge and G.Rushton (eds) *Spatial Choice and Spatial Behaviour*, Ohio State University Press, Columbus, pp. 191–210.

Lieber, S. R. (1978) Place utility and migration, *Geografiska Annaler* **60B**, 16–27.

Lieber, S. R. (1979) An experimental approach for the migration decision process, *Tijdschrift voor Economische en Sociale Geografie* **70**, 75–85.

Lipman, A. and **Russell-Lacy, S.** (1974) Some social psychological correlates of New Town residential localism in D. V. Canter and T. R. Lee (eds) *Psychology and the Built Environment*, Architectural Press, London, pp. 139–47.

Lipset, S. and **Bendix, R.** (1952) Social mobility and occupational career paths, *American Journal of Sociology* **57**, 366–74.

Lipsey, R. G. (1975) *An Introduction to Positive Economics* (4th edn), Weidenfeld and Nicholson: London.

Livingstone, D. N. and **Harrison, R. T.** (1981) Immanuel Kant, subjectivism, and human geography: a preliminary investigation, *Transactions of the Institute of British Geographers* **6**, 359–74.

Lloyd, P. E. and **Dicken, P.** (1972) *Location in Space: a theoretical approach to geography*, Harper and Row: London.

Lloyd, R. and **Jennings, D.** (1978) Shopping behaviour and income: comparisons in an urban environment, *Economic Geography* **54**, 157–68.

Lösch, A. (1954) *The Economics of Location* (trans. W. H. Woglom and W. F. Stolper), Yale University Press: New Haven.

Louviere, J. J. (1973) The dimensions of alternatives in spatial choice processes: a comment, *Geographical Analysis* **5**, 315–25.

Louviere, J. J. (1976) Information-processing theory and functional form in spatial behaviour in, R. G. Golledge and G. Rushton (eds) *Spatial Choice and Spatial Behaviour*, Ohio State University Press, Columbus, pp. 211–48.

Louviere, J. J. (1981) A conceptual and analytical framework for understanding spatial and travel choices, *Economic Geography* **57**, 304–14.

Lowenthal, D. (1961) Geography, experience, and imagination: towards a geographical epistemology, *Annals of the Association of American Geographers* **51**, 241–60.

Lowenthal, D· (1972a) Research in environmental perception and behaviour: perspectives on current problems, *Environment and Behaviour* **4**, 333–42.

Lowenthal, D. (1972b) *Environmental assessment: comparative analysis of four cities*, American Geographical Society Publications on Environmental Perception No. 5: New York.

Lowenthal, D. (1975) Past time, present place: landscape and memory, *Geographical Review* **65**, 1–36.

Lowenthal, D. and **Prince, H. C.** (1964) The English landscape, *Geographical Review* **54**, 309–46.

Lowenthal, D. and **Prince, H. C.** (1965) English landscape tastes, *Geographical Review* **55**, 186–222.

Lowenthal, D. and **Riel, M.** (1972a) The nature of perceived and imagined environments, *Environment and Behaviour* **4**, 189–207.

Lewenthal, D. and **Riel, M.** (1972b) *Milieu and observer differences in environmental associations*, American Geographical Society Publications on Environmental Perception No. 7: New York.

Lowerson, J. and **Myerscough, J.** (1977) *Time and Space in Victorian England*, Harvester Press: Hassocks.

Lowrey, R. A. (1973) A method for analysing distance concepts of urban residents, in R. Downs and D. Stea (eds) *Image and Environment*, Aldine, Chicago, pp. 338–60.

Lynch, K. (1960) *The Image of the City*, MIT Press: Cambridge, Mass.

Lynch, K. (1972) *What Time is This Place?* MIT Press: Cambridge, Mass.

Lynch, K. (1976) Foreword, in G. T. Moore and R. G. Golledge (eds) *Environmental Knowing*, Dowden, Hutchinson & Ross, Stroudsburg, pp. v–viii.

Lynd, R. S. and **Lynd, H. M.** (1956) *Middletown*, Harcourt, Brace and World: New York.

Mabogunje, A. L. (1970) Systems approach to a theory of rural-urban migration, *Geographical Analysis* **2**, 1–18.

McCarthy, D. and **Saegert, S.** (1978) Residental density, social overload and social withdrawal, *Human Ecology* **6**, 253–72.

McClenahan, B. A. (1945) The communality: the urban substitute for the traditional community, *Social Science Research* **30**, 264–74.

McCracken, K. W. J. (1975) Household awareness space and intra-urban migration search behaviour, *Professional Geographer* **27**, 166–70.

McCullock, J. W. Philip, A. E. and **Carstairs, G. M.** (1967) The ecology of suicidal behaviour, *British Journal of Psychiatry* **113**, 313–19.

McDaniel, R. (1975) How information structures influence spatial organisation, in R. Abler *et al.* (eds) *Human Geography in a Shrinking World*, Duxbury, North Scituate, pp. 57–66.

McDermott, P. J. and **Taylor, M. J.** (1976) Attitudes, images and location: the subjective context of decision-making in New Zealand manufacturing, *Economic Geography* **52**, 325–46.

McDonald, N. S. (1979) Hazard perception in northern New

South Wales, in R. L. Heathcote and B. G. Thom (eds) *Natural Hazards in Australia*, Australian Academy of Science, Canberra, pp. 260–9.

McGee, M. G. (1979) Human spatial abilities: psychometric studies and environmental, genetic, hormonal, and neurological influences, *Psychological Bulletin* **86**, 889–918.

McGill, W. and **Korn, J. H.** (1982) Awareness of an urban environment, *Environment and Behaviour* **14**, 186–201.

McGlashan, N. D. (ed.) (1972) *Medical Geography*, Methuen: London.

McHarg, I. (1969) *Design with Nature*, Natural History Press: New York.

Mackay, J. B. (1976) The effect of spatial stimuli on the estimation of cognitive maps, *Geographical Analysis* **8**, 439–52.

Mackay, D. B., Olshavsky, R. W. and **Sentell, G.** (1975) Cognitive maps and spatial behaviour of consumer, *Geographical Analysis* 7, 19–34.

McKay, J. and **Whitelaw, J. S.** (1977) The role of large private and government organizations in generating flows of inter-regional migrants: the case of Australia, *Economic Geography* **53**, 28–44.

MacLennan, D. and **Williams, N. J.** (1979) Revealed space preference theory – a cautionary note, *Tijdschrift voor Economische en Sociale Geographie* **70**, 307–9.

McNee, R. B. (1960) Towards a more humanistic economic geography: the geography of enterprise, *Tijdschrift voor Economische en Sociale Geographie* **50**, 201–6.

McNee, R. B. (1974) A systems approach to understanding the geographic behaviour of organizations, especially large corporations, in F. E. I. Hamilton (ed.) *Spatial Perspectives on Industrial Organization and Decision-making*, Wiley, London, pp. 47–76.

McNeil, E. B. (1970) *The Psychoses*, Prentice Hall: Englewood Cliffs.

McPhail, I. R. (1971) The vote for mayor of Los Angeles in 1969, *Annals of the Association of American Geographers* **61**, 744–58.

McPhail, I. R. (1974) The spatial approach to electoral analysis, *Politics* **9**, 189–94.

Magnusson, D. (ed.) (1981) *Towards a Psychology of Situations: an interactional perspective*, Erlbaum Associates: Hillsdale, N. J.

Malmberg, T. (1980) *Human Territoriality*, Mouton: Hague.

Mangalam, J. J. (1968) *Human Migration*, University of Kentucky Press: Lexington.

Mann, M. (1973) *Workers on the Move*, Cambridge University Press: London.

March, J. G. and **Simon, H. A.** (1958) *Organizations*, Wiley: New York.

Marchand, B. (1972) Information theory and geography, *Geographical Analysis* **4**, 234–58.

Martensson, A. (1977) Childhood interaction and temporal organisation, *Economic Geography* **53**, 99–125.

Martin, A. E. (1967) Environment, housing and health, *Urban Studies* **4**, 1–21.

Martin, J. E. (1981) Location theory and spatial analysis, *Progress in Human Geography* **5**, 258–62.

Maslow, A. (1954) *Motivation and Personality*, Harper & Row: New York.

Massam, B. H. and **Bouchard, D.** (1976) A comparison of observed and hypothetical choice behaviour, *Environment and Behaviour* **8**, 367–74.

Massey, D. (1975a) Is the behavioural approach really an alternative?, in D. Massey and W. I. Morrison (eds) *Industrial Location: alternative frameworks*, Centre for Environmental Studies Conference Paper No. 15, London, pp. 79–86.

Massey, D. (1975b) Behavioural research, *Area* **7**, 201–3.

Massey, D. (1979) A critical evaluation of industrial-location theory, in F. E. I. Hamilton and G. J. R. Linge (eds) *Spatial Analysis, Industry and the Industrial Environment: progress in research and applications. Vol. 1: Industrial systems*, Wiley, Chichester, pp. 57–72.

Matthews, M. H. (1981) Children's perception of urban distance, *Area* **13**, 333–43.

Maurer, R. and **Baxter, J. C.** (1972) Images of the neighbourhood and city among Black-, Anglo-, and Mexican-American children, *Environment and Behaviour* **4**, 351–88.

Maw, R. and **Cosgrove, D.** (1975) *Assessment of demand for recreation – modelling approach*, Polytechnic of Central London, Leisure Model Unit Working Paper No. 2.

Mawby, R. I. (1977) Defensible space: a theoretical and empirical appraisal, *Urban Studies* **14**, 169–79.

May, K. O. (1954) Transitivity, utility and aggregation in preference patterns, *Econometrica* **22**, 1–13.

Mayer, J. D. (1982) Relations between two traditions of medical geography: health system planning and geographical epidemiology, *Progress in Human Geography* **6**, 216–30.

Mays, J. B. (1968) Crime and the urban pattern, *Sociological Review* **16**, 241–55.

Mead, G. H. (1934) *Mind, Self, and Society*, University of Chicago Press: Chicago.

Meinig, D. W. (ed.) (1979a) *The Interpretation of Ordinary Landscapes: geographical essays*, Oxford University Press: New York.

Meinig, D. W. (1979b) Introduction, in D. W. Meinig (ed.) *The Interpretation of Ordinary Landscapes*, Oxford University Press, New York, pp. 1–10.

Meinig, D. W. (1979c) The beholding eye: ten versions of the same scene, in D. W. Meinig (ed.) *The Interpretation of Ordinary Landscapes*, Oxford University Press, New York, pp. 33–48.

Mercer, C. (1975) *Living in Cities: psychology and the urban environment*, Penguin: Harmondsworth.

Mercer, D. (1972) Behavioural geography and the sociology of social action, *Area* **4**, 48–52.

Mercer, D. (1976) Motivational and social aspects of recreation behaviour, in I. Altman and J. F. Wohlwill (eds), *Human Behaviour and Environment*, Plenum Press, New York, pp. 123–61.

Mercer, D. (ed.) (1977) *Leisure and Recreation in Australia*, Sorrett: Melbourne.

Mercer, D. (1980) *In Pursuit of Leisure*, Sorrett: Melbourne.

Mercer, D. (ed.) (1981) *Outdoor Recreation – Australian Perspectives*, Sorrett: Melbourne.

Merry, S. E. (1981) Defensible space undefended: social factors in crime control through environmental design, *Urban Affairs Quarterly* **16**, 397–422.

Meyer, G. (1977) Distance perception of consumers in shopping streets, *Tijdschrift voor Economische en Social Geografie* **68**, 355–61.

Meyer, R. (1980) A descriptive model of constrained residential search, *Geographical Analysis* **12**, 21–32.

Michelson, W. (1970) *Man and his Environment*, Addison Wesley: Reading, Mas.

Michelson, W. (1977) *Environmental Choice, Human Behaviour, and Residential Satisfaction*, Oxford University Press: New York.

Milgram, S. (1970) The experience of living in cities, *Science*

167, 1461–8.
Milgram, S. (1973) Introduction to Chapter II, in W. H. Ittelson (ed.) *Environment and cognition*, Seminar Press, New York, pp. 21 –8.
Miller, F. D. *et al.* (1980) Neighbourhood satisfaction among urban dwellers, *Journal of Social Issues* **36**, 101–17.
Miller, G. A. (1956) The magical number seven, plus or minus two: some limits on our capacity for processing information, *Psychological Review* **63**, 81–97.
Miller, G. A., Galanter, E. and **Pribam, K. H.** (1960) *Plans and the Structure of Behaviour*, Holt: New York.
Miller, J. M. (1961) Residential density: relating people to space rather than to ground area, *Journal of the American Institute of Planners* **27**, 77–8.
Mills, C. W. (1970) *The Sociological Imagination*, Penguin: Harmondsworth.
Milne, G. (1977a) Cyclone Tracy: I. Some consequences of the evacuation for adult victims, *Australian Psychologist* **12**, 39–54.
Milne, G. (1977b) Cyclone Tracy: II. The effects on Darwin children, *Australian Psychologist* **12**, 55–62.
Mintz, N. L. and **Schwarz, D. T.** (1964) Urban psychology and psychoses, *International Journal of Social Psychiatry* **10**, 101–17.
Mitchell, J. C. (ed.) (1969) *Social Networks in Urban Situations*, Manchester University Press: Manchester.
Montague, M. F. A. (ed.) (1968) *Man and Aggression*, Oxford University Press: London.
Moore, E. G. (1972) *Residential mobility in the city*, Association of American Geography Commission on College Geography Resource Paper No. 13: Washington.
Moore, G. T. (1975) Spatial relations ability and developmental levels of urban cognitive mapping: a research note, *Man-Environment Systems* **5**, 247–8.
Moore, G. T. (1976) Theory and research on the development of environmental knowing, in G. T. Moore and R. G. Golledge (eds) *Environmental Knowing*, Dowden, Hutchinson and Ross, Stroudsburg, pp. 138–64.
Moore, G. T. (1979) Knowing about environmental knowing: the current state of theory and research on environmental cognition, *Environment and Behaviour* **11**, 33–70.
Moore, G. T. and **Golledge, R. G.** (1976a) Preface, in G. T. Moore and R. G. Golledge (eds) *Environmental Knowing*, Dowden, Hutchinson and Ross, Stroudsburg pp. xi–xvi.
Moore, G. T. and **Golledge, R. G.** (1976b) Environmental knowing: concepts and theories, in G. T. Moore and R. G. Golledge (eds) *Environmental Knowing*, Dowden, Hutchinson and Ross, Stroudsburg, pp. 3–24.
Moore, P. G. and **Thomas, H.** (1976) *The Anatomy of Decisions*, Penguin: Harmondsworth.
Moore, P. G., Thomas, H., Bunn, D. W. and **Hampton, J. M.** (1976) *Case Studies in Decision Analysis*, Penguin: Harmondsworth.
Moos, R. R. (1976) *The Human Context: environmental determinants of behaviour*, Wiley: New York.
Morgan, B. S. (1976) The basis of family status segregation: a case study of Exeter, *Transactions of the Institute of British Geographers* **1**, 83–107.
Morrill, R. L. (1968) Waves of spatial diffusion, *Journal of Regional Science* **8**, 1–19.
Morrill, R. L. and **Manninen, D.** (1975) Critical parameters of spatial diffusion processes, *Economic Geography* **51**, 269–77.
Morris, D. (1968) *The Naked Ape*, Corgi: London.
Moses, L. N. (1958) Location and the theory of production, *Quarterly Journal of Economics* **72**, 259–72.
Mounfield, P. R., Unwin, D. J. and **Guy, K.** (1982) *Processes of Change in the Footwear Industry of the East Midlands*, University of Leicester Department of Geography: Leicester.
Muller, P. O. (1976) *The outer city*, Association of American Geographers, Commission on College Geography Resource Paper No. 22: Washington.
Mumford, L. (1961) *The City in History*, Secker & Warburg: London.
Murie, A. (1975) *Household movement and housing*, University of Birmingham, Centre for Urban and Regional Studies Occasional Paper No. 28.
Murphy, J. F. (1974) *Concepts of Leisure*, Prentice Hall: Englewood Cliffs.
Murphy, J. F. (1975) *Recreation and Leisure Service: a humanistic perspective*, Brown: Iowa City.
Murphy, P. E. and **Rosenblood, L.** (1974) Tourism: an exercise in spatial search, *Canadian Geographer* **18**, 201–10.
Murray, D. and **Spencer, C. P.** (1979) Individual differences in the drawing of cognitive maps: the effects of geographical mobility, strength of mental imagery and basic graphic ability, *Transactions of the Institute of British Geographers* **4**, 385–91.
Murton, B. J. (1972) Some aspects of a cognitive-behavioural approach to environment: a review, *New Zealand Journal of Geography* **53**, 1–8.
Nalson, J. S. (1968) *The Mobility of Farm Families*, Manchester University Press: Manchester.
Nelson, S. D. (1974) Nature/nurture revisited. I: A review of the biological bases of conflict, *Journal of Conflict Resolution* **18**, 285–335.
New South Wales State Pollution Control Commission (1978) *Recreational Use in Botany Bay*, Government Printer: Sydney.
Newman, O. (1972) *Defensible Space*, Macmillan: New York.
Norberg-Schultz, C. (1971) *Existence, Space and Architecture*, Studio Vista: London.
Norcliffe, G. B. (1974) Territorial influences in urban political space: a study of perception in Kitchener-Waterloo, *Canadian Geographer* **18**, 311–29.
North, D. J. (1974) The process of locational change in different manufacturing organizations, in F. E. I. Hamilton (ed.) *Spatial Perspectives on Industrial Organization and Decision-making*, Wiley, London, pp.213–44.
O'Keefe, J. and **Nadel, L.** (1978) *The Hippocampus as a Cognitive Map*, Oxford University Press: London.
Oliver, J. (1975) The significance of natural hazards in a developing area: a case study from North Queensland, *Geography* **60**, 99–110.
Oliver, J. (1978) Human response to natural disaster, in J. I. Reid (ed.) *Natural Disaster and Community Welfare*, Department of Behavioural Sciences, James Cook University, Townsville, pp. 24–30.
Olsson, G. (1965) *Distance and Human Interaction*, Regional Science Research Institute: Philadelphia.
Olsson, G. (1969) Inference problems in location analysis, in K. R. Cox and R. G. Golledge (eds) *Behavioural problems in geography: a symposium*, Northwestern Studies in Geography **17**, 14–34.
Olsson, G. (1970) Logics and social engineering, *Geographical Analysis* **2**, 361–95.
Olsson, G. (1978) Of ambiguity or far cries from a memorializing mamafesta, in D. Ley and M. S. Samuels (eds) *Humanistic Geography: prospects and problems*,

Maaroufa, Chicago, pp. 109–20.
Onibokun, A. G. (1976) Social system correlates of residential satisfaction, *Environment and Behaviour* **8**, 323–44.
Openshaw, S. (1973) Insoluble problems in shopping model calibration when trip pattern is not known, *Regional Studies* **7**, 367–71.
Orbell, J. M. (1970) An information-flow theory of community influence, *Journal of Politics* **32**, 322–38.
O.R.C.L. (1977) *Analysis methods and techniques for recreation research and leisure studies*, Ontario Research Council on Leisure: Ottawa.
O'Riordan, T. (1973) Some reflections on environmental attitudes and environmental behaviour, *Area* **5**, 17–21.
Orleans, P. (1973) Differential cognition of urban residents: effects of social scale on mapping, in R. Downs and D. Stea (eds) *Image and Environment*, Aldine, Chicago, pp. 115–30.
Ornstein, R. E. (1972) *The Psychology of Consciousness*, Freeman: New York.
Osgood, C. E. (1957) A behaviouralistic analysis of perception and language as cognitive phenomena, in *Contemporary Approaches to Cognition: a symposium at the University of Colorado*, Harvard University Press, Cambridge, Mass, pp. 75–118.
Osgood, C. E., Suci, G. A. and **Tannenbaum, P. H.** (1957) *The Measurement of Meaning*, University of Illinois Press: Urbana.
Outdoor Recreation Resources Review Commission (1962) *Outdoor Recreation for America*, Government Printing Office: Washington.

Pablan, P. and **Baxter, J. C.** (1975) Environmental correlates of school vandalism, *Journal of the American Institute of Planners* **42**, 270–9.
Pacione, M. (1975) Preference and perception: an analysis of consumer behaviour, *Tijdschrift voor Economische en Sociale Geografie* **66**, 84–92.
Pacione, M. (1976) Shape and structure in cognitive maps of Great Britain, *Regional Studies* **10**, 275–83.
Pacione, M. (1978) Information and morphology in cognitive maps, *Transactions of the Institute of British Geographers* **3**, 548–68.
Pacione, M. (1982) Space preferences, locational decisions, and the dispersal of civil servants from London, *Environment and Planning A* **14**, 323–33.
Pahl, R. E. (1966) The rural-urban continuum, *Sociologia Ruralis* **6**, 314–29.
Pahl, R. E. (1968) Is mobile society a myth?, *New Society*, 11 January, pp. 46–8.
Palm, R. (1976a) The role of real estate agents as information mediators in two American cities, *Geografiska Annaler* **58B**, 28–41.
Palm, R. (1976b) Real estate agents and geographical information, *Geographical Review* **66**, 266–280.
Palm, R. I. (1981) Public response to earthquake hazard information, *Annals of the Association of American Geographers* **71**, 389–99.
Park, R. E. (1936) Human ecology, *American Journal of Sociology* **20**, 577–612.
Park, R. E., Burgess, E. W. and **McKenzie, R. D.** (1925) *The City*, University of Chicago Press: Chicago.
Parker, D. J. and **Harding, D. M.** (1979) Natural hazard evaluation, perception and adjustment, *Geography* **64**, 307–16.
Parker, G. (1975) Psychological disturbance in Darwin evacuees following Cyclone Tracy, *Medical Journal of Australia* **1**, 650–2.
Parker, S. (1975) The sociology of leisure: progress and problems, *British Journal of Sociology* **26**, 91–101.
Parker, S. (1976) *The Sociology of Leisure*, International Publishing Service: New York.
Parkes, D. and **Thrift, N.** (1978) Putting time in its place, in T. Carlstein *et al* (eds) *Timing Space and Spacing Time Vol. 1: Making sense of time*, Arnold, London, pp. 119–29.
Parkes, D. and **Thrift, N.** (1980) *Times, Spaces and Places: a chronogeographic perspective*, Wiley: New York.
Parkes, D. and **Wallis, W. D.** (1978) Graph theory and the study of activity structure, in T. Carlstein *et al.* (eds) *Timing Space and Spacing Time Vol. 2: Human activity and time geography*, Arnold, London, pp. 75–99.
Parr, A. R. (1970) Organizational response to community crises and group emergence, *American Behavioural Scientist* **13**, 423–9.
Patmore, J. A. (1970) *Land and Leisure*, David and Charles: Newton Abbot.
Patmore, J. A. and **Collins, M. F.** (1980) Recreation and leisure, *Progress in Human Geography* **4**, 91–7.
Patricios, N. N. (1978) An agentive model of person-environment relations, *International Journal of Environmental Studies* **13**, 43–52.
Pearce, P. L. (1977) Mental souvenirs: a study of tourists and their city maps, *Australian Journal of Psychology* **29**, 203–10.
Peet, R. (1975) The geography of crime: a political critique, *Professional Geographer* **27**, 277–80.
Peet, R. (1976) Further comments on the geography of crime, *Professional Geographer* **28**, 96–100.
Peet, R. (1977) The development of radical human geography in the United States, *Progress in Human Geography* **1**, 240–63.
Peet, R. J. and **Lyons, J. V.** (1981) Marxism: dialectical materialism, social formation and the geographic relations, in M. E. Harvey and B. P. Holly (eds) *Themes in Geographic Thought*, Croom Helm, London, pp. 187–205.
Perry, C. (1929) The neighbourhood unit formula, in W. C. L. Whenton, G. Milgram and M. E. Meyson (eds), *Urban Housing*, Free Press, New York, pp. 36–43.
Phillips, D. R. (1979) Public altitudes to general practitioner services: a reflection of an inverse care law in intra-urban primary medical care? *Environment and Planning A* **11**, 315–24
Phillips, D. R. (1981) *Contemporary Issues in the Geography of Health Care*, Geo Books: Norwich.
Phipps, A. G. (1979) Scaling problems in the cognition of urban distances, *Transactions of the Institute of British Geographers* **4**, 94–102.
Piaget, J. (1970) *Structuralism* (trans. C. Maschler), Basic Books: New York.
Pick, H. L. (1976) Transactional-constructivist approach to environmental knowing: a commentary, in G. T. Moore and R. G. Golledge (eds) *Environmental Knowing*, Downden, Hutchinson and Ross, Stroudsburg, pp. 185–6.
Pickvance, C. G. (1974) Life cycle, housing tenure and residential mobility: a path analytic approach, *Urban Studies* **11**, 171–88.
Pierce, R. C. (1980) Dimensions of leisure, *Journal of Leisure Research* **12**, 5–19, 132–41, 273–84.
Pipkin, J. S. (1981a) The concept of choice and cognitive explanations of spatial behaviour, *Economic Geography* **57**, 315–31.
Pipkin, J. S. (1981b) Cognitive behavioural geography and repetitive travel, in K. R. Cox and R. G. Golledge (eds) *Behavioural Problems in Geography Revisited*, Methuen, London, pp. 145–81.

Pirie, G. H. (1976) Thoughts on revealed preferences and spatial behaviour, *Environment and Planning A* **8**, 947–55.

Plant, J. S. (1957) The personality and an urban area, in P. K. Hatt and A. J. Reiss (eds), *Cities and Society*, Free Press, New York, pp. 647–65.

Pocock, D. C. D. (1973) Environmental perception: process and product, *Tijdschrift voor Economische en Sociale Geografie* **69**, 251–7.

Pocock, D. C. D. (1975) *Durham: image of a cathedral city*, University of Durham, Department of Geography Occasional Paper No. 6.

Pocock, D. C. D. (1976a) A comment on images derived from invitation-to-map exercises, *Professional Geographer* **28**, 161–6.

Pocock, D. C. D. (1976b) Some characteristics of mental maps: an empirical study, *Transactions of the Institute of British Geographers* **1**, 493–512.

Pocock, D. C. D. (1978) The cognition of intra-urban distance: a summary, *Scottish Geographical Magazine* **94**, 31–5.

Pocock, D. C. D. (1979) The novelist's image of the North, *Transactions of the Institute of British Geographers* **4**, 62–76.

Pocock, D. C. D. (1981a) Sight and knowledge , *Transactions of the Institute of British Geographers* **6**, 385–93.

Pocock, D. C. D. (1981b) Place and the novelist, *Transactions of the Institute of British Geographers* **6**, 337–47.

Pocock, D. (ed.) (1981c) *Humanistic Geography and Literature*, Croom Helm: London.

Pocock, D. and **Hudson, R.** (1978) *Images of the Urban Environment*, Macmillan: London.

Popp, H. (1976) The residential location decision process: some theoretical and empirical considerations, *Tijdschrift voor Economische en Sociale Geografie* **67**, 300–5.

Porteous, J. D. (1973) The Burnside gang: territoriality, social space and community planning, *Western Geographical Series* **5**, 130–48.

Porteous, J. D. (1976) Home: the territorial core, *Geographical Review* **66**, 383–90.

Porteous, J. D. (1977) *Environment and Behaviour: planning and everyday urban life*, Addison-Wesley: Reading, Mass.

Potter, R. B. (1976) Directional bias within the usage and perceptual fields of urban consumers, *Psychological Reports* **38**, 988–90.

Potter, R. B. (1977a) The nature of consumer usage fields in an urban environment: theoretical and empirical perspectives, *Tijdschrift voor Economische en Sociale Geografie* **68**, 168–76.

Potter, R. B. (1977b) Spatial patterns of consumer behaviour and perception in relation to the social class variable, *Area* **9**, 153–6.

Potter, R. B. (1979) Perception of urban retailing facilities: an analysis of consumer information fields, *Geografiska Annaler* **61B**, 19–27.

Potter, R. B. (1982) *The Urban Retailing System*, Gower: Aldershot.

Powell, J. M. (1978) *Mirrors of the New World: images and image-makers in the settlement process*, Australian National University Press: Canberra.

Power, J. M. and **Wettenhall, R. L.** (1970) Bureaucracy and disaster. II: Response to the 1967 Tasmanian bushfires, *Public Administration* **29**, 165–83.

Pred, A. (1967) *Behaviour and Location: foundations for a geographic dynamic location theory: Part 1*, Lund Studies in Geography, Series B, No. 27.

Pred, A. R. (1973a) The growth and development of systems of cities in advanced economies, in A. R. Pred and G. E. Törnqvist, *Systems of Cities and Information Flows: two essays*, Lund Studies in Geography, Series B, No. 38, pp.9–82.

Pred, A. R. (1973b) Urbanisation, domestic planning problems and Swedish geographic research, *Progress in Geography* 5, 1–76.

Pred, A. (1977a) *City-systems in Advanced Economies: past growth, present processes and future development options*, Hutchinson: London.

Pred, A. (1977b) The choreography of existence: comments on Hägerstrand's time-geography and its usefulness, *Economic Geography* **53**, 207–21.

Pred, A. (1981) Of paths and projects: individual behaviour and its societal context, in K. R. Cox and R. G. Golledge (eds) *Behavioural Problems in Geography Revisited*, Methuen, London, pp. 231–55.

Pred, A. and **Kibel, B. M.** (1970) An application of gaming simulation to a general model of economic locational processes, *Economic Geography* **46**, 136–56.

Pred, A. and **Palm, R.** (1978) The status of American women: a time-geographic view, in D. A. Lanegran and R. Palm (eds) *An Invitation to Geography*, McGraw-Hill, New York, pp. 99–109.

Prescott, J. R. V. (1969) Electoral studies in political geography, in R. E. Kasperson and J. V. Minghi (eds) *The Structure of Political Geography*, Aldine, Chicago, pp. 376–83.

Preston, V. and **Taylor, S. M.** (1981) Personal construct theory and residential choice, *Annals of the Association of American Geographers* **71**, 437–51.

Preston, V. and **Taylor, S. M.** (1981) The family life cycle, leisure activities and residential area evaluation, *Canadian Geographer* **25**, 45–59.

Prince, H. C. (1971) Real, imagined and abstract worlds of the past, *Progress in Geography* **3**, 1–86.

Proshansky, H. M. (1978) The city and self-identity, *Environment and Behaviour* **10**, 147–69.

Proshansky, H. M., Ittelson, W. H. and **Rivlin, L. G.** (1970a) Basic psychological processes and the environment, in H. M. Proshansky *et al.* (eds) *Environmental Psychology: man and his physical setting*, Holt, Rinehart and Winston, New York, pp. 101–4.

Proshansky, H. M., Ittelson, W. H. and **Rivlin, L. G.** (1970b) Introduction, in H. M. Proshansky *et al.* (eds) *Environmental Psychology: man and his physical setting*, Holt, Rinehart and Winston, New York, pp. 1–6.

Pryor, R. J. (ed.) (1975) *The motivation of migration*, Australian National University, Department of Demography, Studies in Migration and Urbanization No. 1.

Putnam, R. (1966) Political attitudes and the local community, *American Political Science Review* **50**, 640–54.

Pyle, G. F. (1973) Measles as an urban health problem: the Akron example, *Economic Geography* **49**, 344–56.

Pyle, G. F. (1974) *The spatial dynamics of crime*, University of Chicago, Department of Geography Research Paper No. 159.

Pyle, G. F. (1976) Geographic perspectives on crime and the impact of anticrime legislation, in J. Adams (ed.) *Urban Policymaking and Metropolitan Dynamics*, Ballinger, Cambridge, pp. 257–92.

Pyle, G. F. (1979) Expanding North American perspectives on medical geography, *Social Science and Medicine* **13D**, 205–7.

Pyle, G. F. and **Rees, P. H.** (1971) Problems of modelling disease patterns in urban areas: the Chicago example, *Economic Geography* **47**, 475–88.

Quarantelli, E. L. (1966) Organizations under stress, in R. Brictson (ed.) *Symposium on Emergency Operations*, Santa Monica, Rand Corporation, pp. 3–19.

Quarantelli, E. L. and **Dynes, R. R.** (1972) When disaster strikes, *Psychology Today* 5 (9), 66–70.

Raphael, B. (1979) The preventive psychiatry of natural hazard, in R. L. Heathcote and B. G. Thom (eds) *Natural Hazards in Australia*, Australian Academy of Science, Canberra, pp. 330–9.

Rapoport, A. (ed.) (1974) *Game Theory as a Theory of Conflict Resolution*, Reidel: Dordrecht.

Rapoport, A. (1976) Environmental cognition in cross-cultural perspective, in G. T. Moore and R. G. Golledge (eds) *Environmental Knowing*, Dowden, Hutchinson and Ross, Stroudsburg, pp. 220–34.

Rapoport, A. and **Hawkes, R.** (1970) The perception of urban complexity, *Journal of the American Institute of Planners* **36**, 106–11.

Rapoport, R. and **Rapoport, R.** (1975) *Leisure and the Family Life Cycle*, Routledge and Kegan Paul: Henley.

Ravenstein, E. G. (1885) The laws of migration, *Journal of the Royal Statistical Society* **48**, 167–235.

Ravenstein, E. G. (1889) The laws of migration, *Journal of the Royal Statistical Society* **52**, 241–305.

Ray, D. M. (1967) Cultural differences in consumer travel behaviour in East Ontario, *Canadian Geographer* **11**, 143–56.

Reckless, W. C. (1934) *Vice in Chicago*, University of Chicago Press: Chicago.

Rees, J. (1974) Decision-making, the growth of the firm and the business environment, in F. E. I. Hamilton (ed.) *Spatial Perspectives on Industrial Organization and Decision-making*, Wiley, London, pp. 189–211.

Relph, E. (1976) *Place and Placelessness*, Pion: London.

Relph, E. (1981a) Phenomenology, in M. E. Harvey and B. P. Holly (eds) *Themes in Geographic Thought*, Croom Helm, London, pp. 99–114.

Relph, E. (1981b) *Rational Landscapes and Humanistic Geography*, Croom Helm: London.

Reynolds, D. R. (1969) A spatial model for analysing voting behaviour, *Acta Sociologica* **12**, 122–310.

Reynolds, D. R. (1974) Spatial contagion in political influence processes, in K. R. Cox, D. R. Reynolds and S. Rokkan (eds) *Locational Approaches to Power and Conflict*, Halsted, New York, pp. 233–73.

Richmond, A. H. (1973) *Migration and Race Relations in an English city*, Oxford University Press: London.

Rieser, R. (1973) The territorial illusion and behavioural sink: critical notes on behavioural geography, *Antipode* 5, 52–7.

Roberts, K. (1978) *Contemporary Society and the Growth of Leisure*, Longman: London.

Roberts, M. C. and **Rumage, K. W.** (1965) The spatial variations in urban left-wing voting in England and Wales in 1951, *Annals of the Association of American Geographers* **55**, 161–78.

Robinson, M. E. and **Dicken, P.** (1979) Cloze procedure and cognitive mapping, *Environment and Behaviour* **11**, 351–74.

Robinson, W. S. (1950) Ecological correlations and the behaviour of individuals, *American Sociological Review* **15**, 351–6.

Robson, B. T. (1969) *Urban Analysis*, Cambridge University Press: Cambridge.

Rodgers, H. B. (1969) Leisure and recreation, *Urban Studies* **6**, 31–42.

Rokkan, S. (1970) *Citizens, Elections, Parties*, McKay: New York.

Root, J. D. (1975) Intransitivity of preferences: a neglected concept, *Proceedings of the Association of American Geographers* 7, 185–9.

Rose, H. M. (1971) *The Black Ghetto: a spatial behavioural perspective*, McGraw-Hill: New York.

Roseman, C. C. (1971) Migration as a spatial and temporal process, *Annals of the Association of American Geographers* **61**, 589–98.

Rosen, G. (1973) Disease, debility and death, in H. J. Dyos and M. Wolff (eds) *The Victorian City: images and realities*, Routledge, London, pp. 625–68.

Rossi, P. H. (1955) *Why Families Move*, Free Press: Glencoe, Ill.

Royal Commission on Local Government in England (1969) *Community Attitudes Survey*, HMSO: London.

Rumley, D. (1975) Whither electoral geography?, *Annals of the Association of American Geographers* **65**, 342–3.

Rumley, D. (1979) The study of structural effects in human geography, *Tijdschrift voor Economische en Sociale Geografie* **70**, 350–60.

Rumley, D. (1981) Spatial structural effects in voting behaviour: description and explanation, *Tijdschrift voor Economische en Sociale Geografie* **72**, 214–23.

Rumley, D. and **Minghi J. V.** (1977) A geographic framework for the study of the stability and change of urban electoral patterns, *Tijdschrift voor Economische en Sociale Geografie* **68**, 177–82.

Rushton, G. (1969a) Analysis of behaviour by revealed space preference, *Annals of the Association of American Geographers* **59**, 391–400.

Rushton, G. (1969b) The scaling of locational preferences, in K. R. Cox and R. G. Golledge (eds) *Behavioural problems in geography*, Northwestern University Studies in Geography No. 17, pp. 197–227.

Rushton, G. (1976) Decomposition of space-preference functions, in R. G. Golledge and G. Rushton (eds) *Spatial Choice and Spatial Behaviour: geographic essays on the analysis of preferences and perceptions*, Ohio State University Press, Columbus, pp. 119–34.

Rushton, G. (1979) Commentary on behavioural and perception geography, *Annals of the Association of American Geographers* **69**, 463–4.

Saarinen, T. F. (1966) *Perception of drought hazard on the Great Plains*, University of Chicago, Department of Geography Research Paper No. 106.

Saarinen, T. F. (1973a) The use of projective techniques in geographic research, in W. H. Ittelson (ed.) *Environment and Cognition*, Seminar Press, New York, pp. 29–52.

Saarinen, T. F. (1973b) Student views of the world, in R. M. Downs and D. Stea (eds) *Image and Environment*, Aldine, Chicago, pp. 148–61.

Saarinen, T. F. (1974) Problems in the use of a standardised questionnaire for cross-cultural research on perception of natural hazards, in G. F. White (ed.) *Natural Hazards: local, national, global*, Oxford University Press, London, pp. 180–4.

Saarinen, T. F. (1976) *Environmental Planning: perception and behaviour*, Houghton Mifflin: Boston.

Saarinen, T. F. (1979) Commentary-critique of Bunting-Guelke paper, *Annals of the Association of American Geographers* **69**, 464–8.

Sadalla, E. K. (1978) Population size, structural differentiation and human behaviour, *Environment and Behaviour* **10**, 271–92.

Sadalla, E. K. and **Magel, S. G.** (1980) The perception of traversed distance, *Environment and Behaviour* 12, 65–80.

Sadalla, E. K. and **Staplin, L. J.** (1980a) The perception of traversed distance: intersections, *Environment and Behaviour* 12, 167–82.

Sadalla, E. K. and **Staplin, L. J.** (1980b) An information storage model for distance cognition, *Environment and Behaviour* 12, 183–93.

Sagan, C. (1977) *The Dragons of Eden*, Ballantine Books: New York.

Sainsbury, P. (1955) *Suicide in London*, Chapman and Hall: London.

Salins, P. D. (1971) Household location patterns in American metropolitan areas, *Economic Geography* 47, 234–48.

Salling, M. and **Harvey, M. E.** (1981) Poverty, personality, and sensitivity to residential stressors, *Environment and Behaviour* 13, 131–64.

Salter, C. L. and **Lloyd, W. J.** (1976) *Landscape in literature*, Association of American Geographers Commission on College Geography Resource Paper 76–3: Washington.

Samuels, M. S. (1978) Existentialism and human geography, in D. Ley and M. S. Samuels (eds) *Humanistic Geography: prospects and problems*, Maaroufa Press, Chicago, pp. 22–40.

Samuels, M. S. (1981) An existential geography, in M. E. Harvey and B. P. Holly (eds) *Themes in Geographic Thought*, Croom Helm, London, pp. 115–32.

Sanders, R. A. and **Porter, P. W.** (1974) Shape in revealed mental maps, *Annals of the Association of American Geographers* 64, 258–67.

Savage, L. J. (1951) The theory of statistical decision, *Journal of the American Statistical Association* 46, 55–67.

Schmid, C. F. (1960) Urban crime areas, *American Sociological Review* 25, 527–42 and 655–78.

Schmid, C. F. and **Tagishira, K.** (1965) Ecological and demographic ideas: a methodological analysis, *Demography* 1, 194–211.

Schmidt, D. E., **Goldman, R. D.** and **Feimer, W.** (1979) Perceptions of crowding: predicting at the residence, neighbourhood and city levels, *Environment and Behaviour* 11, 105–30.

Schmitt, R. C. (1963) Implications of density in Hong Kong, *Journal of the American Institute of Planners* 24, 210–17.

Schmitt, R. C. (1966) Density, health, and social disorganisation, *Journal of the American Institute of Planners* 32, 38–40.

Schmitt, R. C., **Lane, L. Y. S.** and **Nishi, S.** (1978) Density, health and social disorganization revisited, *Journal of the American Institute of Planners* 44, 201–12.

Schneider, C. H. P. (1975) Models of space searching in urban areas, *Geographical Analysis* 7, 173–86.

Schneider, M. (1959) Gravity models and trip distribution theory, *Papers and Proceedings of the Regional Science Association* 5, 51–6.

Schnore, L. F. (1965) *The Urban Scene*, Free Press: New York:

Schorr, A. L. (1963) *Slums and Social Insecurity*, Department of Health, Education and Welfare: Washington.

Schuler, H. J. (1979) A disaggregate store-choice model of spatial decision-making, *Professional Geographer* 31, 146–56.

Schutz, A. (1960) The social world and the theory of social action, *Social Research* 27, 205–21.

Schutz, A. (1967) *Phenomenology and the Social World* (trans. G. Walsh and F. Lehnert), Northwestern University Press: Evanston.

Scott, P. (1972) The spatial analysis of crime and delinquency, *Australian Geographical Studies* 10, 1–18.

Seamon, D. (1979) *A Geography of the Lifeworld*, St Martin's Press: New York.

Seligman, M. P. (1975) *Helplessness*, Freeman: San Francisco.

Seltzer, J. and **Wilson, S. A.** (1980) Leisure patterns among four day workers, *Journal of Leisure Research* 12, 116–27.

Severy, L. (ed) (1978) *Crowding*, Human Sciences Press: New York. (Special issue of *Journal of Population*).

Shafer, E. and **Mietz, J.** (1968) Aesthetic and emotional experiences rate high with north-west wilderness hikers, *Environment and Behaviour* 1, 186–7.

Shannon, C. E. and **Weaver, W.** (1949) *The Mathematical Theory of Communication*, University of Illinois Press: Urbana.

Shannon, G. W. (1977) Space, time and illness behaviour, *Social Science and Medicine* 11D, 683–9.

Sharrod, D. R. and **Davis, R.** (1974) Environmental determinants of altruism, *Journal of Experimental Social Psychology* 10, 468–79.

Shaw, C. R. and **McKay, H. D.** (1929) *Delinquency Areas*, University of Chicago Press: Chicago.

Shaw, C. R. and **McKay, H. D.** (1942) *Juvenile Delinquency and Urban Areas*, University of Chicago Press: Chicago.

Shaw, R. P. (1975) *Migration Theory and Fact: a review and bibliography of current literature*, Regional Science Research Institute: Philadelphia.

Sheehan, L. and **Hewitt, K.** (1969) *A pilot survey of global natural disasters of the past twenty years*, University of Toronto Natural Hazard Research, Working Paper No. 11.

Shepherd, I. D.H. and **Thomas, C. J.** (1980) Urban consumer behaviour, in J. A. Dawson (ed.) *Retail Geography*, Croom Helm, London, pp. 18–94.

Sherman, R. C., **Croxton, J.** and **Giovanatto, J.** (1979) Investigating cognitive representations of spatial relationships, *Environment and Behaviour* 11, 209–26.

Shevky, E. and **Bell, W.** (1955) *Social Area Analysis*, Stanford University Press: Stanford.

Shevky, E. and **Williams, M.** (1949) *The Social Areas of Los Angeles*, University of California Press: Los Angeles.

Shippee, G., **Burroughs, J.** and **Wakefield, S.** (1980) Dissonance theory revisited: perception of environmental hazards in residential areas, *Environment and Behaviour* 12, 33–52.

Shoard, M. (1980) *The Theft of the Countryside*, Temple Smith: London.

Short, J. R. (1978a) Residential mobility in the private housing market of Bristol, *Transactions of the Institute of British Geographers* 3, 533–47.

Short, J. R. (1978b) Residential mobility, *Progress in Geography* 2, 419–47.

Short, P. (1979) 'Victims' and 'helpers', in R. L. Heathcote and B. G. Thom (eds) *Natural Hazards in Australia*, Australian Academy of Science, Canberra, pp. 448–59.

Siegel, A. W., **Herman, J. F.**, **Allen, G. L.** and **Kirasic, K. C.** (1979) The development of cognitive maps of large-and small-scale spaces, *Child Development* 50, 582–5.

Silk, J. (1971) *Search behaviour: general characterization and review of the literature in the social sciences*, University of Reading, Geographical Paper No. 7.

Sillitoe, K. K. (1969) *Planning for Leisure*, HMSO: London.

Simmel, G. (1957) The metropolis and mental life, in P. K. Hatt and A. J. Reiss (eds) *Cities and Society*, Free Press, New York, pp. 635–46.

Simmons, I. G. (1975) *Rural Recreation in the Industrial World*, Arnold: London.

Simmons, J. (1968) Changing residence in the city: a review of

intra-urban mobility, *Geographical Review* 58, 621–51.
Simmons, J. (1974) *Pattern of residential movement in Metropolitan Toronto*, University of Toronto, Department of Geography Research Publications No. 13.
Simon, H. A. (1952) A behavioural model of rational choice, *Quarterly Journal of Economics* 69, 99–118.
Simon, H. A. (1957) *Models of Man: social and rational*, Wiley: New York.
Simon, H. A. (1959) Theories of decision-making in economics and behavioural science, *American Economic Review* 49, 253–83.
Simon, H. A. (1976) *Administrative Behaviour: a study of decision making processes in administrative organisation* (3rd edn), Free Press: Glencoe.
Simpson-Housley, P. and **Bradshaw, P.** (1978) Personality and the perception of earthquake hazard, *Australian Geographical Studies*, 16, 65–72.
Skinner, B. F. (1971) *Beyond Freedom and Dignity*, Knopf: New York.
Skinner, B. F. (1974) *About Behaviourism*, Jonathan Cape: London.
Slovic, P., Kunreuther, H. and **White, G. F.** (1974) Decision processes, rationality and adjustment to natural hazards, in G. F. White (ed) *Natural Hazards: local, national, global*, Oxford University Press, London, pp. 187–205.
Smith, C. A. and **Smith, C. J.** (1978) Locating natural neighbours in the urban community, *Area* 10, 102–10.
Smith, C. J. (1976) Residential neighbourhoods as humane environments, *Environment and Planning* 8A, 311–26.
Smith, C. J. (1977) *The geography of mental health*, Association of American Geographers, Commission on College Geography Resource Paper No. 76–4: Washington.
Smith, C. J. (1978) Self-help and social networks in the urban community, *Ekistics* 46, 106–15.
Smith, C. J. and **Hanham, R. Q.** (1981) Proximity and the formation of public attitudes towards mental illness, *Environment and Planning A* 13, 147–66.
Smith, D. M. (1971) *Industrial Location: an economic geographical analysis*, Wiley: New York.
Smith, D. M. (1973) *The Geography of Social Well-being in the United States*, McGraw-Hill: New York.
Smith, D. M. (1977) *Human Geography: a welfare approach*, Arnold: London.
Smith, D. M. (1979a) Modelling industrial location: towards a broader view of the space economy, in F. E. I. Hamilton and G. J. R. Linge (eds) *Spatial Analysis, Industry and the Industrial Environment: progress in research and applications: Vol. 1: Industrial systems*, Wiley, Chichester, pp. 37–55.
Smith, D. M. (1979b) *Where the Grass is Greener: living in an unequal world, Penguin: Harmondsworth.*
Smith, G. C. (1976) The spatial information fields of urban consumers, *Transactions of the Institute of British Geographers* 1, 175–89.
Smith, G. C., Shaw, D. J. B. and **Huckle, P. R.** (1979) Children's perception of a downtown shopping centre, *Professional Geographer* 31, 157–64.
Smith, M. A., Parker, S. and **Smith, C. S.** (eds) (1973) *Leisure and Society in Britain*, Allen Lane: London.
Smith, N. (1979) Geography, science and post-positivist modes of explanation, *Progress in Human Geography* 3, 356–83.
Smith, P. F. (1976) *The Syntax of Cities*, Hutchinson: London.
Smith, S. J. (1981) Humanistic method in contemporary social geography, *Area* 13, 293–8.
Smith, S. J. and **Clark, W. A. V.** (1982) Housing market search behaviour and expected utility theory: I. Measuring preferences for housing, *Environment and Planning A* 14, 681–98.
Smith, S. L. J. (1980) Intervening opportunities to urban recreation centres, *Journal of Leisure Research* 12, 64–72.
Smith, T. R., Clark, W. A. V., Huff, J. O. and **Shapiro, P.** (1979) A decision making and search model for intra-urban migration, *Geographical Analysis* 11, 1–22.
Smith, V. and **Wilde, P.** (1977) The multiplier effect of tourism in western Tasmania, in D. Mercer (ed.) *Leisure and Recreation in Australia*, Sorrett, Melbourne, pp. 163–72.
Smith, V. K. and **Kopp, R. J.** (1980) The spatial limits of the travel cost recreational demand model, *Land Economics* 56, 64–72.
Snow, R. E. and **Han, J.** (1981) Density and pathology in Stockholm and Copenhagen, *International Journal of Environmental Studies* 17, 121–7.
Sommer, R. (1969) *Personal Space: the behavioural basis of design*, Prentice Hall: Englewood Cliffs.
Sonnenfeld, J. (1972) Geography, perception, and the behavioural environment, in P. W. English, and R. C. Mayfield (eds) *Man, Space and Environment*, Oxford University Press, New York, pp. 244–50.
Sonnenfeld, J. (1982) Egocentric perspectives on geographic orientation, *Annals of the Association of American Geographers* 72, 68–76.
Speare, A. Jr. (1974) Residential satisfaction as an intervening variable in residential mobility, *Demography* 11, 173–88.
Spector, A. N., Brown, L. A. and **Malecki, E. J.** (1976) Acquaintance circles and communication: an exploration of hypotheses relating to innovation adoption, *Professional Geographer* 28, 267–76.
Spencer, C. and **Weetman, M.** (1981) The microgenesis of cognitive maps: a longitudinal study of new residents of an urban area, *Transactions of the Institute of British Geographers* 6, 375–84.
Spencer, D. (1973) *An evaluation of cognitive mapping in neighbourhood perception*, University of Birmingham, Centre for Urban and Regional Studies Research Memorandum No. 23.
Sprout, H. and **Sprout, M.** (1957) Environmental factors in the study of international politics, *Journal of Conflict Resolution* 1, 309–28.
Stafford, H. A. (1972) The geography of manufacturers, *Progress in Geography* 4, 181–215.
Stamp, L. D. (1964) *The Geography of Life and Death*, Fontana: London.
Starr, C. and **Whipple, C.** (1980) Risks of risk decisions, *Science* 208, 1114–19.
Stea, D. (1969) The measurement of mental maps: an experimental model for studying conceptual places, in K. R. Cox and R. G. Golledge (eds) *Behavioural problems in geography*, Northwestern University Studies in Geography No. 17, pp. 228–53.
Stea, D. (1973) Rats, men and spatial behaviour, all revisited or what animal geographers have to say to human geographers, *Professional Geographer* 25, 106–12.
Stea, D. (1976) Program notes on a spatial fugue, in G. T. Moore and R. G. Golledge (eds) *Environmental Knowing*, Dowden, Hutchinson and Ross, Stroudsburg, pp. 106–20.
Stea, D. and **Blaut, J. M.** (1973) Some preliminary observations on spatial learning in school children, in R. M. Downs and D. Stea (eds) *Image and Environment*, Aldine, Chicago, pp. 226–34.

Stea, D. and **Downs, R. M.** (1970) From the outside looking in at the inside looking out, *Environment and Behaviour* **2**, 3–12.

Stein, M. (1960) *The Eclipse of Community*, Harper and Row: New York.

Steinitz, C. (1968) Meaning and the congruence of urban form and activity, *Journal of the American Institute of Planners* **34**, 233–48.

Stokols, D. (1976) The experience of crowding in primary and secondary environments, *Environment and Behaviour* **8**, 49–86.

Stokols, D. (1978) Environmental psychology, *Annual Review of Psychology* **29**, 253–95.

Stone, G. P. (1954) City shoppers and urban identification, *American Journal of Sociology* **60**, 36–45.

Stouffer, S. A. (1940) Intervening opportunities: a theory relating mobility and distance, *American Sociological Review* **5**, 845–67.

Stouffer, S. A. (1960) Intervening opportunities and competing migrants, *Journal of Regional Science* **2**, 1–26.

Strasser, S. (1963) *Phenomenology and the Human Sciences: a contribution to a new scientific ideal*, Duquesne University Press: Pittsburgh.

Strauss, A. L. (1961) *Images of the American City*, Free Press: New York.

Suttles, G. D. (1972) *The Social Construction of Communities*, University of Chicago Press: Chicago.

Svart, L. (1974) On the priority of behaviour in behavioural research: a dissenting view, *Area* **6**, 301–5.

Sweetser, F. L. (1965a) Factorial ecology: Helsinki, *Demography* **2**, 372–85.

Sweetser, F. L. (1965b) Factor structure as ecological structure in Helsinki and Boston, *Acta Sociologica* **8**, 205–25.

Symanski, R. (1979) Hobos, freight trains, and me, *Canadian Geographer* **23**, 103–18.

Szalai, A. (1966) Trends in comparative time budget research, *American Behavioural Scientist* **10**, 1–31.

Tata, R. J., **Hurn, S.** and **Lee, D.** (1975) Defensible space in a housing project: a case study from South Florida, *Professional Geographer* **27**, 297–303.

Tatalovich, R. (1975) 'Friends and neighbours' voting: Mississippi, 1943–73, *Journal of Politics* **37**, 807–14.

Taylor, C. C. and **Townsend, A. R.** (1976) The local 'sense of place' as evidenced in North-East England, *Urban Studies* **13**, 133–46.

Taylor, I., **Walton, P.** and **Young, J.** (1973) *The New Criminology*, Routledge and Kegan Paul: London.

Taylor, M. J (1973) Local linkage, external economies and the ironfoundry industry of the West Midlands and East Lancashire conurbations, *Regional Studies* **7**, 387–400.

Taylor, M. J. (1975) Organizational growth, spatial interaction and location decision-making, *Regional Studies* **9**, 313–23.

Taylor, M. J. (1977) Corporate space preferences: a New Zealand example, *Environment and Planning A* **9**, 1157–67.

Taylor, M. J. (1978a) Spatial competition and the sales linkages of Auckland manufacturers, in F. E. I. Hamilton (ed.) *Contemporary Industrialization: spatial analysis and regional development*, Longman, London, pp. 144–57.

Taylor, M. J. (1978b) Perceived distance and spatial interaction, *Environment and Planning A* **10**, 1171–7.

Taylor, M. J. (1980) Space and time in industrial linkage, *Area* **12**, 150–2.

Taylor, M. J. and **McDermott, P. J.** (1977) Perception of location and decision-making: the example of New Zealand manufacturing, *New Zealand Geographer* **33**, 26–33.

Taylor, M. J. and **Neville, R. J. W.** (1980) The malleability of managerial attitudes: the case of Singapore's plastics and electronics manufacturers, *Singapore Journal of Tropical Geography* **1**, 55–68.

Taylor, M. J. and **Thrift, N. J.** (1979) A plea for the development of a coherent theoretical approach to the geography of enterprise, *Environment and Planning A* **11**, 973–5.

Taylor, P. J. (1973) Some implications of the spatial organization of elections, *Transactions of the Institute of British Geographers* **60**, 121–36.

Taylor, P. J. (1982) A materialist framework for political geography, *Transactions of the Institute of British Geographers* **7**, 15–34.

Taylor, P. J. and **Johnston, R. J.** (1979) *Geography of Elections*, Penguin: Harmondsworth.

Taylor, R. B. (1981) Perception of density: individual differences, *Environment and Behaviour* **13**, 3–22.

Taylor, R. C. (1969) Migration and motivation: a study of determinants and types, in J. A. Jackson (ed.) *Migration*, Cambridge University Press, Cambridge, pp. 99–134.

Ter Heide, H. (1963) Migration models and their significance for population forecasts, *Milbank Memorial Fund Quarterly* **41**, 56–76.

Theoderson, G. A. (ed.) (1961) *Studies in Human Ecology*, New York: Harper and Row.

Thomas, C. J. (1976) Sociospatial differentiation and the use of services, in D. T. Herbert and R. J. Johnston (eds) *Social Areas in Cities. Vol. II Spatial perspectives on problems and policies*, Wiley, London, pp. 17–64.

Thomas, M. (1980) Explanatory frameworks for growth and change in multiregional firms, *Economic Geography* **56**, 1–17.

Thompson, D. L. (1963) New concept: subjective distance, *Journal of Retailing* **39**, 1–6.

Thompson, E. P. (1978) *The Poverty of Theory and Other Essays*, Merlin Press: London.

Thompson, K. A. (1971) Introductory essay, in G. Gurvitch, *The Social Frameworks of Knowledge* (trans. M. A. and K. A. Thompson), Blackwell, Oxford, pp. ix–xxxvi.

Thorngren, B. (1970) How do contact systems affect regional development?, *Environment and Planning* **2**, 409–27.

Thorngren, B. (1973) Swedish office dispersal, in M. Bannon (ed.) *Office Location and Regional Development*, An Foras Forbartha, Dublin, pp. 9–20.

Thorns, D. C. (1976) *The Quest for Community*, Allen and Unwin: London.

Thorns, D. C. (1980a) Constraints versus choices in the analysis of housing allocation and residential mobility, in C. Ungerson and V. Karn (eds) *The Consumer Experience of Housing*, Gower, Farnborough, pp. 50–68.

Thorns, D. C. (1980b) *The role of the family life cycle in residential mobility*, University of Birmingham, Centre for Urban and Regional Studies Workshop Paper No. 69.

Thrift, N. J. (1977) Time and theory in human geography, *Progress in Human Geography* **1**, 65–101 and 413–57.

Thrift, M. J. (1981) Behavioural geography, in N. Wrigley and R. J. Bennett (eds) *Quantitative Geography: a British view*, Routledge and Kegan Paul, London, pp. 352–65.

Timmermans, H. (1979) A spatial preference model of regional shopping behaviour, *Tijdschrift voor Economische en Sociale Geografie* **70**, 45–8.

Timmermans, H. (1980) Unidimensional conjoint measurement models and consumer decision-making, *Area* **12**, 291–300.

Timmermans, H. (1981) Spatial choice behaviour in different environmental settings: an application of the revealed preference approach, *Geografiska Annaler* **63B**, 57–67.

Timmermans, H., **Van Der Heijden, R.** and **Westerveld, H.** (1982) Cognition of urban retailing structures: a Dutch case study, *Tijdschrift voor Economische en Sociale Geografie* **73**, 2–12.

Timms, D. W. G. (1965) The spatial distribution of social deviants in Luton, England, *Australian and New Zealand Journal of Sociology* **1**, 38–52.

Timms, D. W. G. (1971) *The Urban Mosaic: towards a theory of residential differentiation*, Cambridge University Press: Cambridge.

Titchener, J. L. and **Kapp, F. T.** (1976) Family and character change at Buffalo Creek, *American Journal of Psychiatry* **133**, 295–9.

Tinsley, H. E. and **Kass, R. A.** (1979) The latent structure of the need satisfying properties of leisure activities, *Journal of Leisure Research* **11**, 278–91.

Travis, A. S., **Veal, A. J.**, **Duesbury, K.** and **White, J.** (1981) *The role of central government in relation is the provision of leisure services in England and Wales*, Centre for Urban and Regional Studies, Research Memorandum **86**, University of Birmingham.

Tivers, J. (1977) *Constraints on spatial activity patterns: women with young children*, University of London, King's College Department of Geography Occasional Paper No. 6.

Tolman, E. C. (1932) *Purposive Behaviour in Animals and Men*, Century Crofts: New York.

Tolman, E. C. (1948) Cognitive maps in rats and men, *Psychological Review* 55, 189–208.

Tolman, E. C. (1952) A cognition-motivation model, *Psychological Review* **59**, 389–408.

Tönnies, F. (1887) *Community and Society* (1963 edn) (Trans. C. P. Loomis), Harper: New York.

Törnqvist, G. E. (1968) *Flows of Information and the Location of Economic Activity*, Lund Studies in Geography Series B, No. 30.

Törnqvist, G. E. (1970) *Contact Systems and Regional Development*, Lund Studies in Geography, Series B., No. 35.

Törnqvist, G. E. (1973) Contact requirements and travel facilities in contact models of Sweden and regional development alternatives in the future, in A. R. Pred and G. E. Törnqvist, *Systems of Cities and Information Flows: two essays*, Lund Studies in Geography, Series B, No. 38, 85–121.

Törnqvist, G. E. (1977) The geography of economic activities: some critical viewpoints on theory and application, *Economic Geography* **53**, 153–62.

Törnqvist, G. E. (1978) Swedish industry as a spatial system, in F. E. I. Hamilton (ed.) *Contemporary Industrialization: spatial analysis and regional development*, Longman, London, pp. 86–109.

Townroe, P. M. (1974) Post-move stability and the location decision, in F. E. I. Hamilton (ed.) *Spatial Perspectives on Industrial Organization and Decision-Making*, Wiley, London, pp. 287–307.

Townroe, P. M. (1975) Approaches to the study of industrial location, in D. Massey and W. I. Morrison (eds) *Industrial location: alternative frameworks*, Centre for Environmental Studies Conference Paper No. 15, London, pp. 32–40.

Townsend, A. R. and **Taylor, C. D.** (1975) Regional culture and identity in industrialized societies: the case of north-east England, *Regional Studies* **9**, 379–94.

Trowbridge, C. D. (1913) On fundamental methods of orientation and 'imaginary maps', *Science* **88**, 888–96.

Tuan, Y. F. (1971) Geography, phenomenology, and the study of human nature, *Canadian Geographer* **15**, 181–92.

Tuan, Y. F. (1972) Structuralism, existentialism, and environmental perception, *Environment and Behaviour* **4**, 319–31.

Tuan, Y. F. (1973) Ambiguity in attitudes toward environment, *Annals of the Association of American Geographers* **63**, 411–23.

Tuan, Y. F. (1974a) *Topophilia: a study of environmental perception, attitudes, and values*, Prentice-Hall: Englewood Cliffs.

Tuan, Y. F. (1974b) Space and place: humanistic perspective, *Progress in Geography* **6**, 211–52.

Tuan, Y. F. (1974c) Commentary on 'Values in geography', in A. Buttimer, *Values in geography*, Association of American Geographers Resource paper No. 24, Washington, pp. 54–8.

Tuan, Y. F. (1975a) Images and mental maps, *Annals of the Association of American Geographers* **65**, 205–13.

Tuan, Y. F. (1975b) Place an experiential perspective, *Geographical Review* **65**, 151–65.

Tuan, Y. F. (1976a) Literature, experience, and environmental knowing, in G. T. Moore and R. G. Golledge (eds) *Environmental Knowing*, Dowden, Hutchinson and Ross, Stroudsburg, pp. 260–71.

Tuan, Y. F. (1976b) Humanistic geography, *Annals of the Association of American Geographers* **66**, 266–76.

Tuan, Y. F. (1977) *Space and Place: the perspective of experience*, Arnold: London.

Tuan, Y.F. (1978a) Literature and geography: implications for geographical research, in D. Ley and M. S. Samuels (eds) *Humanistic Geography: prospects and problems*, Maaroufa, Chicago, pp. 194–206.

Tuan Y. F. (1978b) Sign and metaphor, *Annals of the Association of American Geographers* **68**, 363–72.

Tuan, Y. F. (1979) Thought and landscape: the eye and the mind's eye, in D. W. Meinig (ed.) *The Interpretation of Ordinary Landscapes*, Oxford University Press, New York, pp. 89–102.

Turner, A. (1981) National parks and pressure groups in New South Wales, in D. Mercer (ed.) *Outdoor Recreation: Australian Perspectives*, Sorrett, Melbourne, pp. 156–69.

Tversky, B. (1981) Distortions in memory for maps, *Cognitive Psychology* **13**, 407–33.

Udry, J. R. Increasing scale and spatial differentiation: new tests of two theories from Shevky and Bell, *Social Forces* **42**, 404–13.

Ulrich, R. S. and **Addoms, D. L.** (1981) Psychological and recreational benefits of a residential park, *Journal of Leisure Research* **13**, 43–65.

Unkel, M. B. (1981) Physical recreation participation of females and males during life cycle, *Leisure Sciences* **4**, 1–27.

Van Arsdol, M. D., **Camilleri, S. F.** and **Schmid, C. F.** (1958) The generality of urban social area indexes, *American Sociological Review* **23**, 277–84.

Vance, J. E. (1977) *The Scene of Man: the role and structure of the city in the geography of western civilization*, Harper and Row: New York.

Van Doren, C. S., **Priddle, G. B.** and **Lewis, J. E.** (eds) (1979) *Land and Leisure: concepts and methods in outdoor recreation*, Methuen: London.

Van Lierop, W. and **Nijkamp, P.** (1980) Spatial choice and interaction models: criteria and aggregation, *Urban Studies* **17**, 299–311.

Verbrugge, L. M. and **Taylor, R. D.** (1980) Consequences of population density and size, *Urban Affairs Quarterly* **16**, 135–60.

Vickerman, R. W. (1975) *The Economics of Leisure and Behaviour*, Macmillan: London.

Waddell, E. (1977) The hazards of scientism: a review article, *Human Ecology* **5**, 69–76.

Wallace, A. F. C. (1957) Mazeway disintegration: the individual's perception of socio-cultural disorganization, *Human Organization* **16**, 15–19.

Walmsley, D. J. (1972a) *Systems Theory*, Australian National University, Department of Human Geography Publication HG7.

Walmsley, D. J. (1972b) The influence of spatial opportunities on the journey-to-consume: a Sydney case study, *Royal Australian Planning Institute Journal* **10**, 144–8.

Walmsley, D. J. (1973) The simple behaviour system: an appraisal and an elaboration, *Geografiska Annaler* **55B**, 49–56.

Walmsley, D. J. (1974a) Emotional involvement and subjective distance: a modification of the inverse square root law, *Journal of Psychology* **87**, 9–19.

Walmsley, D. J. (1974b) Positivism and phenomenology in human geography, *Canadian Geographer* **18**, 95–107.

Walmsley, D. J. (1975) Normalized distance: an illustration of the interdependence of mobility and opportunity, *Australian Journal of Marketing Research* **8**, 66–8.

Walmsley, D. J. (1976) Territory and neighbourhood in suburban Sydney, *Royal Australian Planning Institute Journal* **14**, 68–9.

Walmsley, D. J. (1977) Congruence of overt behaviour with preference structures, *Psychological Reports* **41**, 1082.

Walmsley, D. J. (1978) Stimulus complexity in distance distortion, *Professional Geographer* **30**, 14–9.

Walmsley, D. J. (1979) Time and human geography, *Australian Geographical Studies* **17**, 223–9.

Walmsley, D. J. (1980) Spatial bias in Australian news reporting, *Australian Geographer* **14**, 342–9.

Walmsley, D. J. (1982a) Personality and regional preference structures: a study of introversion-extraversion, *Professional Geographer* **34**, 279–88.

Walmsley, D. J. (1982b) Mass media and spatial awareness, *Tijdschrift voor Economische en Sociale Geografie* **73**, 32–42.

Walmsley, D. J. Boskovic, R. and **Pigram, J.** (1981) *Tourism and Crime*, University of New England Department of Geography: Armidale.

Walsh, J. A. and **Webber, M. J.** (1977) Information theory: some concepts and measures, *Environment and Planning A* **9**, 395–417.

Wapner, S., Kaplan, B. and **Cohen, S. B.** (1973) An organismic-developmental perspective for understanding transactions of men in environments, *Environment and Behaviour* **5**, 255–89.

Warburton, P. B. (1981) Cognitive images of water resources with specific references to water-based recreation in Leicester, unpublished MA Thesis University of Leicester.

Warnock, M. (1970) *Existentialism*, Oxford University Press: London.

Watson, J. B. (1924) *Behaviourism*, Norton: New York.

Watson, J. W. (1969) The role of illusion in North American geography: a note on the geography of North American settlement, *Canadian Geographer* **13**, 10–27.

Watson, J. W. (1976a) The image of nature in America, in J. W. Watson and T. O'Riordan (eds) *The American Environment: perceptions and policies*, Wiley, New York, pp. 63–75.

Watson, J. W. (1976b) Image regions, in J. W. Watson and T. O'Riordan (eds) *The American Environment: perceptions and policies*, Wiley, New York, pp. 15–28.

Watson, J. W. and **O'Riordan, T.** (eds) (1976) *The American Environment: perceptions and policies*, Wiley: New York.

Watson, M. K. (1978) The scale problem in human geography, *Geografiska Annaler* **60B**, 36–47.

Webber, D. L. (1976) Darwin Cyclone: an exploration of disaster behaviour, *Australian Journal of Social Issues* **11**, 54–63.

Webber, M. J (1969) Sub-optimal behaviour and the concept of maximum profits in location theory, *Australian Geographical Studies* **7**, 1–8.

Webber, M. J (1971) Empirical verifiability of classical central place theory, *Geographical Analysis* **3**, 15–28.

Webber, M. J. (1972) *Impact of Uncertainty on Location*, Australian National University Press: Canberra.

Webber, M. J. (1978) *Information Theory and Urban Spatial Structure*, Croom Helm: London.

Webber, M. M. (1963) Order in diversity: community without propinquity, in L. Wingo (ed.) *Cities and Space*, Johns Hopkins Press, Baltimore pp. 23–56.

Webber, M. M. (1964a) The urban place and the non-place urban realm, in M. M. Webber *et al.* (eds) *Explorations in Urban Structure*, University of Pennsylvania Press, Philadelphia, pp. 79–153.

Webber, M. M. (1964b) Culture, territoriality and the elastic mile, *Papers and Proceedings of the Regional Science Association* **13**, 59–70.

Weber, A. (1929) *Theory of the Location of Industries* (trans C. J. Friedrich), University of Chicago Press: Chicago.

Weinberg, D. H. (1979) The determinants of intra-urban household mobility, *Regional Science and Urban Economics* **9**, 219–46.

Wellman, B. (1979) The community question, *American Journal of Sociology* **84**, 1201–31.

Wellman, B. and **Crump, B.** (1978) *Networks, Neighbourhoods and communities: approaches to the study of the community question*, University of Toronto, Centre for Urban and Community Studies Research Paper No. 97.

Wellman, B. and **Leighton, B.** (1979) Networks, neighbours and communities: approaches to the study of the community question, *Urban Affairs Quarterly* **14**, 363–90.

West, P. C. and **Merriam, L. C.** (1970) Outdoor recreation and family cohesiveness, *Journal of Leisure Research* **2**, 251–9.

Western, J. S. and **Milne, G.** (1979) Some social effects of a natural hazard: Darwin residents and Cyclone Tracy, In R. L. Heathcote and B. G. Thom (eds) *Natural Hazards in Australia*, Australian Academy of Science, Canberra, pp. 488–502.

Westin, A. F. (1967) *Privacy and Freedom*, Atheneum: New York.

Wettenhall, R. L. (1975) *Bushfire Disaster: an Australian community in crisis*, Angus and Robertson: Sydney.

Wettenhall, R. L. and **Power, J. M.** (1969) Bureaucracy and disaster. I: Prelude to the 1967 Tasmanian bushfires, *Public Administration* **28**, 263–77.

Wheatley, P. (1976) Levels of space awareness in the traditional Islamic city, *Ekistics* **42**, 354–66.

White, G. F. (1945) *Human adjustment to floods: a geographical approach to the flood problem in the United*

States, University of Chicago Department of Geography Research Paper No. 29.

White, G. F. (1964) *Choice of adjustments to floods*, University of Chicago, Department of Geography Research Paper No. 93.

White, G. F. (1974) Natural hazards research: concepts, methods, and policy implications, in G. F. White (ed.) *Natural Hazards: local, national, global*, Oxford University Press, London, pp. 3–16.

White, G. F. and **Haas, J. E.** (1975) *Assessment of Research on Natural Hazards*, MIT Press: Cambridge, Mass.

White, G. F. *et al.* (1958) *Changes in urban occupance of flood plains in the United States*, University of Chicago, Department of Geography Research Paper No. 57.

White, P. and **Wood, R.** (1980) *The Geographical Impact of Migration*, Longman: London.

Whitelaw, J. S. and Gregson, J. S. (1972) *Search Procedures in the Intra-urban Migration Process*, Monash University Publication in Geography No. 2,

Whitlock, F. A. (1973) Suicide in England and Wales 1959–63, Part 2: London, *Psychological Medicine* **3**, 411–20.

Whittow, J. (1980) *Disasters: the anatomy of environmental hazards*, Penguin: Harmondsworth.

Whorf, B. L. (1956) *Language, Thought, and Reality* (ed. J. B. Carroll), MIT Press: Cambridge, Mass.

Williams, C. H. (1977) Ethnic perceptions of Arcadia, *Cahiers de Géographie de Québec* **21**, 243–68.

Williams, H. B. (1957) Some functions of communication in crisis behaviour, *Human Organization* **16**, 15–19.

Williams, M. (1979) The perception of the hazard of soil erosion in South Australia: a review, in R. L. Heathcote and B. G. Thom (eds) *Natural Hazards in Australia*, Australian Academy of Science, Canberra.

Williams, N. J. (1979) The definition of shopper types as an aid in the analysis of spatial consumer behaviour, *Tijdschrift voor Economische en Sociale Geografie* **70**, 157–63.

Williams, N. J. (1981) Attitudes and consumer spatial behaviour, *Tijdschrift voor Economische en Sociale Geografie* **72**, 145–54.

Williams, R. (1973) *The Country and the City*, Chatto and Windus: London.

Willis, K. G. (1974) *Problems in Migration Analysis*, Saxon House: Farnborough.

Wilman, E. A. (1980) The value of time in recreation benefit studies, *Journal of Environmental Economics and Management* **7**, 272–86.

Wilmott, P. and **Young, M.** (1960) *Family and Class in a London Suburb*, Routledge and Kegan Paul: London.

Wilner, D. M., and **Walkley, R. P.** (1963) Effect of housing on health and performance, in L. Duhl (ed.) *The Urban Condition*, Simon and Schuster, New York, pp. 215–28.

Wilson, A. G. (1970a) *Entropy in urban and regional modelling*, Centre for Environmental, Studies Working Paper No. 26: London.

Wilson, A. G. (1970b) Advances and problems in distribution modelling, *Transportation Research* **4**, 1–18.

Wilson, A. G. (1971) A family of spatial interaction models and associated developments, *Environment and Planning* **3**, 1–32.

Wilson, A. G. and **Kirkby, M. J.** (1975) *Mathematics for Geographers and Planners*, Clarendon Press: Oxford.

Wilson, B. M. (1980) Social space and symbolic interaction, in A. Buttimer and D. Seamon (eds) *The Human Experience of Space and Place*, Croom Helm, London, pp. 135–47.

Wilson, C. and **Alexis, M.** (1962) Basic frameworks for decisions, W. J. Gove, and J. W. Dryson (eds) *The Making of Decisions: a reader in administrative behaviour*, Free Press, New York, pp. 193–5.

Wilson, E. O. (1978) Introduction: what is sociobiology? in M.S. Gregory, A. Silvers, and D. Sutch (eds) *Sociobiology and Human Nature*, Jossey-Bass, San Francisco, pp. 1–12.

Wingo, L. (1964) Recreation and urban development: a policy perspective, *Annals of the American Academy of Political and Social Science* **352**, 129–40.

Winsborough, H. H. (1965) The social consequences of higher population density, *Law and Contemporary Problems* **30**, 120–6.

Winters, C. (1979) The social identity of evolving neighbourhoods, *Landscape* **23**, 8–14.

Wirth, L. (1928) *The Ghetto*, University of Chicago Press: Chicago.

Wirth, L. (1938) Urbanism as a way of life, *American Journal of Sociology* **44**, 1–24.

Wiseman, R. F. and **Virden, M.** (1977) Spatial and social dimensions of intra-urban elderly migration, *Economic Geography* **53**, 1–13.

Witt, P. A. and **Bishop, D. W.** (1970) Situational antecedents to leisure behaviour, *Journal of Leisure Research* **2**, 64–72.

Wohlwill, J. F. (1970) The emerging discipline of environmental psychology, *American Psychologist* **25**, 303–12.

Wolpert, J. (1964) The decision process in spatial context, *Annals of the Association of American Geographers* **54**, 537–58.

Wolpert, J. (1965) Behavioural aspects of the decision to migrate, *Papers and Proceedings of the Regional Science Association* **15**, 159–72.

Wolpert, J. (1966) Migration as an adjustment to environmental stress, *Journal of Social Issues* **22**, 92–102.

Wolpert, J. (1970) Departures from the usual environment in locational analysis, *Annals of the Association of American Geographers* **60**, 220–9.

Wolpert, J., **Mumphrey, A.** and **Seley, J.** (1972) *Metropolitan neighbourhoods: participation and conflict over change*, Association of American Geographers Commission in College Geography Resource Paper No 16: Washington D C.

Womble, P. and **Studebaker, S.** (1981) Crowding in a national park campground: Katmai movement in Alaska, *Environment and Behaviour* **13**, 557–73.

Wong, K. Y. (1979) Maps in mind: an empirical study, *Environment and Planning* **A11**, 1289–1304.

Wood, L. J. (1970) Perception studies in geography, *Transactions of the Institute of British Geographers* **50**, 129–41.

Wood, P. A. (1975) Are behavioural approaches to industrial location theory doomed to be descriptive?, in D. Massey and W. I. Morrison (eds) *Industrial location: alternative frameworks*, Centre for Environmental Studies Conference Paper No. 15, London, pp. 41–8.

Wright, D. S., **Taylor, A.**, **Davies, D. R.**, **Sluckin, W. G.**, **Lee, S. G. M.** and **Reason, J. T.** (1970) *Introductory Psychology: an experimental approach*, Penguin: Harmondsworth.

Wright, J. K. (1947) Terrae incognitae: the place of the imagination in geography, *Annals of the Association of American Geographers* **37**, 1–15.

Wrigley, N. (1980) An approach to the modelling of shop-choice patterns: an exploratory analysis of purchasing patterns in a British city, in D. T. Herbert and R. J. Johnston (eds) *Geography and the Urban Environment. Vol. III*, Wiley, London, pp. 45–86.

Young, G. (1973) *Tourism: blessing or blight?*, Penguin. Harmondsworth.

Young, M. and **Willmott, p.** (1962) *Family and Kinship in East London*, Penguin: Harmondsworth.

Young, M. and **Willmott, P.** (1973) *The Symmetrical Family*, Penguin: Harmondsworth.

Zehner, R. B. (1972) Neighbourhood and community satisfaction, in J. F. Wohlwill and D. H. Carson (eds) *Environment and the Social Sciences*, American Psychological Association, Washington, pp. 169–83.

Zlutnick, S. and **Altman, I.** (1972) Crowding and human behaviour, in J. F. Wohlwill and D. H. Carson (eds) *Environment and the Social Sciences*, American Psychological Association Washington.

Zorbaugh, H. W. (1929) *The Gold Coast and the Slum*, University of Chicago Press. Chicago.

INDEX

accumulative fragmentalism, 51
action space, 6, 75
  and consumer behaviour, 84
  and industrial location, 105, 106, 107
  and migration, 141–2
  and recreation, 125
activity space, 75, 84, 92
  and migration flows, 141–2
activity system, 75, 97, 99
advertising
  and images, 52, 74, 108
  and recreational behaviour, 125
  see also media
age differences
  in activity patterns, 75, 121
  in cognitive mapping, 72
  in consumer behaviour, 83, 84
  in sensitivity to hazards, 115
  in social interaction, 93–4, 96, 97, 124
agenda setting, 53
alienation, from environment, 157–8
anomie, 27
anthropocentrism, 156–7
areal differentiation, 3
areas, 10, 65, 72
aspirations, 25
  and decision making, 57, 59–60
attitudes, 6, 11, 22

barriers, 10, 65, 72
behaviour
  behaviour in space *vs* spatial behaviour, 7
  behaviour settings, 10
  covert behaviour, 4, 79–80, 89
  discretionary behaviour, 54, 78, 79–80, 97
  information processing and resultant behaviour, 44
  obligatory behaviour, 78, 79–80, 97
  overt behaviour, 4, 12, 61, 74–8, 79–80, 83
  sensate and non-sensate behaviour, 39
behavioural matrix, 8, 57, 58, 101
  see also decision making, information handling
behavioural sink, 128
behaviouralism, 4
behaviourism, 9, 40, 45, 55
belonging, a sense of, 10, 89–91
  see also territoriality, uprootedness
bounded rationality, 5–6, 44, 57, 64
  in hazard adjustments, 109
  in industrial firms, 103–4, 106

brain structure, 9, 10
  and information storage, 44, 46
  hemispheric differences, 47

choice, *see* decision making
chronogeography, 76
class, 13, 18, 34
  and the localization of friendship ties, 94, 96
  class influences on voting, 146, 147, 150
cloze procedure, 68, 72–3
cluster analysis, 32, 33
cognition, 6, 7, 43, 64
  cognition in psychology, 9–10
  cognition of large areas, 49–52
  environmental cognition, 6, 7, 8, 11–14
cognitive dissonance theory, 115
cognitive distance, 68–70, 98
  and consumer behaviour, 88
  and route intersections, 70
  exaggeration of downtown distances, 69, 88
  see also images
cognitive maps, 8–9, 70–3
  as a metaphor, 72
  morphology of cognitive maps, 72
  see also mental maps, sketch maps
communications, 56, 104
  see also information flows
community, 26, 32–5, 48, 89, 118
  community without propinquity, 34, 52, 90
  see also neighbourhood
comparative statics, 12
compensatory theory, 122
conjoint analysis, 87
consciousness, *see* experiential environments, humanistic approaches
constraints
  on consumer behaviour, 88
  on general behaviour, 6, 13
  on information availability, 42
  on migration, 141, 144
  on recreational behaviour, 124
constructive alternativism, 51
constructivism, 45
consumer behaviour, 60–1, 81–8
  consumer information and usage fields, 84
  images of the retail environment, 84–6
  learning and decision making, 60–1, 86–7
  revealed space preferences, 60, 81–2, 88
  stationary purchasing model, 87

traditional models, 81
travel minimization, 81, 87
types of consumer, 88
contact
contact intensive employees, 104, 105
contact landscapes, 107–8
contact space of migrants, 141, 142
contact surfaces in specialized information flows, 106–8
cornucopia phenomenon, 115–16
corporate strategy, *see* organizational decision making
cosmopolites, 94, 149
criticisms, of behavioural approaches, 12–13, 39–40, 153, 155
crowding, 11, 36
and recreation, 120
see also environmental stress, pathology
cultural geography, 39
culture
and cognition, 6, 8, 63, 64
and geographical epistemology, 156
and idealism, 158
and landscape, 67, 159
and social space, 27
and structuralism, 18, 38–9
and the mitigation of the effects of crowding, 129
see also proxemics

decision making, 42, 54–62
as an influence on overt behaviour, 4, 6, 8
in industry, 102, 103–4, 105–6
of consumers, 60, 86–7
see also search behaviour
decision space, of industrialists, 105
defended space, 93, 128
desideratum, 60, 83
determinism, 39, 45, 127
see also environmentalism, spatialism
developmental psychology, 47–8
diffusion, of information and innovations, 52–3
disasters, *see* natural hazards
distance, *see* cognitive distance
districts, *see* areas
drought, perception of, 109

ecological fallacy, 37
ecological psychology, 10, 11
edges, *see* barriers
elections, *see* voting
empirical research in behavioural geography, 5–7
empiricism, 45
entropy, 21–2
environment
behavioural and phenomenal environments, 7, 9, 10, 55–6, 75
meaning of environments, 38, 72, 89
objective environments, 4, 6, 9, 64
perceived environments, 9, 55–6
see also experiental environments, images, perception
environmental knowing, 46–8
inferential, operational, and responsive knowledge, 50
microgenetic, ontogenetic, and phylogenetic perspectives, 41, 46–7
see also cognition, information, learning
environmental psychology, 11, 43, 45
environmental stress, 127–8, 133–4
cognitive overload, 127, 128
crowding, 128, 129, 130, 134
population density, 129
sensory deprivation, 127, 128
stressors, 127–8
see also pathology
environmentalism, 14
see also determinism, spatialism
epistemology
and the basis for environmental knowledge, 14, 43, 45
epistemological errors in structural approaches, 24
geographical epistemology, 156, 161
ethnicity, 29, 32
and local interaction, 94
see also segregation
ethology, 48
evolutionary adaptation, to environment, 46
see also environmental knowing
existentialism, 7, 157–8
experience
and hazard perception, 114–15
and recreational activity, 121, 125–6
see also learning
experiential environments, 43, 153, 155–63
see also topophilia

factorial ecology, 18, 29–32, 36
familiarity theory, 122
feeling, 9, 10
field theory, *see gestalt* psychology
figurative knowledge, 43
flood hazard, 5, 109
frames of reference, 49
and cognitive maps, 72
frames of reference of children, 47–8
images as frames of reference, 10, 65
see also territoriality
freewill, 39
friendship, 93–4

game theory, 37, 58
gatekeepers, 52
gemeinschaft, 33–4
gender differences
in activity systems, 75, 97
in spatial orientation ability, 46
geographic inference problem, 13, 37
geosophy, 7
gesellschaft, 33–4
gestalt psychology, 7, 47
cloze procedures, 72–3
decision making, 42
perceived and behavioural environments, 7, 10, 55
transactional-constructivism, 45
gravity model, 19, 39
cognitive gravity model, 20
criticisms, 20
probabilistic gravity model, 81

habit, 54
in recreation, 125
habitat theory, 159
helplessness, 133–4
hermeneutic approaches, 155
high-rise living, 128, 132, 137
historical geography, 7, 67
holism
and models of man, 38–9

and structural marxism, 22, 23
in humanistic approaches, 156–7
home, 49, 94, 97
as a venue for recreation, 120
see also territoriality
homo psychologicus, 13
human ecology, 4
and pathology, 18, 127, 132
Chicago School, 25–6, 32, 89
criticisms, 27
humanistic approaches, 4, 7, 153–63
criticisms, 162–3

idealism, 7, 12, 45, 158
imageability, 10, 42, 65
of shopping centres, 85
images, 6, 8, 64
and environmental information, 7, 8–9, 11, 42
environmental images, 8–9, 10, 12, 38, 63–78
government images of hazards, 116
methodological difficulties in image measurement, 67–8, 70
of landscape, 7
of political parties, 147
of the retail environment, 85–6
urban images, 66, 98–9
see also legibility
impedance function, 19
individualism, 23, 38–40
industrial linkages, 103, 105–6
industrial location, 100–8
behavioural approaches, 100–3
information processing and decision making, 102, 103–6
specialized information, 106–8
types of location decision, 103
information
about natural hazards, 113–15
and consumer behaviour, 84–5
and migration, 141
environmental information, 8, 41, 42–53
generic information, 46, 53
information fields, 49, 141
information handling ability, 44
information overload, 49, 84
private information, 53, 148, 150
public information, 53, 107
specialized information, 106–8
specific information, 46, 53
information flows, 4, 52–3
and regional economic growth, 104, 107–8
in industry, 104–6
spatial bias, 104, 148
information theory, 17, 44
inner city
and crime, 132–3
and mental illness, 131–3
and residential satisfaction, 137–8
see also urban living
intellectual development, 46–8, 72
see also environmental knowing
intentionality, 155, 157, 160
interactionalism, 45
intersubjectivity, 155, 156–7, 159
intervening opportunities model, 20
inverse square root law, 70

landmarks, 10, 65, 94, 98
landscape, 3, 7
interpretation of landscapes, 67, 158–60
language, 70
law of *large numbers*, 58–9
learning, 4, 6, 123
and decision making, 55–6
by consumers, 86–7
environmental and place learning, 49–51
spatial learning, 59–60, 106
stimulus-response theories, 9, 39, 49–50, 55
vicarious learning, 44
lebenswelt, 157, 161
legibility, of images, 65
leisure and recreation, 118–26
and the life cycle, 124–5
and residential mobility, 125
and resource management, 120–6
decision making, 121–3
definitions, 119–20
demand, 120–1
tourism, 120
life cycle, dimension of urban spatial structure, 29–32
life path, 37, 76–7
see also time
life style, 25, 27
and migration, 140–1
and suburbia, 94
lifeworld, *see lebenswelt*
literature
and images, 67
landscape in literature, 160, 161
localities, 94, 149
locational analysis, 3, 4, 19, 37, 38
criticisms, 100–1
normative location theory, 100

markov models, 37, 86–7
marxism
critical, 22
criticisms, 23–4
scientific, 22
structural, 17, 22–4, 38–9
materialism, 12
materialist view of the mind, 45
media, 52–3
and migration, 142
and voting, 146, 148, 150
mental illness, *see* pathology
mental maps, 11, 43, 63–4
and action space, 75
criticisms, 68
see also cognitive maps, sketch maps
migration, 135–44
and the life cycle, 138–9
and social mobility, 139
and voting, 148
decision making, 6, 139–41
information used by migrants, 141–4
laws of migration, 135
reasons for migration, 136–8
search, 142–4
mind, 41
as a black box in perception studies, 4, 8, 42, 43, 56
information processing, 56
innate structuring capacities, 22
philosophy of mind, 14, 45

stimulus-response learning, 39, 42
models
aggregate, 13, 17, 19, 37–8, 58–9
decision making, 59–62
logit and probit, 22
normative, 3
of man, 37–40
of spatial structure, 25–32
positive, 4
spatial interaction, 17, 19–22, 81
structural, 19, 22–4
morbidity, 129–32
motivation, 6, 54, 61–2
in corporate strategy, 62, 103–4
in recreation, 121–3
movement imagery, 60, 83
multidimensional scaling, 72, 82, 86–7
multiplier effect, 108, 125
see also information flows
myths, 7

nativism, 45
natural areas, *see* community
natural hazards, 5, 109–17
adaptation and adjustment, 110–3
definition, 111–12
emotional aftermath, 116–17
government responses, 116
human responses, 113–17
methodological problems in hazard studies, 112–13
paradigm for the study of hazards, 109
prevention and mitigation, 109–10, 111, 114
warnings, 113, 115
navigation, *see* orientation
need, 9, 10
hierarchy of needs, 121–2
need arousal, 44
neighbourhood, 34, 91–7
influence of voting, 146, 148–50
labelling of delinquent neighbourhoods, 133
neighbourhood quotient, 96, 97
perceived neighbourhoods, 94–7
types of neighbourhood, 34, 95–7
see also community
neodualism, 45, 64
neural nets, 46
see also brain structure
Newtonian physics, 17, 19, 20, 21
nodes, 10, 65, 68, 72
noise, and pathology, 36

offices, 105, 106–8
operative knowledge, 43
organization theory, 62, 101–3
see also theory of the firm
organizational decision making, 61–2, 101, 103–4
orientation, within the city, 98

participant observation, 156–7
pathology, 127–34
and access to health care, 130
and housing standards, 36, 129–30
and urbanization, 25, 27
crime and delinquency, 36, 132–4
mental illness, 35–6, 131–2
pathogenic areas, 129
social pathology, 35–6
spatial patterns of pathology, 35, 89, 128–9, 130–1
see also environmental stress
paths
in city images, 10, 65, 67
in distance distortion, 70
perception, 7, 8, 12, 83
and mental maps, 43, 63–4
and preferences, 60
and the behavioural environment, 9
by organizations, 105
in environmental psychology, 11
in *gestalt* psychology, 7, 10, 55
of the environment, 4, 5, 6
see also environment
periodicity of behaviour, 79–80
personal community theory, 123, 124
see also socialization and behaviour
personal construct theory, 10, 51–2, 85–6
personal geographies, 7
and geographical epistemology, 156
personal space, *see* proxemics
personality, 6, 8, 11, 73
and natural hazards, 115
phenomenology, 45, 157, 161–2
place
a sense of place, 160–11
and architectural psychology, 10
attachment to place, 7, 34, 94, 157–8
place identity, 90, 91
place utility, 6, 42, 59, 136, 139–40
placelessness, 161
significance of place in the city, 89
political geography, 145
population potential surfaces, 20
post-industrial society, 107–8, 118–19, 125–6
potential models, 20
preferences, 12, 59, 60
and appraisive images, 73–4
between multi-dimensional alternatives, 87
for recreational venues, 121–3
preference surfaces, 11, 74, 85
repressed preferences, 13, 88, 123, 124, 125
revealed space preferences, 81–2, 88
transitivity of preferences, 59–87
probability, in decision making, 57–9
problem solving, 54
see also decision making
profit maximization, 62, 100
see also rational economic man
projective techniques, 68
prospect-refuge theory, 159
proxemics, 49
psychologism, 13, 161

quantitative revolutions, 3, 12

rational economic man
and distance minimization, 4, 81
and normative models, 3, 39, 56–7
and the behavioural matrix, 8
unreality, 44, 100
see also motivation
rationalims, 45
'ratomorphism', 9, 55
realism, 45

recall of behaviour, methodological problems, 112–13
recreation, *see* leisure and recreation
reductionism, 9
reification of concepts, in structural approaches, 23
repertory grid technique, 51–2, 85–6
  see also personal construct theory
residential differentiation, 26, 27, 31, 32, 33
  residential desirability and appraisive images, 73
  residential mobility, 135–44
  residential satisfaction, 136–8
retailing
  information about retail environment, 84–5
  law of retail gravitation, 21
risk and uncertainty, 6, 57–9
  in natural hazards, 5, 109–11
  minimization by firms, 101, 103

satisficing, 6, 42, 56–7, 60, 62
schemata
  in environmental cognition, 6, 8–9, 11, 53, 64, 73
  socio-spatial schemata, 10, 65, 95–6, 97
schizophrenia, 131
scientific paradigms, in behavioural geography, 12
scientism, 111
search behaviour, 4, 54, 60
  by consumers, 84–5, 87
  in industrial location, 105
  in migration, 140, 141–4
  space covering *vs* organizing behaviour, 142
segregation, 26, 28–9
  and neighbourhoods, 91
  and voting, 147
sentiment, 27
sex, *see* gender differences
shopping centres, 84–6
simple behaviour system, 59
situations, 13
  psychology of situations, 10
sketch maps, 65, 70–3
  methodological problems, 67–8
  sequential, 67, 70
  spatial, 70
  see also cognitive maps, mental maps
skid row, 35, 132
social areas, 27–32
  social area analysis, 28–32
social interaction, 93–4
social milieu, 10, 25, 89
  and image formation, 64
  and local communities, 32
  and pathology, 36
social network analysis, 93
  and voting, 147–9
social pathology, *see* pathology
social physics, *see* Newtonian physics
social problems, *see* environmental stress, pathology
social reality, levels of, 161–3
social space, 18, 25, 29, 90, 91
social status
  and activity systems, 97
  and consumer behaviour, 84
  and hazard adjustment, 114, 115
  and urban images, 13, 98
socialization, and behaviour, 10
  see also personal community theory
  sociobiology, 9
sovereignty of decision makers, 6, 42, 88, 144
  space searchers, 44, 52
  space sitters, 44
  spatial structures, 25–36
    see also urban morphology
spatialism, 14
  see also determinism, environmentalism
statistical mechanics, 17, 20–2
statistically average man, 17, 19, 120
stereotypes, 67, 74, 108
stress, 59
  and migration, 136–7, 139–41
  see also environmental stress
structuralism, 7, 17–18, 22, 38
subjective distance, *see* cognitive distance
subjectivity, *see* intersubjectivity
suburbia, 137
  and crime, 132
  and social interaction, 94
  and voting, 146
suicide, 132
symbolic interaction theory, 161–2
symbolism
  and urban socio-spatial structure, 27, 65, 67
  in the environment, 11, 44, 156
  of landscape, 159
  of place, 160–1
  of residential location, 137
systems theory
  organizations as systems, 102–3, 104
  systems perspective on hazard adjustment, 109

taken-for-granted world, 13, 161–2
  and human territoriality, 48
  and landscape, 158–9
  in phenomenology, 157
telecommunications, 104
teleology, 23, 39
terrae incognitae, 7, 56
territoriality, 11, 41–2, 48–9
  and defensible space, 128
  see also belonging, home
theory of the firm, 101
  see also organization theory
time, 76, 119
  as a constraint on behaviour, 37, 77–8
  discretionary time, 118–19
  sequencing of activities in time, 78
  time budget studies, 78, 97–8
  time geography, 6, 76–8
  time-space prisms, 77
topophilia, 7, 67, 160–1
  see also experiential environments
transactional-constructivism, 41, 45–8, 63
transcendental structures, 38

uprootedness, 158
  see also belonging
urban ecology, *see* human ecology, pathology
urban living, 89–99
  a sense of belonging, 89–91
  changing nature of urban living, 28
  coping with urban life, 26–7
  neighbourhoods, 91–7
  orientation within the city, 97–9

structure of the urban environment, 25–35
see also pathology, inner city
urban morphology, and urban images, 66, 98–9
urban villages, 94
urbanism, 26–7, 89
utility, 22, 59, 61
subjective expected utility, 59

value systems, 7, 8, 10, 25, 56, 60, 83
and recreation, 121
in humanistic approaches, 156
verstehen, 157, 158, 160, 162–3
voting, 4, 145–51
areal-structural analyses, 145–7
behavioural analyses, 145, 147–50
conversion and transplantation thesis, 146
friends and neighbours effect, 149–50
geography of representation, 150
malapportionment and gerrymandering, 150
neighbourhood effect, 148–9
societal cleavages and political parties, 146–7

well-being, 49, 101, 127
wilderness, 67, 120